All photographs, unless otherwise noted, are by Junius Beebe III, Katya Kallsen, Allan Macintyre, and Julie Swiderski of the Digital Imaging and Visual Resources Department, Harvard Art Museum. P. 23, Henry Lie, Straus Center for Conservation and Technical Studies; p. 89, Craigen Bowen, Straus Center for Conservation and Technical Studies; p. 180, © 2008 The Munch Museum/The Munch-Ellingsen Group/ARS, New York; pp. 181, 185, 191, 214, © 2008 Estate of Pablo Picasso/ARS, New York; pp. 182, 183, 193, © 2008 Succession H. Matisse/ARS, New York; pp. 189, 194, 216, 226, 227, © 2008 ARS, New York/ADAGP, Paris; p. 195, reproduced by permission of the Elie Nadelman Estate; pp. 197–99, 202, 204, 205, 207, 208, 217, 233, © 2008 ARS, New York/VG Bild-Kunst, Bonn; p. 200, © 2008 Mondrian/Holtzman Trust, c/o HCR International, Warrenton, VA; p. 201, © 2008 Georgia O'Keeffe Museum/ARS, New York; p. 203, © 2008 The Josef and Anni Albers Foundation/ARS, New York; p. 209, © 2008 Man Ray Trust/ARS, New York/ADAGP, Paris; p. 211, © T. H. Benton and R. P. Benton Testamentary Trusts/UMB Bank Trustee/Licensed by VAGA, New York, NY; p. 212, © 2008 ARS, New York/SOMAAP, Mexico City; p. 213, © Estate of Ben Shahn/Licensed by VAGA, New York, NY; p. 215, © 2008 Successió Miró/ARS, New York/ADAGP, Paris; p. 218, © 2008 ARS, New York; p. 219, © 2008 The Pollock-Krasner Foundation/ARS, New York; p. 220, Aaron Siskind Foundation; p. 221, © 2008 The Franz Kline Estate/ARS, New York; pp. 222, 223, © Estate of David Smith/Licensed by VAGA, New York, NY; p. 224, © The Center for American History, The University of Texas at Austin; p. 225, © Robert Frank, from *The Americans*; p. 226: © George Brecht; © Albert M. Fine Papers, Special Collections Department, University of Iowa Libraries, Iowa City, IA; © Ken Friedman; © Shigeko Kubota/Licensed by VAGA, New York, NY; Fredric Lieberman, by permission of the artist; George Maciunas, by permission of Ken Friedman; © Claes Oldenburg; © Yoko Ono; © Willem de Ridder; James Riddle, by permission of Ken Friedman; © Paul Sharits Estate, Christopher Sharits; © Robert Sheff; © Robert Watts Estate; p. 228, © 1958 Morris Louis; p. 229, © Richard Misrach, courtesy Fraenkel Gallery, San Francisco, Marc Selwyn Fine Art, Los Angeles, and Pace/MacGill Gallery, New York; pp. 230, 231, © Jasper Johns/Licensed by VAGA, New York, NY; p. 232, © 2008 Andy Warhol Foundation/ARS, New York/Trademarks, Campbell Soup Company. All rights reserved; p. 234, © Georg Baselitz; p. 235, © Philip Guston; p. 236, © The Estate of Diane Arbus LLC; p. 237, © Lee Friedlander, courtesy Fraenkel Gallery, San Francisco; p. 238, © The Estate of Eva Hesse/Galerie Hauser & Wirth; p. 239, © Gerhard Richter; p. 240, © Anselm Kiefer, courtesy Gagosian Gallery; p. 241, © Tacita Dean; p. 242, © Nan Goldin, courtesy of the artist; p. 243, © Gary Schneider; p. 244, © Louise Bourgeois/Licensed by VAGA, New York, NY; p. 245, Courtesy Barbara Krakow Gallery; p. 246, © Robert Gober, courtesy of the artist and Matthew Marks Gallery, New York; p. 247, © Carrie Mae Weems; p. 248, courtesy of Shōmei Tomatsu and Tepper Takayama Fine Arts; p. 249, © Succession Raghubir Singh; p. 250, © Fang Lijun; p. 251, © Cai Guo-Qiang; p. 252, © Ed Ruscha; p. 253, © 2008 Andreas Gursky/ARS, New York/VG Bild-Kunst, Bonn. Courtesy Gallery Monika Sprueth/Philomene Magers, Cologne; p. 254, © Rauschenberg Estate/Licensed by VAGA, New York, NY; p. 255, © Paul McCarthy, courtesy of the artist and Hauser & Wirth Zurich London. Photo by Ann-Marie Rounkle; p. 256, © Ellen Gallagher.

The publishers have made every effort to contact all copyright holders for works. All those we have been unable to reach are invited to write to the publishers so that a full acknowledgment may be given in subsequent editions.

Servant Girls' Dormitory (Jean-Honoré Fragonard), 117
Shahn, Ben, 213
Sheeler, Charles, 206
Sideboard Dish (Jacob Bodendeich), 105
Silk Panel: Yalis and Makaras within an Ogival Lattice (Indian), 52
Silsbee, Case, & Co,. 152
Singh, Raghubir, 249
Siqueiros, David Alfaro, 212
Siskind, Aaron, 220
Six Etchings from the Series "Ornamenti e grotteschi," (Stefano della Bella), 113
Six Heads (Jean-Antoine Watteau), 110
Smith, David, 222, 223
Smith, Kiki, 245
Solidus of Pulcheria (Byzantine), 19
Southworth & Hawes, 147
Spencer Albums (Jean and Pierre-Jean Mariette), 112–13
Sphinx (Etruscan), 9
Standing Bodhisattva Maitreya (Zanabazar, attrib.), 103
Standing Buddha (Thai), 31
Standing Male Nude (John Singer Sargent), 184
Standing Nude Woman (Pablo Picasso), 185
Steelyard: Empress Bust Weight, Crossbeam, and Collar with Chains (Byzantine), 28
Stigmatization of Saint Francis (Taddeo Gaddi), 48
Still Life: Basket of Fruit (Pierre Bonnard), 216
Still Life with Apples (Henri Matisse), 193
Still Life with Bric-a-Brac (William Michael Harnett), 137
Still Life with Watermelon (Sarah Miriam Peale), 136
Story of the Bodhisattva Medicine King (Japanese), 42
Stoughton Cup (John Coney), 128
Striding Man (Egyptian), 4
Studies for "Home of the Welder": Wife as Locomotive Parts (David Smith), 222
Study for the Figure of Christ (Peter Paul Rubens), 94
Submerged Gas Pumps, Salton Sea (Richard Misrach), 229
Summer Scene (Frédéric Bazille), 158
Susannah Speakman Inman (Robert Feke), 121

Tabernacle (Spanish), 91
Tablet Case with Multiple Impressions of Seal with Presentation Scene (Neo-Sumerian), 6
Tahmina Comes into Rustam's Chamber (Islamic), 51
Taju, Shaykh, attrib., 111
Tamehiro, Reizei, 64
Tetradrachm of Demetrios Poliorketes (Greek), 18
Tetradrachm of Katane (Greek), 16
Theseus Painter, attrib., 11
This is Eddie Carmel, a Jewish giant, with his parents in the living room of their home in the Bronx, New York (Diane Arbus), 236
Three (Philip Guston), 235
Tiepolo, Giovanni Battista, 116
Tile with Palmette Blossoms, Flowers, and Serrated Leaves (Islamic), 84
Titian, 73; attrib., 72
To the Convalescent Woman (Triptych) (Erich Heckel), 202
Tomatsu, Shōmei, 248
Toulouse-Lautrec, Henri de, 173
Trajan (Roman), 22–23
Trees Near a Pool of Water (Titian), 73
Tripod Ewer with Strap Handle (Chinese), 2
Tucker, Harriet Ann, 146
Turner, Joseph Mallord William, 139
Two Standing, Braying Camels Laden with Goods (Chinese), 32
Two Studies of Napoleon, Nude, Crowning Himself (Jacques-Louis David), 130
Two-Tiered Cabinet with Relief Decorations (French), 75

Untitled (American), 164
Untitled (Harry Annas), 224
Untitled (Mary Georgiana Caroline Cecil Filmer), 150
Untitled (Arshile Gorky), 218
Untitled (Eva Hesse), 238
Untitled (Lewis Wickes Hine), 186–87
Untitled (Frances Benjamin Johnston), 186–87
Untitled (George Henry Seeley), 192
Untitled (Ben Shahn), 213
Untitled (Harriet Ann Tucker), 146
Untitled (Yokosuka) (Shōmei Tomatsu), 248
Upper Deck (Charles Sheeler), 206
U.S. 90, en route to Del Rio, Texas (Robert Frank), 225

van Gogh, Vincent, 170, 171
Vanity of the Artist's Dream (Charles Bird King), 149
Veneziano, Agostino, 78
Victoria Maharani with the Princess Royal (Indian), 151
Virgin and Child (Alessandro Algardi), 96
Virgin and Child in a Landscape (Girolamo Mazzola Bedoli), 76
Virgin with Saints of the Dominican Order (Agostino Veneziano), 78
Virgin with the Sleeping Christ Child (Orazio Gentileschi), 93
Voyage of the Cardinal Infante Ferdinand of Spain from Barcelona to Genoa in April 1633, with Neptune Calming the Tempest (Peter Paul Rubens), 95

Wall Hanging (Anni Albers), 203
Warhol, Andy, 232
Watteau, Jean-Antoine, 110
Wedgwood, Josiah, 129
Weems, Carrie Mae, 247
Whistler, James Abbott McNeill, 162
Wilderness I (Jasper Johns), 231
Willow-Branch Avalokiteshvara (Korean), 49
Womb World Mandala (Japanese), 43
Wooded Landscape with a Distant View toward the Sea (Pieter Bruegel the Elder), 88–89
Wreck of the Old 97 (Thomas Hart Benton), 211

You Became a Scientific Profile/A Negroid Type/An Anthropological Debate/& A Photographic Subject (Carrie Mae Weems), 247
Young Man in a Blue Cloak (Aqa Riza [Riza 'Abbasi]), 83
Youth and Girl, Each Offering the Other a Fruit (Italian), 61
Yu Tŏk-chang (Su-un and Ka-san-ŭng), 109

Zanabazar, attrib., 103
Zhu Da (Bada Shanren), 106
Zuccaro, Taddeo, 77

Harvard / Handbook
Art Museum

Harvard Art Museum / Handbook

Edited by Stephan Wolohojian

Harvard Art Museum
Cambridge, Massachusetts

Harvard University Press
Cambridge, Massachusetts

Funding for this publication has been provided by the José Soriano Fund and the Melvin R. Seiden and Janine Luke Fund for Publications and Exhibitions, two endowment funds at the Harvard Art Museum.

Published by the Harvard Art Museum

Director of Design & Publications: Katie Andresen
Editor in Chief: Evelyn Rosenthal
Project Coordination: Danielle Carrabino
Editing: Carolann Barrett, Patricia O'Connell, & Evelyn Rosenthal
Design: Katie Andresen
Production Management: Becky Hunt
Production: Kim Cafasso, Becky Hunt, & Michael Seitz
Printing: Meridian Printing, East Greenwich, RI

Front cover: Enthroned Lion-Headed Deities, Egyptian (p. 1); Fra Angelico, Christ on the Cross between the Virgin and Cardinal Torquemada and Saint John the Evangelist (p. 57); Bizarre Silk Panel, French (p. 108); Richard Misrach, Submerged Gas Pumps, Salton Sea (p. 229); back cover: Ellen Gallagher, Abu Simbel (p. 256); Sadiqi Beg, Figures from the Annunciation (p. 80); Jackson Pollock, No. 2 (p. 219); front flap: Tacita Dean, Banewl (p. 241); Aubrey Beardsley, Isolde (p. 172); Large Jade Disk, Chinese (p. 15); back flap: Andreas Gursky, Los Angeles (p. 253); Ammi Phillips, Harriet Leavens (p. 132); Gustav Klimt, Pear Tree (p. 188)

Library of Congress Cataloging-in-Publication Data

Harvard Art Museum.
Harvard Art Museum handbook / edited by Stephan Wolohojian.
p. cm.
Includes index.
ISBN 978-1-891771-50-7 (alk. paper)
1. Harvard Art Museum—Catalogs. 2. Art—Massachusetts—Cambridge—Catalogs. I. Wolohojian, Stephan. II. Title.
N526.A58 2008
708.1444--dc22

2008028548

vi Director's Foreword
viii Acknowledgments
ix Introduction
xviii List of Contributors
1 Selected Works
257 Resources
258 Index of Artists and Works
262 Illustration Credits

Director's Foreword

This handsome volume is one of the first publications to appear since the Fogg, Busch-Reisinger, and Sackler museums have been united on equal ground under the name Harvard Art Museum. The separate identities, collections, histories, and founding philosophies of each—while proudly maintained—are now more closely intertwined, in deeper conversation with one another, and more reflective of the visual, historical, and intellectual links that have always existed among them, only obscured by our current physical divides and space limitations. These great assemblages of art, gathered together to further Harvard's educational mission, represent an unparalleled teaching resource that expands the university's traditional emphasis on learning through numbers and words to embrace visual learning.

The Harvard Art Museum is dedicated to unleashing the multiplicity of ideas embedded in its collections for the benefit of students, faculty, and the wider communities we serve. As with the clarification of our identity and bringing our collections together in more meaningful ways, the Art Museum will soon undergo a historic renovation and transformation resulting in a state-of-the-art physical facility, one that will match the value and importance of our mission and collections. The driving inspiration behind this effort is a deep-rooted commitment to close and repeated looking, an intellectual, emotional, and visual transaction that ultimately reveals what is often hard to see.

This is also the first publication to bring all the collections together in a true handbook form. Earlier versions in 1927, 1931, 1936, 1985, 1990, 1991, 1996, and 2007 served a variety of purposes, and seem an almost instinctual response to milestones in our institutional history. This effort stands apart from them for two reasons. First, it places in tandem many of the best known works with some of the least known, creating dialogues and juxtapositions both unexpected and revelatory. Second, many of the analyses and descriptions were written by curatorial and conservation interns under the supervision of the Art Museum's curators and conservators. The results are immensely gratifying for a university museum: As one reads through entries, it is possible to sense critical looking and thinking evolving and sharpening, recalibrating as eye and mind grapple with image and object.

This handbook would not have become a reality without the inspired imagination and leadership of Stephan Wolohojian, the Landon and Lavinia Clay Curator of Painting, Sculpture, and Decorative Arts, who served as head of the Interns Seminar during 2006–2007 and fall 2007. It was his idea, his encouragement of the interns, and his dedication to this museum that made this book possible.

Thomas W. Lentz
Elizabeth and John Moors
Cabot Director

Acknowledgments

An endeavor such as this requires the collaboration and generous help of many. Almost every department of the Harvard Art Museum has worked toward realizing this handbook. However, the following deserve special acknowledgment for their support and expertise: Carolann Barrett, Jay Beebe, Richard Benefield, Craigen Bowen, Kim Cafasso, Maureen Donovan, Meg Howland, Becky Hunt, Katya Kallsen, Chris Linnane, Allan Macintyre, Katrina Meyer, Patricia O'Connell, Tara Phillips, Lizzy Ramhorst, Michael Seitz, David Sturtevant, Julie Swiderski, and Bradford Wm. Voigt. Beyond the museum, thanks are due to Sylvan Barnet, William Burto, Alexis Gregory, Emily Rauh Pulitzer, and Helen Rundell at the Pulitzer Foundation for the Arts.

In addition to these, several people must be particularly thanked. This project would never have been possible without the support and encouragement of Thomas W. Lentz, and the book would never have materialized without the careful editorial attention of Evelyn Rosenthal, the compelling design of Katie Andresen, and the energetic devotion of Danielle Carrabino, who made coordinating this complex enterprise look easy.

Introduction

Representations: A Survey of the Harvard Art Museum Collections

Stephan Wolohojian

Selecting a group of objects to represent a collection is no easy task. The Harvard Art Museum has one of the largest and most important collections in the United States. As a teaching museum within a major university, every work in its care is important for its pedagogical mission. In this setting, the fragment from an Attic red-figure vase, usually kept in a storeroom, is as crucial for teaching as a vessel on display in the galleries. Depending on students' interests, it might be as rewarding and life altering for some to analyze the chemical composition of the pigments found on a palette once used by John Singer Sargent as it is for others to analyze his preparatory studies or finished paintings in the collection. That said, the museum, with the support of its generous benefactors, has always believed that the finest works can have a transformative effect on students and, for over a century, its galleries have been filled with works from every part of the world that have had an indelible impact on generations of students and members of the general public alike.

For the past decade, the Harvard Art Museum has maintained an active internship program. Each year about a dozen graduate students and young conservators arrive from around the globe to work in one of the museum's curatorial departments or in its Straus Center for Conservation and Technical Studies. These promising scholars participate in a seminar, run by a curator, that examines museum practice while introducing them to the complex workings of the museum.

The 2006–2007 seminar was presented with the task of creating a handbook of the museum's collections. Before even debating what works would be included, we began by analyzing the category itself. We lifted handbooks that weighed several pounds and stretched the notion of a "handbook" to an unwieldy size, and studied others that required magnifying lenses to look at the tiny illustrations. We diligently read through some that offered readers a history of the universe, and others that described the history of their institutions with detailed stories of their benefactors' lives. Although we found many virtues in the books we examined, we ultimately decided that our handbook would respond to the experience of looking at individual objects much as one does in the galleries, and that each page would present one work, accompanied by information that was similar to that found in gallery labels.

With the basic format determined, we turned to the difficult task of establishing a list of objects. This task is made all the more difficult as museum collections expand and grow. We began by asking the simple question many visitors ask when they are in the galleries: If I had to pick one work from the collection, which would it be, and why? We quickly realized that choosing objects for an introduction to a collection was not the straightforward exercise we had imagined, and that trying to distill a balanced selection of only a few hundred works from a collection approaching three hundred thousand was a considerable challenge. We rightly recognized as well that our criteria for selecting works, based on specialized knowledge, whether in paper conservation or in ancient bronze sculpture, might not necessarily lead to a representative and balanced overview of the full range of the collection. This brief survey seeks to present some of the Art Museum's best-known and most beloved works along with lesser-known works in order to introduce the reader to the museum's far-reaching collections.

The handbook does not divide works by museum department or by medium but presents the collection as a whole, in roughly chronological order. This allows the reader to see connections between works from different cultures, or to get a sense of the strength of the museum's holdings of individual artists or in certain periods. The progression is occasionally broken to focus on particular objects or resources at the museum. In some instances, these expanded pages highlight conservation treatments or technical analyses; in others they focus on works of special interest, such as prints from the Spencer Albums, or the museum's extensive holdings of works by Lyonel Feininger and the complementary material in the artist's archives that are housed at the Busch-Reisinger Museum. As with any work in the collection, these archives are available to the public for study, and more information on such resources can be found in the appendix at the end of this volume.

There has not been a true handbook of the Fogg collection since 1936. Although that guide reveals what a young university art museum was able to put together in its first decades, it was published before some of the most distinguished gifts and bequests were made and is, needless to say, both out of print and out of date. No works from the legendary bequests of Grenville L. Winthrop or Maurice Wertheim are there included, nor, obviously, are the generous gifts of more recent benefactors and those of countless others who have contributed to the collections. The last handbook of the Busch-Reisinger's collection appeared in 1991, and there has never been a guide to the Sackler

Museum's holdings. Although works from these collections have appeared in larger books about the collections and in dedicated catalogues, we are pleased to introduce the museum's holdings in an integrated presentation with new photography illustrating some of these works for the first time in color. Whether you are familiar with the works in the Harvard Art Museum or this is a first look at its significant collections, we hope that this handbook will invite you to seek out its resources, which are preserved for our benefit and for future generations.

List of Contributors

AA Amy Auer, Curatorial Intern, Islamic and Later Indian Art
AJA Adam Aja, Andrew W. Mellon Curatorial Intern, Ancient Art
ALC Alvin L. Clark Jr., Jeffrey E. Horvitz Research Curator, Drawings
AM Andreya Mihaloew, Agnes Mongan Curatorial Intern, Ancient Art
ARK Anne Rose Kitagawa, Assistant Curator of Japanese Art, Asian Art
BF Brendan Fay, Agnes Mongan Curatorial Intern, Photographs
CS Celka Straughn, Senior Research Assistant, Harvard Art Museum / Project Zero Research Collaboration
CU Craig Uram, Samuel H. Kress Conservation Intern, Straus Center for Conservation, Objects Lab
DC Danielle Carrabino, Theodore Rousseau Curatorial Intern, Painting, Sculpture, and Decorative Arts
EL Eve Lambert, Charlotte and Irving Rabb Curatorial Intern, Modern and Contemporary Art
EMR Elisabeth Ramhorst, Curatorial Assistant, Busch-Reisinger Museum
ER Elizabeth Rudy, Andrew W. Mellon Curatorial Intern, Painting, Sculpture, and Decorative Arts
FW Francine Weiss, Curatorial Intern, American Painting, Sculpture, and Decorative Arts
HC Harry Cooper, Curator of Modern Art
HH Heather Hess, Stefan Engelhorn Curatorial Intern, Busch-Reisinger Museum
JP Jacob Proctor, Ruth V S Lauer Curatorial Assistant, Prints
KM Kimberly Masteller, Assistant Curator, Islamic and Later Indian Art
MAM Melissa Moy, Assistant Curator of Chinese Art, Asian Art
MB Morwenna Blewett, Advanced-Level Conservation Intern, Straus Center for Conservation, Paintings Lab
MM Mary McWilliams, Norma Jean Calderwood Curator of Islamic and Later Indian Art
MS Miriam Stewart, Assistant Curator of Drawings
PK Penley Knipe, Associate Conservator of Photographs and Works of Art on Paper, Straus Center for Conservatic
SG Supriya Gandhi, Andrew W. Mellon Curatorial Intern, Islamic and Later Indian Art
SK1 Sandra Kelberlau, Advanced-Level Conservation Intern, Straus Center for Conservation, Paintings Lab
SK2 Solveig Köbernick, Michalke Curatorial Intern, Busch-Reisinger Museum
SKS Suzanne Karr Schmidt, Lynn and Philip A. Straus Curatorial Intern, Prints
TS Theresa Smith, Advanced-Level Conservation Intern, Straus Center for Conservation, Paper Lab
VS Valeria Sergueenkova, Andrew W. Mellon Curatorial Intern, Ancient Art
WL Willemijn Lindenhovius, Lynn and Philip A. Straus Curatorial Intern, Drawings
WR William Robinson, Maida and George Abrams Curator of Drawings
YFY Yao-Fen You, Theodore Rousseau Postdoctoral Fellow, Painting, Sculpture, and Decorative Arts
YH Yasmin Hilloowala, Norma Jean Calderwood Curatorial Intern, Islamic and Later Indian Art

1 Bronze; male: h. 20 1/4 in. (51.4 cm); female: h. 26 11/16 in. (67.8 cm). Arthur M. Sackler Museum, Bequest of Grenville L. Winthrop, 1943.1121.A, B.

Enthroned Lion-Headed Deities
Egyptian, Late Period
Dynasty 26
c. 664–525 BC

These large statuettes of lion-headed deities, perhaps representing the goddess Wadjet and the god Horus, are of similar date, style, and quality but from the hands of different artists. Their clenched fists once held separately cast attributes. The male deity wears a short kilt and elaborate four-banded collar, the female an ankle-length dress. The male's eyes are highlighted with gold foil. The thrones bear hieroglyphic inscriptions and are incised with lion-headed figures and Horus falcons. Their hollow interiors may have held mummified ichneumon, an Egyptian mongoose known to hunt the serpents associated with the lion-headed deities. Remains of these animals have been discovered in similar bronze statuettes. The Art Museum's statuettes are notable for a different kind of discovery: In the 1950s, the previously unknown mineral chalconatronite was found in their interiors. AJA

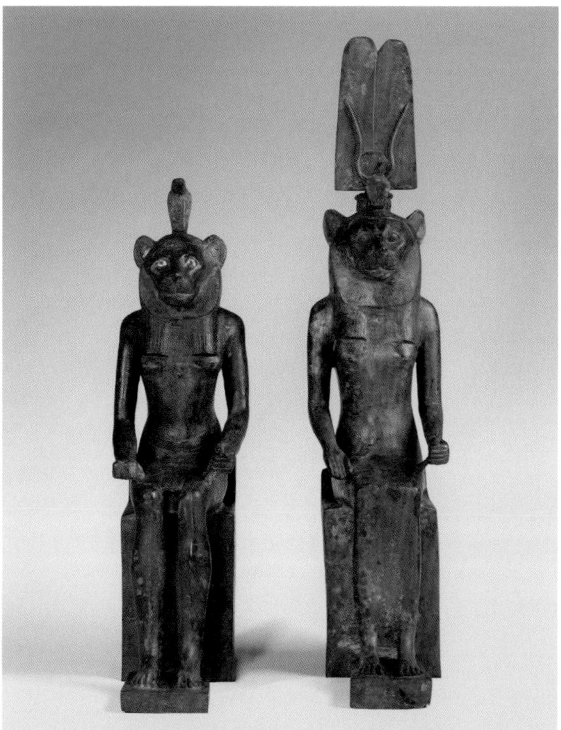

2 Buff and light gray earthenware with incised decoration on the handle, 21 1/16 x 6 11/16 x 5 3/4 in. (53.5 x 17 x 14.6 cm). Arthur M. Sackler Museum, Partial gift of the Walter C. Sedgwick Foundation and partial purchase through the Ernest B. and Helen Pratt Dane Fund for the Acquisition of Oriental Art, 2006.170.119.

Tripod Ewer with Strap Handle

Chinese, Neolithic to Shang period, Erlitou culture (1900–1350 BC)

Probably from northwestern Henan or southern Shanxi province

Supported by three hollow legs of rounded conical form, this elongated ewer with strut-braced strap handle was almost certainly made for ritual use. Earthenware wine vessels of this form have been unearthed at sites associated with the Erlitou culture in China's central plain region, widely regarded as the cradle of Chinese civilization. Named after the village where remains of this complex hierarchical society were first discovered, Erlitou culture predates the establishment of the Shang dynasty, a period celebrated for its highly sophisticated bronze ritual vessels (see opposite page). Ceramic containers such as this ewer served as models in both form and function for Shang bronze vessels; Erlitou may thus be considered a temporal bridge from the Neolithic period to China's great Bronze Age. MAM

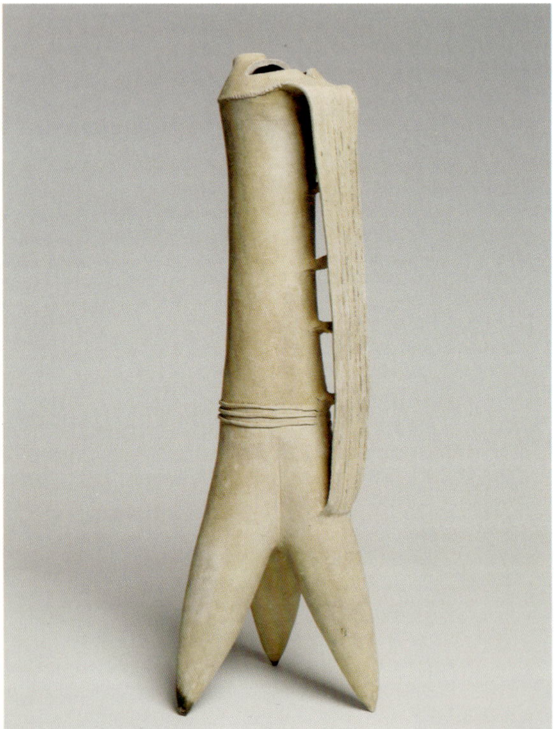

3 Cast bronze with pale green patina, 9 13/16 x 12 3/8 x 4 3/16 in. (25 x 31.5 x 10.6 cm). Arthur M. Sackler Museum, Bequest of Grenville L. Winthrop, 1943.52.103.

Ritual Wine-Pouring Vessel with Tiger and Owl Decor Chinese, Shang dynasty 13th century BC

This impeccably cast pouring vessel, or *guang*, is a masterpiece of Shang-dynasty metalwork. Intended to decant wine, this container takes the form of a blunt-snouted tiger standing back-to-back with an owl. The heads of both animals feature prominently on the removable lid, while their bodies are skillfully rendered on the vessel's lower portion. *Leiwen*, or "lightning pattern" squared spirals, enliven the interstices between the tiger and owl and impart a rhythmic animation to the piece. / The ruling class of China's Shang dynasty (c. 16th–11th century BC) used such intricately decorated vessels for ritual offerings of food and wine to ancestral spirits. The importance of these rituals fostered the large-scale production of bronzes, whose method of piece-mold manufacture required a high degree of technical skill and artistic imagination. Among the ancient bronzes that survive today, the guang is a relatively rare form and one of the few that does not derive from a ceramic prototype. MAM

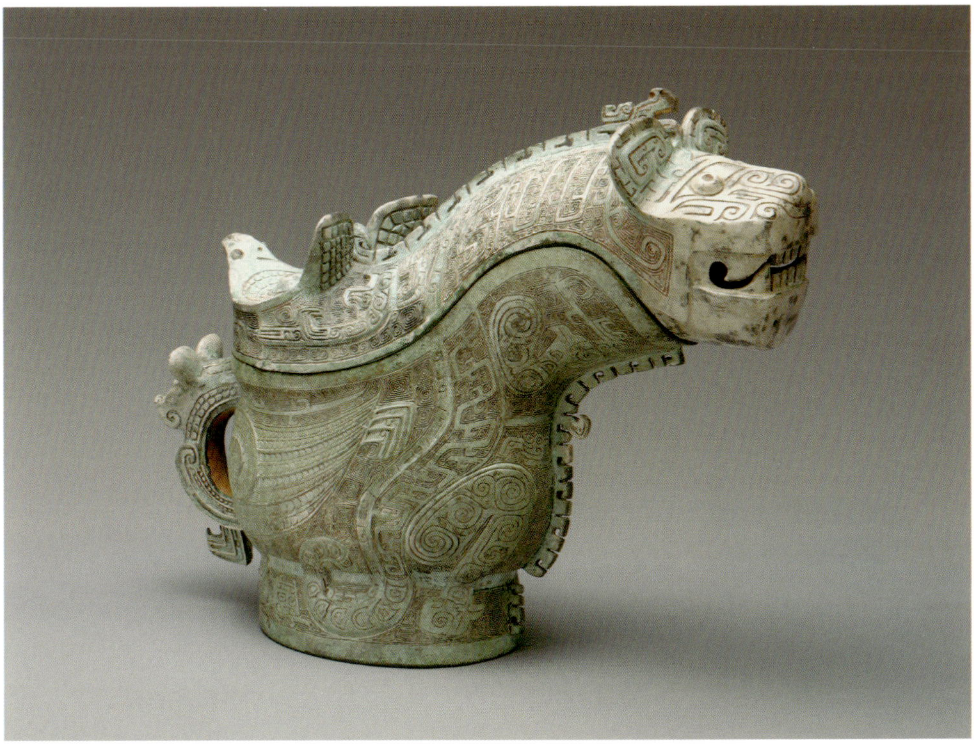

Wood, with remains of paint; h. 13 in. (33 cm). Arthur M. Sackler Museum, Gift of Nanette Rodney Kelekian, 1996.136.

Striding Man
Egyptian, Old Kingdom
Dynasty 6
c. 2150 BC

Several ancient Egyptian tombs contained carved wooden sculptures that represented the deceased. In the Old Kingdom and the following First Intermediate Period, these sculptures often took the form of a youthful striding male. Although the pose seems static with the weight evenly distributed, the convention of placing the left foot forward implies movement. The arms of this statuette were carved separately and attached with dowels, as was common for larger works. Many statuettes were painted or covered with painted plaster. Occasionally, linen garments were added and additional details such as jewelry painted on. Traces of black survive on this figure's wig, and white on the thumbnails and toenails. AJA

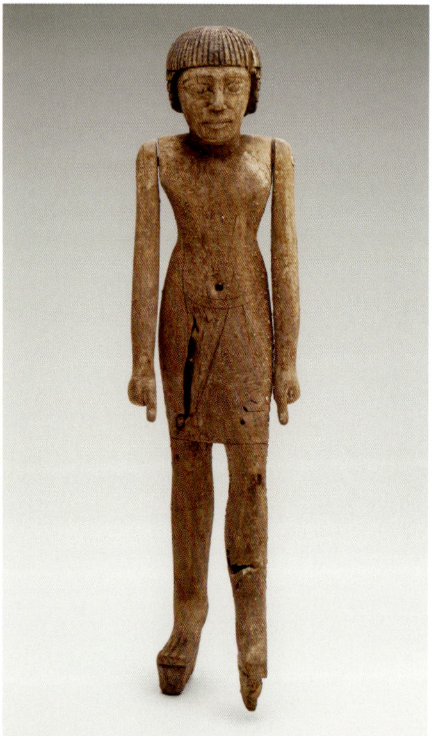

5 Limestone, with remains of paint; 16 3/4 x 22 11/16 in. (42.5 x 57.7 cm). Arthur M. Sackler Museum, Gift of Mr. and Mrs. Samuel H. Lindenbaum, 1983.96.

Queen Arsinoë II as Hathor
Egyptian, Ptolemaic
after 270 BC

This relief fragment, probably from a temple, illustrates how the Macedonian rulers who governed Egypt after Alexander's conquest and the founding of Alexandria chose to appear to the local population: not in Greek fashion but by adopting traditional Egyptian modes of representation. Arsinoë II (c. 316–270 BC), the sister-wife of Ptolemy Philadelphos, wears rich jewelry and holds a lily scepter. On her elegantly coiffed wig sits a vulture headdress, topped by a composite crown. This elaborate crown, created for her and reused in images of later queens including the famous Cleopatra VII, consists of ram's horns, the Red Crown of Lower Egypt, and the sun disk and bull's horns of Hathor. This representation was probably created after the death and deification of Arsinoë II. The finely carved details of the sunk relief were once painted. AJA

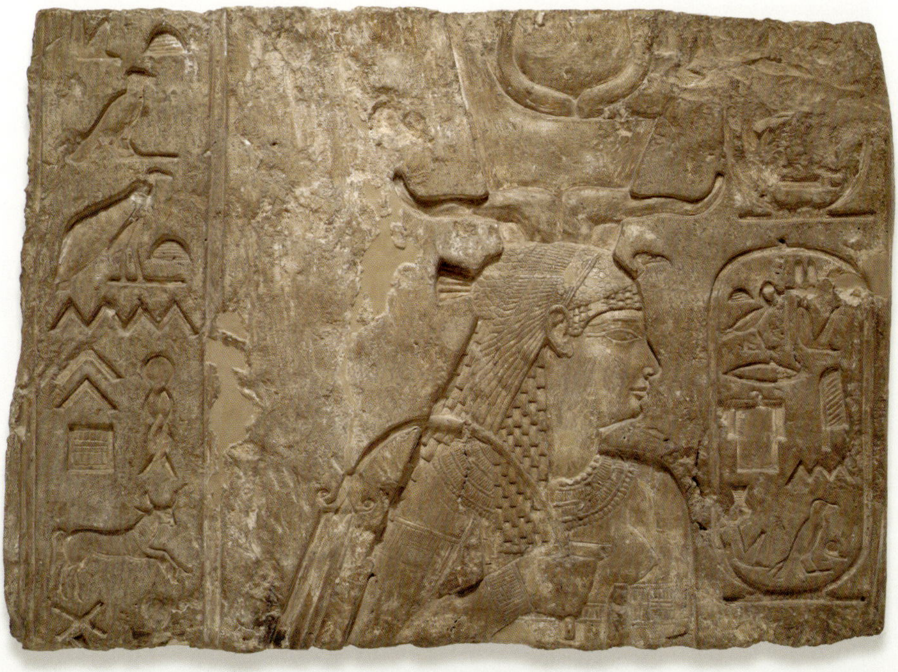

6 / Tablet case: Clay, 1 3/4 x 2 3/16 in. (4.4 x 5.5. cm). Arthur M. Sackler Museum, Gift of Nanette Rodney Kelekian, 1983.108. Seal: Hematite; inscribed PA-AZU, son of SAGTAR-bani; h. 1 in. (2.4 cm). Arthur M. Sackler Museum, Marian H. Phinney Fund, 1993.183.

Tablet Case with Multiple Impressions of Seal with Presentation Scene, Neo-Sumerian, Ur III period probably reign of King Shulgi, 2094–2047 BC

Cylinder Seal: Presentation Scene Mesopotamian, Isin-Larsa period, c. 2017–1800 BC

In ancient Mesopotamia (modern-day Iraq), documents were inscribed on damp clay tablets and generally left to air-dry. For protection, many tablets were additionally enveloped in clay cases, which could also be inscribed with information, including duplicate texts of the document sealed inside. Carved cylinder seals were often rolled across the clay to leave impressions denoting individual or institutional ownership and ensuring authenticity or legitimacy of the text. / The tablet case illustrated here bears the rolled impression of such a cylinder seal. The impressed scene is similar to the one depicted on a slightly later seal of hematite, also shown. A goddess stands behind the seal owner and presents him to a seated king. The seal is pierced lengthwise so it could be strung and worn as a personal adornment or attached to a garment. AJA

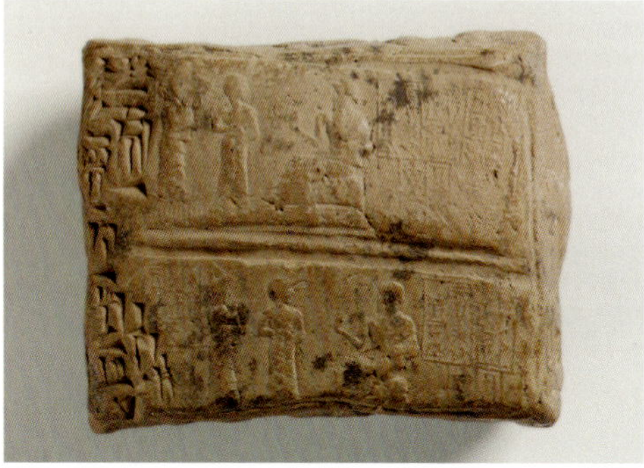

Above: tablet case; below: seal, modern impression

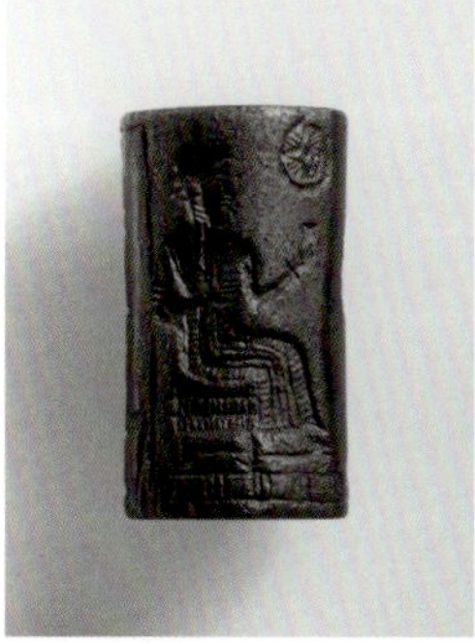

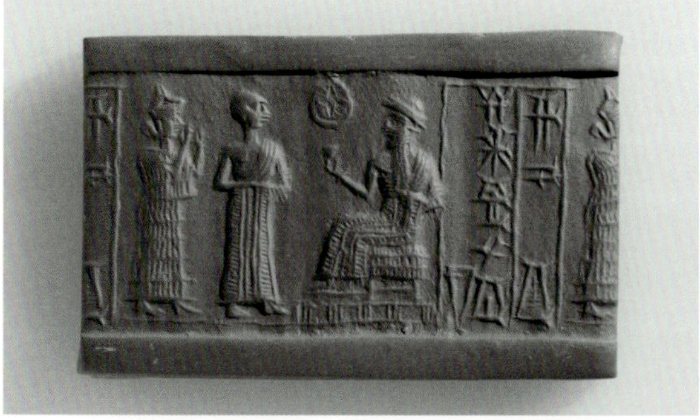

7 Alabaster, 25 13/16 x 19 7/8 in. (65.5 x 50.5 cm). Arthur M. Sackler Museum, Gift of Mrs. Percival Lombard, Mrs. John Bartol, Miss D. Bartol, Mr. and Mrs. F. R. Grace, and the Alpheus Hyatt Purchasing Fund, 1940.13.

Head of a Winged Genie
Neo-Assyrian
reign of Ashurnasirpal II
c. 883–859 BC

The walls of the palaces of the Neo-Assyrian kings bore elaborate relief decoration, including scenes of battle and hunt. This fragment was originally mounted to the right of the royal throne base in the throne room of Ashurnasirpal II's Northwest Palace at Nimrud (ancient Kalhu) in northern Iraq. Traces of wings are visible behind the genie, or protective spirit, who wears the horned cap of a deity. This figure originally stood as one of several winged attendants holding ritual objects accompanying the ruler, and flanking a representation of the Sacred Tree. Across the genie's body ran Ashurnasirpal II's "standard inscription," written in cuneiform and listing the titles and achievements of the king. The relief once bore polychrome decoration. AJA

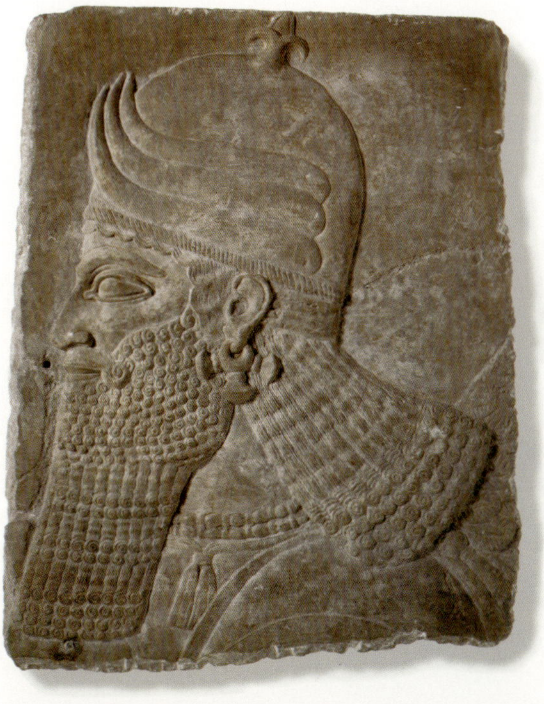

Cast bronze, h. 5 1/4 in. (13.3 cm). Arthur M. Sackler Museum, Bequest of Grenville L. Winthrop, 1943.1162.

Openwork Pin Head
Iranian, Luristan
c. 800–600 BC

Luristan bronzes, named after the region in western Iran where they are found, include weapons, tools, finials, pendants, pins, and horse harness ornaments. Many are decorated with stylized representations of humans, animals, or composite creatures. Although some bronzes have been discovered within sanctuary and settlement contexts, most probably come from graves. / This openwork finial was the decorative head of a large pin likely destined for ceremonial use. The scene is divided into two registers. The upper register depicts a central anthropomorphic figure on a rosette between two slightly smaller figures standing on lions. The lower register depicts a fourth anthropomorphic figure between lions with gaping mouths. Part of the iron pin shaft remains at the bottom. AJA

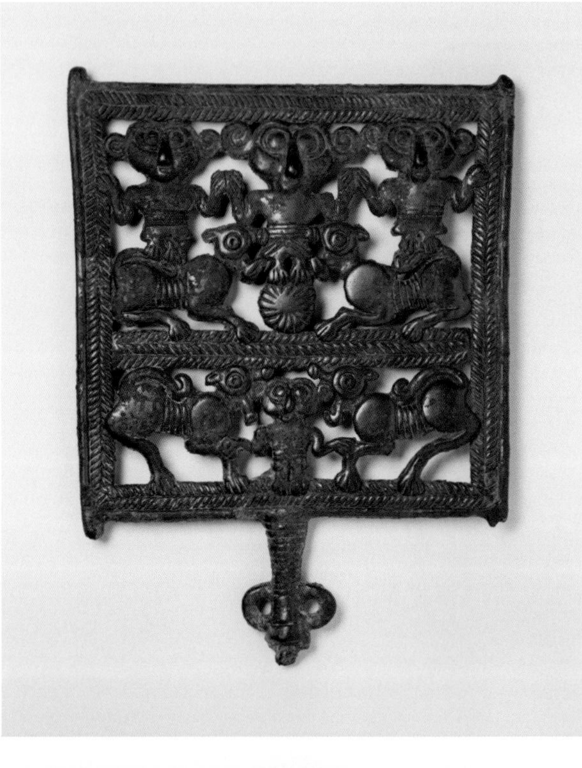

9 Nenfro (volcanic stone), h. 21 in. (53.3 cm). Arthur M. Sackler Museum, David M. Robinson and Marian H. Phinney Funds and the William Hayes Fogg Art Museum Discretionary Fund for the Ancient Art Department, 1984.195.

Sphinx
Etruscan
c. 540–530 BC

This fragmentary sphinx, combining the body of a winged lion with the head of a woman, was probably one of a pair that decorated the entrance to a monumental Etruscan tomb. Sphinxes, as well as other mythical and real creatures, were popular funerary decorations in the Etruscan tradition and were perhaps seen as apotropaic figures whose liminal nature (part beast, part human) made them appropriate companions for the deceased's transition from life to death. Here the rendering of head and wings shows the influence of East Greek art, which predominated in the second half of the sixth century BC. Vulci, where the sphinx was probably carved, was a center of sculpture production. VS

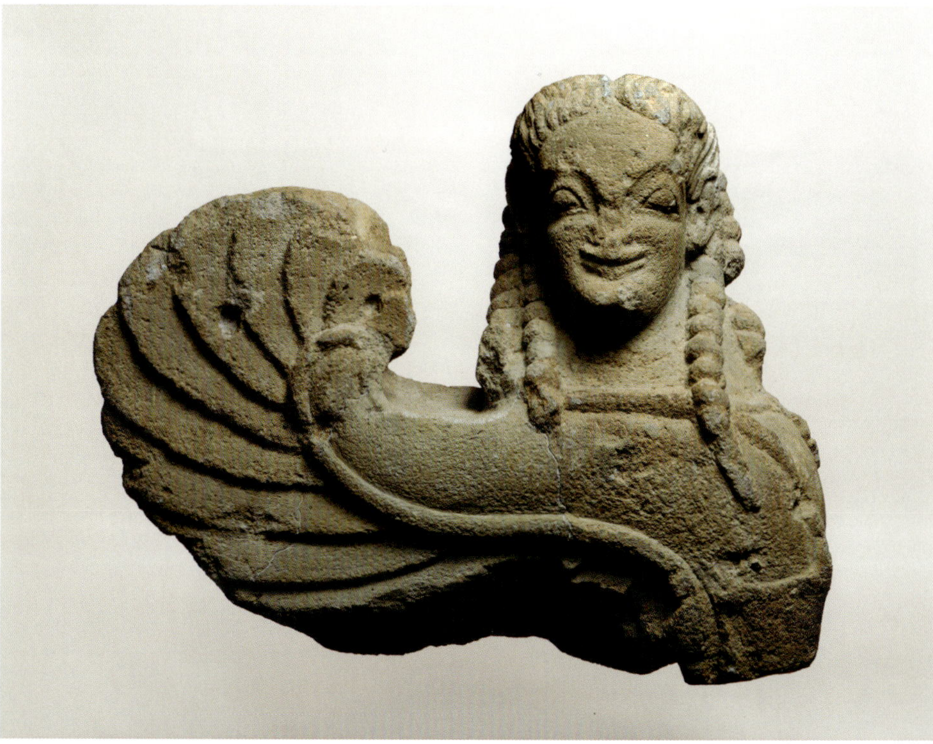

Terracotta, h. 3 1/8 in. (8 cm). Arthur M. Sackler Museum, Purchase through the generosity of Claude Grenier in honor of James Cuno, 2002.283.

Aryballos in the Shape of a Hare

Greek, Proto-Corinthian

c. 630 BC

The production of mold-made vessels in figural shapes, a technique borrowed from the East, became a major industry in Corinth by the late seventh century BC. Popular forms include squatting men, phalli, pomegranates, sphinxes, sirens, and animals such as the lion, ram, duck, and hare. Small *aryballoi* served as containers for scented oils and were often deposited in tombs and sanctuaries. The delicate stippling of the fur and the painted ears, paws, and facial features indicate the work of a skilled painter. Actual hares were common gifts between male lovers in ancient Greece; this aryballos could have fulfilled a similar function. AJA

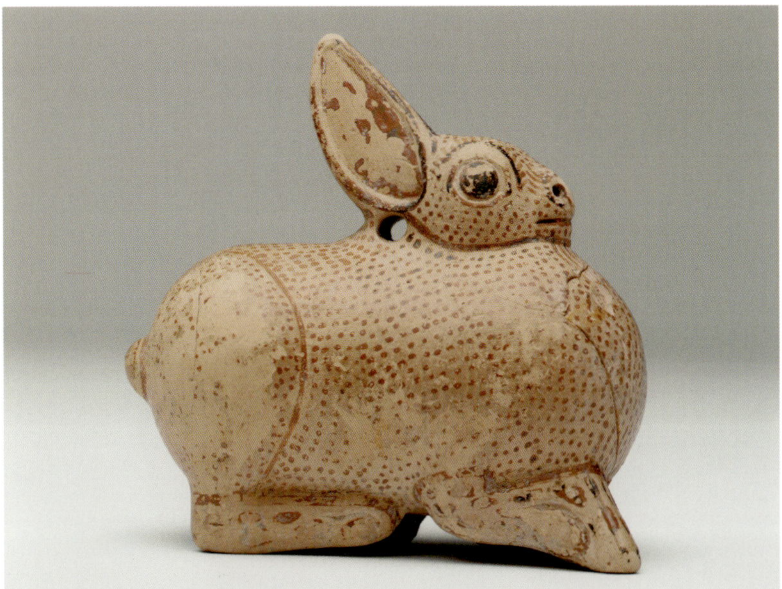

11 Terracotta; h. 6 7/8 in. (17.4 cm), diam. 8 11/16 in. (22 cm). Arthur M. Sackler Museum, Bequest of David M. Robinson, 1960.321.

Black-Figure Skyphos: Preparation of Clay or Agricultural Scene Attributed to the Theseus Painter Greek, Attic c. 510–500 BC

Workshops in and around Athens were the leading producers of Greek pottery in the sixth and fifth centuries BC. This large Attic *skyphos*, or drinking cup, is thought to show either the preparation of clay for potting or the winnowing of grain. The trapezoidal mounds in the center of the front and back could depict clay or perhaps grain at two stages of the winnowing process. Laborers in loincloths are seen either working the clay or gathering the grain under the scrutiny of overseers standing near herms—semiabstract images of the commerce god, Hermes. The roadside herms and stylized foliage place the scenes outdoors. / This vessel is attributed to the Theseus Painter, a painter of pottery in the black-figure style at a time when the popularity of this decorative method was being supplanted by the newer red-figure technique. AM

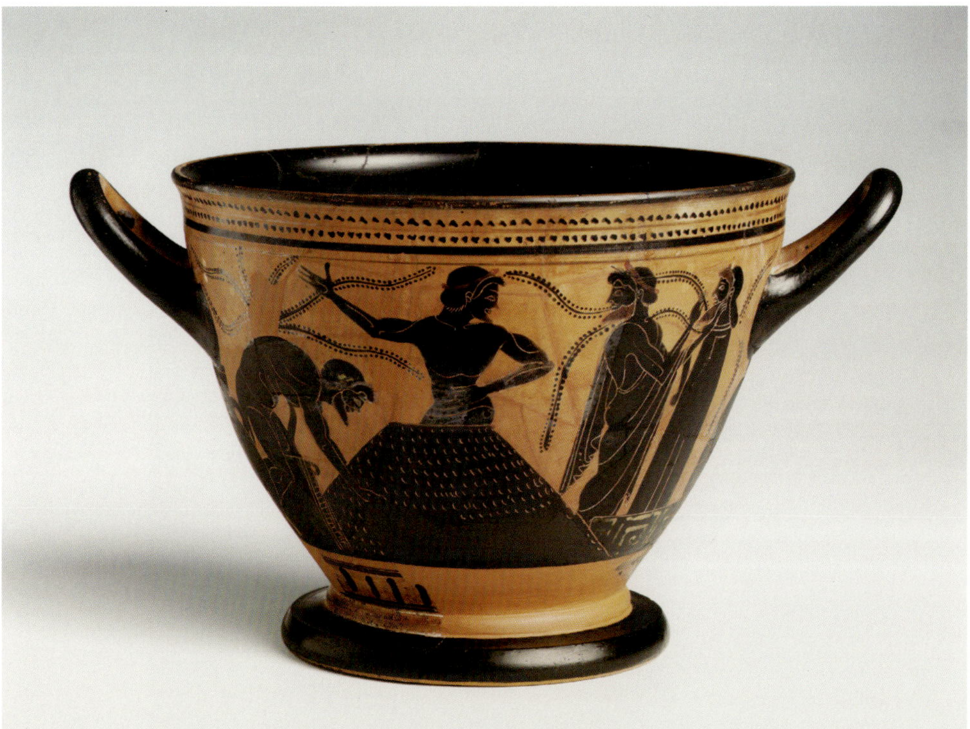

12 Terracotta; h. 17 1/4 in. (43.8 cm), diam. 18 7/8 in. (48 cm). Arthur M. Sackler Museum, Gift of Frederick M. Watkins, 1960.236.

Red-Figure Kalyx Krater: Return of Hephaistos to Olympos

Attributed to the Kleophrades Painter Greek, Attic, c. 500 BC

After the divine smith Hephaistos was cast from Mount Olympos, Dionysos was the only god able to coax him back to the home of the gods. He did this with the help of wine and his band of riotous satyrs, creatures who were half-man, half-horse. / This vessel, known as a krater, was used for mixing wine with water, a quintessentially Greek practice. Such a highly decorated pot was no doubt destined for use at the *symposion*, a male drinking party that would often have ended with a drunken procession similar to the mythological one depicted here. The vase has been attributed to the Kleophrades Painter, one of the greatest of the second generation of vase painters to work in the red-figure technique. AM

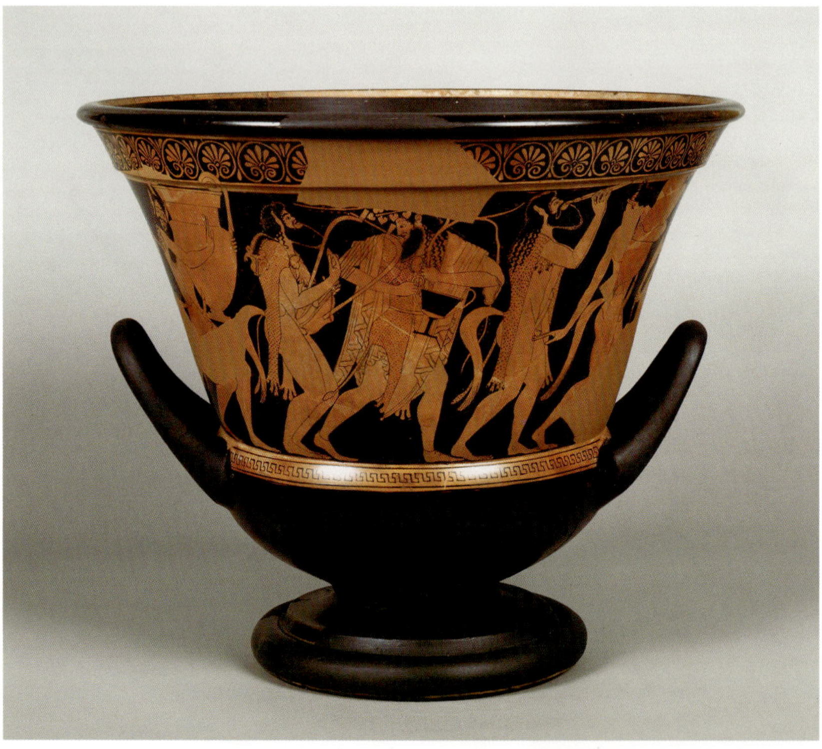

13 Terracotta; h. 11 13/16 in. (30 cm), diam. 13 3/16 in. (33.5 cm). Arthur M. Sackler Museum, Transfer from the Alice Corinne McDaniel Collection, Department of the Classics, Harvard University, 2007.104.4.

Red-Figure Bell Krater: Phlyax Scene
Attributed to the McDaniel Painter Greek, South Italy, Apulian
c. 370 BC

In the fourth century, red-figure wares made in South Italy provided stiff competition for imported Attic pottery, eventually replacing it in the local markets. *Phlyax* vessels, produced in greatest numbers in the workshops of Apulia and Paestum, are thought to show scenes from performances of Attic comedy in South Italy or of South Italian parodies of Attic tragedy. The actors, known as *phlyakes*, are depicted in masks and padded suits and often sport exaggerated phalli. Their appearance on such vases, along with components of stage buildings and sets, provides valuable insight into ancient Greek theater production. / The McDaniel Painter, an otherwise anonymous Apulian vase painter, derives his name from this krater's attribution to his hand. Typical of his work are the thin laurel leaves below the rim of the vessel and the small meander pattern below the scene. AM

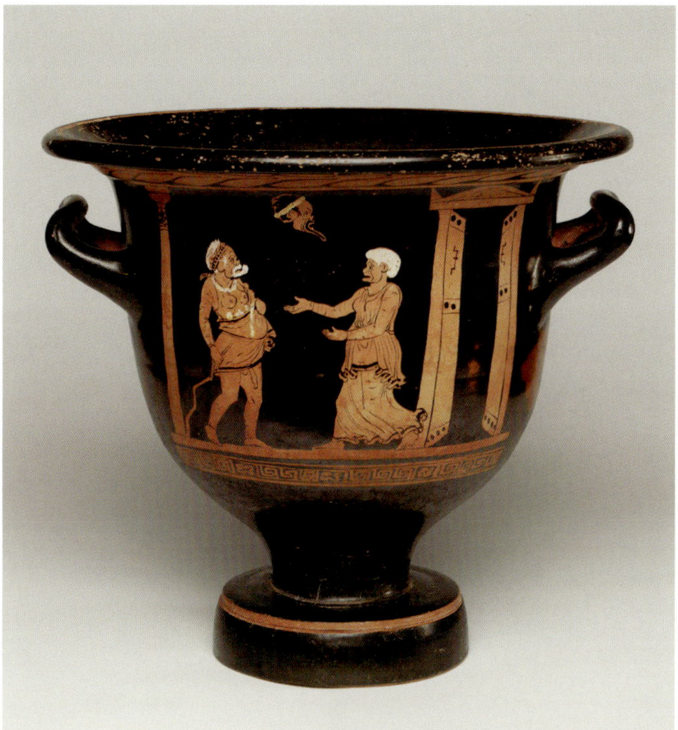

Highly polished, translucent brown and honey-colored nephrite; 5 1/8 x 3 1/16 x 3/16 in. (13 x 7.8 x 0.5 cm). Arthur M. Sackler Museum, Bequest of Grenville L. Winthrop, 1943.50.468.

Jade Configuration of Dragon, Bird, and Snake
Chinese, Warring States period 4th–3rd century BC

Admired for its durability, color, translucence, and luster, jade has been used to fashion objects for ritual and personal adornment in China since at least the fifth millennium BC. A native variety of silicate known as nephrite was the most common jade stone used in ancient China. Nephrite is extremely hard and must be cut, drilled, and polished using abrasive sands of even greater hardness than itself—a labor-intensive technique first devised by Neolithic lapidaries. Later artisans honed the technique, creating even more complex jade forms with increasingly elaborate ornamentation. The jades illustrated here date to China's late Bronze Age known as the Warring States period (5th–3rd century BC) and represent the pinnacle of jade artistry in ancient China. / The serpentine plaquelike pendant is composed of a dragon's head at one end and a bird grasping a snake with its beak at the other; it is decorated nearly identically on both sides. Though pictured vertically, the piece would

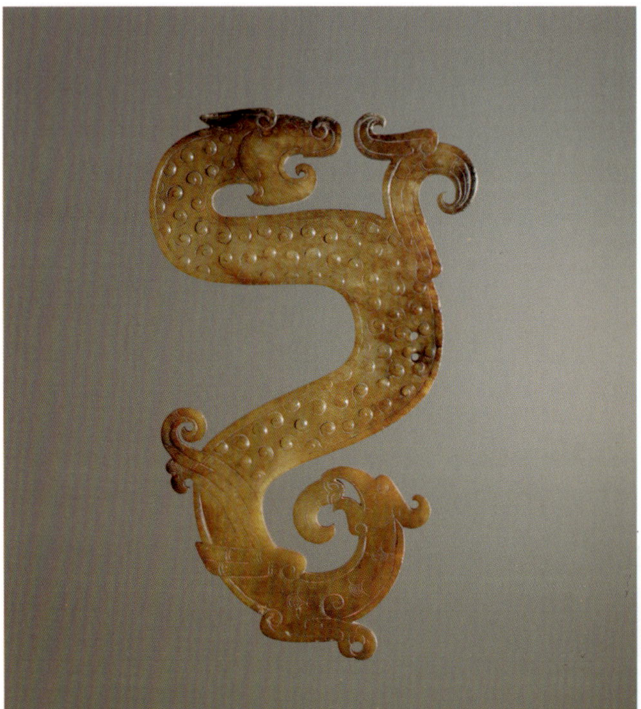

15 Clouded, translucent grayish green nephrite with light brown markings on one side and areas of dark brown and grass-green on the other; diam. 8 1/8 in. (20.6 cm), depth 1/4 in. (0.6 cm). Arthur M. Sackler Museum, Bequest of Grenville L. Winthrop, 1943.50.649.

Large Jade Disk
Chinese, Warring States period
4th century BC

have been suspended horizontally from a thin cord, as evidenced by two small threading holes midway between the dragon's and bird's heads. / The disk traces its form to the Neolithic era, when jades of this shape were interred in the graves of important figures. The tiny raised bumps and incised curls are characteristic of Warring States-period jades and distinguish this spectacular disk from its earlier counterparts. A jade of this size and quality could only have been made for an elite member of society. In later years, the Qianlong Emperor (r. 1736–95) composed a poem in its praise and ordered the verse engraved on its outer edge. These and hundreds of other archaic Chinese jades are part of the Art Museum's Grenville L. Winthrop collection, which is considered one of the finest collections of such material in the world. MAM

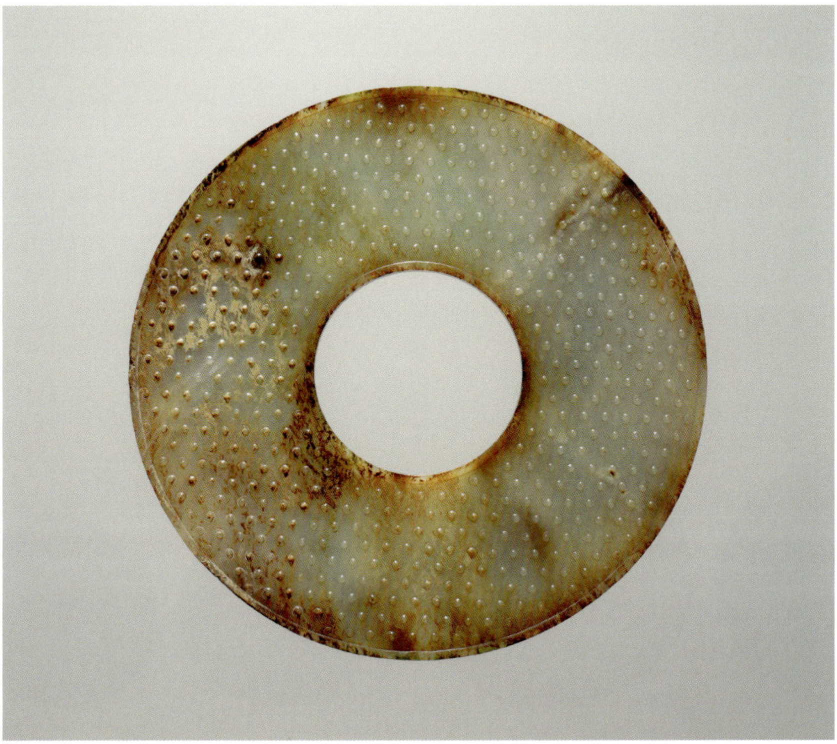

Dekadrachm: Silver, signed Kimon, 42.94 g. Tetradrachm: Silver, signed Herakleidas, 17.51 g. Arthur M. Sackler Museum, Bequest of Frederick M. Watkins, 1972.212, .134.

Dekadrachm of Syracuse
Greek, Sicily
c. 405 BC

Tetradrachm of Katane
Greek, Sicily
c. 405 BC

This dekadrachm is one of the great masterpieces of classical Greek art. Dekadrachms such as these are thought to be the coinage of the tyrant Dionysios of Syracuse (r. 405–367 BC), probably struck to finance his military campaigns against the Carthaginians. The obverse shows a galloping quadriga driven by a charioteer, crowned by a small flying Victory. The elegant profile of the nymph Arethusa on the reverse bears the engraver's signature on the headband: KIM, for Kimon. Harvard houses the world's largest collection of dekadrachms from Syracuse. / The head of Apollo on the obverse of the tetradrachm is an early and particularly successful representation of the human face in frontal view. Just legible to the right, around the edge, is the signature of the die-engraver Herakleidas. The reverse shows the popular galloping quadriga. Katane, north of Syracuse, is a Sicilian city whose coinage marked a high point in classical Greek art. VS

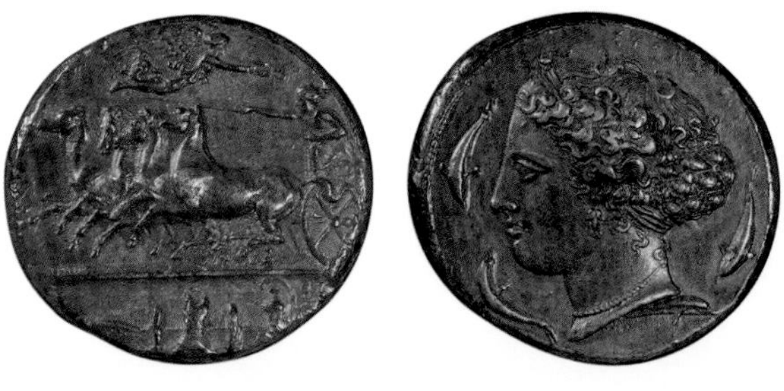

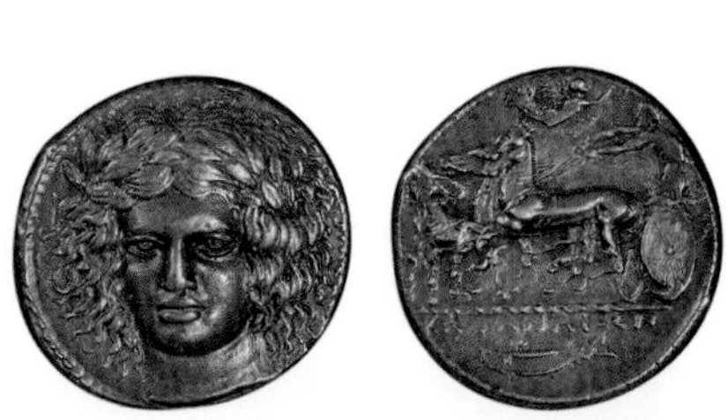

17 Marble, 37 5/8 x 19 3/8 in. (95.5 x 49.2 cm). Arthur M. Sackler Museum, Alpheus Hyatt Purchasing and Gifts for Special Uses Funds in memory of Katherine Brewster Taylor, as a tribute to her many years at the Fogg Museum, 1961.86.

Grave Stele of a Young Girl, "Melisto" Greek, Attic
c. 340 BC

Child mortality was a common occurrence in the ancient world, and sculpted gravestones (stelae) often marked children's tombs in the classical and Hellenistic periods. The young girl represented on this stele from Attica is shown smiling as she clutches a doll while teasing her Maltese dog with a pet bird. A wreath, perhaps in bronze, was originally attached to the girl's hair through the holes next to her head. The scene is generic, but the careful composition and the sensitive depiction of the girl's chubby face make this a particularly fine example. The inscription below the pediment identifies her as "Melisto, daughter of Ktesikrates from the deme [district] of Potamos." VS

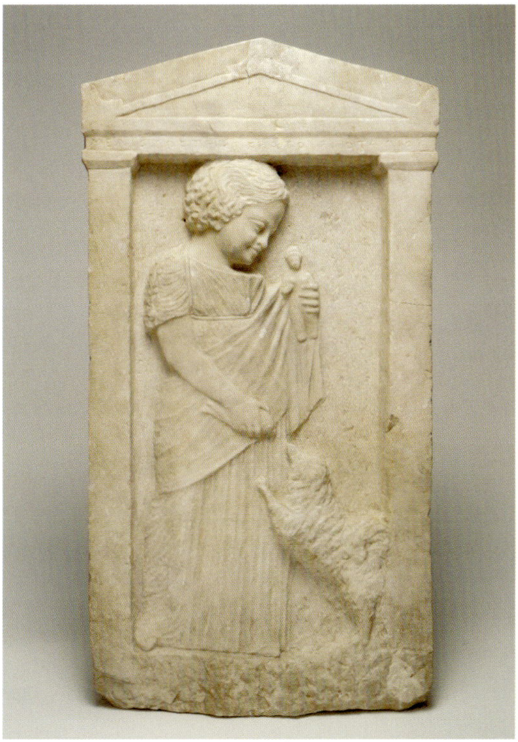

Tetradrachm: Silver, 17.13 g. Denarius: Silver, 3.76 g. Arthur M. Sackler Museum, Bequest of Frederick M. Watkins, 1972.156, .244.

Tetradrachm of Demetrios Poliorketes
Greek, from the mint of Salamis, Cyprus
c. 300–295 BC

Denarius of Marcus Iunius Brutus and Lucius Plaetorius Caestianus
Roman, Republican, 43–42 BC

Demetrios Poliorketes ("besieger of cities") was one of Alexander the Great's Successors (Diadochoi) in Macedonia. In a gesture of political propaganda, he commemorated on this coin his greatest success, the naval victory at Salamis in 306 BC over Ptolemy of Egypt. On the obverse, a Victory standing on the prow of a ship blows a trumpet; on the reverse is the sea god Poseidon with Demetrios's name and title of king—the latter still a novelty in the Greek world. / The denarius is also explicitly related to a historical event—the murder of Julius Caesar on the Ides of March, 44 BC. The obverse shows the head of Brutus, one of the assassins. Only one other living Roman had ever been portrayed on coins when the Senate voted to feature Caesar's portrait on coinage, an act suggestive of monarchic privilege that precipitated his death. The reverse shows the daggers of the two assassins, now "liberators," with a *pileus* (cap of freedom) between them. VS

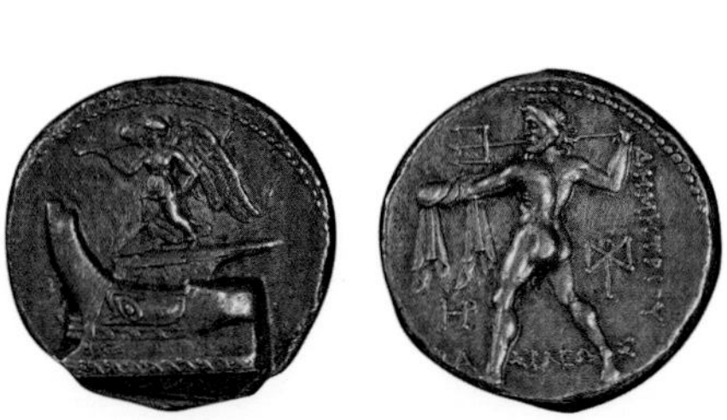

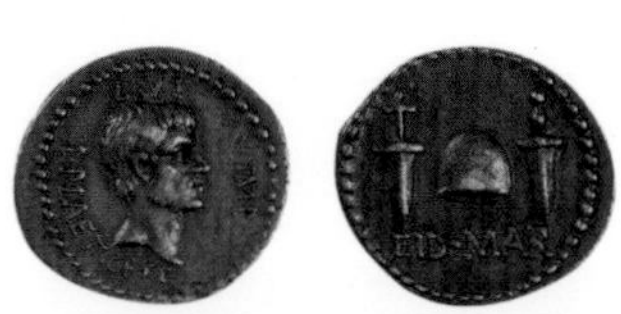

Drachm: Bronze, 29.7 g. Arthur M. Sackler Museum, Marian H. Phinney Fund, 2004.11. Solidus: Gold, 4.49 g. Arthur M. Sackler Museum, Bequest of Thomas Whittemore, 1951.31.4.157.

Drachm of Lucius Verus, with the Nile and the Nilometer
Roman Provincial, from the mint of Alexandria
AD 162–63

Solidus of Pulcheria
Byzantine, from the mint of Constantinople
AD 420–22

This bronze drachm demonstrates the richness of coin designs ("types") in Roman provincial coinage. The obverse shows the emperor's portrait; the reverse is a complex representation of the Alexandrian landscape. A personification of the river Nile reclines, crowned with lotus and holding a cornucopia and a reed. The exergue features a swimming crocodile and the background a nilometer, to measure the annual flood and thus predict crop revenue. The gamma (Greek number *3*) at left dates the coin to the third year of the emperor's reign. / This solidus exemplifies the new prominence of imperial women on Byzantine coinage. The obverse shows Augusta Aelia Pulcheria, sister of the emperor Theodosius II. The hand of God crowns her, sanctioning her power on earth. On the reverse, Victory holds a decorated cross commemorating the one Pulcheria erected at the site of the Crucifixion in AD 420. The inscription records the vows to her in honor of her twentieth anniversary. VS

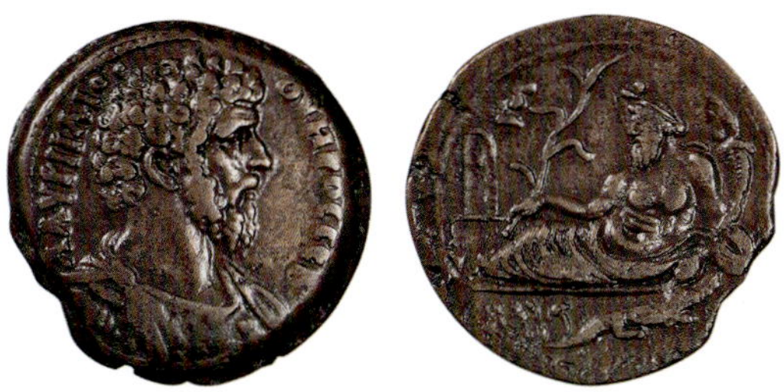

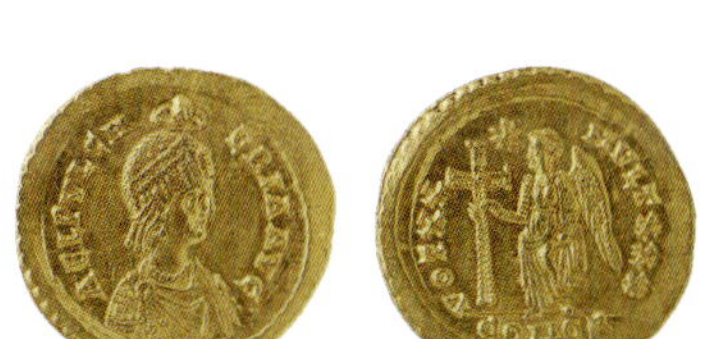

 Parian marble, h. 48 7/16 in. (123 cm). Arthur M. Sackler Museum, Bequest of Mrs. K. G. T. Webster, 1926.48.

Meleager Roman copy of a Greek original (c. 340 BC) attributed to Skopas of Paros

c. AD 70–100

Meleager, the tragic Greek hero, is depicted here resting after his momentous triumph over the destructive Calydonian boar. Skopas, to whom the original statue has been attributed, was among the most renowned sculptors of the classical period. Harvard's *Meleager* includes many of the characteristic features associated with his style, such as the deep-set and expressive eyes, furrowed brow, and tousled hair. / The Romans had an insatiable appetite for Greek statuary. Beginning in the late third century BC, not only were thousands of Greek statues carried to Rome to decorate houses and public spaces but many copies and variants of famous works were also produced. This statue is one of more than thirty identified copies of Skopas's Meleager. AM

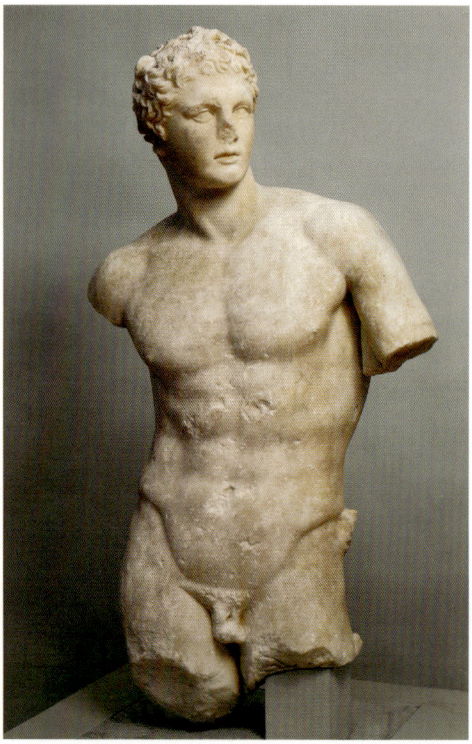

21 Bronze, h. 9 1/8 in. (23.2 cm). Arthur M. Sackler Museum, Gift of John W. Straus in honor of David Mitten, 2007.221.

Demosthenes Roman copy of a Greek original (c. 280 BC) by Polyeuktos of Athens

100 BC–AD 100

Demosthenes, perhaps the greatest Athenian orator, argued vehemently against Macedonia's increasing domination of Greece as Philip II rapidly gained territory and power there. This statuette is the most complete surviving replica of Polyeuktos's full-sized portrait of Demosthenes, although about fifty copies of the work are known. The bronze original was erected in the Athenian agora forty-two years after Demosthenes' suicide, at a time when Athens was briefly free of Macedonian rule. The early Hellenistic period saw the development of what has been called the psychological portrait, a likeness with individualized features meant to convey the character or personality of the subject. With its furrowed brow, concerned and contemplative gaze, and clasped hands, Polyeuktos's portrait was meant to capture the orator's perseverance and the essence of his internal and external struggles. AM

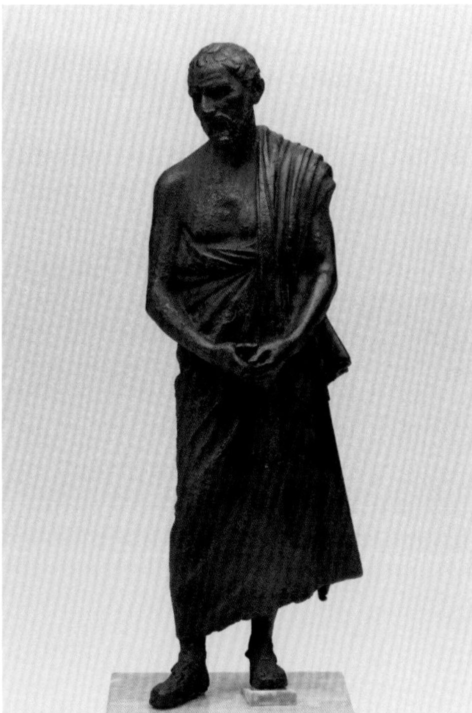

Carrara marble, h. 75 3/16 in. (191 cm). Arthur M. Sackler Museum, Alpheus Hyatt Purchasing Fund, 1954.71.

Trajan
Roman
c. AD 120, with modern restorations

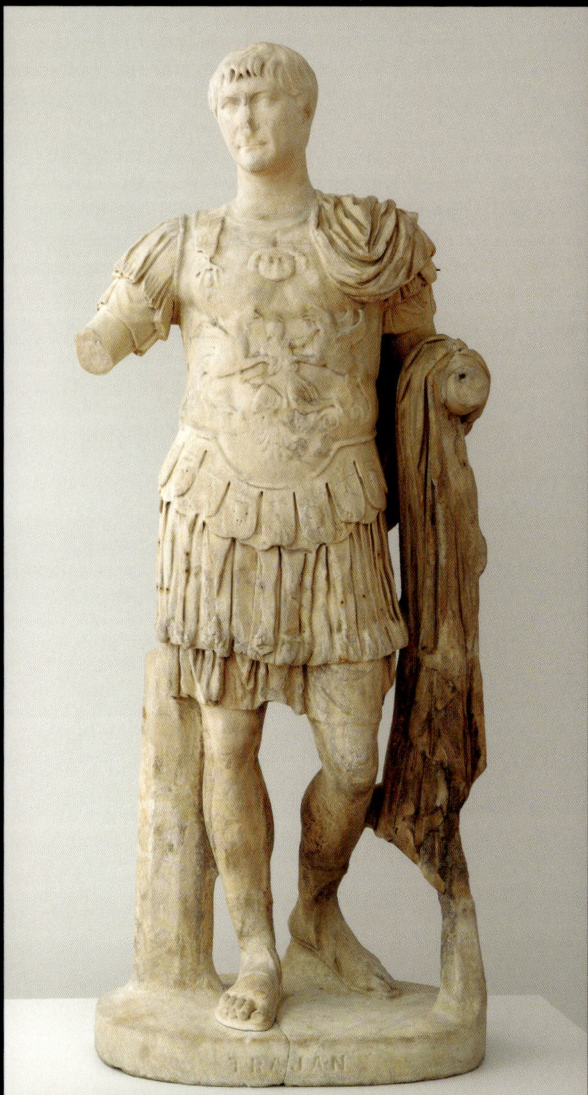

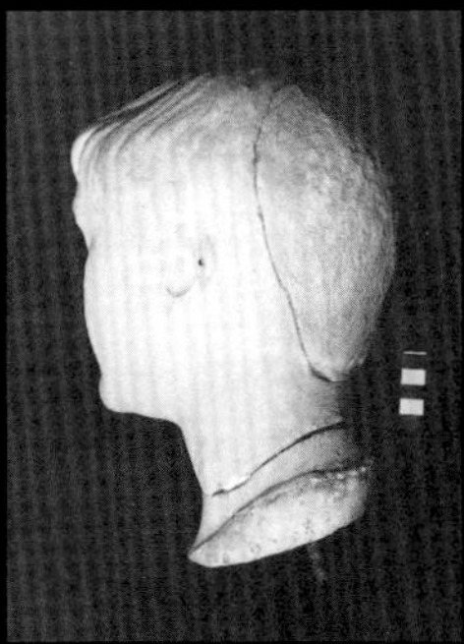
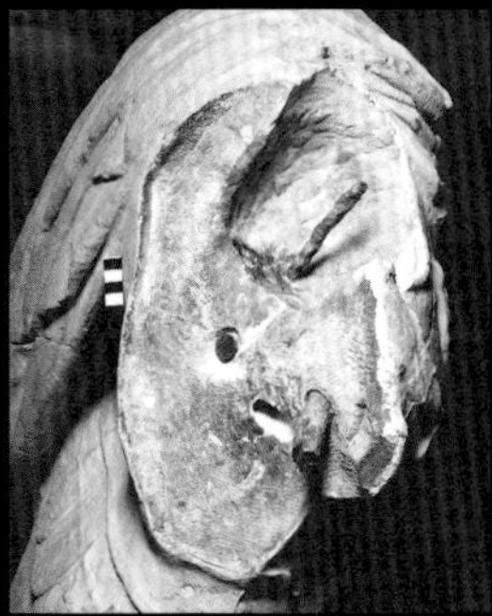
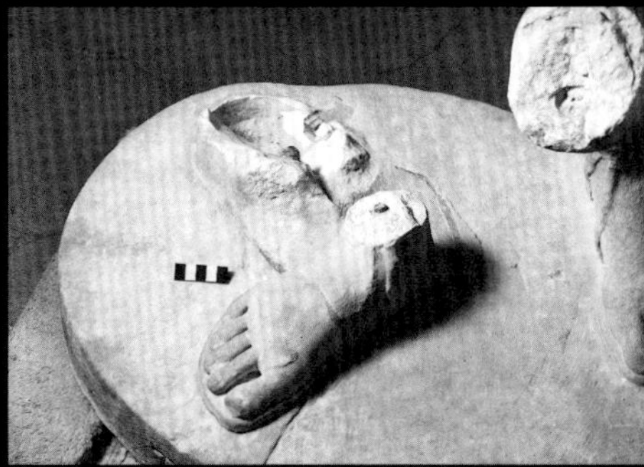

Marcus Ulpius Traianus, of Roman Spanish ancestry, was emperor from AD 98 to 117. During his reign, Rome reached its greatest geographical extent. This is the largest ancient marble sculpture in the museum's collection and depicts Trajan, as he was known, in ceremonial armor. His elaborate parade cuirass (breastplate) is decorated with heroic motifs symbolizing the wars on the eastern frontiers of the empire. An Amazon or Arimasp battles two griffins. The bovine skulls on the leather flaps of the cuirass suggest that the statue may have been commissioned posthumously. / From 1983 to 1985, conservators at the museum's Straus Center for Conservation and Technical Studies disassembled the statue for cleaning and repair of poorly aligned earlier restorations. Core samples were analyzed to distinguish original parts from later restorations. Only the main stone mass—including right leg and ankle, left leg to the knee, and drapery down to the thigh—can confidently be called original. The head may be original but was carved separately. The neck, right shoulder and arm, end of the drapery at the back, lower left leg and drapery at the front, base including both feet, and possibly the back of the head are later restorations. The support at the right of the figure has been recut. A trace of red pigment on the left rear of the tunic may be the remains of original polychromy. AJA & CU

24 / Encaustic on linden wood, 13 7/8 x 8 7/8 in. (35.3 x 22.5 cm). Arthur M. Sackler Museum, Gift of Dr. Denman W. Ross, 1923.60.

Portrait of a Lady with Earrings
Roman, Egypt, Antinoöpolis
c. AD 130–40

Many Greeks living in Egypt after the conquest by Alexander the Great adopted traditional Egyptian funerary practices, mummifying their dead and providing them with three-dimensional mummy masks and coffins. Beginning early in Egypt's Roman period, local Hellenized elites in the Fayum area of northern Egypt and in centers such as Antinoöpolis replaced these masks with naturalistic portraits of the deceased. As was the custom, this one was painted on a wooden panel using encaustic, a mixture of pigments and wax. It might have initially decorated the house of this well-to-do woman. Upon her death, it was inserted, at face level, into her elaborate mummy wrappings. / Evidence suggests that mummies were kept in the home for several generations to preserve the family memory of the dead. The portraits owe their carefully preserved states to their eventual burial in the dry Egyptian sands. AM

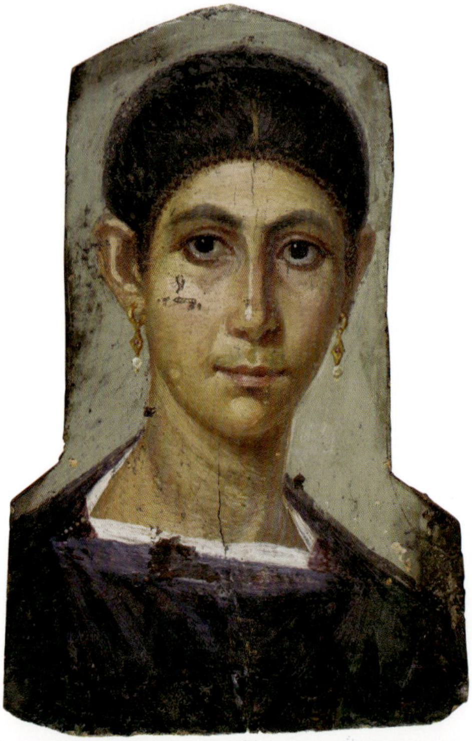

25 / Bronze, with traces of gilding; h. 14 3/16 in. (36 cm). Arthur M. Sackler Museum, Gift of Mr. C. Ruxton Love Jr., 1956.19.

Head of Julia Domna
Roman
AD 193–217

Julia Domna, born in Emesa in Syria, was the second wife of the emperor Septimius Severus and ruled with him from AD 193 to 211. She was the mother of the emperors Caracalla and Geta and two daughters, and was an influential figure in the political and intellectual life of the empire. / Julia Domna's beauty is well known from official portraiture on coinage and monuments. She appears as a young woman with a prominent nose and thick wavy hair parted down the center. Her hair is usually fashioned into a bun at the back of her head, sometimes covered with a veil. Minute traces of gold leaf discovered on the neck of this bronze indicate that the head was originally gilded. Holes in the ear lobes held separate earrings, and a separately cast bun was once attached at the back of the head. The head was part of a full-scale statue or bust. AJA

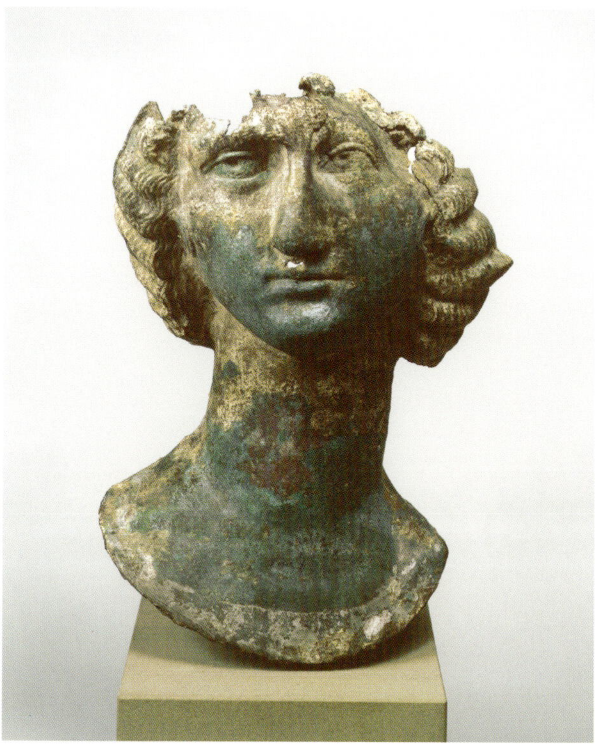

Pentelic marble; left end, 24 13/16 x 21 11/16 in. (63 x 55 cm); front, 25 1/16 x 76 1/2 (63.5 x 194 cm). Arthur M. Sackler Museum, Gift of Edward Forbes, 1899.9.A–C, Bequest of Charles W. Gould, Esq., 1932.49.A–B.

Sarcophagus: Amazonomachy
Roman
late 2nd–early 3rd century AD

Throughout the Roman Empire in the second century AD and afterward, burial in highly ornamental sarcophagi became desirable. Decorative schemes were probably chosen to convey messages about the deceased contained within. Here the theme of the Amazonomachy, a mythological battle between the Greeks and the Amazon women, would have conjured thoughts of heroism and the victory of civilized over barbarian forces. Production centers in Attica and Asia Minor dominated the market, and works from each place appealed to different patrons. Sculpted of marble from the region of Athens, this sarcophagus is of the Attic variety, which typically had three of four sides decorated in high, intricate relief. AM

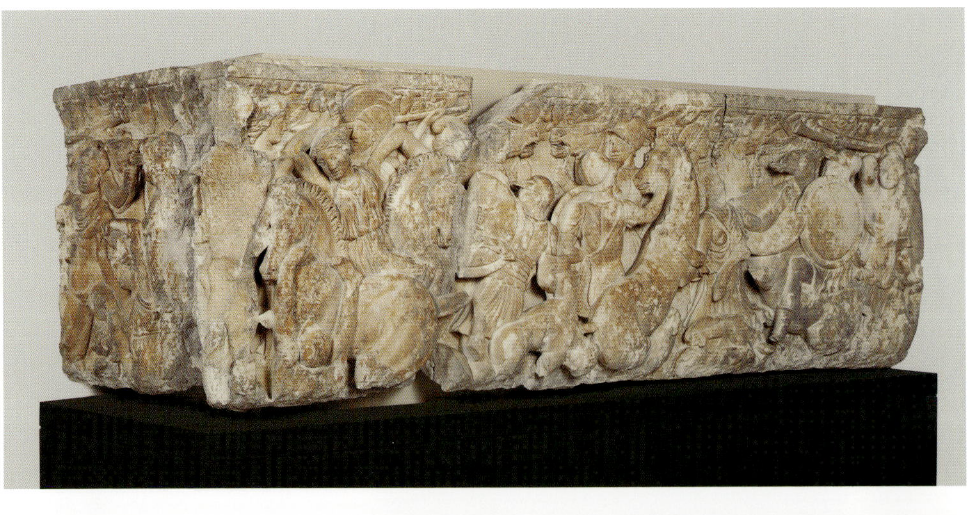

27 / Limestone, 28 1/8 x 22 1/16 in. (71.5 x 56 cm). Arthur M. Sackler Museum, Gift of Alden Sampson, Richard Norton, and Edward W. Forbes, 1908.3.

Funerary Relief of a Woman
Roman, Palmyra
c. AD 150

Funerary portrait slabs from Palmyra, a thriving city along the east–west trade route in Roman Syria, adorned the front end of stone coffins that were inserted in rows into the walls of buildings housing the dead. Although somewhat individualized, the funereal portraiture of Palmyra is characterized by the figures' frontality, stiff postures, and angular sculptural modeling. / This large-eyed and highly bejeweled woman was undoubtedly a member of a prominent Palmyrene family. In a formula typical of these monuments, the Aramaic inscription to her right directly addresses the woman and then identifies her as the daughter of Hayran. She is flanked by two sons who are named in additional inscriptions. The regular appearance of children on these sepulchral reliefs suggests a comforting sentimentality on the part of the Palmyrenes but also points to the high incidence of child mortality in antiquity. AM

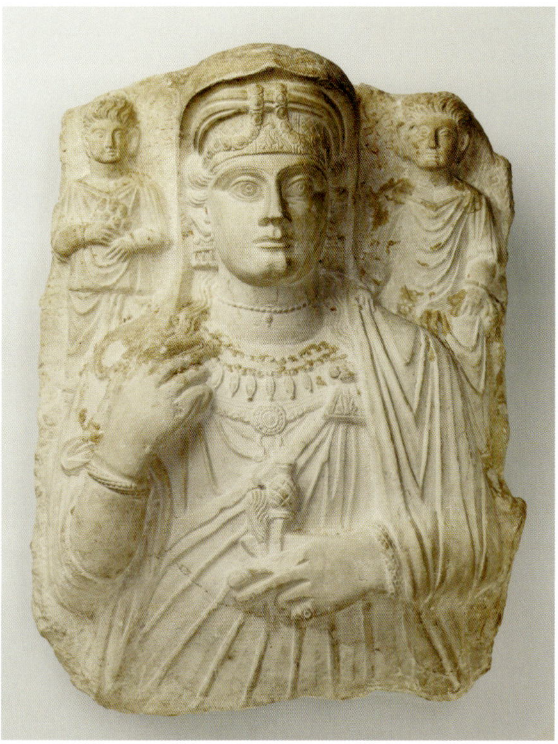

Bronze and lead; h. of bust 8 1/4 in. (21 cm), l. of beam 15 9/16 in. (39.5 cm), l. of chains 17 3/16 in. (43.5 cm), wt. of bust 1441 g. Arthur M. Sackler Museum, Transfer from the Alice Corinne McDaniel Collection, Department of the Classics, Harvard University, 2007.104.3.A–C.

Steelyard: Empress Bust Weight, Crossbeam, and Collar with Chains
Byzantine
5th–7th century

This steelyard with lead-filled counterweight would have been used to weigh marketplace goods of up to 85 pounds, depending on the fulcrum position (the pivot point of the lever). The bar has three graduated scales corresponding to three fulcra; two are preserved with their original hooks, but the fulcrum closest to the center, which would have been used to weigh lighter goods, is missing. To weigh an item, a merchant hung the steelyard by one of the fulcrum hooks and suspended the commodity from the twin hooks attached by chains to the shorter arm. The position of the counterweight on the longer (calibrated) arm in balance indicated the weight of the merchant's goods. The counterweight is shaped as the bust of an empress, a symbolic guarantee of the correctness of the weight and the fairness of the transaction. VS

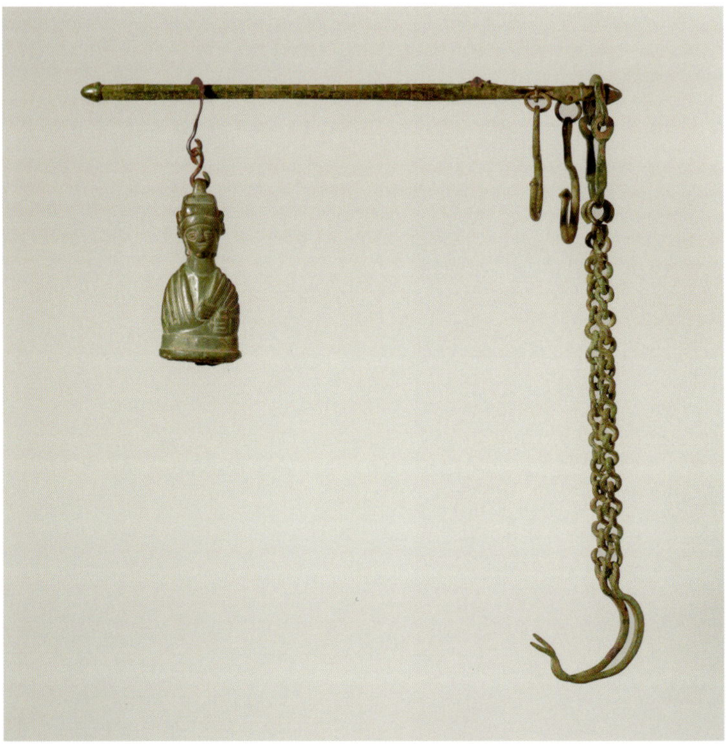

Wool and linen; two fragments: 18 7/8 x 14 9/16 in. (48 x 37 cm) and 12 5/8 x 17 5/16 in. (32 x 44 cm). Arthur M. Sackler Museum, Gift of Mrs. John D. Rockefeller Jr., 1939.112.1, .2.

Saint Theodore
Byzantine, Coptic
c. 500–600

Christians living in Egypt during Byzantine times produced artworks in many media, including decorative and intricately woven textiles. This stern-gazed figure has been identified as Saint Theodore through the inscription on the border fragment (not shown) and by comparing the image on this textile with contemporary icons and mosaics of the saint, whose most conspicuous attribute is his dark, pointed beard. The subject matter of this tapestry suggests it was hung in a church, and the quality of detail on both obverse and reverse indicates that both sides were intended to be viewed. Because this piece entered the Harvard Art Museum's collections in a fragmentary state, questions remain about the overall composition of the work. AM

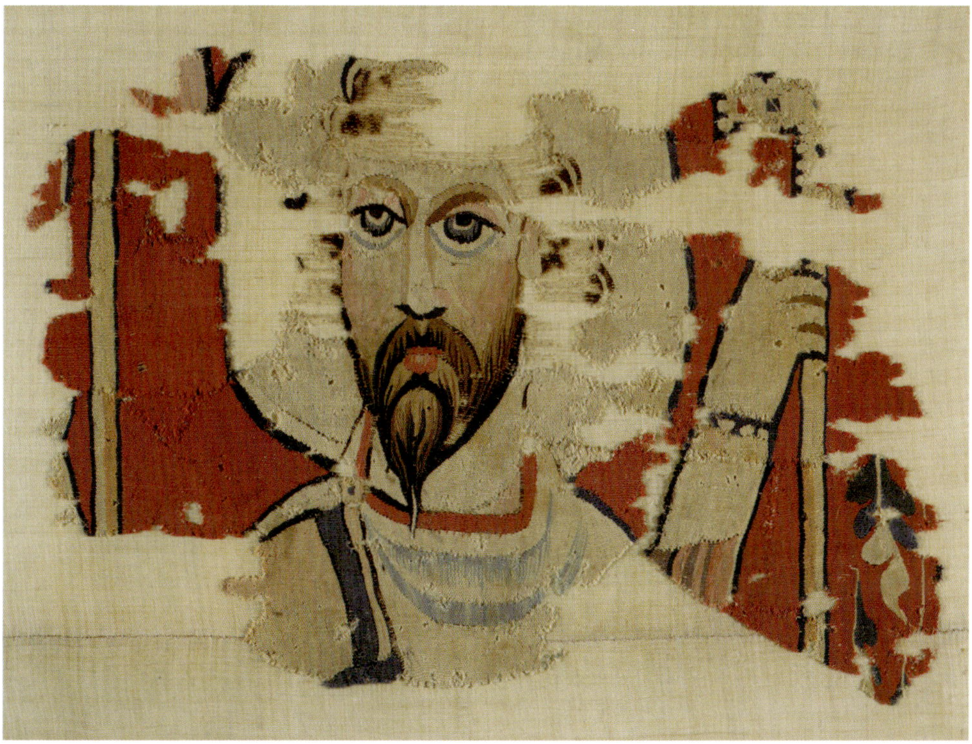

Gilt bronze, Gandhara type; $12\,5/8$ x $9\,7/16$ x $5\,1/8$ in. (32 x 24 x 13 cm). Arthur M. Sackler Museum, Bequest of Grenville L. Winthrop, 1943.53.80.A.

Seated Buddha Shakyamuni with Flaming Shoulders Chinese, Northern and Southern dynasties period 3rd–4th century

This gilt-bronze sculpture depicts the historical Buddha Shakyamuni seated on a rectangular throne flanked by a pair of small lions and two donor figures. The Buddha's hands form a mudra (hand gesture) indicating meditation, while eight triangular points emanating from his shoulders represent flames—a visible manifestation of the body heat associated with meditation. Whereas the Buddha's facial features, mustache, hair, and robes suggest the artistic influence of Gandhara—an ancient kingdom that included parts of present-day Pakistan, Afghanistan, and northwestern India—the lions and donor figures are Chinese in style and indicate a Chinese origin. Introduced to China from India during the first century AD, Buddhism gradually grew in popularity, necessitating the creation of objects of devotion such as this. Scholars continue to debate the precise dating of this work; it is the earliest Chinese Buddhist sculpture in the Art Museum's illustrious collection. MAM

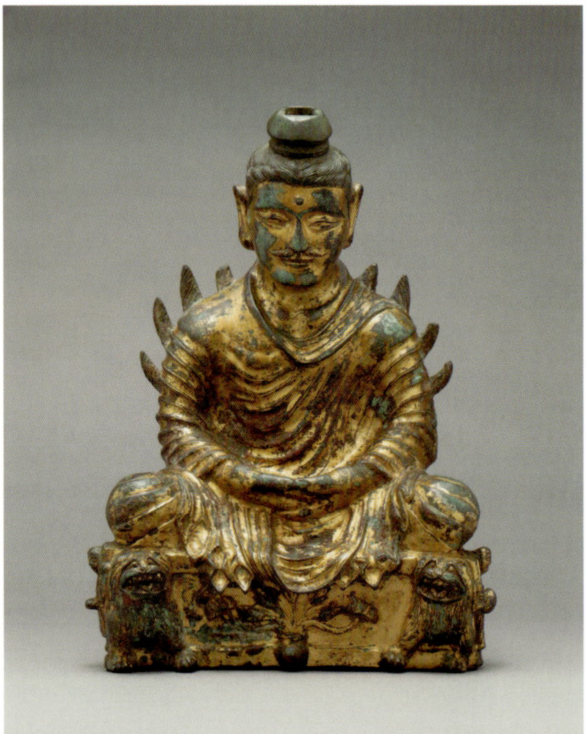

31 Greenish gray limestone, Mon-Gupta style; 23 x 10 x 3 1/2 in. (58.4 x 25.4 x 8.9 cm). Arthur M. Sackler Museum, The Louis Sidney Thierry Memorial Fund and the Ernest B. and Helen Pratt Dane Fund for the Acquisition of Oriental Art, 1988.427.

Standing Buddha Thai, Dvaravati period 7th–8th century

Despite the loss of the head, forearms, and lower legs, this otherwise majestic figure is recognized as an image of the Buddha in the guise of a monk. A finely incised line at the abdomen and subtle ridges at the neck and shins indicate the edges of the upper and lower garments that compose the figure's monastic robes. Although intended to be viewed primarily from the front, this figure was conceived as a freestanding sculpture, as evidenced by its gently modeled back. The forearms would most likely have projected forward in a symbolic gesture associated with the historical Buddha Shakyamuni. / Created during the Dvaravati period, when Buddhism first flourished in Thailand and Indian sculptural styles were introduced, this sculpture reflects the influence of the late fifth-century Gupta style, with its exquisitely subtle modeling, harmonious composition, and delicate balance between areas of light and shadow. MAM

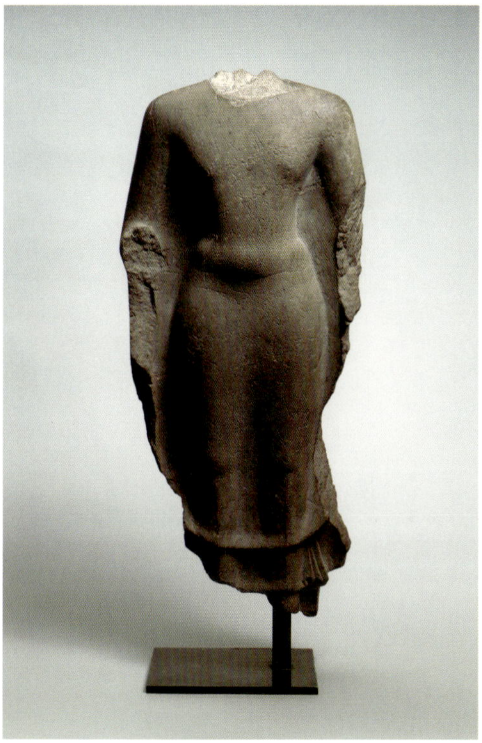

Molded, medium gray earthenware with cold-painted pigments over white ground; white camel: 13 3/16 x 9 13/16 x 7 11/16 in. (33.5 x 25 x 19.5 cm); buff camel: 13 3/4 x 10 13/16 x 6 1/2 in. (35 x 27.5 x 16.5 cm). Arthur M. Sackler Museum, Gift of Anthony M. Solomon, 2003.193.

Two Standing, Braying Camels Laden with Goods
Chinese
Northern Qi period (550–577)

Bactrian camels were a familiar sight along the Silk Road, a network of ancient trade routes that crossed the Eurasian steppes, linking China to the Mediterranean. Accustomed to the desert terrain of Central Asia, these pack animals were an ideal means of transportation that epitomized the influx of foreign products, people, and ideas into Chinese territories. The cosmopolitan character of northern China from the Han (206 BC–AD 220) through Tang (618–907) dynasties was frequently captured in funerary art. It was customary to bury the deceased in tombs with an array of ceramic representations of the people, animals, and objects of daily life believed to be necessary for comfort in the afterlife. These camels, which probably originated from a larger set, are made of low-fired earthenware embellished with mineral pigments applied after firing. A tomb dating to 559 yielded similar camel sculptures, supporting the attribution of this pair to the Northern Qi period. MAM

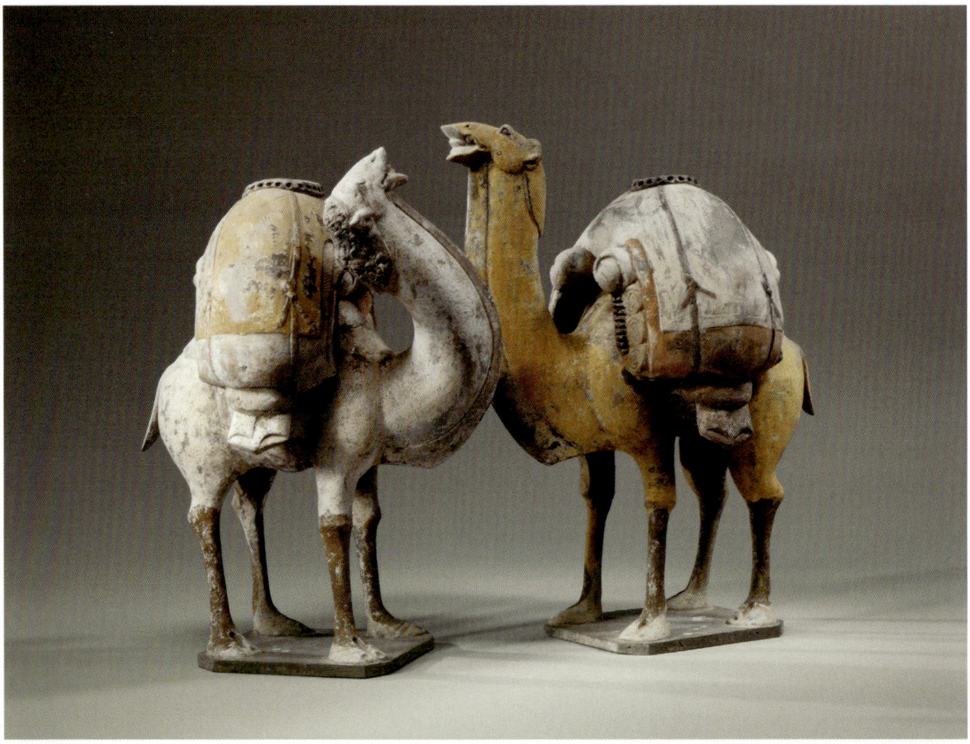

33 Kaya-type ware: gray stoneware with combed and openwork decoration and natural ash glaze; jar and stand: h. 25 11/16 in. (65.2 cm), diam. 11 7/16 in. (29.1 cm). Arthur M. Sackler Museum, Partial gift of Maria C. Henderson and partial purchase through the Ernest B. and Helen Pratt Dane Fund for the Acquisition of Oriental Art, 1991.516.

Ceremonial Stand and Round-Bottomed Jar
Korean, Three Kingdoms period Silla Kingdom mid-6th century

Reportedly recovered from a tomb near Kyŏngju, the ancient capital of Korea's Silla Kingdom (57 BC–AD 668), this robust jar and stand were almost certainly used in the ritual offering of food and wine to nourish the spirit of a deceased nobleman. The bowl-like top section of the openwork stand was designed to support a round-bottomed vessel, such as this jar with everted lip. Turned on a potter's wheel in several sections assembled together before firing, the stand was then carefully pierced to create geometric openwork and embellished with combed details within its horizontal friezes. The same combed decoration can be found on the jar's neck and shoulder. Although both vessels are technically unglazed, they bear a considerable amount of kiln gloss, which occurred when ash from the wood being burned to fuel the kiln fell onto the surface of the wares as they were fired, making this an especially handsome ensemble. MAM

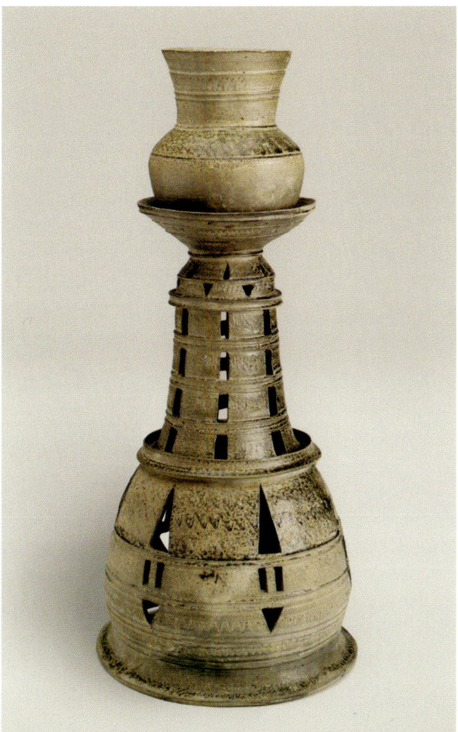

Fragment of a wall painting: pigments on gesso, 14 7/8 x 11 1/2 in. (37.8 x 29.2 cm). Arthur M. Sackler Museum, First Fogg Expedition to China (1923–1924), 1924.43.

Bust of an Attendant Bodhisattva
Chinese, Tang dynasty early 8th century

From the south wall of Mogao Cave 320, Dunhuang, Gansu province

Although Buddhism did not immediately thrive when it was first introduced to China in the first century AD, its influence eventually spread, resulting in a proliferation of Chinese Buddhist art. Inspired by the rock-cut Buddhist shrines of India, Chinese emperors and wealthy devotees began to sponsor the construction of elaborate cave temples. This work and the one opposite originate from two such sites. / The famous Mogao Caves near Dunhuang host an array of colorful wall paintings and clay sculptures that reflect the confluence of Indian, Central Asian, Tibetan, and Chinese artistic traditions. From the fourth to the fourteenth century, nearly five hundred caves were carved into the cliffs and transformed into richly adorned shrines. The walls were plastered with a clay mixture, providing an even surface for artists to paint lively Buddhist scenes. This *Bodhisattva* is a section of a Tang-dynasty (618–907) mural that featured this and other adoring figures attending the Buddha. MAM

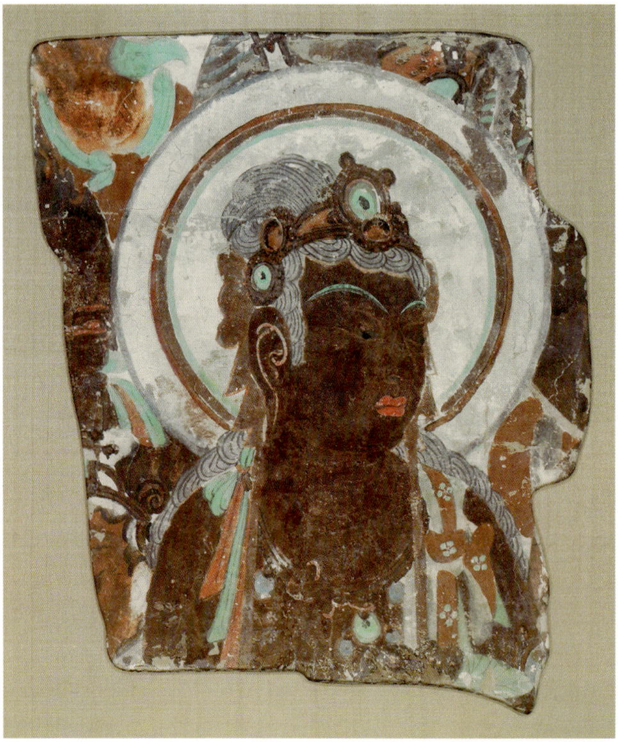

35 Light gray sandstone with traces of polychromy, $43\frac{1}{8}$ x $29\frac{1}{2}$ x $18\frac{1}{2}$ in. (109.5 x 75 x 47 cm). Arthur M. Sackler Museum, Bequest of Grenville L. Winthrop, 1943.53.22.

Seated Buddha (probably Shakyamuni) Chinese, Tang dynasty early 8th century

From the north wall of Tianlongshan Cave 21, near Taiyuan, Shanxi province

This magnificent stone *Seated Buddha* once graced the main wall of an eighth-century grotto at Tianlongshan. From the early sixth century through the Tang dynasty, approximately twenty-five caves were hewn into the sandstone cliffs at Tianlongshan and embellished with Buddhist images carved in high relief directly into the rock. Although this massive Buddha appears fully carved in the round, its unfinished back side indicates that it was once attached to the wall. The broad chest and shoulders, rounded face, and ample neck folds reflect the shift toward a preference for fleshier depictions of the Buddha in the eighth century. MAM

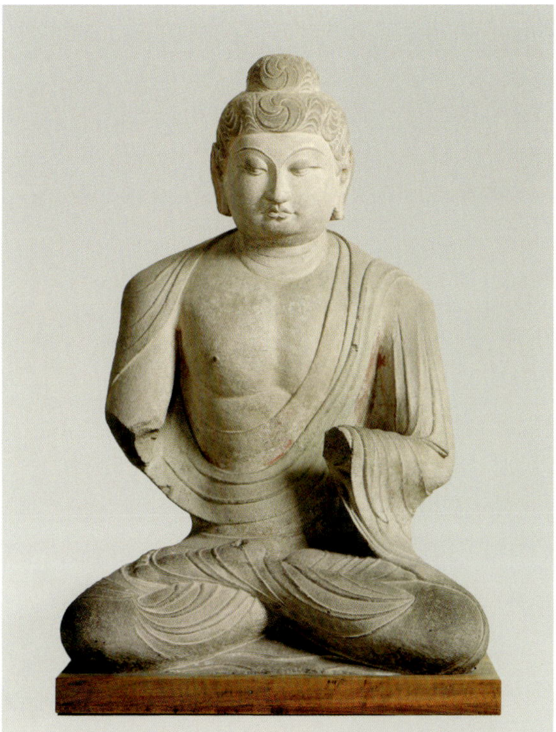

Lushan ware: light gray stoneware with dark brown glaze and light blue splashes; h. 8 11/16 in. (22.1 cm), diam. 7 1/8 in. (18.1 cm). Arthur M. Sackler Museum, Partial gift of Peter W. Scheinman in honor of James Cuno and partial purchase through the Ernest B. and Helen Pratt Dane Fund for the Acquisition of Oriental Art, 2002.91.

Calabash-Shaped Bottle with Blue Splashes

Chinese, Tang dynasty

8th–9th century

Probably from the Duandian kiln, Lushan county, Henan province

Modeled after the double-lobed form of the calabash gourd, this bottle anticipates the transition from the Tang-dynasty (618–907) taste for geometric shapes to the Song-dynasty (960–1279) preference for naturalistic forms. Turned on the wheel in sections that were luted together after drying, the clay body was coated with a thick, opaque brown glaze that extends to the edge of the foot ring. A milky blue glaze suffusion, probably created using wood ash, was brushed over the dark glaze in a careful yet seemingly spontaneous manner. Whereas many contemporaneous celadons and white wares were decorated with incised or carved designs under their glazes, the opacity of this dark brown glaze rendered such a technique impractical. The splashes of color on this type of ware were an inspired alternative to decorating dark-glazed stonewares and reflect the inventiveness of Tang potters. MAM

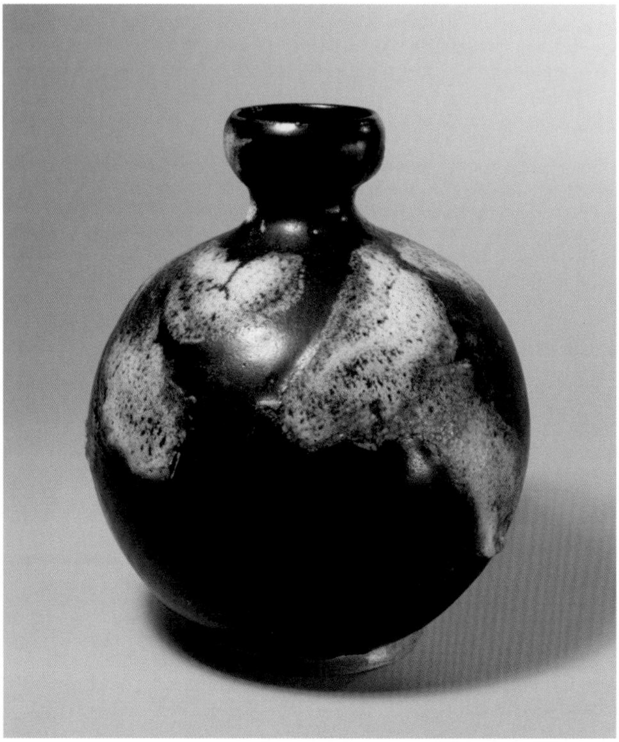

37 Earthenware with overglaze painting, diam. 8 1/2 in. (22 cm). Arthur M. Sackler Museum, Gift of Elizabeth S. Ettinghausen in memory of Richard Ettinghausen and in honor of Mary A. McWilliams, 2006.207.

Bowl with Flower and Scallops
Islamic, Iraq, Basra
ʿAbbasid period
9th century

The blue rosette freely painted in bright cobalt on the white background of this bowl signals a development of far-reaching consequences in ceramic decoration. Blue-and-white wares represent one of the most important themes in the long ceramic dialogue between eastern and western Asia. Ninth-century potters in the Iraqi port town of Basra are sometimes credited with originating the blue-and-white color scheme for ceramics, obtaining cobalt from sources inside Iran. The creamy white ground of the bowl, however, is a response to the white-bodied luxury wares imported from China. Unable to produce high-fired stoneware and porcelain, the Muslim potters instead employed a tin glaze that turned opaque white upon firing. These Basra wares stand as the first generation of a vast, extended family of blue-and-white ceramics. MM

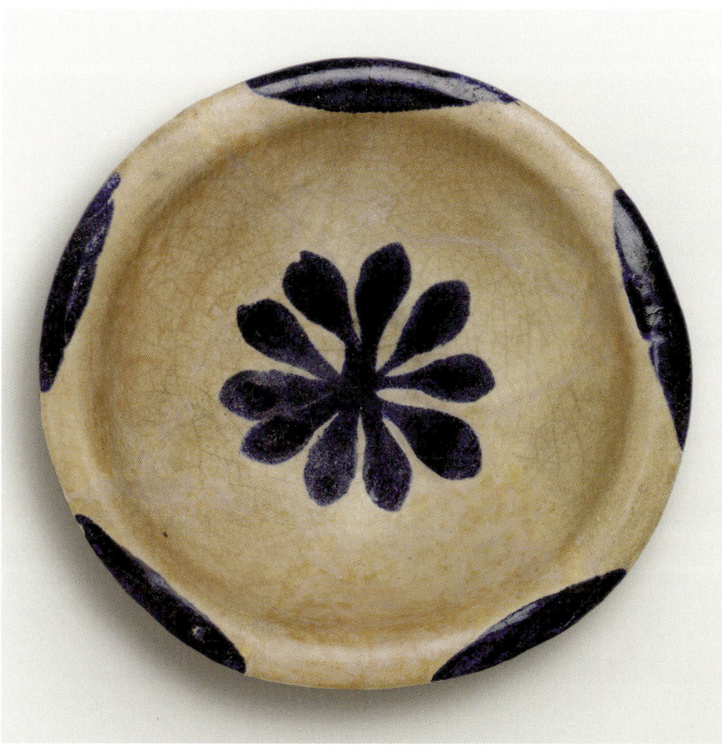

Ink and gold on parchment, 7 3/16 x 10 3/16 in. (18.2 x 25.9 cm). Arthur M. Sackler Museum, Anonymous gift in memory of Rudolph Meyer Riefstahl (1880–1936), 1956.197.

Folio from a Qur'an, Sura 49:16 Islamic, North Africa or Near East, 'Abbasid period 9th–10th century

According to Islamic tradition, the Qur'an, the holy book of Muslims, was revealed in oral form to the Prophet Muhammad in the Arabic language early in the seventh century. At that time, written Arabic did not provide marks to distinguish between letters of the same shape or to indicate the presence of short vowels. A need for accurate recording and proper recitation of the Qur'an led to the codification of the Arabic language and script. Some of the resulting changes are evident in this folio. Here pronunciation is indicated by colored dots; the triangle of six gold dots (lower left) is a marker indicating the end of verse 16. The technique in which letters are exaggerated horizontally (*mashq*) is illustrated in the top line, which forms a single compound word, *bidinikum*, meaning "with your religion." The strong, bold letters reflect the splendor of the divine text. YH

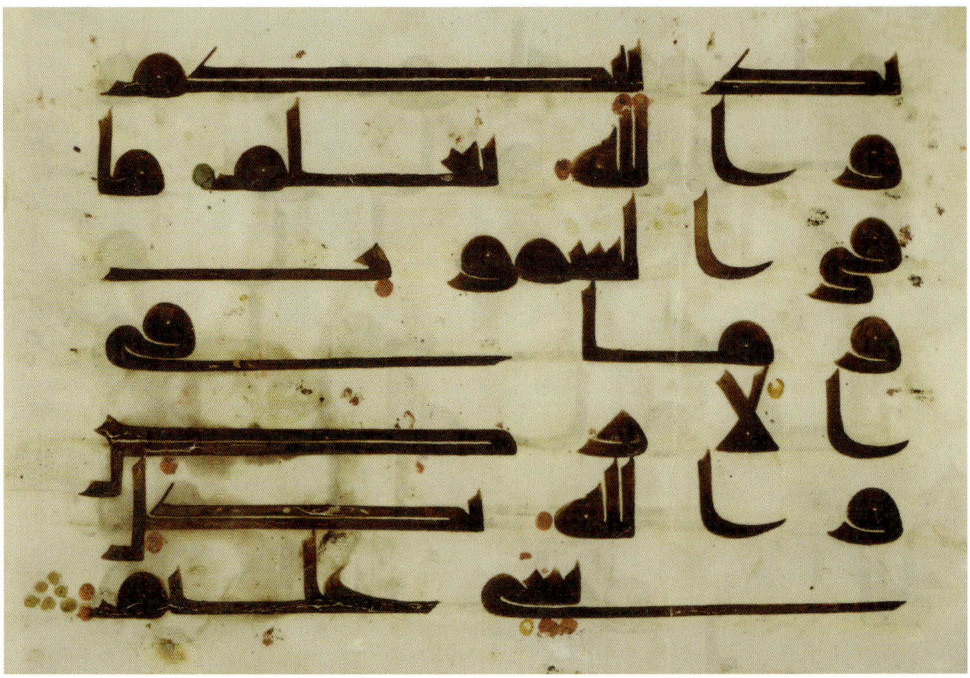

39 Earthenware with underglaze slip painting; inscribed (outside) Modesty is a branch of faith, and faith is in paradise. Bliss; (inside) Greed is a sign of poverty. Peace; h. 3 3/4 in. (9.6 cm), diam. 10 9/16 in. (26.9 cm). Arthur M. Sackler Museum, The Norma Jean Calderwood Collection of Islamic Art, 2002.50.88.

Bowl with Hadith Inscriptions
Islamic, Iran, Nishapur, or Uzbekistan, Samarkand Samanid period 10th century

The epigraphic wares created under the Samanid dynasty (819–999) in northeastern Iran and Uzbekistan rank among the most visually potent ceramics in the history of the industry. Samanid potters perfected a decorative technique that used colored slips (colored clay in solution). First the bowl was coated with a white slip to cover its buff or pinkish earthenware body. Arabic verses in the Kufic script were then painted in colored slips. The entire piece was covered with a lead-based glaze that became transparent when fired. On this bowl the quotation written in black about modesty is ascribed to the Prophet Muhammad and found in the Hadith. The inner inscription is a saying attributed to ʿAli ibn Abi Talib, Islam's fourth caliph and the first Shiʿi imam. AA

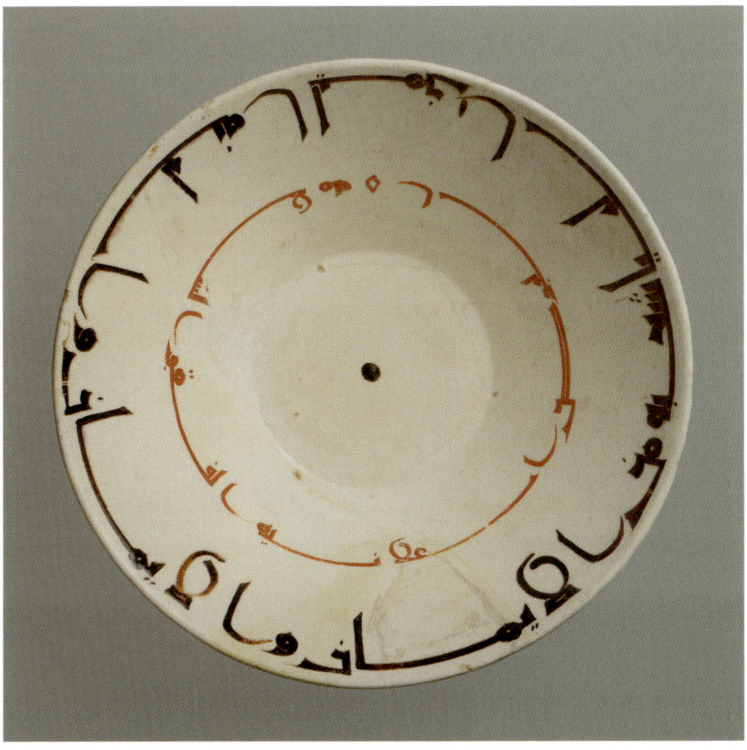

Marble, $11\frac{5}{8}$ x $10\frac{1}{4}$ x $10\frac{1}{4}$ in. (29.5 x 26.1 x 26.1 cm). Fogg Museum, Gift of Meta and Paul J. Sachs, 1922.132.

Capital with Four Scenes from the Story of Samson
French, Avignon
1150–75

This capital originally topped a column that once stood in the cloister of Notre-Dame-des-Doms in Avignon. It represents the Fogg's renowned collection of Romanesque sculpture, which includes architectural as well as freestanding sculpture. All four sides of the capital narrate scenes from the life of the Old Testament hero Samson. In this scene, a monumental Samson wrestles a lion, a contest interpreted as prefiguring the triumph of Christ over Satan. / The deep undercutting and use of a drill have created a play between light and dark, rendering the relief particularly expressive. The columns were probably arranged with the capitals at eye level, where this exquisitely carved detail could be appreciated. DC

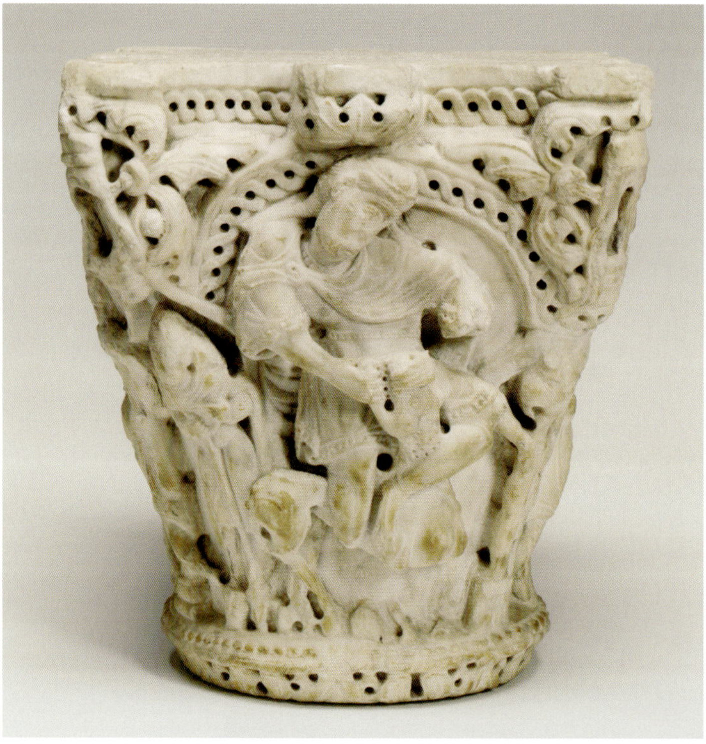

41 Incised celadon ware: light gray stoneware with celadon glaze over incised decoration; h. 8 3/8 in. (21.3 cm), diam. 5 9/16 in. (14.2 cm). Arthur M. Sackler Museum, Bequest of Hervey E. Wetzel, 1919.205.

Segmented Maebyŏng Bottle
Korean, Koryŏ dynasty mid-12th century

After experimenting with high-fired Chinese-style glazes for centuries, by the eleventh century Korean potters had fully mastered the technique of producing celadon wares—light gray stonewares with transparent bluish green glazes. By the second half of the twelfth century they began to develop uniquely Korean shapes, styles, and decorative techniques, as embodied in this magnificent bottle. Although the name and shape of the Korean *maebyŏng* derive from the Chinese *meiping*—a tall broad-shouldered bottle with constricted waist and foot—this example is segmented to suggest the lobes of a ripening melon, reflecting the Korean taste for natural forms. Within each vertical segment are incised images of blossoming and fruiting branches. The clear, slightly crackled glaze displays a jadelike green that appears bluish green at one moment and grayish green the next—a hue so esteemed that even a twelfth-century Chinese emissary described Korean celadons as "first under heaven." MAM

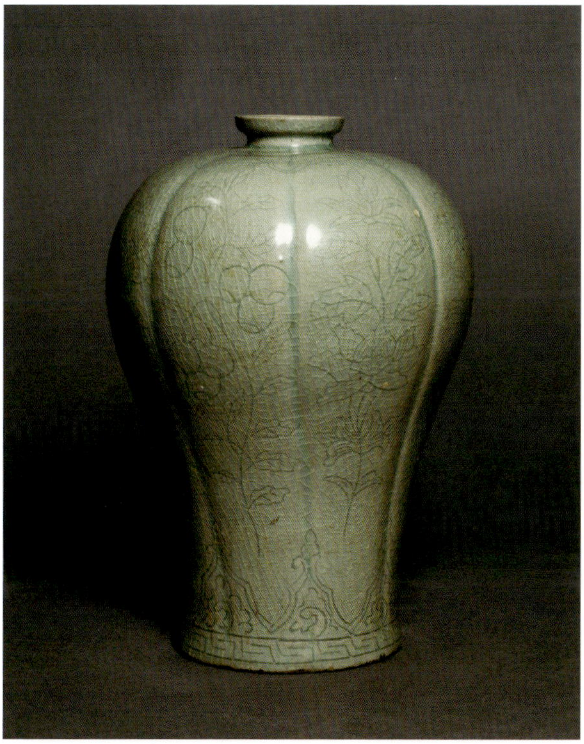

42 Handscroll fragment mounted as a hanging scroll: ink on dyed paper decorated with ink, colors, silver pigment, scattered gold- and silver-leaf, and cut-gold ruled lines; 9 3/16 x 17 5/16 in. (25 x 44 cm). Arthur M. Sackler Museum, Gift of Mrs. Donald F. Hyde, 1977.202.

Story of the Bodhisattva Medicine King

From Chapter 23 of the *Lotus Sutra*

Japanese, Heian period

c. 1150

For more than a millennium the *Lotus Sutra* (*Myōhō-renge-kyō*) provided Japan's most common doctrine of fate and salvation. Piety, salted by a love of luxury, had long inspired Buddhists to produce elegant scriptures, but Heian-period (794–1185) aristocrats raised this custom to unprecedented heights. To make this exquisite example, lustrous paper was dyed and decorated with sprayed silver pigment and flecks of gold and silver foil. Gold strips were added to form columns and delicate paintings of lotus plants (symbolizing enlightenment) to enliven the top and bottom margins. Finally, the text was brushed with great flourish from top to bottom and right to left, seventeen characters to a column. This section formed the end of a long horizontal handscroll that was later cut down and remounted. It tells the story of a deity who twice offered himself in sacrifice to the Buddha and was twice restored—miraculous events that led witnesses to higher levels of enlightenment. ARK

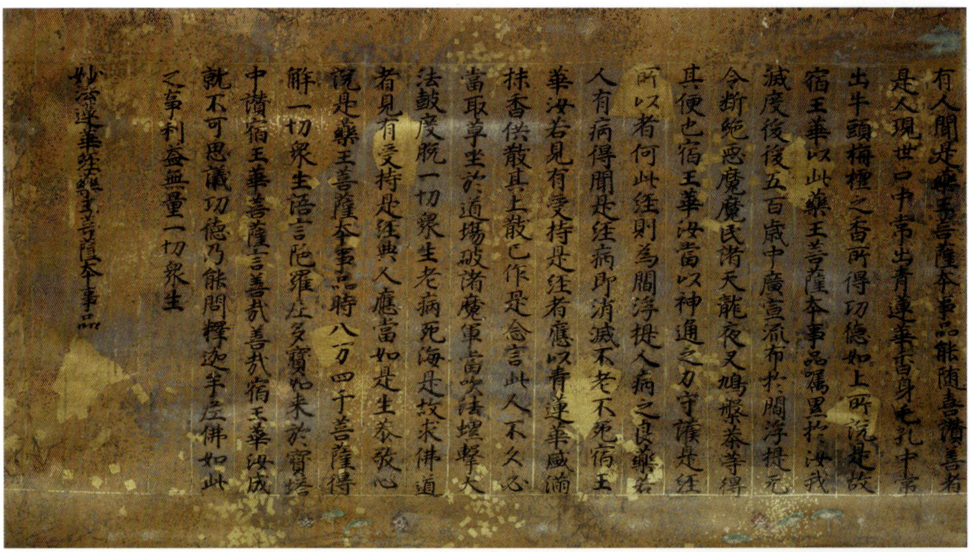

Hanging scroll: gold and color on indigo-dyed silk, 35 9/16 x 31 1/8 in. (90.3 x 79 cm). Promised gift of Sylvan Barnet and William Burto in honor of John M. Rosenfield, TL40552.

Womb World Mandala
Japanese, Kamakura period mid-13th century

Esoteric Buddhism relies on a secret transmission of understanding through elaborate rituals that help the practitioner become one with the eternal Buddha Vairochana. Art is of prime importance because it is believed to convey sacred truths that have no other means of transmission. The arduous path to enlightenment is divided into stages through which the devotee navigates using visual diagrams known as mandalas, which map the complex relationships among deities. / This *Womb World Mandala* is structured like a palace viewed from above, with a central "hall" surrounded by chambers and outer gateways. In the central lotus sits Vairochana, with eight related deities on surrounding petals. The figures that populate the adjacent halls are all manifestations of the central cosmic Buddha. Esoteric devotees meditate on such paintings to align themselves with the divine, and must visualize traveling through each quadrant during the spiritual journey toward the center. ARK

Ink, opaque watercolor, and gold on paper; 12 1/4 x 8 3/8 in. (31.1 x 21.3 cm). Arthur M. Sackler Museum, Fund for the Acquisition of Islamic Art, 1982.40.

Folio from a Qur'an, Sura 4: 161–62
Islamic, Iran
Saljuq-Atabeg period
late 12th–early 13th century

The attenuated, vertical, and angular script of this Qur'an folio is commonly known as eastern Kufic. The red and blue marks furnish the text with pronunciation points, and letters of similar shape are distinguished from one another by the black dots. The gold roundel on the top line indicates the end of verse 161. The written word is surrounded by a rich decorative background of whole and split palmettes over a tightly packed tapestry of tiny scrollwork. Variations on this ornamentation appeared in other media, as is evident on the *Charger with Courtly Couple* (see opposite page). YH

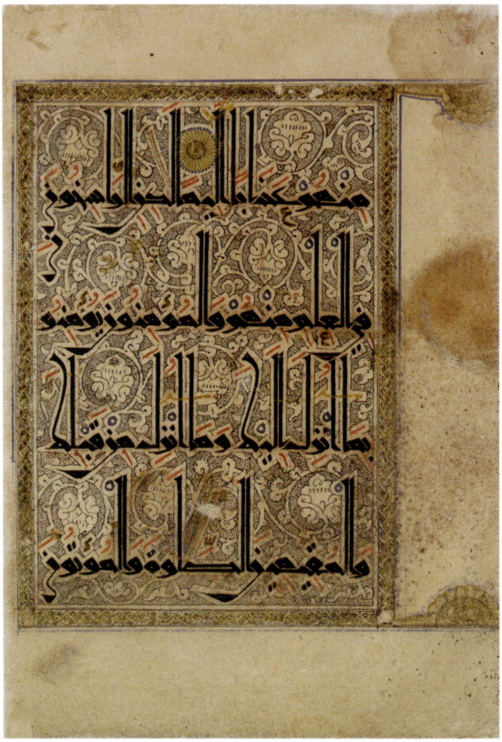

45 Fritware with overglaze luster painting, h. 2 1/2 in. (6.3 cm), diam. 10 3/8 in. (26.4 cm). Arthur M. Sackler Museum, The Norma Jean Calderwood Collection of Islamic Art, 2002.50.56.

Charger with Courtly Couple Encircled by Bands of Poetry
Islamic, Iran, Kashan
Saljuq-Atabeg period
c. 1200

Literature, painting, and the industrial arts often intersected in medieval Persian culture, resulting in the creation of striking works of art. On this elaborate dish, a seated couple—whose graceful gestures, ornate dress, and moonlike faces convey courtly tastes—has been rendered in a costly and unforgiving technique known as luster painting. Because of abrasion, the inscriptions on the walls and rim of the charger will never be fully recovered, but enough can be deciphered to determine that the texts express romantic longing. The verses belong to a type of popular Persian poetry that, with lute or flute accompaniment, was recited at literary gatherings, where vessels such as this charger may have been used. MM

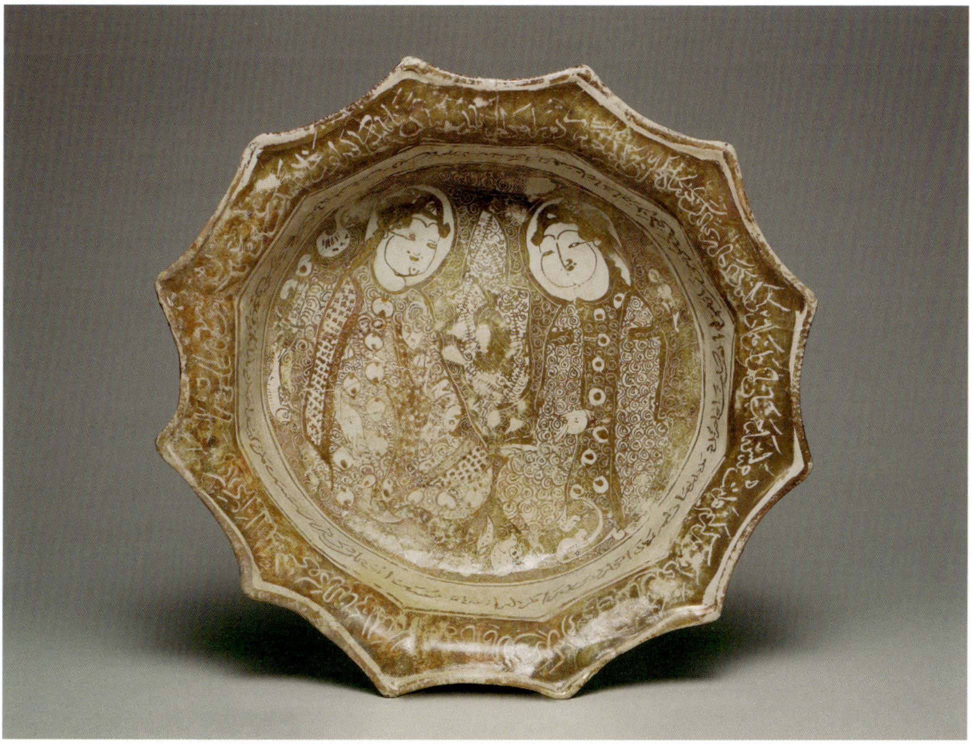

Carved Japanese cypress, assembled-woodblock construction with polychromy and rock-crystal inlaid eyes; 2
9 3/4 x 9 in. (67.9 x 24.8 x 22.9 cm). Arthur M. Sackler Museum, Promised gift of Walter C. Sedgwick in memory o
Sedgwick Sr. and Ellery Sedgwick Jr., 99.1979.1.

Prince Shōtoku at Age Two

Japanese, Kamakura period

c. 1292

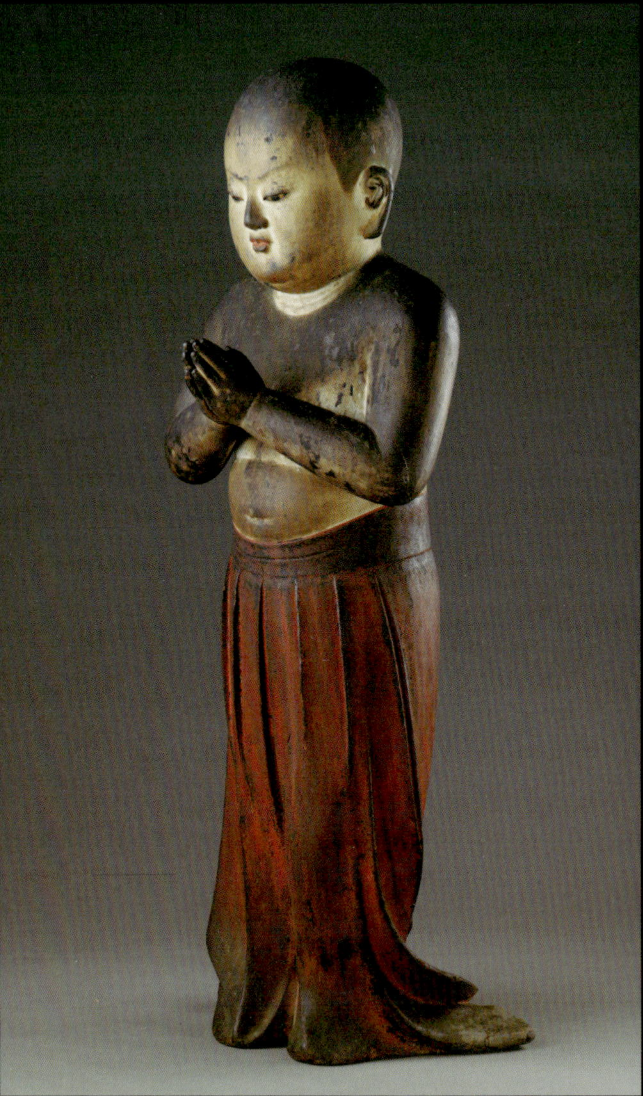

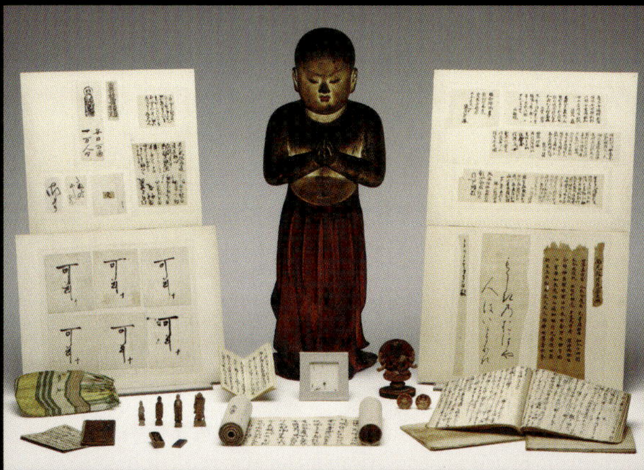

Shōtoku Taishi (572–621) was an important political and cultural figure, instrumental in the dissemination of Buddhism in Japan. This statue, the oldest datable work of its type and one of the most important Japanese sculptures in the United States, shows him as a toddler, when he was said to have chanted the Buddha's name and joined his hands in prayer, miraculously causing a tiny religious relic to appear. The sculptor has ingeniously blended adult and childlike characteristics to convey the prince's innocence and spiritual equipoise. The image was likely carved by a master of the Kei school, the Nara-based lineage responsible for the most celebrated Kamakura-period (1185–1333) statues. / The assembled-woodblock method of construction allowed access to a sculpture's interior, where crystals were inserted to impart an uncanny lifelike quality to the eyes. The technique also created a cavity where practitioners could place small devotional items. Most statues have lost their original dedicatory objects, but this one survived undisturbed, offering a fascinating time capsule of medieval Japanese Buddhism: More than seventy items were found inside, including relics, miniature devotional sculptures, printed and handwritten texts, a multicolored silk bag, and Sanskrit paper charms. These were intended to spiritually activate the image and establish a bond between the deified prince and those who commissioned his likeness. ARK

Tempera and gold on panel, 83 1/2 x 58 7/8 in. (212.1 x 149.5 cm). Fogg Museum, Friends of the Fogg Art Museum Fund, 1929.234.

Taddeo Gaddi
Italian, c. 1300–1366
The Stigmatization of Saint Francis
c. 1325–30

This monumental painting was certainly intended for an altar of a Franciscan church, which remains unidentified. The four-part punched design of the saint's halo has helped in assigning this work to Taddeo Gaddi, one of the leading followers of Giotto, on whose oeuvre this composition is based. The panel represents one of the most important scenes in the life of the saint—when Christ appeared to him as a seraphim and inflicted his wounds—made popular in the early development of the Franciscan order in the thirteenth century. Here Gaddi shows a concern for the emotional response and modeled figure of Francis that was new for the times and reflected the devotional practices of the Franciscans. The iconic figure of the saint that was once the norm for altarpieces has been abandoned in favor of his depiction in a narrative scene set within a naturalistic landscape. DC

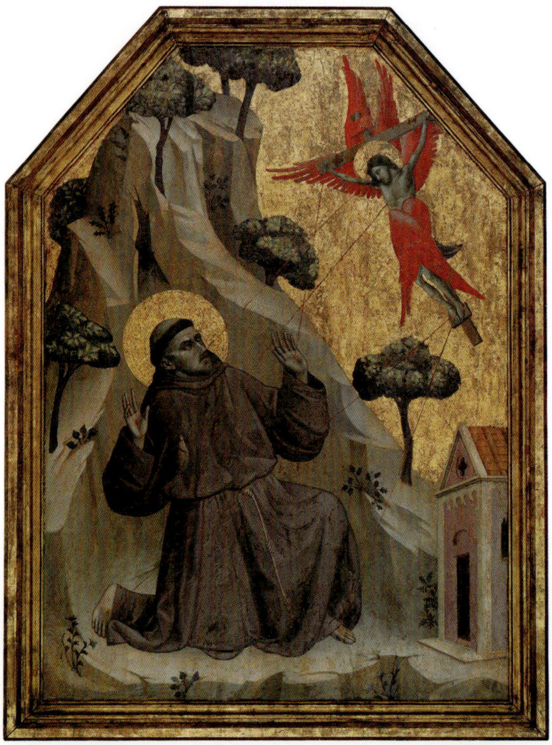

49 Hanging scroll: ink, colors, and gold pigment on silk; 62 13/16 x 32 1/2 in. (159.6 x 82.5 cm). Arthur M. Sackler Museum, Bequest of Grenville L. Winthrop, 1943.57.12.

Willow-Branch Avalokiteshvara Korean, Koryŏ dynasty mid-14th century

Bodhisattvas are Buddhist saints who postpone their own enlightenment in order to help others along the same spiritual path. This scroll depicts the most popular such deity, the Bodhisattva of Compassion, Avalokiteshvara. Surrounded by a moonlike nimbus, he sits on an outcropping of gold-edged rock above a pool from which emerge lotus buds—Buddhist symbols of rebirth. Below, a tiny figure, the youthful wisdom-seeker Sudhana, stands in a pose of supplication. This iconography, known as the "Willow-Branch Avalokiteshvara" (after the small willow stem in the *kundika* water vessel behind the deity), seems to have been most popular in fourteenth-century Korea. Although the imagery is based on Tang-dynasty (618–907) Chinese prototypes, the fascination with transparency, seen in the deity's diaphanous robe and luminous rosary, and the use of gold pigment rather than applied gold leaf are hallmarks of the finest Koryŏ-period (913–1392) Korean paintings. ARK

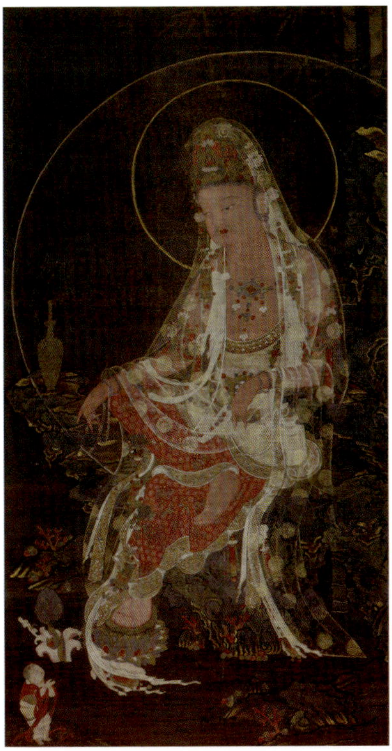

50 Ink, opaque watercolor, gold, and silver on paper; 19 3/4 x 15 9/16 in. (50.2 x 39.5 cm). Arthur M. Sackler Museum, Gift of Edward W. Forbes, 1955.167.

Iskandar's Iron Cavalry Battles King Fur of Hind

Folio from a manuscript of the *Shahnama* by Firdawsi

Islamic, Iran, Ilkhanid period c. 1330–40

This dramatic battle scene was originally part of a monumental and magnificently illustrated manuscript of the *Shahnama* (Book of Kings), believed to have been produced for Abu Sai'd, the last of the Ilkhanid rulers of Iran. The text of the *Shahnama*, completed by the Persian poet Firdawsi early in the eleventh century, presents the histories of the great kings and heroes, mythical and historical, of ancient Iran. With lavish amounts of silver (now tarnished) and gold, this painting depicts the decisive moment in the battle between Iskandar (Alexander the Great) and King Fur of Hind (India). To break the king's massive front line, Alexander's councilors ordered the construction of iron horses filled with oil. When ignited on the battlefield, the horrific iron cavalry confused Fur's war elephants, which ultimately resulted in Alexander's victory. AA

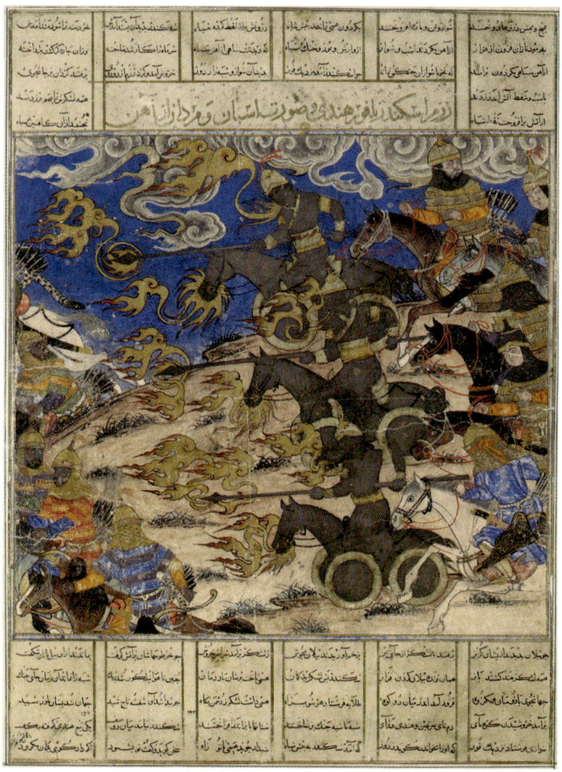

51 Opaque watercolor and gold on paper, 8 3/16 x 4 1/8 in. (20.8 x 10.5 cm). Arthur M. Sackler Museum, Gift of Mrs. Elise Cabot Forbes and Mr. Eric Schroeder, and Annie S. Coburn Fund, 1939.225.

Tahmina Comes into Rustam's Chamber

Folio from a manuscript of the *Shahnama* by Firdawsi

Islamic, Afghanistan, Herat Timurid period c. 1410

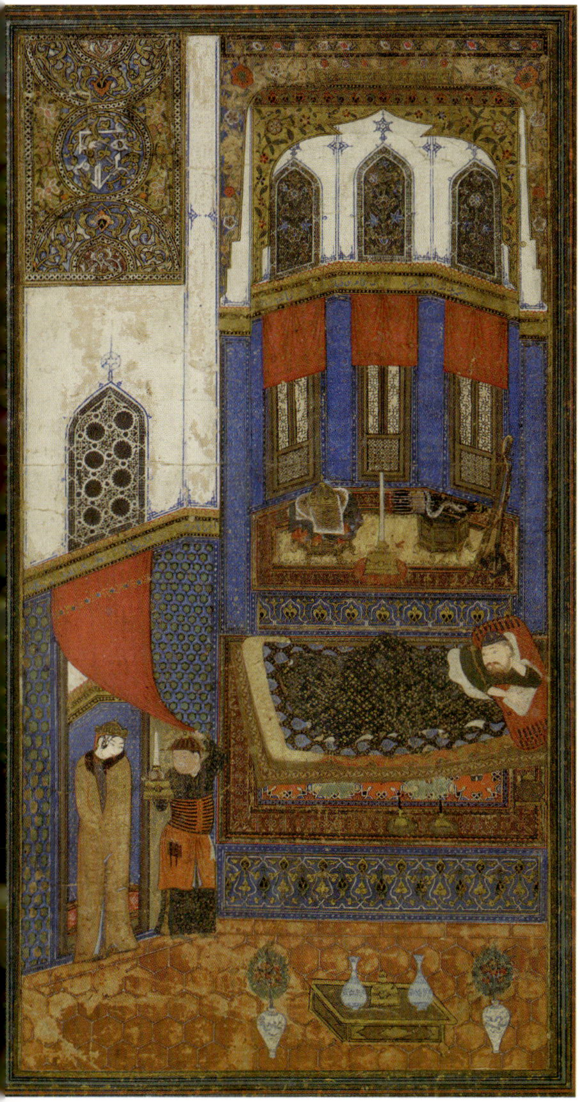

Beneath a brilliant red curtain, the young Tahmina enters Rustam's bedroom and changes the course of Persian epic history. These mythical lovers inhabit a luxurious space ornamented with geometric tiles, latticed windows, patterned textiles, gleaming metalwork, and blue-on-white ceramics. The sophistication of the painting, including its division of space into flat, angular planes and its incorporation of tightly packed detail, reveals the refinement achieved by Persian artists after Timur's rule. / Illustrating a scene from the *Shahnama*, this domestic encounter stands in contrast to the battle scene from the imperial Ilkhanid *Shahnama* (see opposite page), and it points to an interest among Timurid patrons and artists in the epic's romantic as well as heroic passages. In this case, the romance will turn to tragedy: Suhrab, the son born from this union, will lead a Turanian army into Iran and fall in battle at the hands of the greatest Iranian hero, his father, Rustam. KM

Silk, lampas weave: 4+1 (1) satin foundation with supplementary weave bound in 1S2 twill; warp 29 in. (73.7 cm), weft 24 7/8 in. (63.2 cm). Arthur M. Sackler Museum, Francis H. Burr and William H. Prichard Memorial Funds, 2007.140.

Silk Panel: Yalis and Makaras within an Ogival Lattice
Indian, Gujarat, Sultanate period 15th–16th century

Enclosed by an elaborate lattice, hybrid beasts snarl and paw the air. Despite their apparent ferocity, they are auspicious motifs. The blue creature with elephant and crocodile features resembles the Hindu *makara*, a mythical being associated with life-giving water. The yellow "lion" with blue wings recalls the protective *yali* that can be found ornamenting thrones and entryways in southern India. / This panel (reproduced below with warps running horizontally) belongs to an eclectic group of silk textiles that, at this writing, represent the earliest pattern-woven textiles that can be attributed to India. As such, they mark a significant departure from India's ancient tradition of applying patterns to cotton fabrics after weaving. The complex weave structures of this group, either lampas or samite, suggest external influences on indigenous production. MM

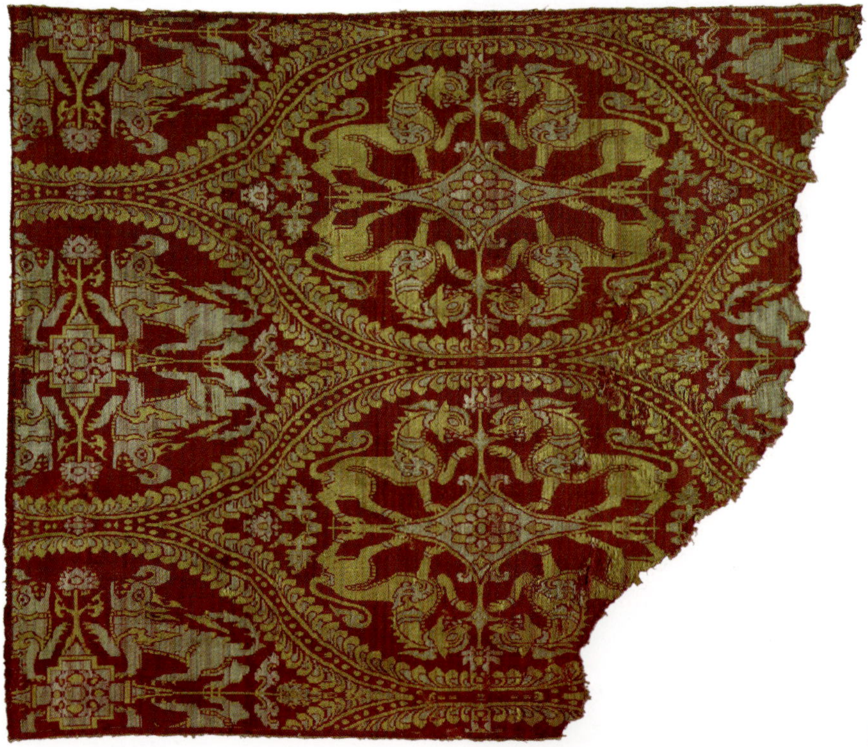

53 / Cast bronze, 6 7/8 x 5 1/2 x 2 5/8 in. (17.5 x 14 x 6.7 cm). Arthur M. Sackler Museum, Friends of the Fogg Art Museum Fund, 1964.44.

Incense Burner in the Form of a Lion
Indian, Deccan, Sultanate period
15th century

This energetic lion combines the tradition of zoomorphic metalwork from the Islamic world and the sculptural heritage of India. In the Middle East the lion is an ancient symbol for imperial power. With its paw raised in a salute, it is an enduring motif on temple and secular architecture throughout India. / The plump features, horns, and bulging eyes are particularly reminiscent of the *yali*, a mythical horned lion (see opposite page for this motif on a textile). Incense was placed in the opening in the lion's back, now missing its lid. Smoke escaped first through the array of holes on the lion's mane, which resemble a beaded necklace, and then through the mouth with its movable tongue. YH

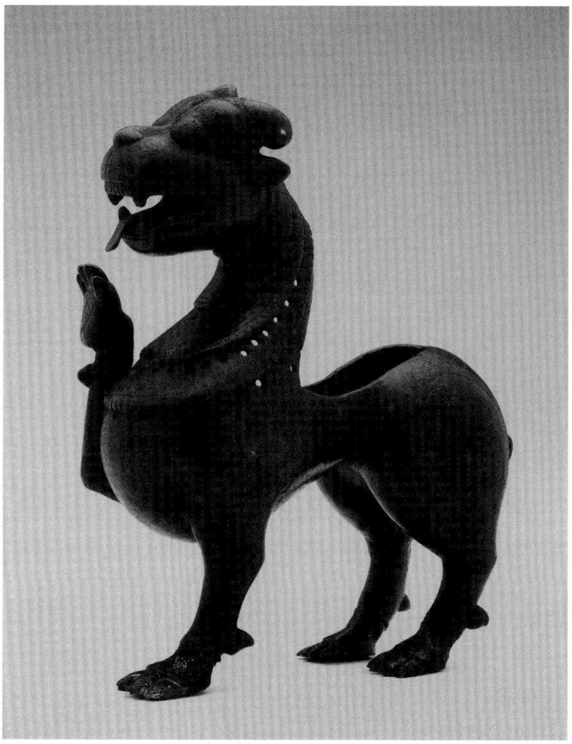

Blue-and-white ware: porcelain with decoration painted in underglaze cobalt blue; h. 2 3/4 in. (7 cm), diam. 15 15/16 in. (40.5 cm). Arthur M. Sackler Museum, Purchase through the generosity of the Ralph C. Marcove International Understanding Through Arts and Crafts Foundation, 2005.110.

Charger with Blossoming-Peony Decor

From kilns at Jingdezhen, Jiangxi province

Chinese, Ming dynasty early 15th century

By the early fifteenth century, potters at the Jingdezhen kilns in Jiangxi province had perfected the technique of creating high-fired pure white porcelains decorated with bright blue cobalt designs under a clear glaze. Widely esteemed for their beauty and durability, Jingdezhen blue-and-white wares were produced for both domestic and foreign markets. As the charger here is of a shape and size not used in China, it most likely was fashioned for a foreign buyer. Although the form originated elsewhere, the double-peony decorative pattern is purely Chinese. / Blue-and-white wares fashioned during the reigns of the Yongle (1403–24) and Xuande (1426–35) emperors are especially admired for their superb potting, magnificent color, lustrous glaze, and exquisitely painted decoration, making them among the most sought-after wares by collectors today. The quality of the cobalt color and painted designs on this charger suggest a probable Yongle-period date of manufacture. MAM

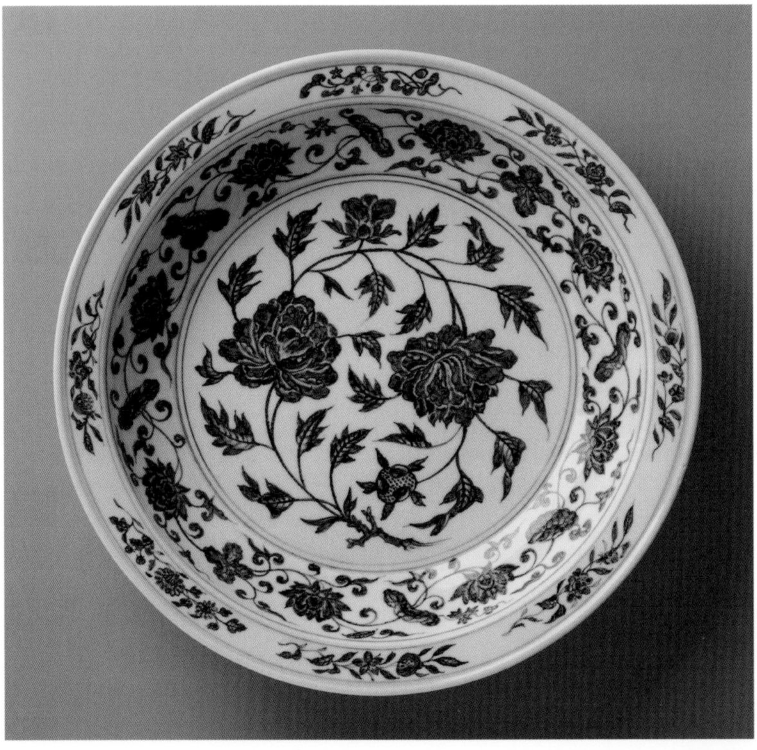

55 Numbered Jun ware: light gray stoneware with purple and blue glazes, a Chinese *3* impressed on bases; flowerpot: h. 7 $^{1}/_{16}$ in (17.9 cm), diam. 10 $^{5}/_{16}$ in (26.2 cm); basin: h. 2 $^{13}/_{16}$ in. (7.2 cm), diam. 9 in. (22.8 cm). Arthur M. Sackler Museum, Gift of Ernest B. and Helen Pratt Dane, 1942.185.5, .51.

Foliate Flowerpot and Basin

Chinese, probably Ming dynasty 15th century

This flowerpot and basin sport vibrant blue and purple glazes similar to those found on classic Jun wares of the Song dynasty (960–1279). They are marked, however, with the Chinese numerals that appear on later numbered Jun wares—an assortment of planters, basins, and vases bearing Jun-type glazes, distinctive shapes, and numbers ranging from 1 to 10 impressed into the undersides of the vessels before firing. The numbers denoted size (with 1 designating the largest) and facilitated the pairing of pots and basins. The flowerpot and basin here are a perfect match in shape, color, and size. These utilitarian wares became prized possessions collected by members of the Qing dynasty (1368–1644), as evidenced by the palace inscriptions incised into the glazed undersides of these types of wares. Although neither of these pieces bears such an inscription, the Art Museum possesses around sixty examples of numbered Jun, fourteen with palace markings. MAM

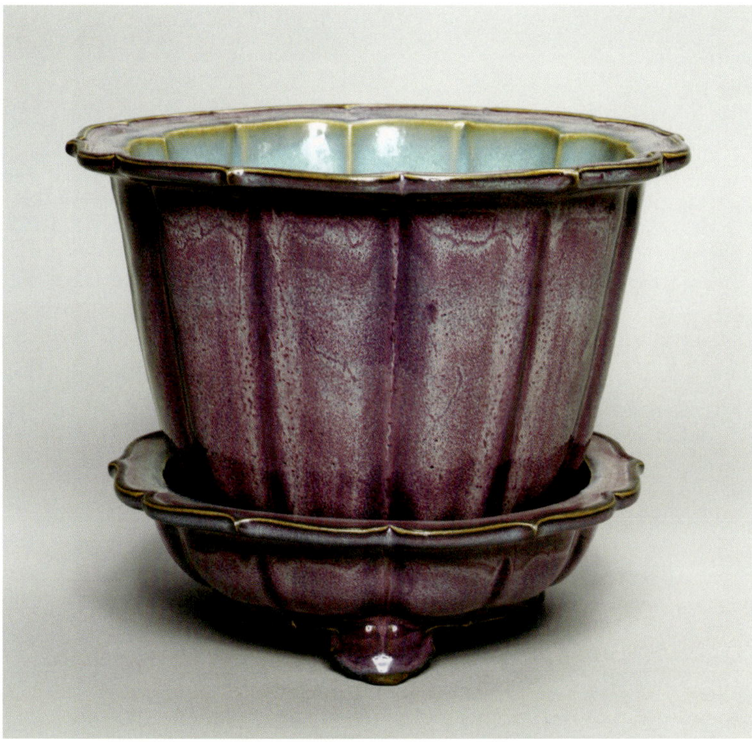

Tempera and gold on panel, 13 1/2 x 17 in. (34.3 x 43.2 cm). Fogg Museum, Gift of Paul J. Sachs, "A testimonial to my friend Edward W. Forbes," 1922.172.

Master of the Osservanza
Italian, active 1425–50
The Descent into Limbo
c. 1440–44

The Master of the Osservanza has paid homage here to his two great Sienese predecessors, Duccio and Sassetta. Duccio first painted this subject in his *Maestà* (1308–11); in his version, the Master of the Osservanza gives greater prominence to illusionistic space and atmosphere. The influence of Sassetta's style is evident in the naturalistic folds of drapery. / This panel is from a narrative predella of an altarpiece whose other panels are in collections around the world. In this scene from the apocryphal Acts of Pilate, Christ descends into Limbo to save the souls who had died before his Resurrection. The jewellike colors and the technique of glazed gold create the effect of a vibrant aura emanating from Christ. DC

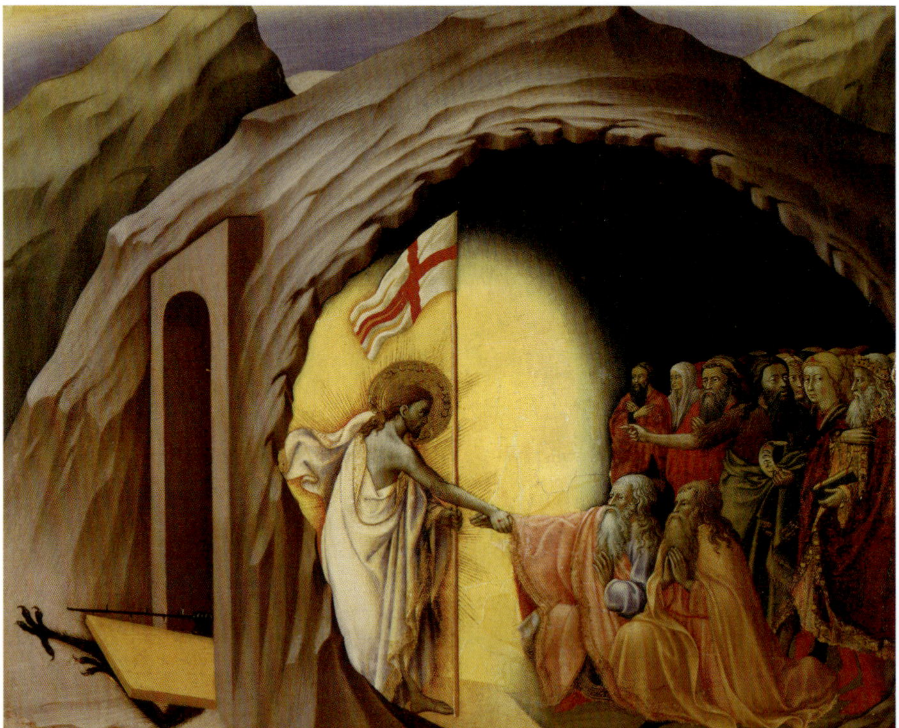

 Tempera and gold on panel, 38 1/16 x 16 3/4 in. (96.6 x 42.5 cm). Fogg Museum, Hervey E. Wetzel Bequest Fund, 1921.34.

Fra Angelico, Italian, c. 1400–1455 Christ on the Cross between the Virgin and Cardinal Torquemada and Saint John the Evangelist, c. 1446

The Dominican monk Fra Angelico was a pivotal painter of the early Renaissance. In this painting, the central panel of a triptych, he has demonstrated the Renaissance concern for modeled drapery, the human body, and the naturalistic effects of light. The simplicity of this composition mirrors the Dominican devotion to individual contemplation and the order's love of this subject, which appears numerous times in the artist's famous fresco decoration of the monastery of San Marco in Florence (1440–45). / At the foot of the cross, a donor kneels in prayer as a model for the viewer. His Dominican habit and cardinal's hat have recently helped identify this figure as Juan de Torquemada (1388–1486). Not to be confused with his more famous nephew, the Inquisitor Tomaso de Torquemada, this cardinal may have been in Rome at the same time as Fra Angelico, and he supported the convent where the artist resided in Florence. DC

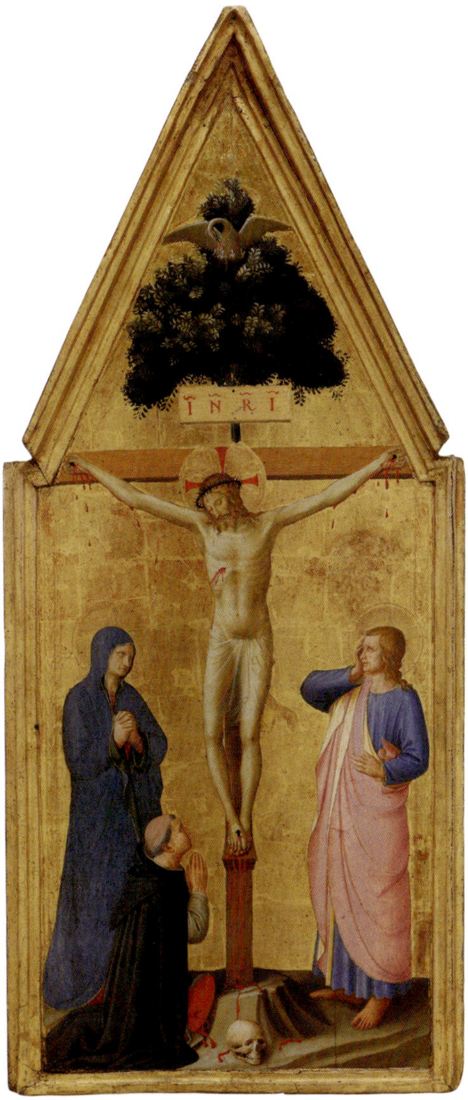

Gilt silver, 4 1/4 x 4 x 2 11/16 in. (10.8 x 10.2 x 6.8 cm). Arthur M. Sackler Museum, Gift of Ralph C. Marcove, M.D., 1997.254.

Seated Buddha Shakyamuni Flanked by Standing Bodhisattvas Korean, Chosŏn dynasty mid-15th century

Cast in silver and brilliantly gilded, this exquisite triad depicts the historical Buddha Shakyamuni seated on a lotus throne flanked by attendant bodhisattvas Manjushri and Samantabhadra—saintly figures who represent the Buddha's wisdom and compassion, respectively. The Buddha's left hand rests in his lap; his right extends downward, a gesture symbolizing "calling the earth to witness" at the moment of enlightenment, when he triumphed over temptation and realized supreme truth. As most surviving Buddhist sculptures depict single deities, triads are extremely rare. That this one was cast in silver (rather than the more typical bronze) and then sheathed in gold indicates its exalted status. Once believed to be Chinese, this piece was recently reattributed to fifteenth-century Korea on the basis of its serenely simplified figures, drapery style, and ring-punched surface decoration. It is by far the finest of the three such triads known to be extant. ARK

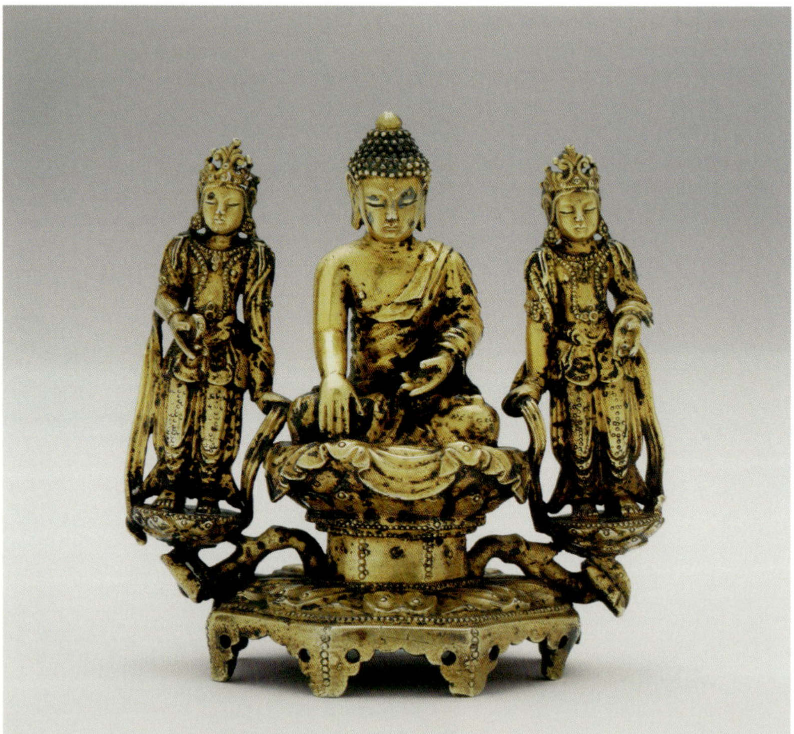

Tempera on panel, 62 5/8 x 74 3/4 in. (159.1 x 189.9 cm). Fogg Museum, Gift of Edward W. Forbes to honor the memory of Richard Norton, 1963.111.

Filippo Lippi
Italian, 1406–1469
Saint Jerome in the Desert with Saints John the Baptist and Ansanus, c. 1455

Fra Filippo Lippi took his vows as a Carmelite monk in Santa Maria del Carmine in Florence in 1421, precisely during the time when Masaccio and Masolino were decorating the Brancacci Chapel. Lippi's style echoes Masaccio's monumentality but adds sensitive coloring and graceful line. / This painting is from the Dragoni Chapel of the Carmelite church of San Bartolomeo in Prato, where Lippi was a member of the order (1452–67). The three saints are placed within a pyramidal composition in the desert, their attributes echoed in their natural surroundings. Saint Jerome beats his chest with a rock, much like the one embedded in the stone in the foreground. Saint Ansanus holds his heart above a similarly shaped bush, while the dried river is an allusion to baptism, referring to both Saint John and Saint Ansanus, known as the "Baptist of Siena." DC

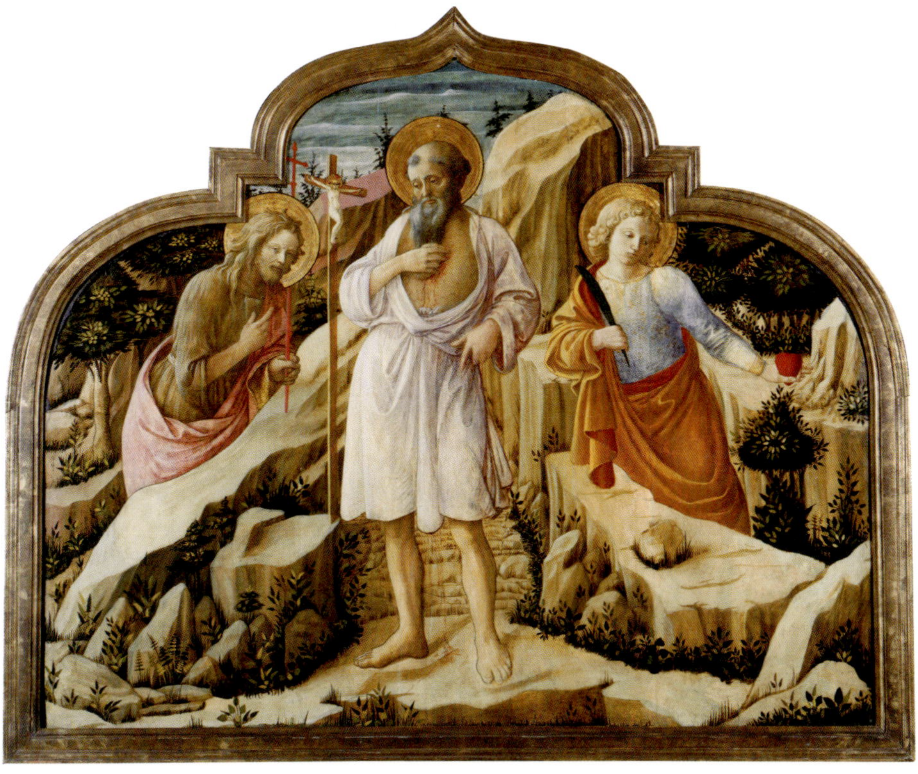

Gold; part A, diam. 5 1/8 in. (13 cm), depth 5 1/2 in. (14 cm); part B, diam. 5 1/8 in. (13 cm), depth 5 5/8 in. (14.3 cm). Fogg Museum, Bequest of Grenville L. Winthrop, 1943.1072.A, B.

Earplugs with Relief Decorations Chimu, Peru c. 14th–15th century

The Chimu culture, which thrived in Peru from the eleventh century until the Incan conquest in 1475–76, produced a variety of ornate art objects, such as these gold earplugs. Chimu versatility in handling gold is evident in the intricate relief pattern on the disks, the small gold beads that decorate the outer edges, and the incised carving in the cylinders. The fronts of the disks show five warrior figures in profile carrying weapons, alternating with five menacing feline figures. Given their large size, these decorative objects—inserted through the lobes to distend them—would have been worn by a man of considerable status. In fact, the coastline in Peru known as the Costa de la Oreja (Ear Coast) may refer to the distended ears of the Chimu. DC

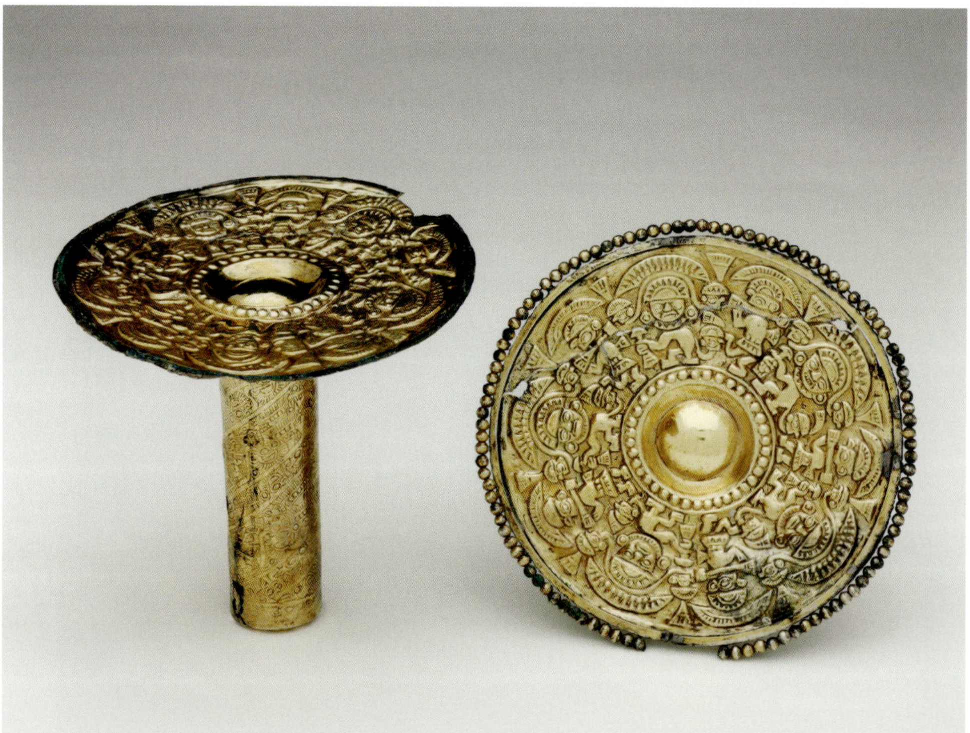

61 Engraving with drawn additions in brown ink, diam. 4 3/4 in. (12 cm). Fogg Museum, Gift of William Gray from the collection of Francis Calley Gray, G2936.

Youth and Girl, Each Offering the Other a Fruit Italian, c. 1470

This unusual secular roundel from late-fifteenth-century Florence not only depicted courtly love but also enabled it. Lovers pasted decorative engravings such as these onto small round boxes, which they then exchanged as gifts. In this image, the courting couple in their garden paradise give each other presents of ripe fruit. Although this impression was never affixed to a box, an early owner personalized it by drawing the Medici insignia of six *palle* balls on the central shield; perhaps the engraving belonged to a member of that family. It is one of twenty-four similar roundels from the same Florentine workshop that are now known as *Otto Prints*, after their eighteenth-century owner, Leipzig merchant Ernst Peter Otto. SKS

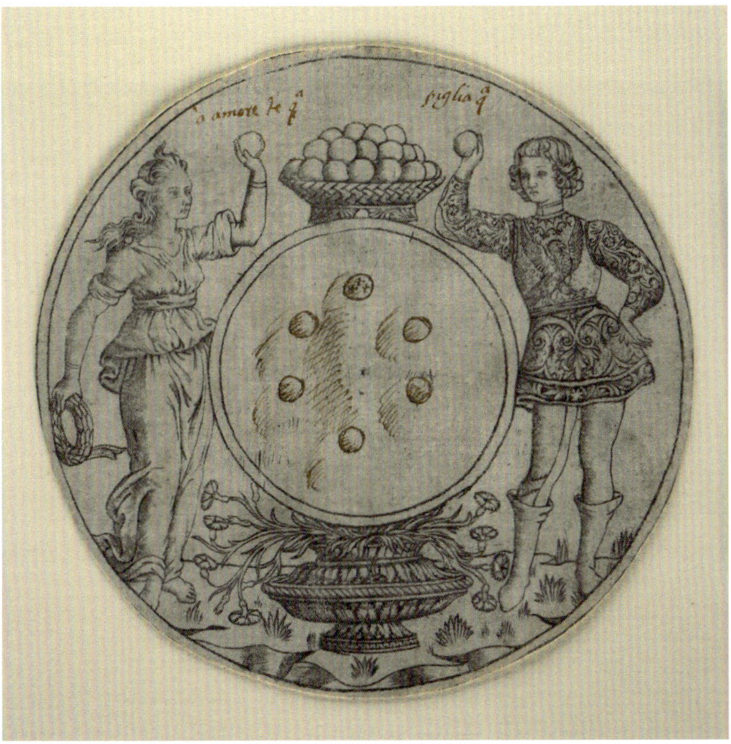

Oil on oak panel, 14 15/16 x 10 7/16 in. (37.9 x 26.5 cm) and 14 15/16 x 10 5/8 in. (37.9 x 27 cm). Fogg Museum, The Kate, Maurice R., and Melvin R. Seiden Special Purchase Fund in honor of Seymour and Zoya Slive, 2001.170, .171.

Albrecht Bouts Netherlandish, 1451–1549 The Man of Sorrows and The Mater Dolorosa mid-1490s

These panels pairing Christ shown as the Man of Sorrows with the Virgin Mary as the Mater Dolorosa (sorrowful mother) may not have been conceived of or produced as a diptych, a work consisting of two panels of the same shape and size that are hinged so that they can be opened and closed. But they were paired at some point in their history and have survived as such. Questions concerning their original format, however, do not diminish their broader function as objects of private meditative devotion. A rise in piety in the Netherlands during the fourteenth and fifteenth centuries stimulated the production of images such as these of the weeping Christ and his grief-stricken mother. Images of this type, brilliantly embellished with poignant details—for example, the tears trickling down the Virgin's cheeks—were intended to elicit the viewer's compassion for Christ's suffering. YFY

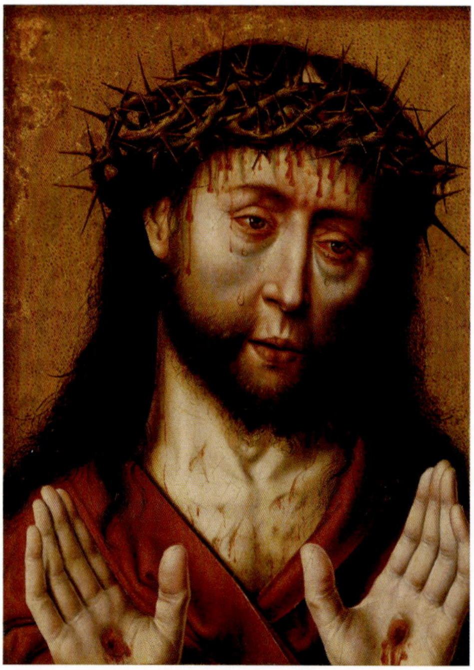

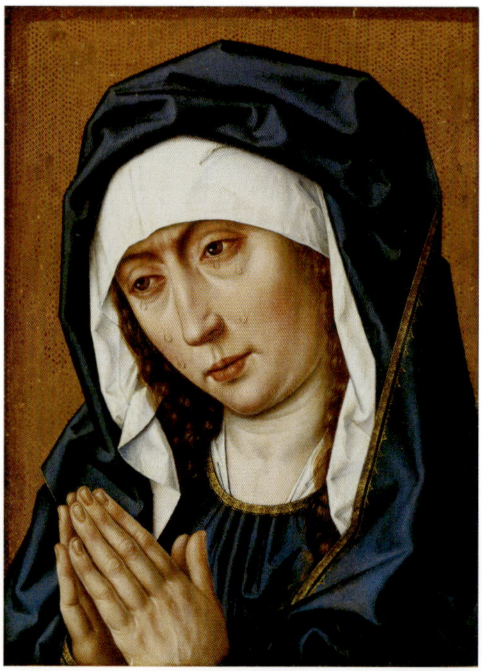

63 / Tempera on unprimed linen, 22 1/2 x 13 3/4 in. (57.2 x 34.9 cm). Fogg Museum, Friends of the Fogg Art Museum Fund, 1930.2.

Studio of Sandro Botticelli
Italian, 1445–1510
Salvator Mundi
c. 1490–99

This finely executed painting combines the iconography of the blessing Christ as Savior of the World with the Northern tradition of Christ as Man of Sorrows displaying his wounds, to evoke awe and pity simultaneously in the viewer. The unusual support of this painting on unprimed linen and its awareness of Northern iconography reflect the artistic and cultural exchanges occurring in Florence in the second half of the fifteenth century. / Botticelli painted this work while under the influence of sermons by the fanatical Dominican preacher Girolamo Savonarola (see page 70) concerning the suffering of Christ during the Passion. DC

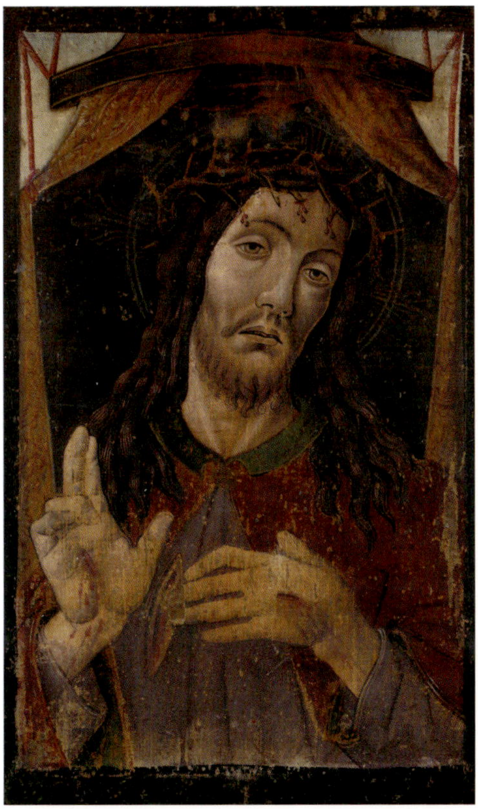

Oil on panel, 31 9/16 x 50 7/8 in. (80.1 x 129.3 cm). Fogg Museum, Alpheus Hyatt Purchasing Fund and Friends of Art, Archaeology, and Music, 1940.85.

Piero di Cosimo
Italian, c. 1462–c. 1515
The Misfortunes of Silenus
c. 1500

Inspired by a passage in Ovid's *Fasti* (3.735), this painting shows three scenes of the mythological story in which Silenus, a follower of Bacchus, disastrously mistakes a wasp's nest for a beehive. The painting and its pendant, *The Discovery of Honey* (Worcester Art Museum), are visual puns on the last name of its patron, Guidantonio Vespucci, which means "little wasps." / Surprisingly, there are no wasps visible in the painting. Infrared reflectography has shown that some compositional elements drawn in by the artist were not realized at the painting stage, including ambiguous marks near the tree branch in the center of the painting that may represent wasps or a wasp's nest. DC & MB

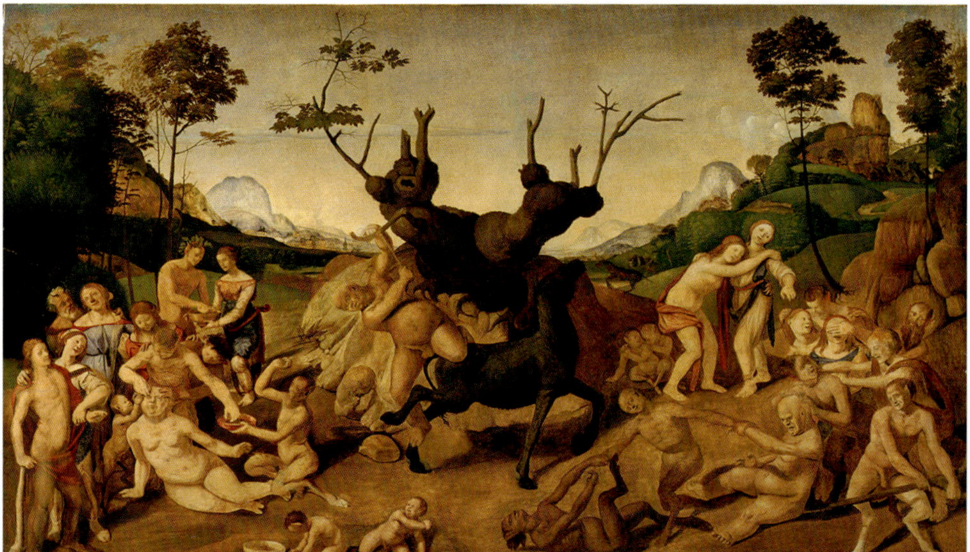

65 17th of a series of 54 paired leaves in an album: ink, color, and gold on paper; 9 9/16 x 14 3/8 in. (24.3 x 36.5 cm). Arthur M. Sackler Museum, Bequest of the Hofer Collection of the Arts of Asia, 1985.352.17.A–B.

Tosa Mitsunobu, illustrator
Japanese, 1434–1525
Reizei Tamehiro, calligrapher
Japanese, 1450–1526
The Picture Contest Chapter 17 of the *Tale of Genji*
Muromachi period, datable to 1509

It is impossible to overemphasize the importance of the *Tale of Genji* in Japanese cultural history. This romantic eleventh-century novel focuses on the ideal Heian-period (794–1185) man—a prince dubbed the "Shining Genji." Harvard's album, with an illustration and textual excerpt for each chapter, is now thought to contain the earliest extant complete painted-album-leaf-format version of this seminal work. Textual research and evidence discovered during conservation have shed fresh light on its age and authorship, the circumstances of its production, and its original and subsequent formats. Inscribed backing sheets corroborate that a wealthy warrior commissioned texts by six prominent courtly calligraphers; they also identify the provincial temple to which the ensemble was donated and suggest that it was once pasted onto a pair of screens. Scholarly perception of this set has altered significantly, resulting in a fascinating addition to the Japanese artistic canon. ARK

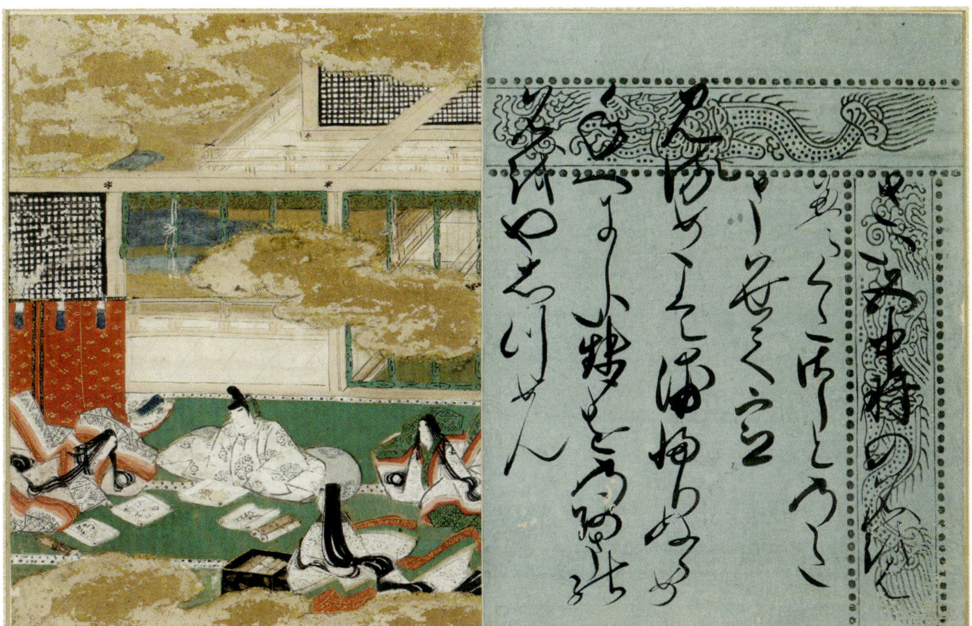

Engraving, 12 13/16 x 8 13/16 in. (32.6 x 22.4 cm). Fogg Museum, Gift of Marjorie B. Cohn in honor of Jakob Rosenberg, M24944.

Albrecht Dürer German, 1471–1528 Nemesis, or The Large Fortune c. 1502

Albrecht Dürer called this winged allegory Nemesis, or divine fury, in his travel journal. She possessed the ability to create chaos throughout the orderly world beneath her feet. Her attributes—the bridle, chalice, and unstable globe perch—come from a Latin poem by Florentine classical scholar Angelo Poliziano. Dürer's best friend, humanist Willibald Pirckheimer, likely introduced the text to Dürer, and Pirckheimer's abbess sister, Caritas, may have served as the model for Nemesis's countenance. Combining humanist learning with virtuosic artistry, Dürer also endowed Nemesis with a carefully observed Germanic physique, mapped onto the ideal proportions of Vitruvian symmetry. SKS

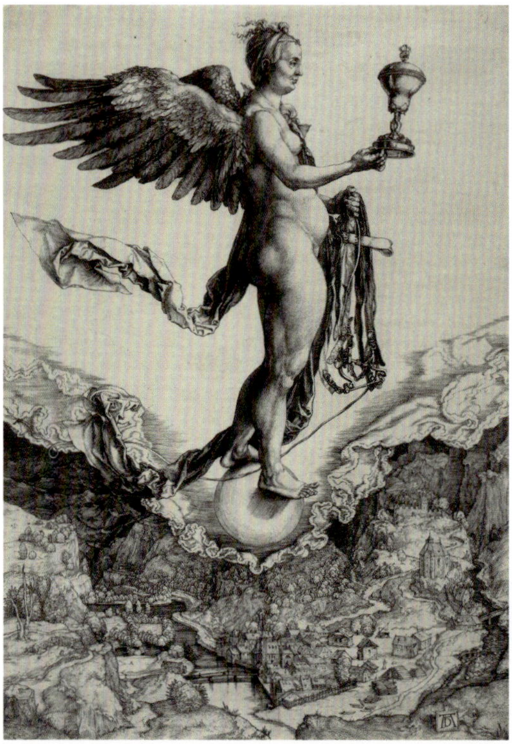

67 Brown ink on white antique laid paper, 11 7/16 x 8 1/4 in. (29 x 21 cm). Fogg Museum, Bequest of Meta and Paul J. Sachs, 1965.339.

Albrecht Dürer
German, 1471–1528
The Lamentation of Christ
1521

In 1520 Albrecht Dürer traveled from his hometown of Nuremberg to the Netherlands. He kept a journal documenting mundane transactions, meetings with artists, and impressions of the cultural treasures of the Flemish cities. His journal also records the spiritual stress that affected him during the religious crisis precipitated by Martin Luther. Dürer's intense religious feeling during this period might account in part for the originality and powerful emotional tenor of the *Lamentation* and other pen-and-ink drawings dated between 1520 and 1523 that rank among his most moving representations of Jesus's suffering and death. Executed with a rigorously systematic technique of parallel and crosshatched lines, these drawings are fully resolved compositions characterized by shallow pictorial spaces, relieflike figure groupings, and extreme emotions expressed with simple gestures. We do not know whether Dürer considered this group to be a series or discrete, independent works of art. WR

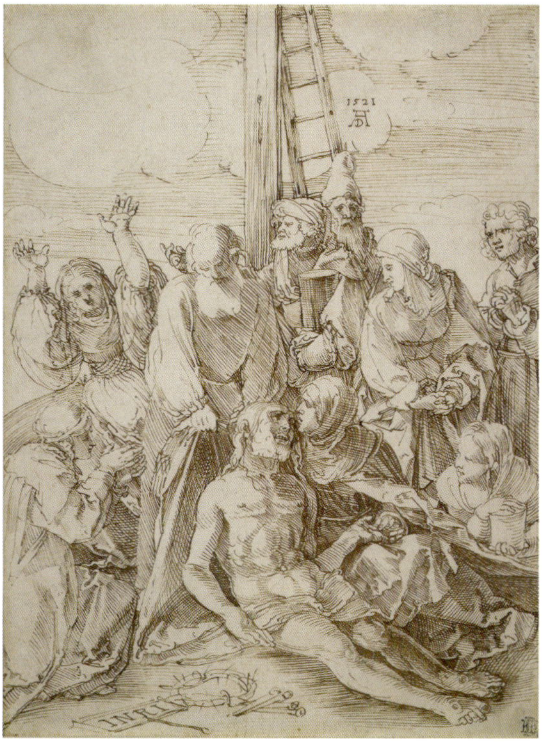

Oil and gold leaf on oak panel, 42 11/16 x 36 1/4 in. (108.5 x 92 cm). Fogg Museum, Anonymous gift and the Kate, Maurice R., and Melvin R. Seiden Special Purchase Fund in honor of Philip A. and Lynn Straus, 1997.2.

Jan Provoost
Netherlandish, 1462/5–1529
Last Judgment
c. 1505

The Bruges painter Jan Provoost executed a number of different versions of the theme of the Last Judgment. In the Fogg panel, the emphasis is on the resurrection of the dead before Christ judges all souls. Clarion trumpets announce the apocalyptic moment, and the resurrected figures—their bodies still stiff and ashen—look upward to Christ, who is flanked by the Virgin Mary and Saint John the Evangelist. The original location of the Fogg painting is unclear. It could have hung in a church or in a town hall or courtroom. In secular settings, Last Judgment pictures functioned as images promoting moral rectitude and proper civic behavior. YFY

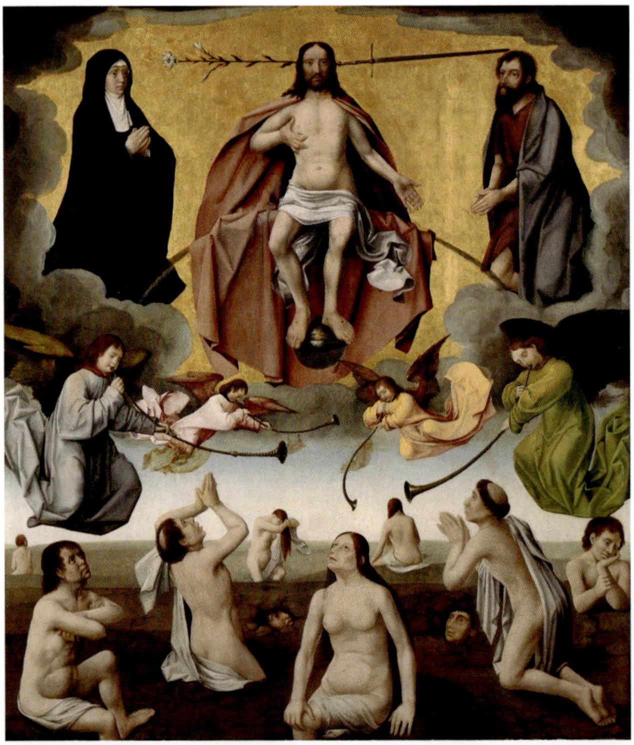

Ink, opaque watercolor, gold, and silver on paper; 23 1/16 x 17 3/16 in. (58.5 x 43.7 cm). Arthur M. Sackler Museum, Gift of Stuart Cary Welch, Jr., 1999.302.

Attributed to Aqa Mirak
Persian, 16th century
Day of Judgment

Folio from a manuscript of the *Falnama* by Jaʿfar al-Sadiq

c. 1555

This folio from a *Falnama*, a book of augury opened at random to predict fortunes, strikingly depicts the Day of Judgment according to Shiʿi Muslim tradition. The unusually grand dimensions of the page and the rich detail of the painting suggest a powerful patron. Seated above are eleven of the twelve Shiʿi imams, successors to the Prophet Muhammad, along with Fatima, his daughter, depicted as a flame. The Prophet, kneeling under a green banner, and his son-in-law ʿAli ibn Abi Talib, the first Shiʿi imam, intercede for the dead, accompanied by the archangels Jabraʾil, Mikhaʾil, and Israfil. Veils cover the faces of Muhammad and his family, as is customary in Ottoman and Persian miniatures. The sinners portrayed below include liars with protruding tongues and thieves whose hands have been amputated. This illustration would have originally faced a page of text revealing its corresponding fortune. SG

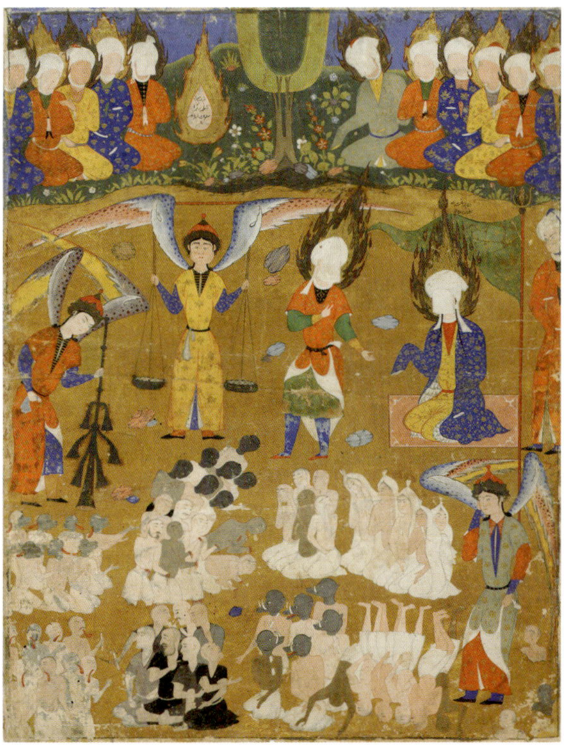

Bronze with dark brown patina, diam. 2 15/16 in. (7.4 cm), depth 5/16 in. (0.8 cm). Fogg Museum, Purchase through the generosity of Alexis Gregory, 2001.252.

Medal of Girolamo Savonarola
Italian, Florence
c. 1500

As part of the Italian Renaissance revival of classical antiquity, influential figures were represented on medals in profile, as Roman emperors were on coins. This bronze example was dedicated to Girolamo Savonarola (1452–1498), the Dominican religious zealot whose sermons warned the people of Florence against the evils of a society based on material wealth and corruption, leading to such extreme measures as the Bonfires of the Vanities in 1497 and 1498. The friar is rendered on the obverse with his distinctive profile, wearing a hooded habit. The inscription, "Girolamo Savonarola of Ferrara, most learned man and blessed prophet," attests to his predictions and foreshadows his eventual execution as a false prophet. On the reverse a hand holding a dagger above Florence—a vision from a sermon of January 13, 1495—accompanies the inscription "The sword of the Lord over the land quickly and swiftly." This prophecy was later interpreted as a warning against the French invasion of Florence. DC

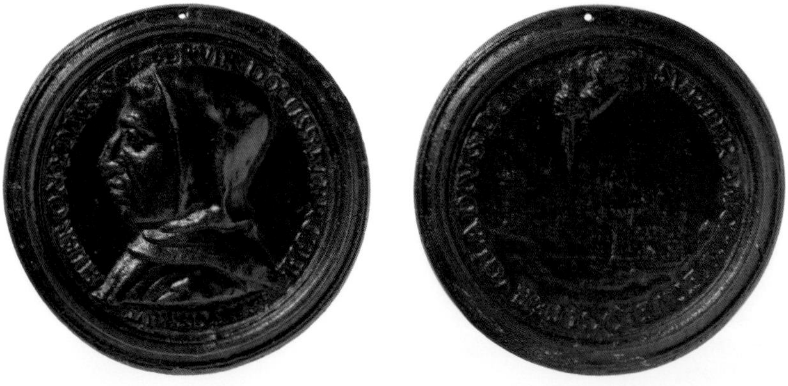

Linden wood, h. 46 1/4 in. (117.5 cm). Busch-Reisinger Museum, Antonia Paepcke DuBrul Fund and Special Gifts of Friends of Charles L. Kuhn, BR69.214.

Tilman Riemenschneider and Workshop German, 1450–1531 Saint Anthony Abbot c. 1510

In the years before Tilman Riemenschneider created his statues, wooden figures were routinely painted in bright polychrome colors. Rather than relinquish the finishing touches to the painter's guild, Riemenschneider and his workshop developed an elegant new Gothic vocabulary of deep-cut curves and softly draping fabrics. While emphasizing linden wood's natural color and patterns, the artists sometimes augmented it with subtle tinted glazes. / The plank used for this sculpture was so thin that Saint Anthony's hands had to be added separately to grasp his attributes, the staff and book. The thinness also suggests the saint formed part of a larger group of high-relief panels for an altarpiece rather than an independent devotional image. SKS

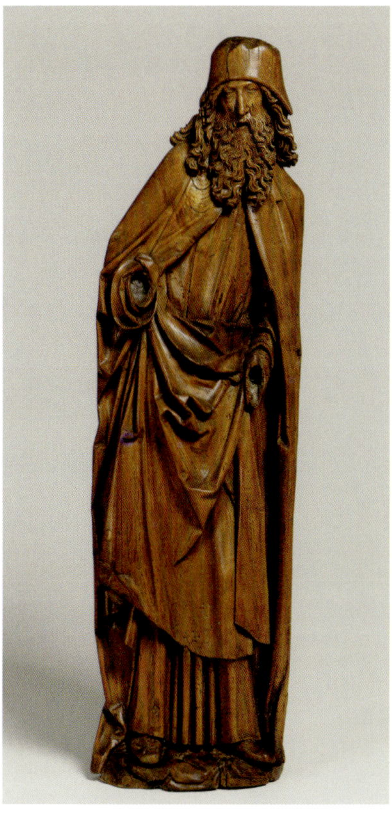

Oil on panel, 18 1/16 x 17 3/8 in. (45.9 x 44.2 cm). Fogg Museum, Kate, Maurice R., and Melvin Seiden Special Purchase Fund in honor of Konrad Oberhuber and Sydney Freedberg, Richard Norton Memorial Fund, and Richard Norton Fund, 2007.106.

Attributed to Titian
Italian, c. 1490–1576
An Idyll: A Woman with a Child and a Halberdier in a Landscape
1505–10

Although the composition of this painting is clearly related to Giorgione's *Tempest*, his famous landscape that also includes a seated mother and child with a man standing guard, this panel is considered by many scholars to be an early work by Titian. The artist explores the possibilities of the relatively new medium of oil paint as he builds his composition through layers of saturated color to create subtle effects of light, as seen in the sky, the leaves of the tree, the drapery, and the reflections on the armor of the halberdier. This luminous effect is a hallmark of Titian's poetic approach to landscape and was emulated by other Venetian artists at the beginning of the sixteenth century. DC

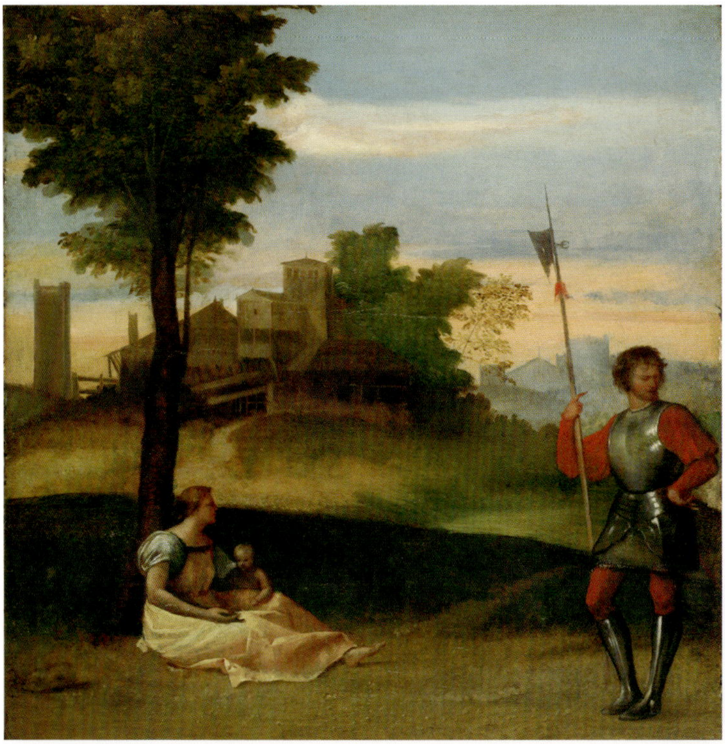

73 Brown ink over charcoal on cream antique laid paper, $9\frac{9}{16}$ x $8\frac{1}{8}$ in. (24.3 x 20.6 cm). Fogg Museum, Bequest of John and Alice Steiner, 2004.67.

Titian
Italian, c. 1490–1576
Trees Near a Pool of Water
c. 1530

Few drawings by Titian survive. This is one of a small number of landscapes in pen and ink that are plausibly attributed to the Venetian master. The superior quality of the drawing lies in the artist's almost painterly skill in using different weights of ink to define volume and depth, whereby denser areas are balanced by the use of the blank page. Atmospheric effects are captured in the patterned play of light and shadow in the foliage and in the reflective pool of water below. This creates a sense of movement and conveys the artist's interest in the constant flux of nature. DC

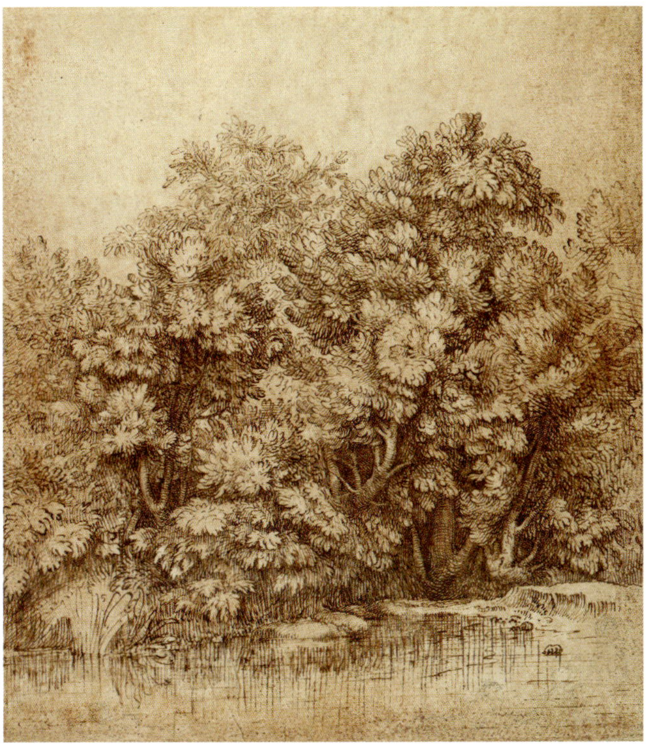

Black chalk on beige antique laid paper, 6 1/8 x 6 1/16 in. (15.6 x 15.4 cm). Fogg Museum, Bequest of Charles A. Loeser, 1932.152.

Michelangelo Buonarroti
Italian, 1475–1564
Goldsmith's Designs and Other Studies
1521

A prolific draftsman, Michelangelo upheld the notion of Florentine *disegno* (drawing and design) as the initial intellectual moment of artistic creation. On this sheet, the artist carefully sketched his ideas for two bronze lamps featuring fantastic creatures. The attention to detail and precise lines would have helped the craftsmen who fabricated the lamps follow the master's designs. Other light sketches on the page include an eye, a man with a lyre, a man with his right arm raised, and a mourning woman. This last figure may be connected with a sketch of a sarcophagus on the reverse of the page. That drawing has been identified as a study for the Magnifici Tomb, an abandoned project for the Medici Chapel. DC

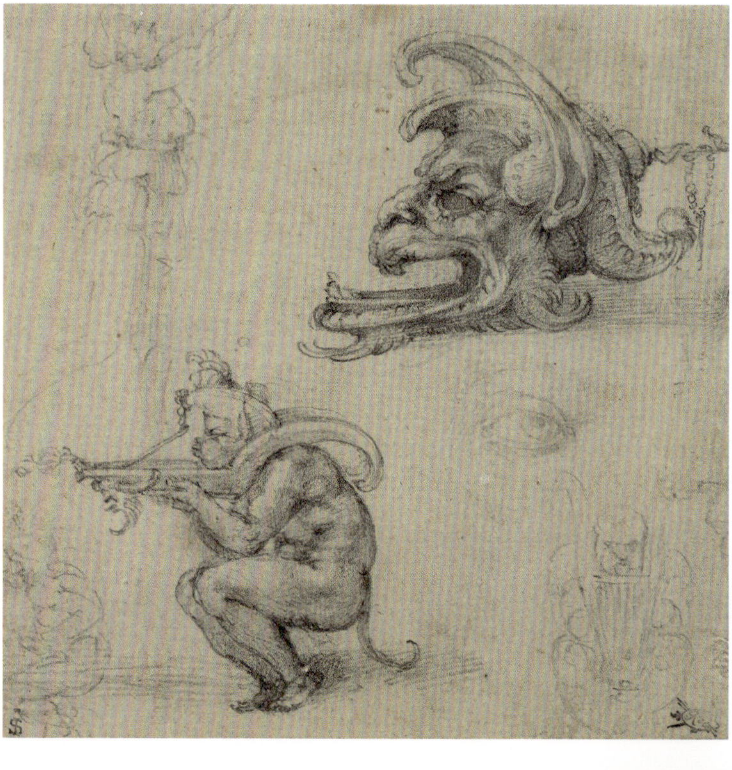

Walnut with black marble inserts, 84 3/8 x 49 3/4 x 21 1/4 in. (214.3 x 126.4 x 54 cm). Fogg Museum, Gift of Anne H. and Frederick Vogel III, Class of 1957, with their children, Alicia H. Vogel and Frederick Vogel IV, Class of 1990, 1997.88.B.

Two-Tiered Cabinet with Relief Decorations

French, Île-de-France c. 1570–80

The classicizing design and rich decoration of this two-tiered cabinet is typical of late sixteenth-century French furniture. Venus and Mars, carved in relief, adorn the smaller doors above, Juno and Minerva the larger doors below. Nymphs recline languidly in the frieze of the slightly recessed upper part; sea monsters swim in opposite directions in the drawer fronts of the protruding lower part. Black marble inlay adds to the sumptuousness of the piece. The emphasis on sensuous nude figures and grotesque ornament testifies to the spread of the Italianate court style, which arose from the design and decor of the royal palace at Fontainebleau and circulated through prints. YFY

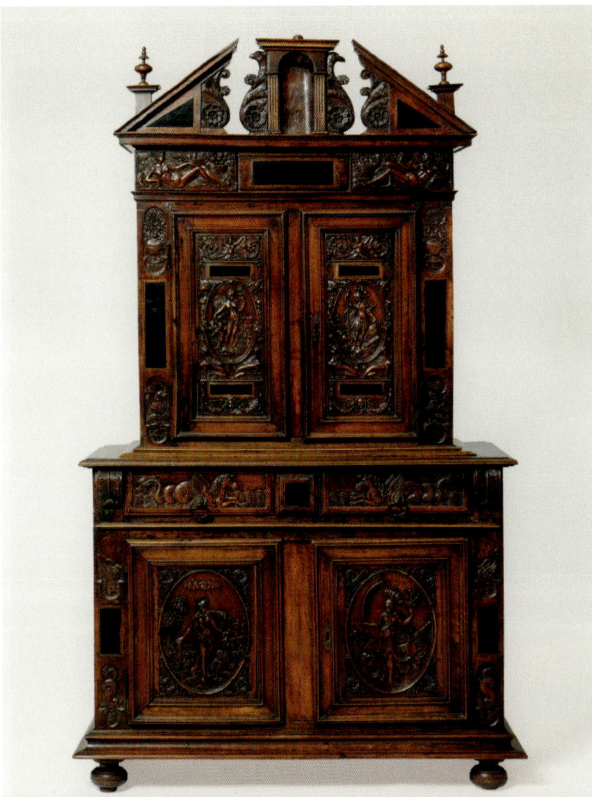

Oil on panel, 14 x 18 1/2 in. (35.6 x 47 cm). Fogg Museum, Gift in part of Barbara B. Paine and purchase in part from Mrs. Ernest Angell Trust Fund and Richard Norton Fund, 1972.22.

Girolamo Mazzola Bedoli Italian, c. 1505–c. 1569 The Virgin and Child in a Landscape c. 1536–37

Bedoli became the leading painter in Parma in 1540, following the death of Parmigianino. Bedoli is best known for his altarpieces and frescoes, but this smaller painting was probably privately commissioned and served a more devotional function. The details of this intimate scene are best appreciated when this work is viewed closely. The Virgin encourages us to join her in quietly adoring her sleeping child. We quickly become lost in the vibrant colors of the sumptuous drapery and creamy flesh tones of these foreground figures. The curve of their bodies is echoed in the natural setting of the scene, which gives way to a distant and atmospheric background. DC

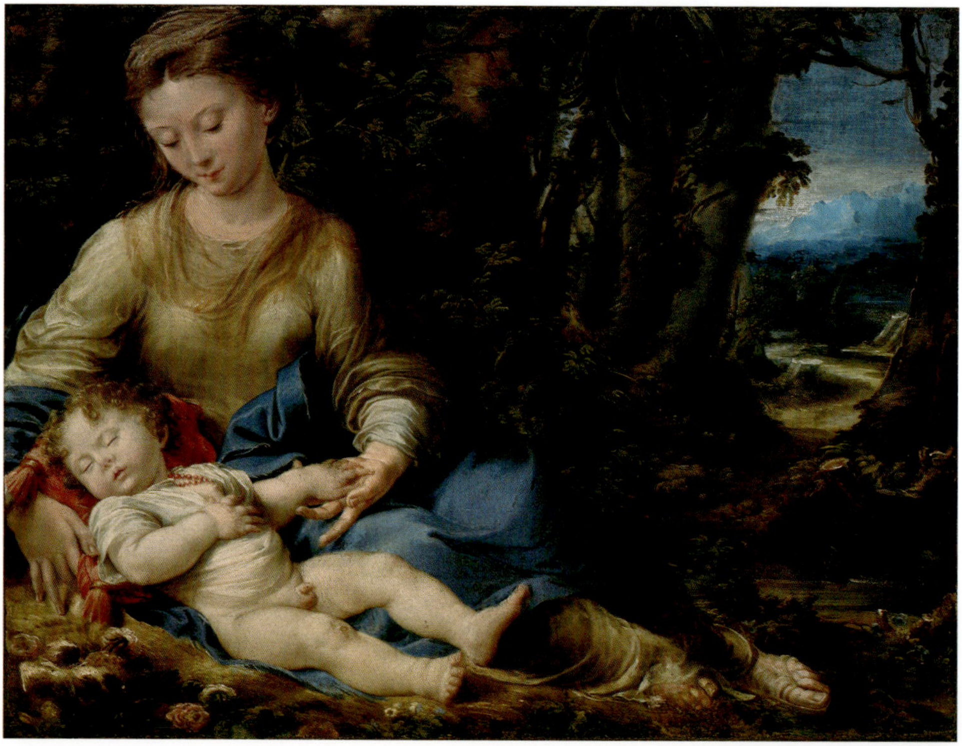

77 Black and brown ink, gray wash, and white gouache over red chalk on cream antique laid paper; $10\frac{1}{2} \times 6\frac{15}{16}$ in. (26.6 x 17.6 cm). Fogg Museum, Bequest of Charles A. Loeser, 1932.299.

Taddeo Zuccaro
Italian, 1529–1566
Nude Youth
1550–55

A native of the Marches region, Taddeo Zuccaro went to Rome at age fourteen to begin his artistic training by studying the art of Michelangelo and especially Raphael. The naturalism of these High Renaissance masters is here blended with a mannerist sensibility, seen in the gentle sway of the body, the exaggerated muscular anatomy, and the elongated fingers. The dynamic and varied ink lines define the pose of this figure, and wash and cross-hatching create a more pictorial effect. Zuccaro experimented with the position of the legs in what may have been a preliminary study for a painting whose location is now unknown. The drawing is layered with other figural studies, including a man drawn in red chalk and upside down in relation to the main figure, and another lightly sketched silhouette, oriented vertically at the left. DC

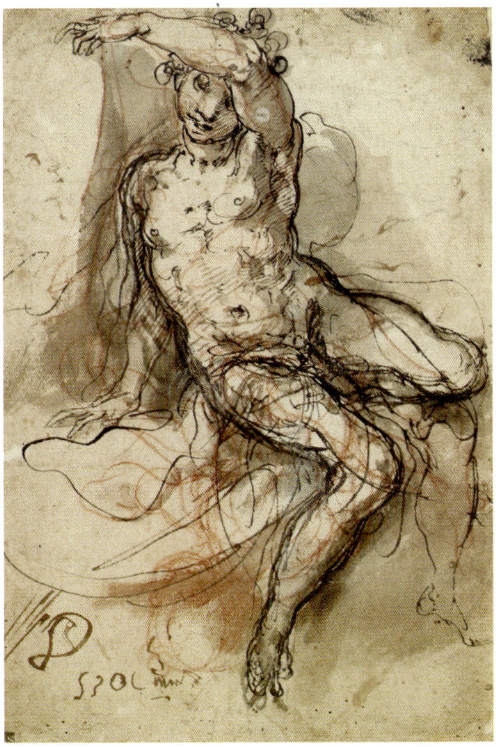

Engraving, printed *à la poupée* in red and blue ink; 15 11/16 x 9 in (39.8 x 22.9 cm). Fogg Museum, Anonymous Fund for the Acquisition of Prints Older than 150 Years, 2007.32.

Agostino Veneziano
Italian, c. 1490–active until 1536
Virgin with Saints of the Dominican Order
c. 1525

Agostino Veneziano was active in Marcantonio Raimondi's Roman printmaking workshop. This Madonna is the earliest-known sheet printed *à la poupée*. That process involves printing multiple colors from a single plate, using small fabric bundles, or dolls, to dab on each color of ink. Veneziano highlighted the Madonna and Child in red ink, leaving the rest of the composition blue. Other impressions survive in pure black, suggesting that these color choices were highly symbolic: blue and red allude to Mary's purity. Barely visible pinholes might have resulted from tacking the sheet onto a wall; thus, the Virgin's rosy aura could have enhanced the engraving's use as a devotional panel. SKS

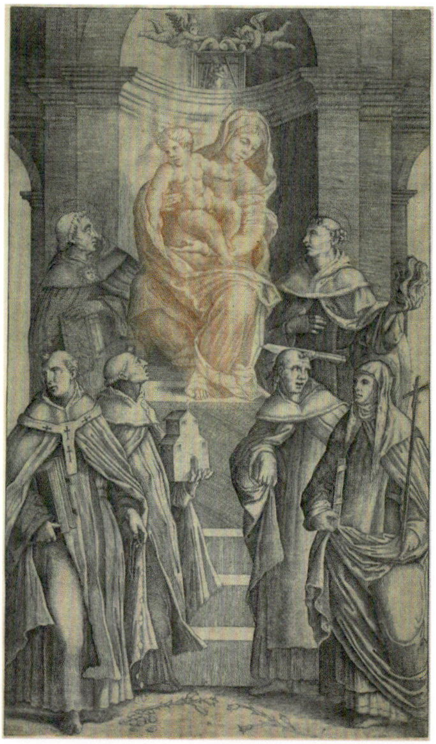

79 Oil on canvas, 35 3/8 x 27 5/16 in. (89.9 x 69.4 cm). Fogg Museum, Gift of Edward W. Forbes in memory of Alice F. Cary, 1964.4.

Lorenzo Lotto
Italian, c. 1480–1556
Friar Angelo Feretti as Saint Peter Martyr
1549

This painting exemplifies Lotto's skill as a portraitist. Records indicate that this iconic saint is actually a portrait of the Dominican monk Angelo Feretti of Ancona. Holding the New Testament in one hand, the saint gestures toward the martyr's palm and an inscription in the lower right of the painting: CREDO IN UNUM DEUM (I believe in one God). This phrase echoes the beginning of the Apostles' and Nicene creeds and the words Peter wrote in his own blood during his martyrdom. This inscription, along with the artist's signature and the cleaver in the saint's head, had been overpainted and were revealed with the restoration of the painting at Harvard in 1923. DC & MB

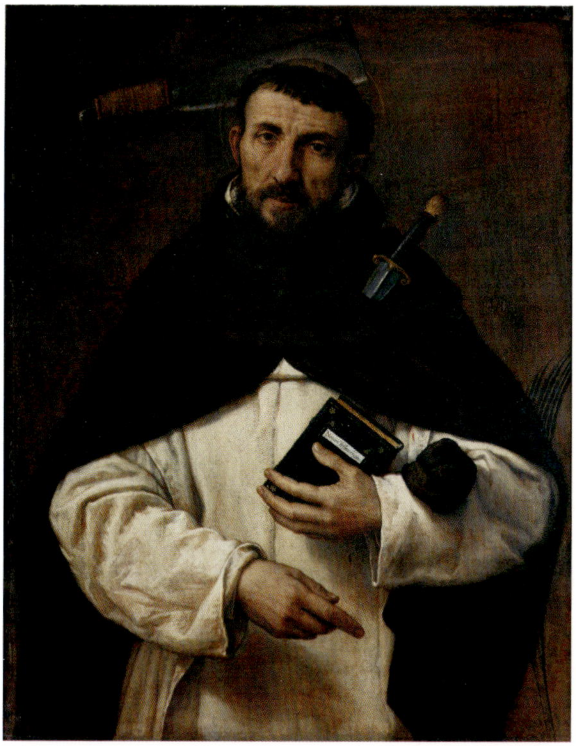

Black ink and opaque watercolor on off-white paper; inscribed These two figures are in the manner of the Frankish masters: drawn while in the service of the one giving asylum to those seeking the right path, the Wonder of the Age, Khwaja Ghiyath Naqshband. Written by the servant [of God] Sadiqi, the Librarian; 12 3/16 x 8 3/16 in. (31 x 20.8 cm). Arthur M. Sackler Museum, Gift of Stuart Cary Welch, Jr., 1999.289.

Sadiqi Beg
Persian, 1533/34–1609/10
Figures from the Annunciation
c. 1590

In this carefully modeled and tinted drawing, two figures based on the Virgin Mary and the archangel Gabriel—the primary actors in the Christian Annunciation—have somewhat surprisingly come to rest upon a Persian album page. These quiet figures are enlivened by Sadiqi Beg's attentive hand. Heavy drapery and angular folds give way to gentle pink faces and flowing hair through the combination of tiny brushstrokes and translucent washes. / Shah ʿAbbas appointed Sadiqi Beg the head of the imperial library-atelier, a position he maintained until 1598, when Riza ʿAbbasi was assigned to the post (see page 83). Copied from an engraving by the Flemish artist known as the Master of the Banderoles, this graceful work is one of the earliest known examples of experimentation with European sources in Persian art. KM

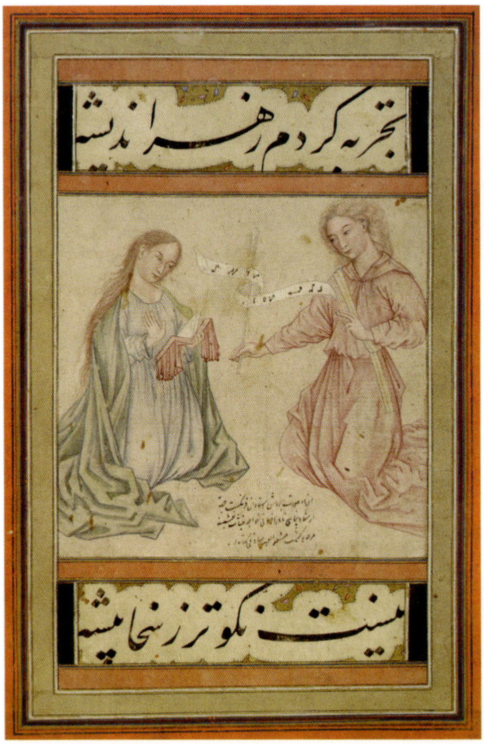

81 Etching, 15 15/16 x 11 in. (40.5 x 28 cm). Fogg Museum, Gray Collection of Engravings Fund, G4784.

Melchior Lorch
German, c. 1527–after 1588
Ismael, Persian Ambassador at Constantinople in 1557
after 1559

Melchior Lorch traveled to Constantinople in 1554 on a diplomatic mission for the Holy Roman Emperor Ferdinand I. After his return in 1559, Lorch published a poem, book, and several prints illustrating Turkish costumes and habits. As the Latin and Arabic legend notes, this etching was a "viva effigies,"or living image, of the Persian ambassador to Suleiman the Magnificent. Lorch probably made sketches from life and completed the etching on his return to Europe. His keen interest in foreign costume is evident: Lorch particularly elaborates Ismael's bejeweled and feathered headdress, which he revisited in a full-length etching in 1569. SKS

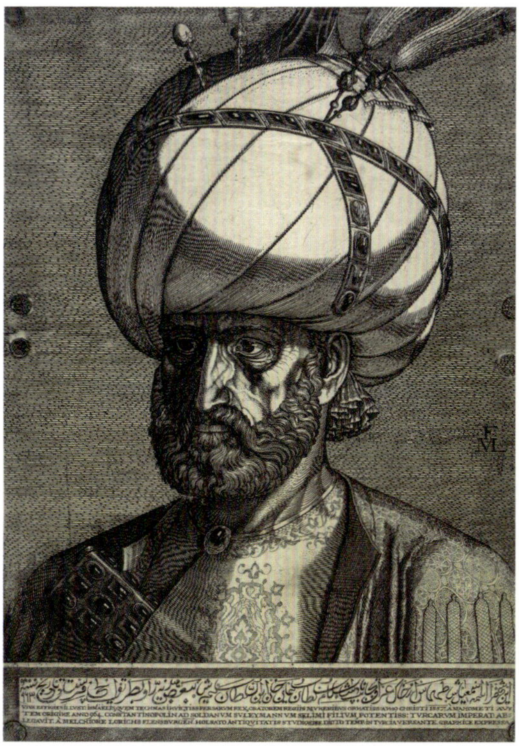

Gunmetal with iron insets, 8 5/16 x 8 1/4 x 9 1/16 in. (22.7 x 21 x 23 cm). Fogg Museum, Gift of Mrs. John D. Rockefeller Jr. (Abby Aldrich Rockefeller), 1937.38.

Commemorative Head of a King
Nigerian, Edo-speaking
Kingdom of Benin
16th century

Rulers of Benin, called *obas*, were represented by large copper alloy heads that were placed on ancestral altars in homage to the intelligence, character, judgment, and leadership that they brought to their role as monarchs. This work portrays the oba's fringed headdress and collar, simulating coral beads. The large opening at the top of the sculpture originally held a carved elephant tusk, which signified the ruler's function as an intercessor between the worlds of the living and the dead. ER

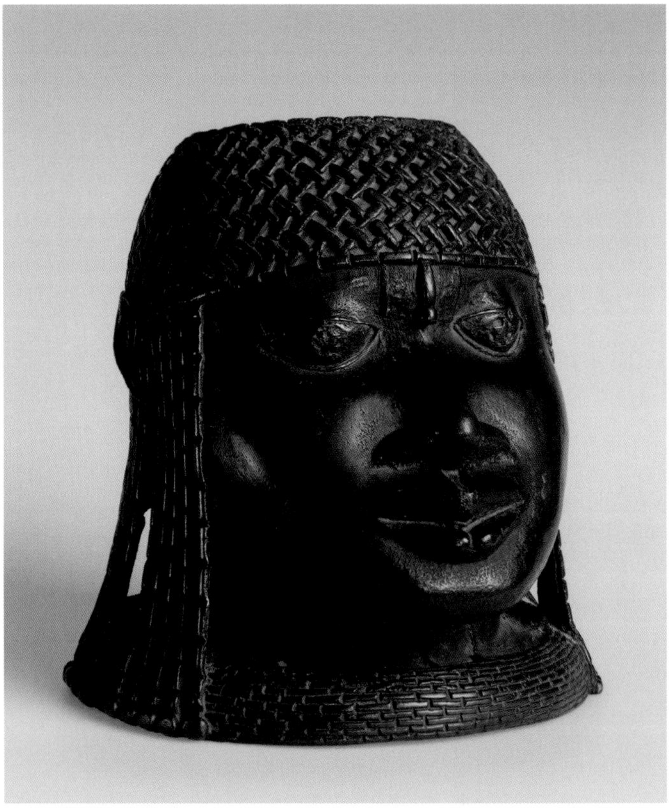

83 Ink, opaque watercolor, and gold on paper; inscribed (left) work of the most humble Aqa Riza; seal (lower center) 'Abbas, the servant of the King of Holiness, year 995 [AD 1587]; 6 15/16 x 2 7/8 in. (17.6 x 7.3 cm). Arthur M. Sackler Museum, Sarah C. Sears Collection, 1936.27.

Aqa Riza (Riza 'Abbasi) Persian, c. 1565–1635 Young Man in a Blue Cloak 1587

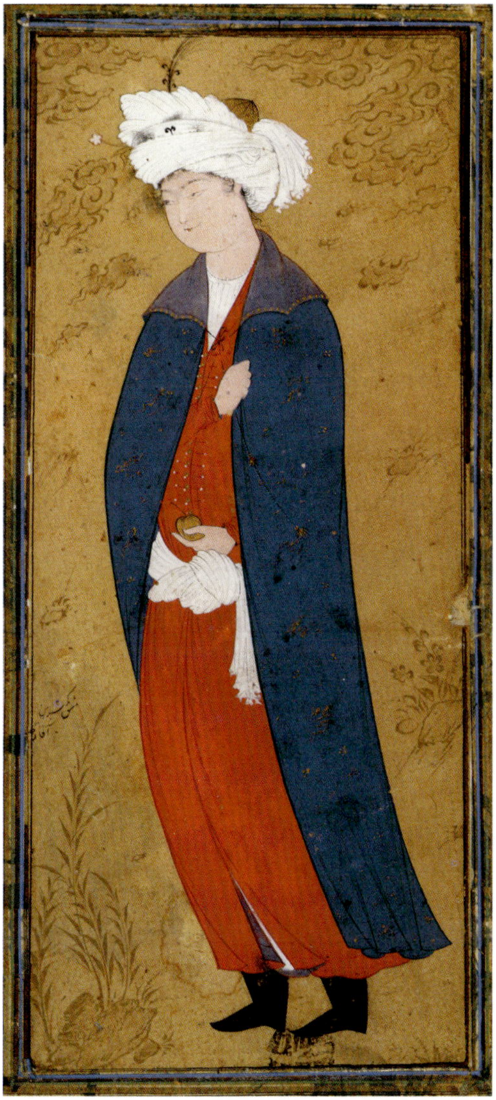

Bright-eyed and smiling, a fashionable young courtier is here rendered with a harmony of curves and the punch of primary colors. This painting of an elegant youth swaying slightly on his black boots is among the earliest known works by Aqa Riza, one of the most influential artists who worked during the reign of the Safavid dynasty in Iran (1501–1722). A master of rhythmic line and a confident colorist, Riza was also known as Riza 'Abbasi, an honorific indicating his status at the court of Shah 'Abbas I (r. 1587–1629). Although he also produced many illustrations for manuscripts over his long career, Riza is best known for his single-page paintings that brilliantly capture the Safavid social world. MM

Fritware with underglaze painting, 15 3/8 x 26 3/8 in. (39 x 67 cm). Arthur M. Sackler Museum, Gift of John Goelet, 1960.17.

Tile with Palmette Blossoms, Flowers, and Serrated Leaves
Islamic, Turkey, Iznik
Ottoman period
c. 1570–80

Cobalt blue, emerald green, a thick tomato red, and turquoise make the stunning Iznik tiles instantly recognizable. The production of decorative building tiles emerged at Iznik (ancient Nicaea) in the mid-sixteenth century, along with new palettes and motifs, leading to a truly Ottoman style. / This tile exemplifies the *saz* leaf-and-rosette style that developed in the 1540s and 1550s. Curling, serrated leaves, rosettes, and palmettes are connected by undulating tendrils, giving the decoration a sense of movement. Borders of scalloped arches and Chinese-style cloud scrolls frame the interior decoration. While the saz style developed decades earlier, this striking color palette did not come to fruition until later in the century. Imperial Ottoman patronage of the manufacture of these brilliant tiles helped elevate them to the status of a high art form. YH

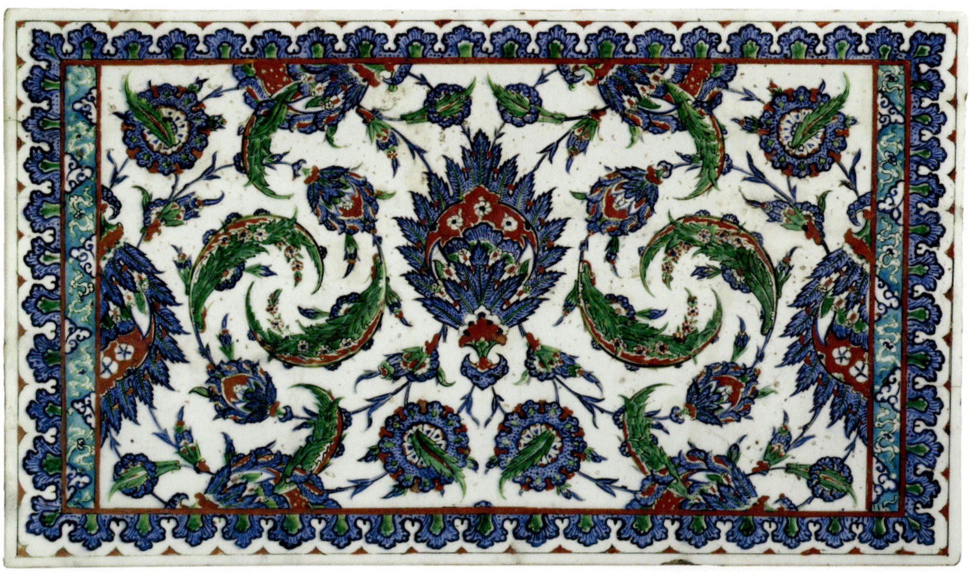

85 / Fritware with molded decoration and underglaze painting in cobalt blue, h. 2 15/16 in. (7.5 cm), diam. 16 7/16 in. (41.7 cm). Arthur M. Sackler Museum, The Gweneth Knight Memorial Fund, 2005.83.

Large Dish with Flying Cranes
Islamic, Iran, Safavid period
c. 1620

For centuries Muslim artists decorated vessels with inscriptions believed to confer blessings on the owners. Deliberately or not, this dish continues the tradition, although Daoist symbols borrowed from China have here replaced inscriptions. The cranes, cloud bands, and peach sprays (underside), painted in multiple shades of cobalt against a pure white ground, convey wishes for long life. / During the sixteenth and seventeenth centuries, European merchants vastly expanded the trade in Chinese blue-and-white ceramics, supplying markets from the Coral Sea to the Atlantic Ocean. Members of Iran's Safavid dynasty (1501–1722) were particularly avid, discriminating collectors of Chinese blue-and-whites. This royal taste, coupled with official encouragement of domestic industries after 1600, inspired Persian potters to produce in the blue-and-white idiom some of their finest wares ever. MM

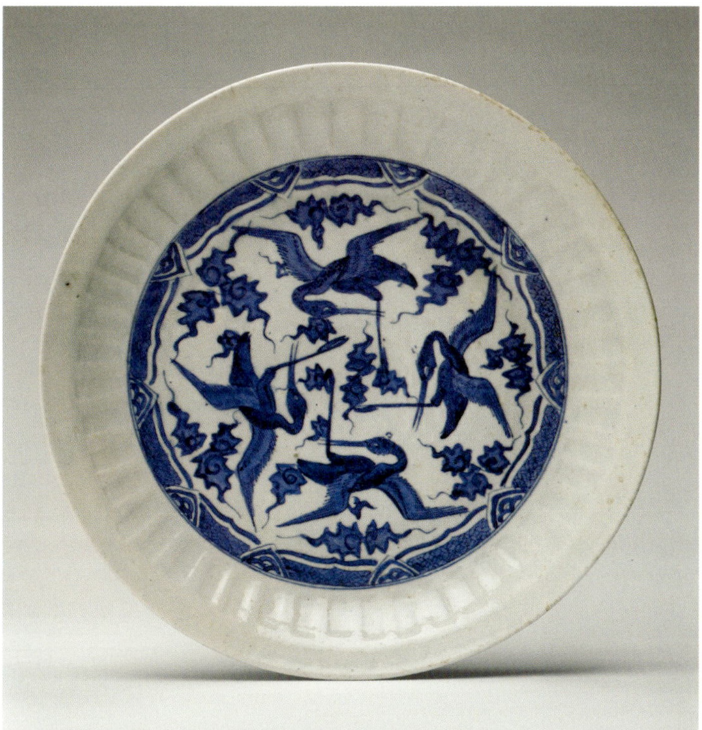

86 Ink, opaque watercolor, and gold on paper; 5 1/2 x 3 in. (14 x 7.6 cm). Arthur M. Sackler Museum, Gift of John Goelet, formerly in the collection of Louis J. Cartier, 1960.117.173.

Attributed to Mahesh
It's the Day for the Garden!
Folio from a manuscript of the *Divan* by Anvari
Islamic, Pakistan, Lahore
Mughal period
1588

The *chaharbagh*, a fourfold garden divided by water channels, became an important aesthetic expression of imperial authority for the Mughals, as well as a source of pleasure. The tiny, detailed painting of gardeners tending a chaharbagh complements a verse by the twelfth-century Persian poet Anvari: "It's the day for merrymaking in the garden, / It's the day for the pageant of rose and basil, / The earth is infused with aromatic amber, / The skirt of the breeze spreads fragrance."

This sixteenth-century manuscript of Anvari's *Divan* (collected poems) includes new verses created for the emperor Akbar, under whom Mughal painting developed a distinctive style, emphasizing naturalism. Elements such as the banana tree at the bottom right highlight the garden's Indian location. Akbar's son, the emperor Jahangir, who very likely had this manuscript in his library, recalls Anvari's verse in his memoirs as epitomizing an enjoyable garden party that he attended. SG

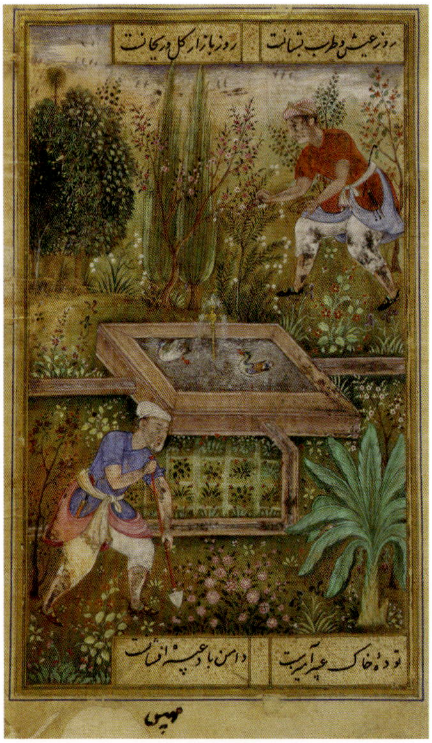

87 Knotted wool pile on cotton warp and weft, 270 x 96 in. (685.8 x 243.8 cm). Arthur M. Sackler Museum, Gift of Joseph V. McMullan, 1957.137. Detail reproduced below.

Garden Carpet
Islamic, Northwestern Iran
c. 1800

Gardens in Islamic societies have often served as metaphors of paradise. References to paradise as a garden are found in the Qur'an as well as in Persian and Arabic poetry. In fact, *pairidaeza*, the ancient Iranian term for a walled garden, is the source for the Greek *paradeisos*. Persian carpets have incorporated the fourfold *chaharbagh* design since the sixteenth century, simulating the heavenly garden within the bounds of a courtly craft. This carpet (detail below) exemplifies the genre of a paradisiacal garden captured in eternal bloom through an artistic medium. Trees and shrubs depict the seasons, their variegated forms ranging from autumn leaves to spring blossoms. A central stream feeds secondary rivulets, both replete with fish. Typical of the later garden carpets of Kurdistan, in northwestern Iran, this piece represents one-quarter of a chaharbagh. The carpet's vast scale lends itself particularly well to the theme of a garden recreated indoors. SG

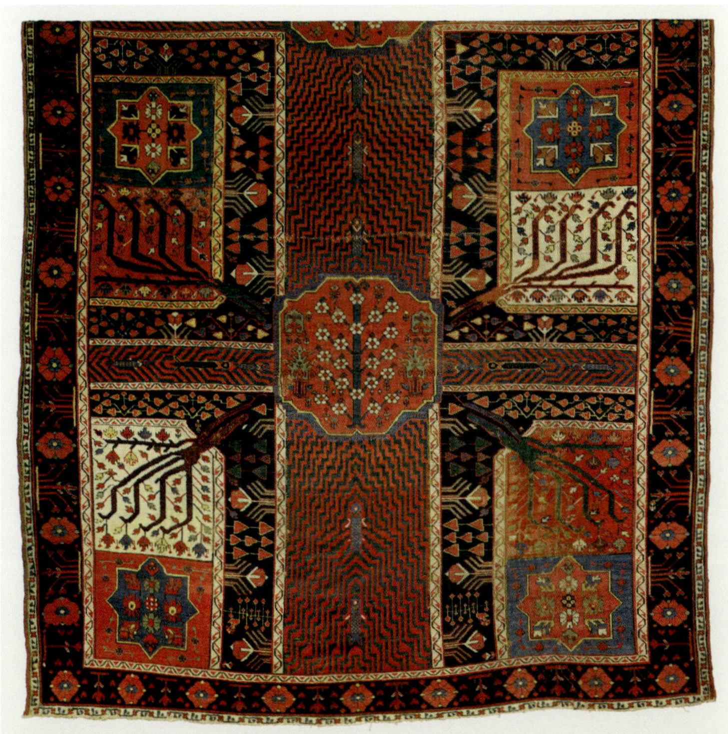

Brown ink, brown wash, white gouache, and black chalk on blue antique laid paper, signed in brown ink, 10 1/4 x 13 1/2 in. (26 x 34.4 cm). Fogg Museum, The Maida and George Abrams Collection, 1999.132.

Pieter Bruegel the Elder
Flemish, c. 1525/30–1569
Wooded Landscape with a Distant View toward the Sea
1554

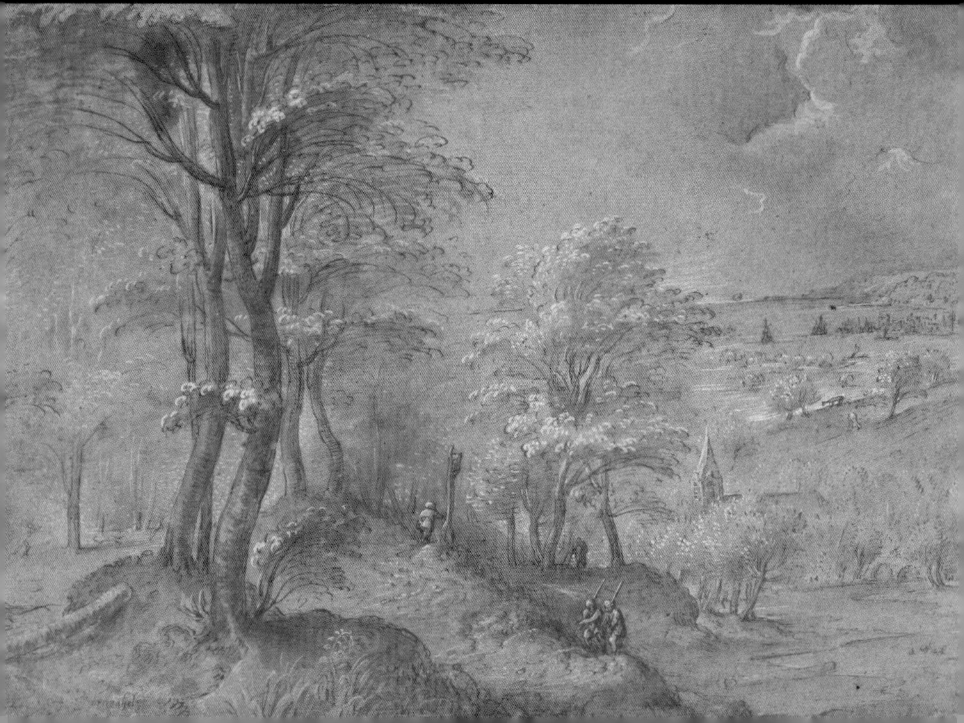

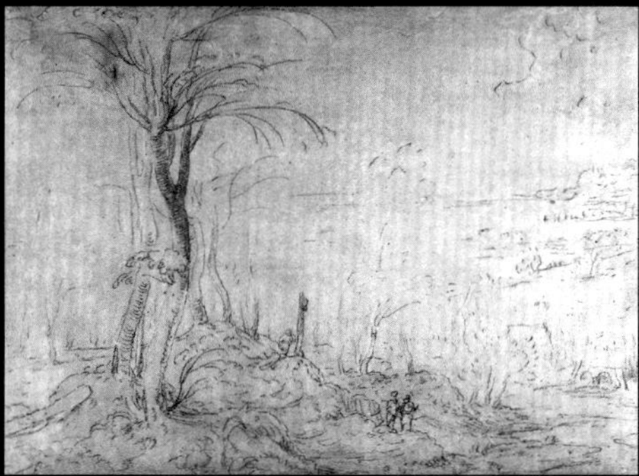

Infrared reflectogram

About sixty drawings by Pieter Bruegel the Elder are known to survive today. This is one of two on blue paper, and the only drawing he finished with white gouache. Bruegel worked in ink, wash, and gouache over a preliminary sketch in black chalk. The drawing dates from the final months of the artist's three-year journey to Italy (1552–54). While the panoramic composition belongs to an established tradition in Netherlandish art, the dynamic construction of space, serpentine trees, and free, vigorous penwork attest to Bruegel's study of landscape prints and drawings by Venetian artists, particularly Titian and Domenico Campagnola. / The infrared reflectogram above was taken with special photographic equipment sensitive in the near-infrared portion of the spectrum. While colorants, such as pigments and dyes, are relatively transparent and therefore invisible in infrared light, materials that contain carbon, such as charcoal, chalk, and graphite, are absorbed and appear dark in reflectograms. Thus, preparatory designs or underdrawings in black chalk show up clearly because the colorants (ink wash and gouache, in this case) painted on top of them have been rendered invisible. This image shows the surprisingly extensive and detailed chalk sketch that underlies the finished composition, revealing how Bruegel developed his design. WR & PK

Left: chiaroscuro woodcut, 4 5/8 x 5 13/16 in. (11.7 x 14.7 cm), Fogg Museum, Light-Outerbridge Collection, Gift of Robert M. Light and Anonymous Fund for the Acquisition of Prints Older than 150 Years, M26576. Right: woodcut on blue paper with white gouache, 4 1/2 x 5 5/8 in. (11.5 x 14.3 cm), Fogg Museum, Gray Collection of Engravings Fund, G7448.

Hendrick Goltzius
Dutch, 1558–1617
Landscape with Farmhouse
c. 1597–1600

Hendrick Goltzius was a mannerist artist renowned for his sophisticated engraving style, but he also produced woodcuts in an intricate process called chiaroscuro that approximated the shading of multitone drawings. One version (at left) of this quintessentially Dutch scene with its stork and defecating dog was made in three stages. Each ink—black, light green, and dark green—required a separate woodblock and a new pass through the printing press. The other impression combines the main block—printed in black on blue paper—with hand-painted white heightening. This soft finish makes the gradations of volume here markedly more subtle than in the version with crisp tone blocks. / Goltzius designed these woodcut variations to replicate the appearance of drawings, which were beginning to be prized as artworks in their own right. These woodcuts were some of his final prints: Goltzius gave up most of his printmaking activities around 1600 in favor of painting. SKS & TS

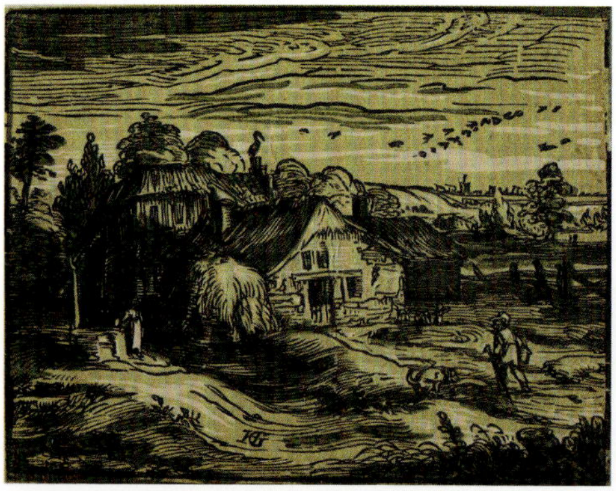

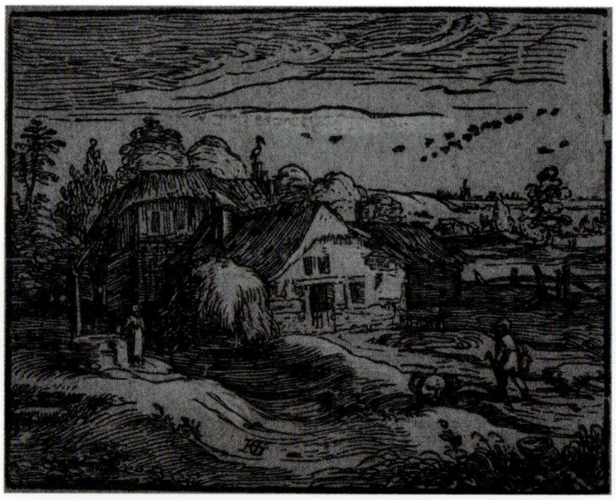

91 / Pine wood, polychromed and gilded; part A, 36 1/4 x 54 3/4 x 19 3/4 in. (92 x 139 x 50.2 cm); part B, 21 1/2 x 44 x 13 1/2 in. (55 x 112 x 34 cm); part C, 32 3/4 x 19 1/4 x 10 1/2 in. (83 x 49 x 27 cm). Fogg Museum, Gift of Mrs. Samuel D. Warren, 1946.60.A–C.

Tabernacle
Spanish
16th century

This portion of a sixteenth-century Spanish altarpiece originally served as the tabernacle (*custodia*) of a church's high altar (*retablo mayor*). The Host would be locked inside until the priest retrieved it for consecrating and for administering Communion to his congregation. Around the tabernacle, the high altar, also ornately carved, painted, and gilded, would stretch from floor to ceiling, attached to the wall. / In the fifteenth through seventeenth centuries, while Spain oversaw a vast empire, many Spanish parishes had high altars built for and fitted into the apses of their churches. Workshops employed designers, carpenters, carvers, gilders, and painters to contribute specific skills to the production of large altars. This tabernacle is a superb example of *estofado*, a technique whereby the sculpture is entirely gilded and painted over, followed by the scratching away of some of the paint to reveal the gold underneath. SK1

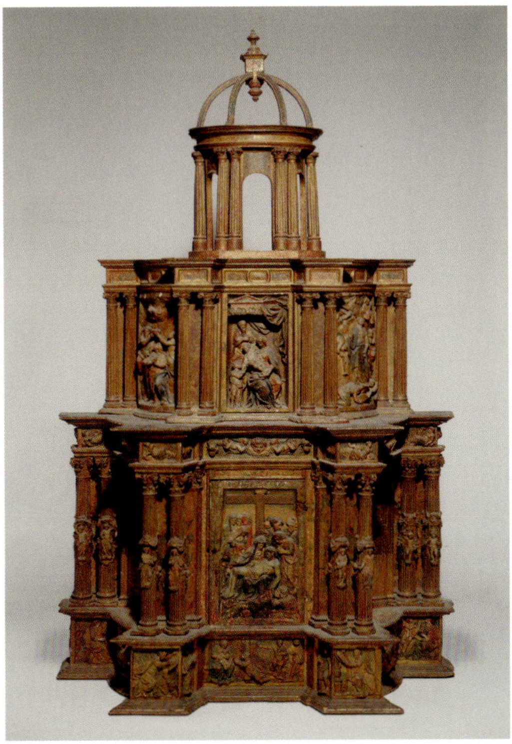

 Linden wood, h. 10 3/8 and 9 13/16 in. (26.4 and 25 cm). Busch-Reisinger Museum, Association Fund, BR59.33, .32.

Death with Outstretched Right Hand and Death with Left Hand Raised German, Upper Rhine 1600–1650

Affecting the *contrapposto* stances of classical sculpture, the two gruesome but elegant statuettes personify Death as partly decomposed cadavers. Snakes writhe amid the decay, animating the exposed flesh and bones. Most likely, the now-broken arms once held bows while the sashes worn diagonally across the torsos originally supported quivers; bows and arrows were common attributes in sixteenth- and seventeenth-century depictions of Death. Exquisitely carved small sculptures representing Death such as these were highly prized by Renaissance and Baroque collectors, who valued them at once as objects of artistic virtuosity and as reminders of the transience of earthly life. YFY

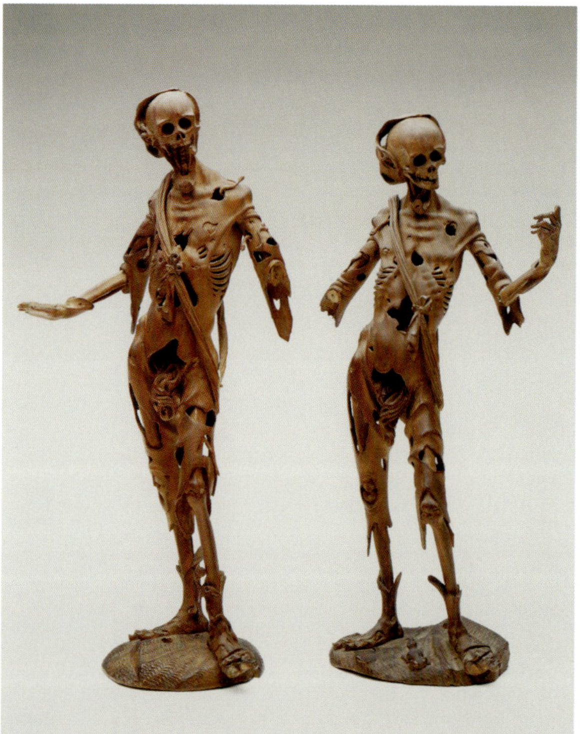

Oil on canvas, 39 5/16 x 33 9/16 in. (99.8 x 85.3 cm). Fogg Museum, Gift through William A. Coolidge in memory of Marian Lady Bateman, 1976.10.

Orazio Gentileschi
Italian, 1563–1639
The Virgin with the Sleeping Christ Child
c. 1610

A follower of Caravaggio, Orazio has created a sense of drama by setting this brilliantly lit scene of monumental figures against a dark background. He added his own stylistic mark through the use of saturated colors, elegant fabrics, and idealized beauty. / The tender moment of the Virgin adoring her sleeping baby foreshadows Christ's death. The child rests on a white sheet over Mary's lap, much in the same way a body would be placed over a shroud. The Virgin acts as the sacrificial altar, and she seems to protect her child with the veil, recalling the humeral veil that is used in carrying the ritual vessel containing the Eucharist. DC

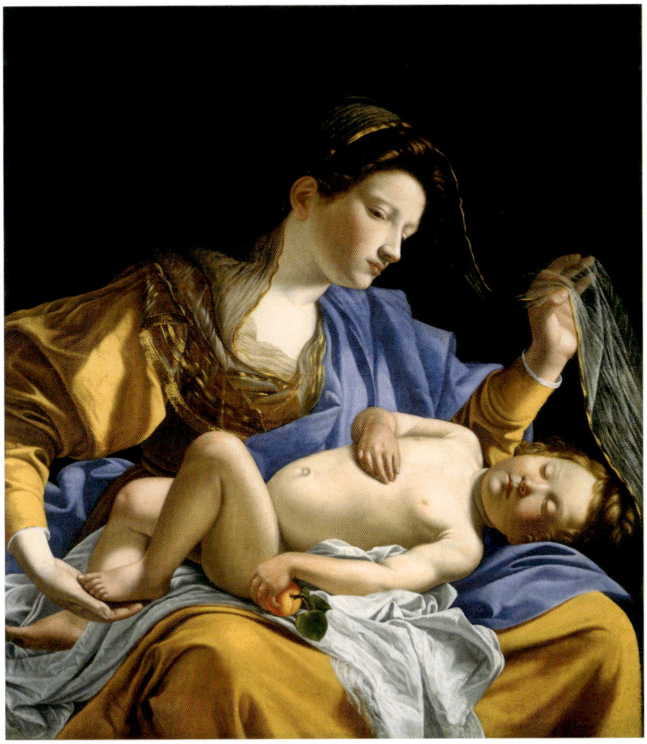

Black and white chalk on light tan antique laid paper, 15 7/8 x 11 11/16 in. (40.3 x 29.7 cm). Fogg Museum, Gift of Meta and Paul J. Sachs, 1949.3.

Peter Paul Rubens
Flemish, 1577–1640
Study for the Figure of Christ
1610

In June 1610, Rubens secured the commission to paint a monumental triptych of the Elevation of the Cross for the high altar of the Antwerp Church of St. Walburga. Following his preferred working method, he established the composition in an oil sketch on panel and then drew detailed studies in chalk for the principal figures. For the body of Christ in his colossal altarpiece, Rubens closely followed this study from a model, reproducing the vigorous contours, articulation of the muscular arms and torso, disposition of light and shadow, facial expression, and the powerful torsion of the body that twists and strains heroically above the burly executioners who struggle to lift the cross. In the painting, Christ appears full-length and wears the canonical beard and crown of thorns. WR

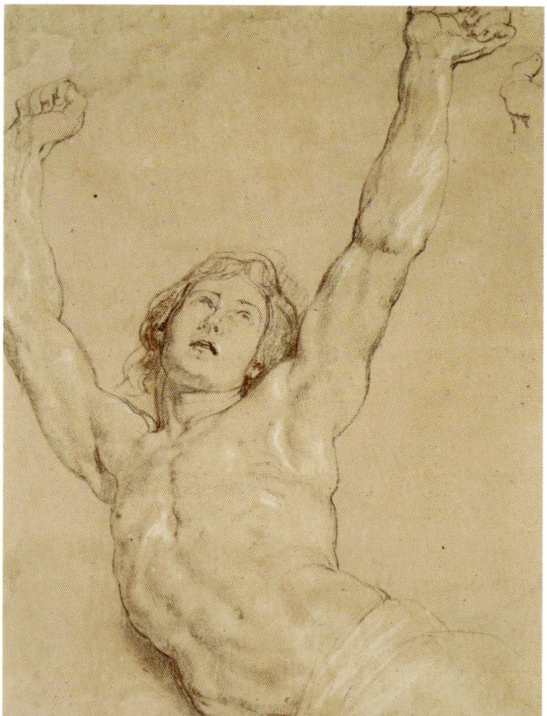

 Oil on panel, 19 1/4 x 25 1/4 in. (48.9 x 64.1 cm). Fogg Museum, Alpheus Hyatt Purchasing Fund, 1942.174.

Peter Paul Rubens
Flemish, 1577–1640
The Voyage of the Cardinal Infante Ferdinand of Spain from Barcelona to Genoa in April 1633, with Neptune Calming the Tempest
1635

The Cardinal Infante Ferdinand, brother of King Philip IV of Spain, was welcomed to Antwerp in 1635 as the new governor of Flanders with an elaborate celebration. Rubens and his workshop were entrusted with creating the decorations for this event, including a series of monumental Roman-inspired triumphal arches and a Stage of Welcome. / This small oil sketch served as the study for the left side panel of the arch, inspired by a line from the *Aeneid* (1.135), describing Neptune calming the turbulent waves. Aeneas's troubled voyage is a metaphor for Ferdinand's own stormy trip from Barcelona to Genoa in 1633. Neptune is depicted ordering the northern wind, Boreas, to make way for the calming southern and western winds, Auster and Zephyr. Allegorically, Spain, to the southwest of the Netherlands, is shown dominating the threatening North. Such preliminary studies record Rubens's initial concept for the final work, executed by workshop assistants. DC

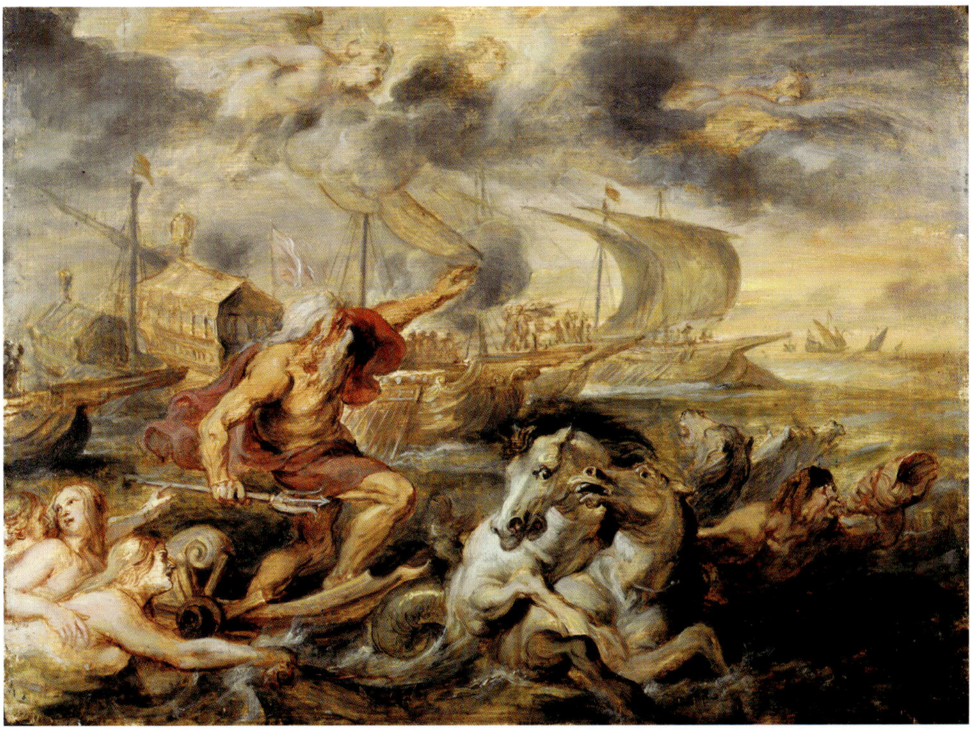

Bronze with dark brown patina, 21 1/8 x 11 15/16 x 8 1/16 in. (53.7 x 30.3 x 20.5 cm). Fogg Museum, Partial and promised gift of Alexis Gregory in honor of James Cuno, 2002.320.

Alessandro Algardi
Italian, 1598–1654
Virgin and Child
1625–50

Algardi began his career restoring ancient sculpture in Rome before creating his own classically inspired works. His style set him apart from the more "High Baroque" sculpture of Gian Lorenzo Bernini, his main rival in Rome. They vied for papal patronage in seventeenth-century Rome, with Bernini as the preeminent sculptor under Pope Urban VIII (1623–44) and Algardi as the favorite of Pope Innocent X (1644–55). / Algardi's attention to detail is illustrated in this finely modeled small bronze. Casts and copies of his sculptures were disseminated throughout Europe as teaching tools, and his influence continued well into the eighteenth century. DC

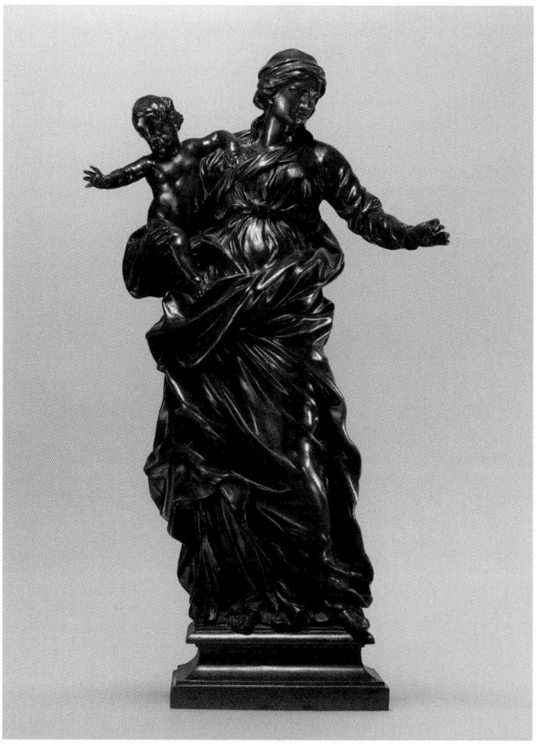

97 / Low-fired clay with gilding, 20 11/16 x 15 x 7 in. (52.6 x 38.1 x 17.8 cm). Fogg Museum, Alpheus Hyatt Purchasing and Friends of the Fogg Art Museum Funds, 1937.51.

Gian Lorenzo Bernini
Italian, 1598–1680
Saint Longinus
c. 1628

This work is one of fifteen clay *modelli* and *bozzetti* attributed directly to Gian Lorenzo Bernini at the Fogg, which houses the largest collection of its kind in the world. This modello served as an early study for Bernini's colossal marble statue (1638) in Saint Peter's basilica. Bernini captured Longinus at the dramatic moment of his Christian conversion, just after he pierced Jesus's side with his lance. He throws back his arms, mirroring the Crucifixion and prefiguring his own martyrdom. / This modello is significant not only for its composition and emotional impact but also because it was gilded. Cross-sectional microscopy by the Straus Center for Conservation and Technical Studies has revealed the absence of a dirt layer between the terracotta and gilding layers, suggesting that the gilding was applied shortly after firing. This may indicate that the modello was made specifically as a presentation model for papal approval or was quickly elevated to the status of a finished work of art. DC & CU

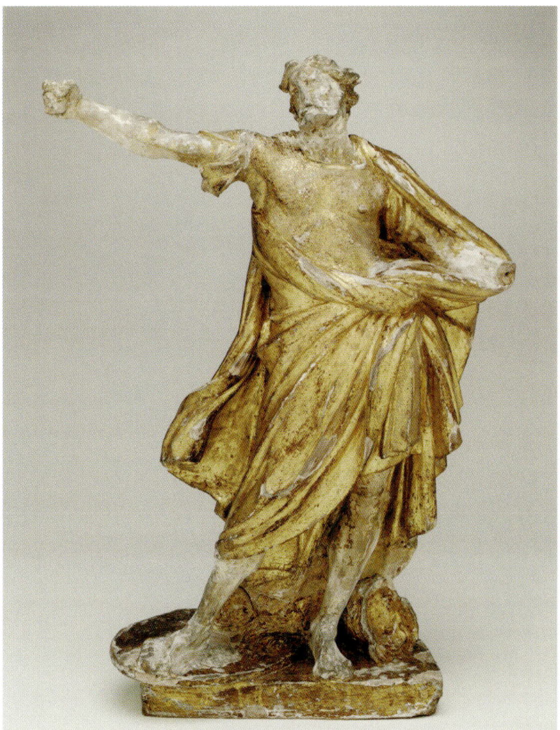

Etching and drypoint, 5 11/16 x 7 3/8 in. (14.5 x 18.8 cm). Fogg Museum, Anonymous Fund for the Acquisition of Prints Older than 150 Years, M23935.

Rembrandt van Rijn
Dutch, 1606–1669
The Hog
1643

Rembrandt's renowned facility with etching and drypoint, as well as his interest in experimental draftsmanship, is magnificently on display in this early state of one of his most impressive nature studies. The light sketchlike etching the artist used to delineate the background peasant figures heightens the strength of his study of the trussed sow in the foreground. Rembrandt reinforced the shadows under her belly with a series of velvety drypoint lines, increasing the sense of her weight and utter immobility. No piglets suckle at her exposed nipples; perhaps, no longer fertile, she has been bound in preparation for slaughter. SKS

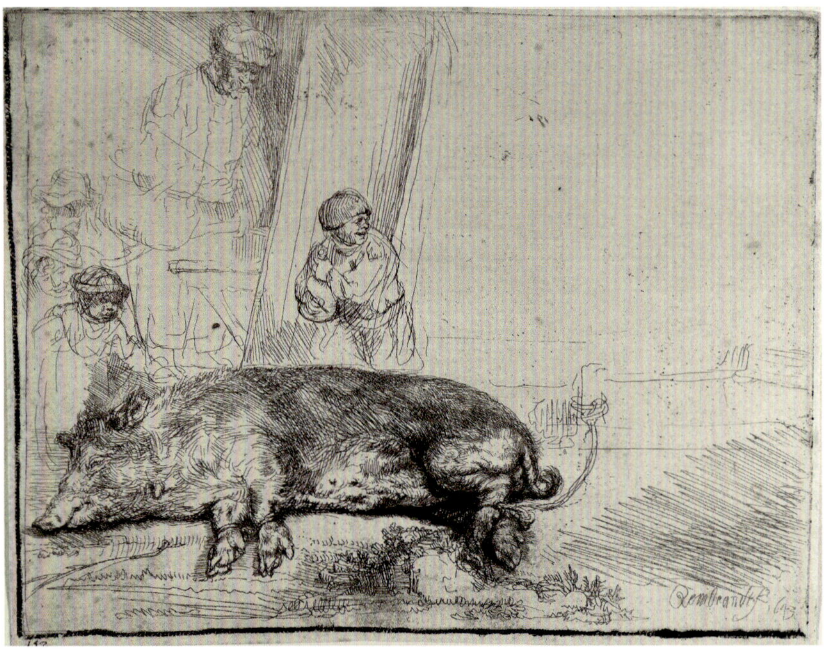

Brown ink, brown wash, and white gouache on cream antique laid paper; 4 5/16 x 8 11/16 in. (10.9 x 22.1 cm). Fogg Museum, The Maida and George Abrams Collection, Gift of George Abrams in memory of Maida Abrams, 2004.181.

Rembrandt van Rijn
Dutch, 1606–1669
A Farm on the Amsteldijk
1650–52

When Rembrandt and his pupils left Amsterdam to draw in the countryside, they occasionally walked south along the Amstel River. This farmstead stood some eight kilometers from the city on the road that flanked the river. Rembrandt sketched the property at least five times and from three sides. The distinctive hump of the barn roof rises at the center, while the lower structure with the living quarters nestles behind the trees and dovecote to the left. In the nearby buildings, the interplay of pen lines, reserves of white paper, and delicate washes brilliantly conveys fleeting shadows and the textures of thatched roofs and weathered planks shimmering in bright sunlight. Rembrandt combines meticulously rendered details with a summarily sketched setting of still water and flat meadows. WR

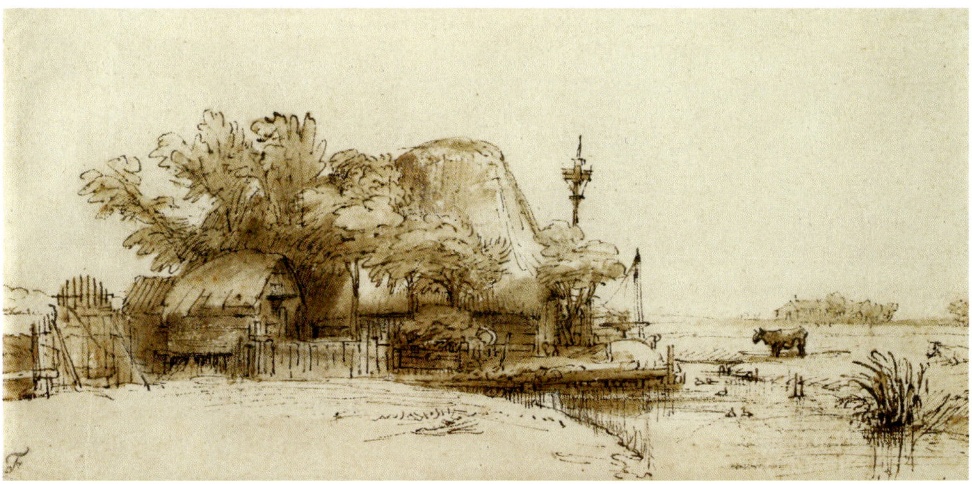

Brown ink and brown wash over traces of black chalk, squared in red chalk, on off-white antique laid paper; 9 x 14 3/4 in. (22.9 x 37.5 cm). Fogg Museum, Gift of Mr. and Mrs. Donald S. Stralem, 1958.290.

Nicolas Poussin
French, 1594–1665
The Infant Bacchus Entrusted to the Nymphs of Nysa; The Deaths of Echo and Narcissus, c. 1657

Connections between related paintings and drawings are not always clear, and works on paper are not always preparatory to the canvas. Most of Nicolas Poussin's extant drawings are composition studies, and they often reveal the evolution of his ideas and of the formal elements of his designs. / This very finished late sheet—the trembling line suggests his older hand—is one of the masterpieces of the artist's draftsmanship. However, its relationship to the Fogg's painting remains unclear, as significant changes in the drawing include Apollo ascending in his chariot, the reversal of Pan, the alteration of Mercury's gesture, and the submergence of Narcissus. Accordingly, this sheet may have been a rejected *modello* for the Fogg canvas, an elaboration of the painted design for the contemporary etching by Giovanni Verini, or the *ricordo* of a similar painting mentioned in eighteenth-century sources. ALC

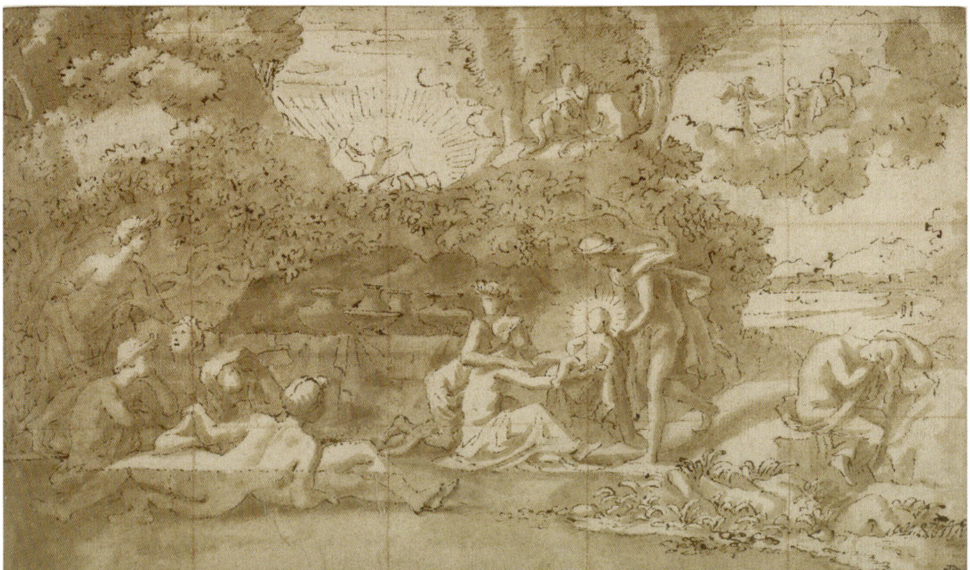

101 Oil on canvas, 48 1/4 x 71 1/16 in. (122.6 x 180.5 cm). Fogg Museum, Gift of Mrs. Samuel Sachs in memory of her husband, Samuel Sachs, 1942.167.

Nicolas Poussin
French, 1594–1665
The Infant Bacchus Entrusted to the Nymphs of Nysa; The Deaths of Echo and Narcissus, 1657

Poussin created this work for his friend and fellow painter Jacques Stella in 1657. Two mythological stories from classical texts by Ovid and Philostratus are here collapsed into a single scene, juxtaposing life and death. Zeus rests in the clouds after having just given birth to Bacchus from his thigh, while Mercury entrusts the baby to the care of Dirce and the nymphs of Nysa, and Pan celebrates the birth. Meanwhile, the darker right side of the painting, where Echo's unrequited love for Narcissus turns her to stone as he becomes a flower, warns against sterility and death. Landscape is treated with the same importance as the figures in the narrative scene, ultimately using the metaphor of the lushness of nature to comment on human mortality. DC

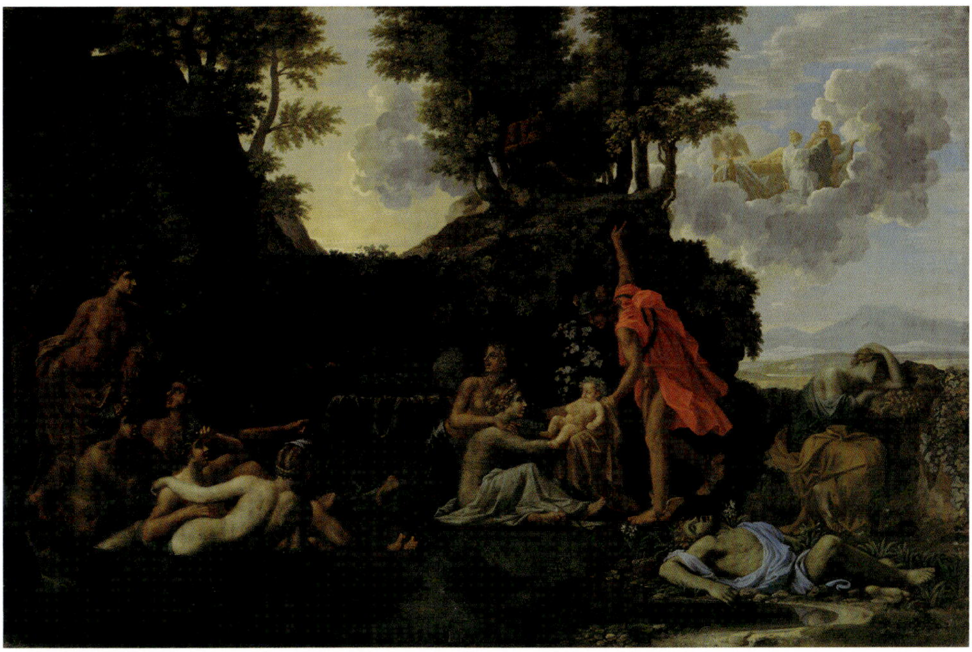

102 Lacquer on wood with *Kōdaiji*-style decoration in gold and silver using the low-relief and high-relief sprinkled design, "pear-skinned" and "pictorial pear-skinned" ground, and linear incising techniques; modern silver fittings; l. 8 9/16 in. (21.8 cm), w. 2 3/8 in. (6.1 cm), h. 2 1/2 in. (5.7 cm). Arthur M. Sackler Museum, The Elaine Ehrenkranz Collection of Japanese Lacquer Boxes; Gift of Elaine Ehrenkranz, 1996.242.12.

Kōdaiji Scroll Box with Lozenge and Crest Design

Japanese, Momoyama period late 16th century

Japanese lacquer, or *urushi*, is made from the viscous sap of the *Rhus verniciflua* tree, which is applied to an object in paper-thin layers to provide an impermeable barrier and lustrous foundation for decoration. A major Japanese innovation was the development of the *maki-e*, or "sprinkled design," technique in which tiny particles of cut gold are sprinkled onto an uncured lacquer surface to create pictorial compositions. The decoration on this extraordinary scroll box (*fubako*) typifies a style that became popular with Japan's warrior elite during the turbulent Momoyama period (1568–1615): Sprinkled-gold lozenges alternate with fields of black lacquer to emblazon surfaces enlivened by stylized floral crests and more naturalistic renderings of the Seven Plants of Autumn. The combination of chrysanthemum and paulownia crests suggests that this box was made for Toyotomi Hideyoshi (1537–1598), a warlord whose military campaigns helped unify Japan in the early seventeenth century. ARK

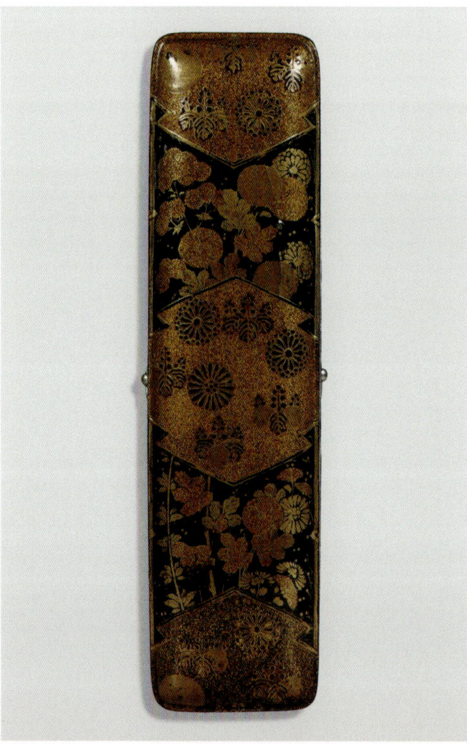

103 Gilt bronze with polychomy, 24 9/16 x 8 7/16 x 7 5/8 in. (62.4 x 21.5 x 19.4 cm). Arthur M. Sackler Museum, Gift of John West, 1963.5.

Attributed to Zanabazar
Mongolian, 1635–1723
Standing Bodhisattva Maitreya
second half of 17th century

Maitreya, the Future Buddha destined to reign over a coming age of reason, is depicted here as a youthful bodhisattva, or saintly being. His crown is adorned with a stupa (Buddhist reliquary) and he proffers the Elixir of Immortality in his left hand. The restrained stance and gesture are elevated by the sinuous depiction of this Nepalese-inspired figure, which wears only minimal adornment. This work is attributable to Mongolia's most celebrated sculptor, the Tibetan Gelugpa-order Lama Zanabazar; it is likely modeled on a statue he made to be paraded through the Mongolian capital (Urga) during the annual Maitreya Festival. Zanabazar himself is credited with promulgating that festival, and this is among the finest sculptures attributed to him. Maitreya worship held special appeal for the Mongols because of its promise of a coming new age, which they equated with a reestablishment of their formerly glorious empire. ARK

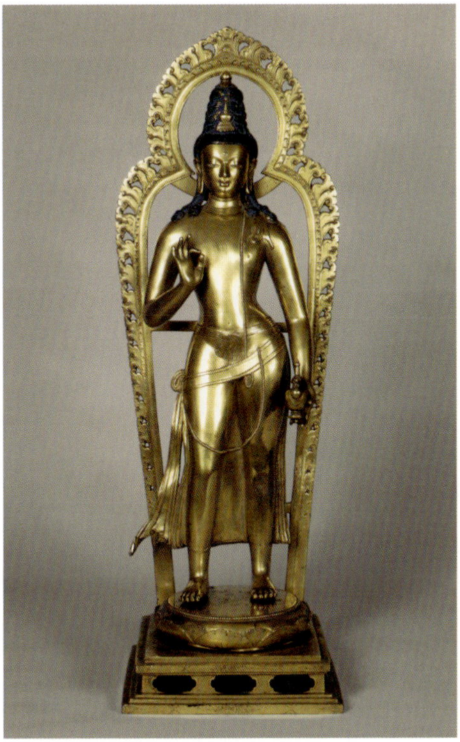

104 Opaque watercolor, gold, and beetle-wing cases on paper; inscribed (top) in Takri script guru mana; 9 3/16 x 13 in. (23.4 x 33 cm). Arthur M. Sackler Museum, Gift of John Kenneth Galbraith, 1972.74.

A Nayika and Her Lover

Folio from a *Rasamanjari* series

Indian, Kashmir, Basohli
c. 1660–70

Immediately recognizable for their vibrant color fields and wide-eyed, bejeweled figures, early painted works from Basohli greatly influenced painting in the Himalayan foothills of northern India. Among the finest examples from Basohli are those in the circa 1660 album of the *Rasamanjari* (Blossom Cluster of Delight), the source of this folio. Written by Bhanudatta in the fourteenth century, the *Rasamanjari* exemplifies *nayika bheda* literature, which presents *nayakas* (heroes) and *nayikas* (heroines) in poignant situations. Here, the nayaka, depicted with blue skin—conflating his identity with the god Krishna—has returned to his beloved after a tryst with another. Sinking beneath her fine clothes and heavy jewels (the gemstones are crafted from beetle wings), the distraught nayika brings her hand to her head. While gestures help to carry this narrative, color intensifies the mood, making the confrontation highly emotional. The top inscription refers to the nayika's intense pride. KM

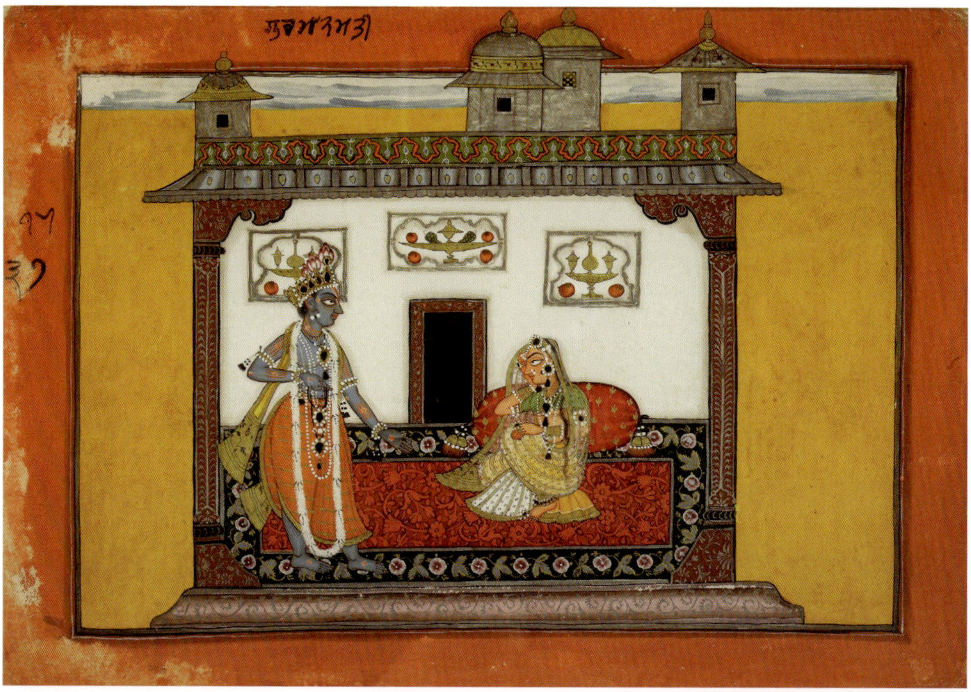

105 / Silver gilt, $1\frac{3}{8} \times 17\frac{5}{8} \times 13\frac{3}{4}$ in. (3.5 x 44.8 x 34.9 cm), 1072 g. Fogg Museum, Paul Clarke Stauffer Fund, 2003.278.

Jacob Bodendeich
German (active London by 1661, no record after 1688)
Sideboard Dish
1676

This oval dish would have been admired as a centerpiece in Restoration England. German-born goldsmith Bodendeich, whose initials mark the underside of the dish, was active in London and known for his excellence in chasing, embossing, and casting. This is one of several objects by Bodendeich based on classical mythology. The lacy foliate design encloses a central scene representing Hercules drawing his bow to shoot Nessus, the centaur who is abducting Deianira. Bodendeich may have been inspired by artists such as Stefano della Bella and Rubens and by a 1557 edition of Ovid's *Metamorphoses* illustrated by Bernard Solomon. DC

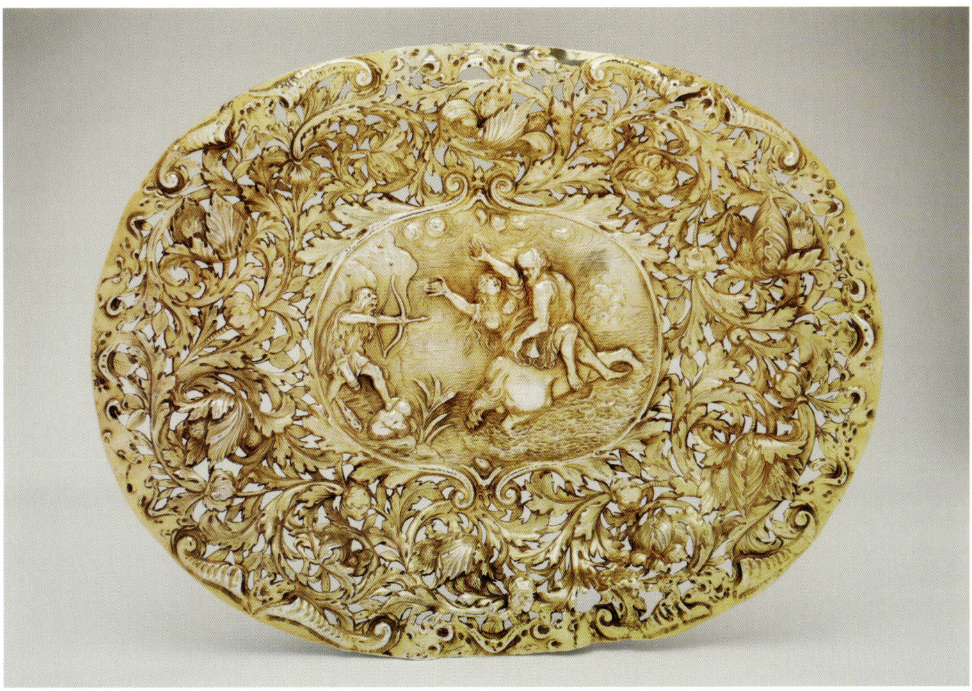

Hanging scroll: ink on paper; signed Bada Shanren; 29 x 17 3/4 in. (73.6 x 45.1 cm). Arthur M. Sackler Museum, Gift of Earl Morse, Harvard Law School Class of 1930, 1964.94.

Zhu Da (Bada Shanren) Chinese, 1626–1706 Moon and Melon Qing dynasty 1689

This stark rendering of a slightly misshapen watermelon against a full moon is a subtle yet poignant work of political opposition. A descendant of the imperial family of the Ming dynasty (1368–1644), Zhu Da (known by his sobriquet Bada Shanren) refused to serve or even acknowledge the existence of the Qing dynasty (1644–1911), established by ethnic Manchus. After the Ming defeat, he fled to a Buddhist monastery, where he wrote poetry and practiced painting and calligraphy. He created this work approximately one year after an uprising against the Manchus failed. Scholars suggest that the melon with its many seeds symbolizes a robust royal lineage that could survive dynastic change and represents the artist's loyalty to the Ming. The moon is believed to refer to the last Ming emperor. The enigmatic poem inscribed on the painting conveys the artist's feelings of hopelessness and fear that a rebellion against the Qing would never succeed. MAM

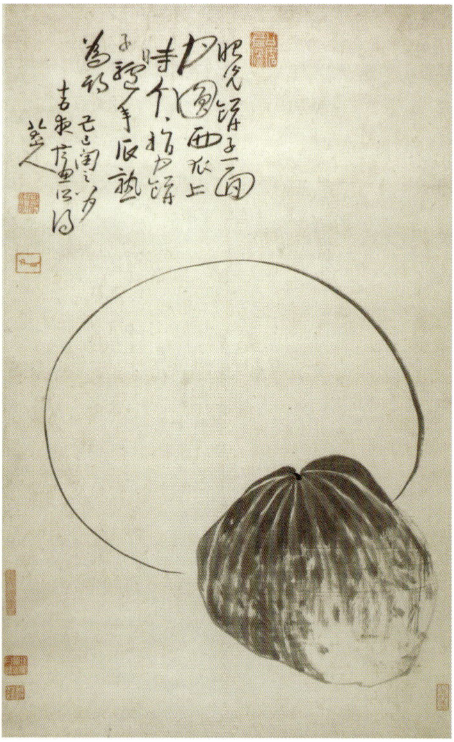

Hand-colored ukiyo-e woodblock print in *hosoban* format: ink, colors, and metal filings on paper; 11 5/16 x 5 3/8 in. (28.7 x 13.6 cm). Arthur M. Sackler Museum, Gift of the Friends of Arthur B. Duel, 1933.4.1588.

Attributed to Torii Kiyomasu II
Japanese, 1694–1763
Actor Arashi Wakano I as Aburaya Osome

From the series *Comparison of Three Young Beauties*

Edo period, c. mid-1720s

The peace established by the Tokugawa Shogunate during the Edo period (1615–1868) had a galvanizing effect on Japanese urban culture. Previously, the literary and visual arts were dominated by members of the courtly, religious, and warrior elites, but during this long and prosperous era a new class of urban merchants fostered vibrant new forms of expression. The wider dissemination of printing contributed to the development of lighthearted fiction and images of the "floating world," or ukiyo-e, in which fashionable courtesans, Kabuki actors, and Sumo wrestlers celebrated a playful, devil-may-care attitude. Here an actor of the all-male Kabuki theater plays a romantic female role. The lilting black outline and bold patterns were printed from a single carved wooden block; colors were brushed in by hand, and glue and sprinkled metal filings were applied to describe the gold brocade of the splendid floral obi (sash) that secures the figure's elegant kimono. ARK

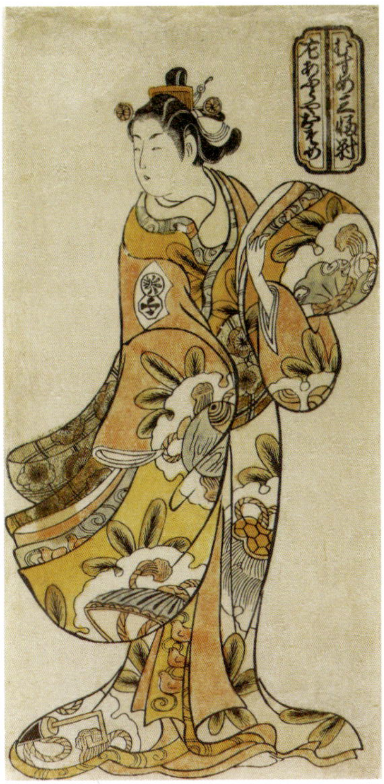

Silk and metallic threads (*filé* and *frisé*), 110 x 21 1/2 in. (279.4 x 54.6 cm). Fogg Museum, Bequest of Nettie G. Naumburg, 1930.385. Detail reproduced below.

Bizarre Silk Panel
French
1707–8

This swath of luxurious fabric would have been used for upholstery or clothing. The design—which features a polychrome assortment of archways, garden vistas, large vases, fruit, and birds—exemplifies the "bizarre" style for its fanciful components. In order to increase the attractiveness of their products to clients, eighteenth-century textile manufacturers mimicked designs that were being imported from east Asia and were immensely popular. The preponderance of gnarled vines in this fabric speaks to the contemporary taste for decorative elements that appeared Chinese or Japanese to European customers. ER

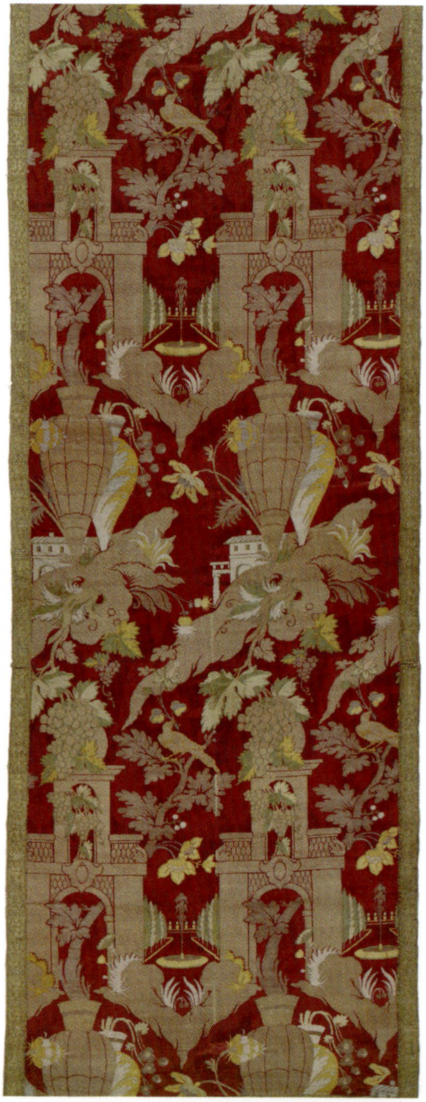

109 Eight-panel folding screen: ink on paper; two artist seals, Su-un and Ka-san-ŭng; each painting: 32 1/16 x 19 1/4 in. (81.4 x 48.8 cm). Arthur M. Sackler Museum, Ernest B. and Helen Pratt Dane Fund for the Acquisition of Oriental Art, Richard Norton Memorial Fund, 2000.232.

Yu Tŏk-chang (Su-un and Ka-san-ŭng) Korean, 1675–1756

Bamboo through the Four Seasons

Chosŏn dynasty, mid-18th century

The first two paintings on this folding screen, at top right, depict new shoots and bamboo stalks emerging in spring. In the next pair, lush plants endure strong summer winds. The relative sparseness, dry ink tones, and overlapping mist in the pair at bottom right convey the feeling of autumn. The last pair depict old, broken bamboo stalks with hints of new shoots in one painting and snow-laden branches in the other, completing the seasonal cycle. / Yu Tŏk-chang, one of Korea's most prominent Chosŏn-dynasty (1392–1910) literati artists, was inspired by earlier Chinese literati painters. Here, however, he exhibits a distinctly Korean style of bamboo painting after that of Yi Chŏng (1554–after 1626), in which two tones of ink distinguish fore- and background subjects, angular mists abruptly interrupt a motif, and selected plants appear as thick stumps with sharp, broken edges—characteristics that differ markedly from established Chinese models. ARK

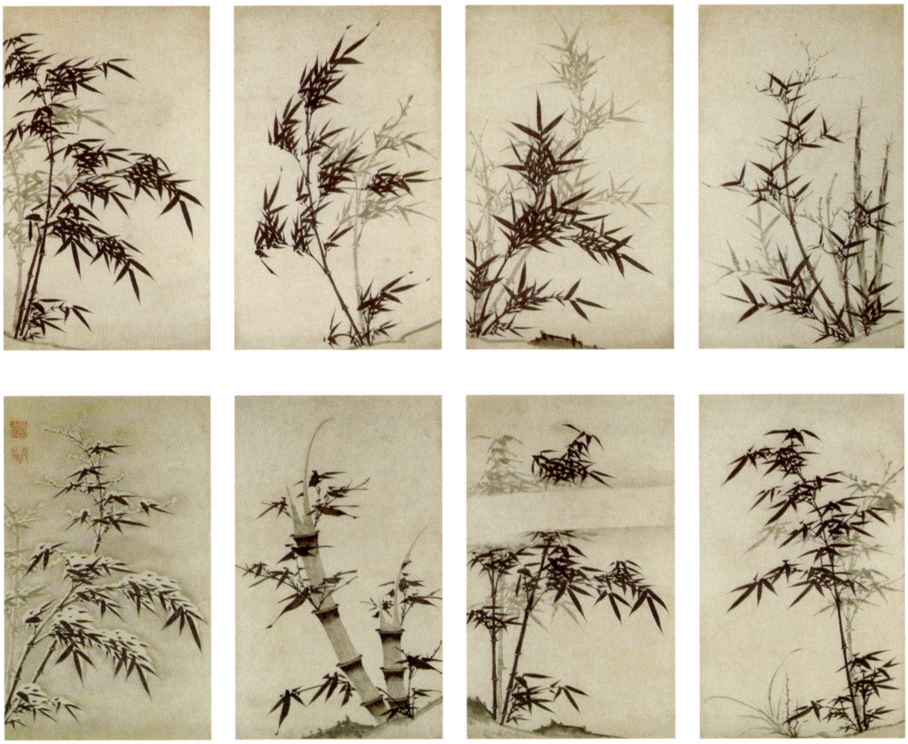

Black, red, and white chalk on tan antique laid paper; 8 3/4 x 8 9/16 in. (22.2 x 21.7 cm). Fogg Museum, Bequest of Meta and Paul J. Sachs, 1965.336.

Jean-Antoine Watteau
French, 1684–1721
Six Heads
c. 1714

Figure studies of various kinds dominate the drawn oeuvre of Jean-Antoine Watteau, who often remarked that he preferred drawing to painting. He later returned to these studies for many of the figures found in his paintings. The adroit delicacy of the artist's touch is evident in works like *Six Heads*, in which the elegance and sophisticated placement of the elements endow the drawing with a visual power equivalent to a full-blown composition. Watteau's achievement is even more remarkable in that this is one of his earliest sheets of head studies and one of his first attempts to draw with the mixture of red, black, and white chalks that is referred to as the *trois-crayons* manner. He eventually raised this technique to a such a level of mastery that it became synonymous with his name. ALC

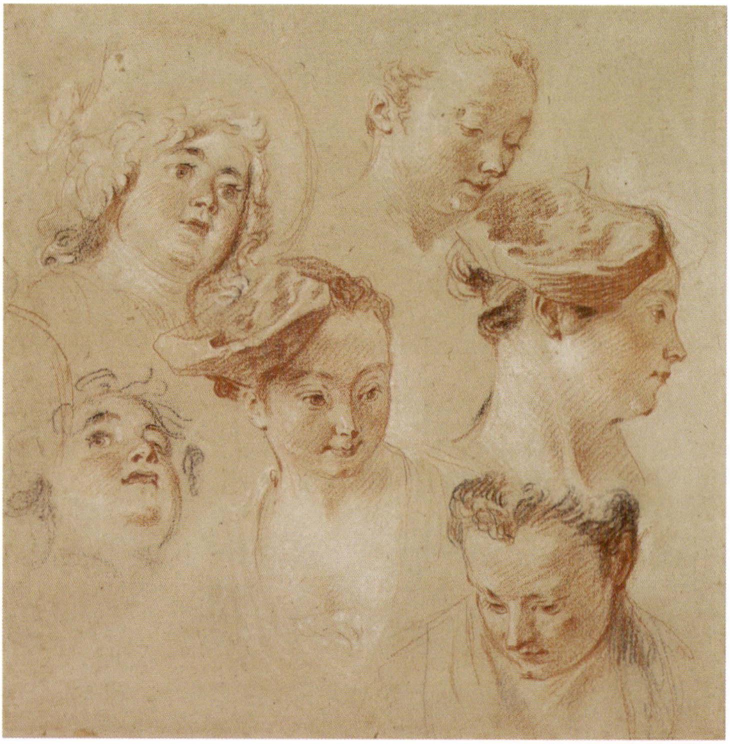

111 Black and red-brown ink over charcoal underdrawing on beige laid paper, 20 3/16 x 22 5/16 in. (51.3 x 56.7 cm). Arthur M. Sackler Museum, Gift of Stuart Cary Welch, Jr., 1999.286.

Attributed to Shaykh Taju
Five Views of an Elephant Combat
Indian, Rajasthan, Kota
c. 1730

Staged fights between captive elephants were a favorite sport of Indian nobility. This series of robust and fluid sketches tracks the motions of several pairs of dueling elephants. These superb studies accentuate the massive proportions of their animal subjects and transform their violent movements into graceful forms. Although imperial Mughal painters executed splendid naturalistic studies of elephants, the dynamism and draftsmanship of elephants produced by Kota artists were unsurpassed by other Rajput masters. KM

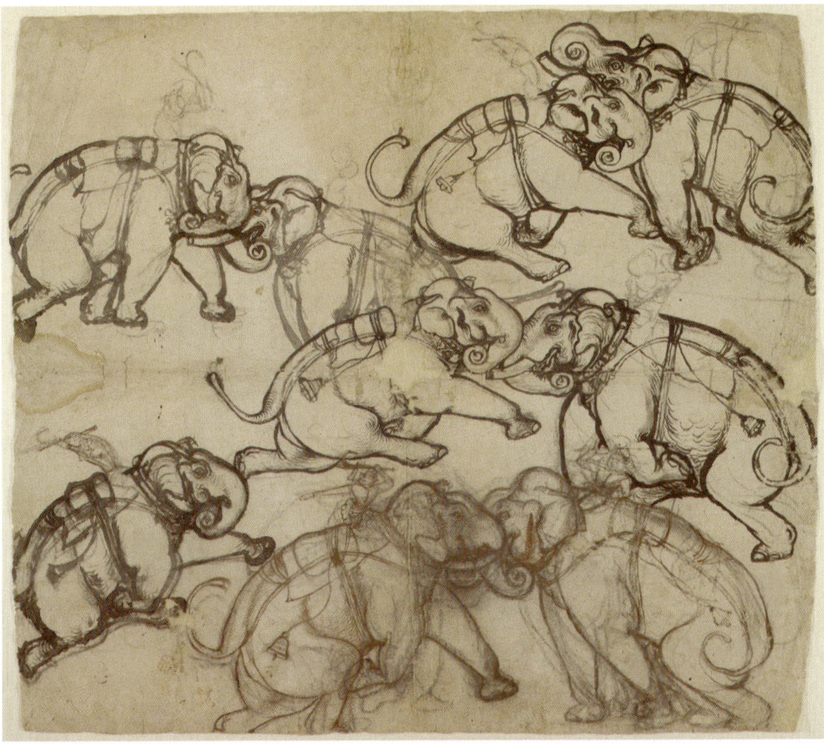

12 / Eleven red morocco leather–bound volumes, 22 [illegible] x [illegible] in. ([illegible] x [illegible] cm), Fogg Museum, various credit lines.

Jean and Pierre-Jean Mariette
French, 1660–1742 and 1694–1774
Spencer Albums
c. 1720

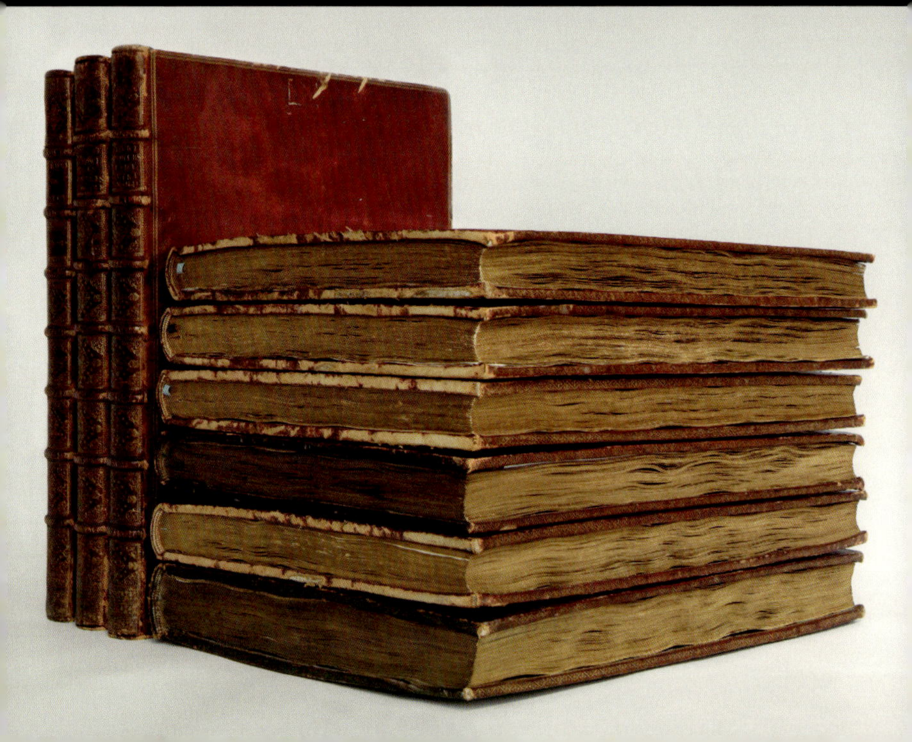

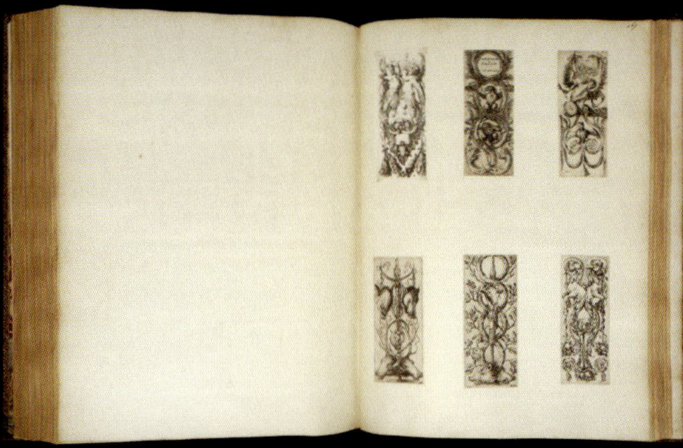

Stefano della Bella (Italian, 1610–1664). *Six Etchings from the Series "Ornamenti e grotteschi,"* c. 1648, from Spencer Album 7. Fogg Museum, Gray Collection of Engravings Fund, by exchange, S7.167.1–.6.

Many works on paper have survived in albums from the early modern period, when they were first collected as part of encyclopedic cabinets of curiosities. The Parisian publisher family Mariette compiled over 3,500 Italian, French, and Netherlandish prints for the Earls Spencer around 1720. Harvard's eleven Spencer Albums include two Jacques Callot tomes, one on Stefano della Bella, and eight more containing works by Antonio Tempesta, the Caracci, and other Italian artists, and an expansive group of Netherlandish landscapes. Carefully laid into fine French paper and bound in red morocco leather, the prints remain in pristine condition today. / The Mariettes indexed their prints by school, pursuing several artists exhaustively. The massive della Bella album contains impressions of the bulk of his 1,052 etchings. His oeuvre encompassed everything from large history scenes to tiny didactic playing cards for the young Louis XIII. These grotesque ornament prints from a series of twelve appealed to both the collector's whims and his imagination. SKS

Etching, 16 1/4 x 24 13/16 in. (41.2 x 63 cm). Fogg Museum, Loan from the Fine Arts Library, Harvard University, 43.1987.55.

Giovanni Battista Piranesi
Italian, 1720–1778
The Arch of Titus
1748

Piranesi completed his virtuosic, massive etching series of ancient Roman architectural monuments by the late 1770s, although he had been selling them in small sets for decades. During his European Grand Tour in 1767, Thomas Palmer (Harvard class of 1761) purchased ninety-nine Piranesi prints, very likely from the artist himself, and in the 1770s, he gave them to Harvard. The Arch of Titus in this print was constructed around AD 81 to commemorate the sack of Jerusalem in AD 70. Perhaps Palmer wanted to share his new wealth of knowledge from his touristic conquest of Europe with his alma mater. SKS

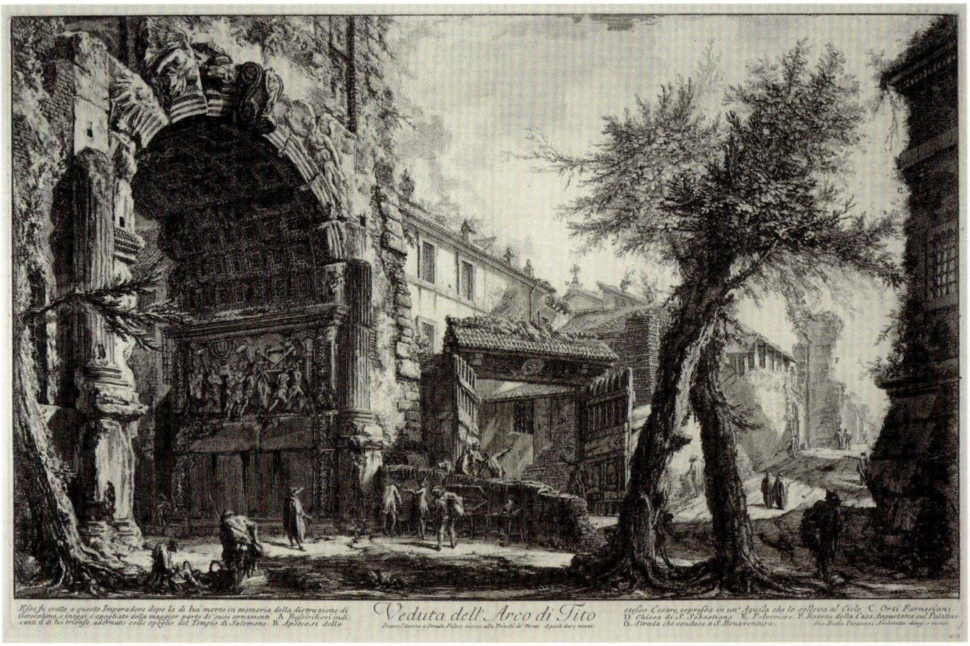

 Oil on canvas, 43 1/8 x 58 7/16 in. (109.6 x 148.5 cm). Fogg Museum, Bequest of Grenville L. Winthrop, 1943.106.

Canaletto
Italian, 1697–1768
Piazza San Marco, Venice
c. 1730–35

Canaletto's paintings were popular with wealthy travelers who voyaged throughout Western Europe on the Grand Tour. The topographic accuracy and anecdotal details of his scenes convinced them that they were seeing exact images of places they had visited. This painting depicts one of the most famous sites in Venice, which was a requisite stop on the tour. It is one of a pair of paintings purchased by the Duke of Leeds during his trip to Italy in 1734. The pendant painting (Detroit Institute of Art) shows the Piazza San Marco from the opposite direction. ER

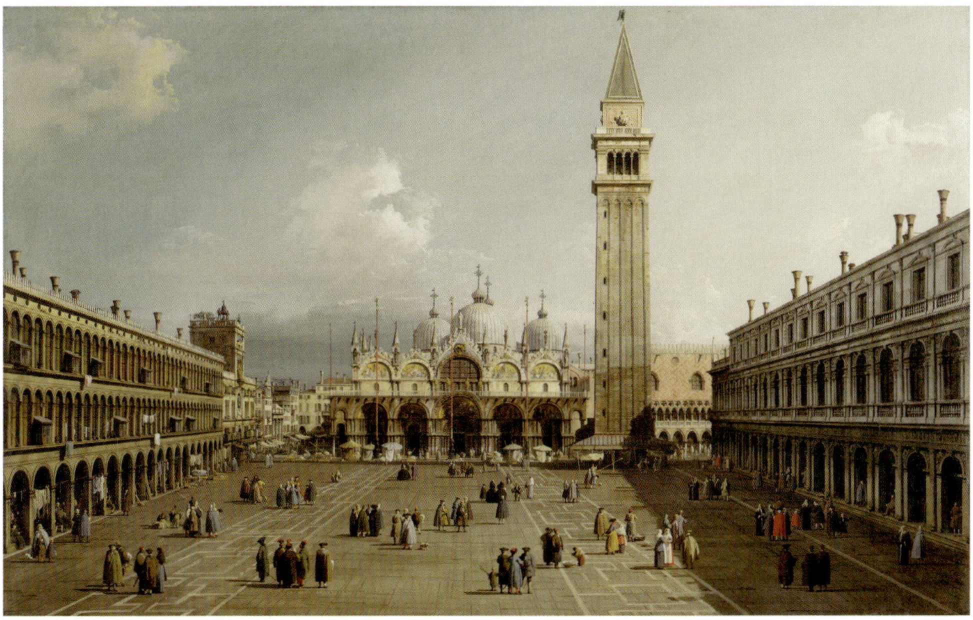

Brown ink and brown wash over black chalk on white antique laid paper, 17 x 11 5/8 in. (43.2 x 29.5 cm). Fogg Museum, Bequest of Meta and Paul J. Sachs, 1965.417.

Giovanni Battista Tiepolo Italian, 1696–1770 Holy Family Enthroned with Saints Sebastian, Catherine of Alexandria, and Francis, c. 1735

Heir to the great Venetian tradition of history painting, Giovanni Battista Tiepolo also ranks among the most brilliant draftsmen of the eighteenth century. Fully resolved ink-and-wash compositions comprise a fundamental category of his drawings. Autonomous works of art rather than working studies, they represent countless variations on canonical religious subjects and attest to the virtuosity of his technique and his inexhaustible inventiveness and expressivity. As early as 1732, a Venetian author wrote that such drawings confirmed Tiepolo's "extraordinarily fertile imagination," and were held "in high esteem" and collected "in the most distant countries." / In this pristine work from about 1735 and other drawings of the Virgin and Child with saints, Tiepolo devised original compositional solutions for one of the most venerable themes in Italian art. WR

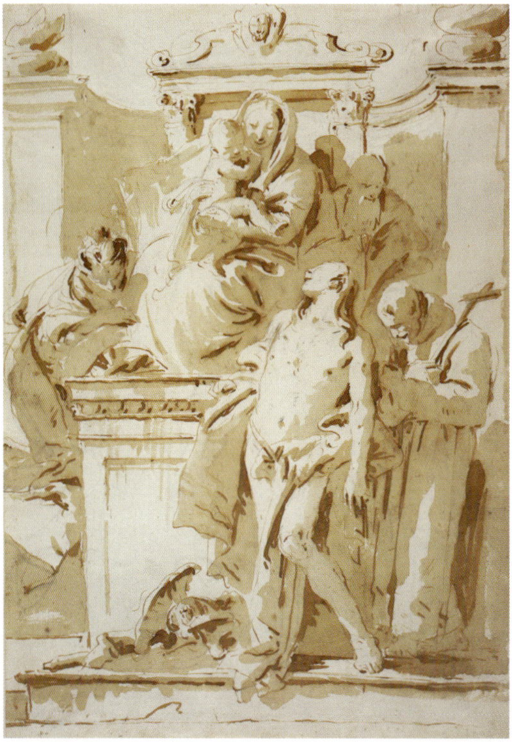

117 Brown wash over graphite and touches of brown ink on cream antique laid paper, 9 7/16 x 14 7/16 in. (23.9 x 36.7 cm). Fogg Museum, Gift of Charles E. Dunlap, 1954.106.

Jean-Honoré Fragonard French, 1732–1806 The Servant Girls' Dormitory c. 1770

Jean-Honoré Fragonard's enormous skill as a draftsman makes this delightful genre scene appear as effortless as it is amusing. His ubiquitous, busy graphite underdrawing prepared the composition for his carefully orchestrated blend of chiaroscuro and transparence with the brown wash and his incisive accents with brown ink. While this playful depiction of young ladies relaxing and preparing for bed certainly enchanted most of Fragonard's wealthy male clients, it is also a poignant reminder of the early age at which children in the eighteenth century began working. The tickling and spanking at the far right, the moment of discovery and comparison in the center, and the conversation that can't wait until morning on the left are all typical moments in the lives of young adolescents. ALC

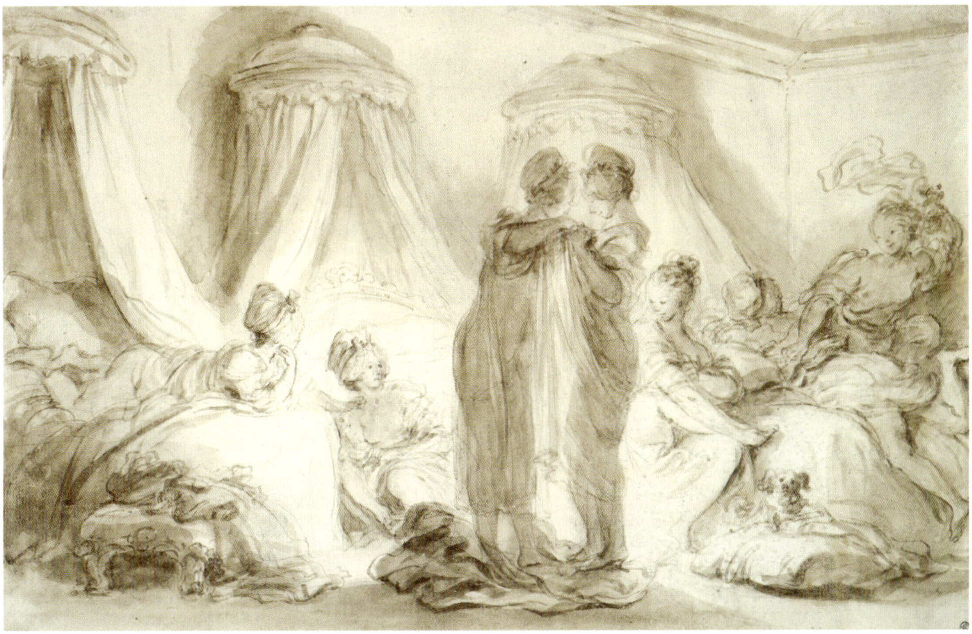

Hard-paste porcelain with polychrome enamel decoration and gilding, h. 4 1/8 in. (10.5 cm). Busch-Reisinger Museum, Gift of Mr. and Mrs. Edward M. Pflueger, BR61.18.

Meissen Porcelain Manufactory
German
Putto as Hercules
c. 1780

Wielding a cudgel, with the pelt of the Nemean lion flowing down his back, this putto wears the attributes of Hercules, a symbol of princely virtue. A shield with the Saxon-Lithuanian-Polish coat of arms nearly topples the cherubic figure. Together they link the putto directly to Augustus the Strong, the first patron of the Meissen factory. Arcanists at Meissen, near Dresden, were the first Europeans to discover the secret of hard-paste porcelain, which until the eighteenth century had been available only as a costly import from East Asia. Even a tiny figure such as this would have been a luxurious symbol of status. HH

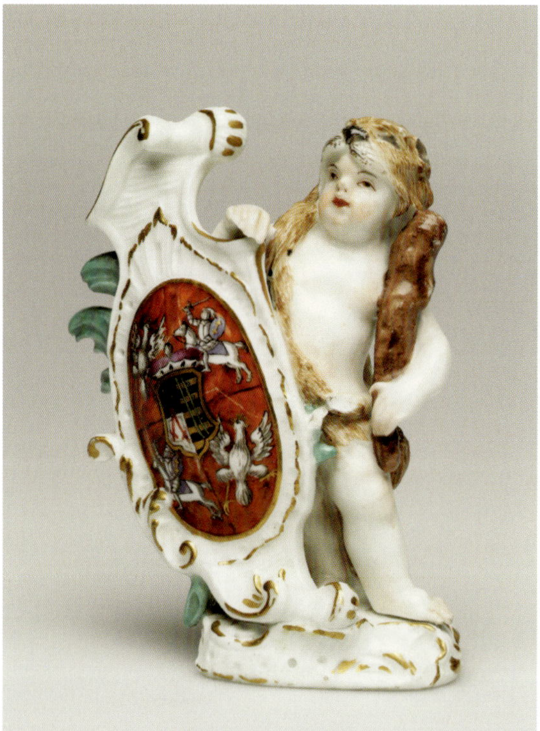

119 Blue-and-white ware: porcelain with decoration painted in underglaze cobalt blue; h. 17 7/16 in. (44.3 cm), diam. 13 3/4 in. (35 cm). Arthur M. Sackler Museum, Gift of Marie-Hélène Weill and Claudia Weill Teller, 2003.291.

Broad-Shouldered Jar with Dragon Decor
Korean, Chosŏn dynasty mid-18th century

By the mid-fifteenth century, after assimilating ceramic techniques learned from the Chinese, Korean potters were able to produce blue-and-white wares using local sources of clay and limited supplies of cobalt imported from China at great expense. Such rare and costly wares were reserved for the exclusive use of the Chosŏn-dynasty court (1392–1910). Invasions by Japan and war with China devastated the Korean ceramics industry in the late sixteenth and seventeenth centuries. It was not until the mid-eighteenth century, with the reestablishment of official kilns patronized by the court, that Korea's manufacture of porcelain wares fully revived. The fine potting and extraordinarily skillful painted designs on this massive jar strongly suggest that this piece was made at an official kiln. The dragons chasing after flaming jewels, a decorative motif borrowed from the repertory of both Daoist and Buddhist art, are auspicious symbols of the pursuit of wisdom. MAM

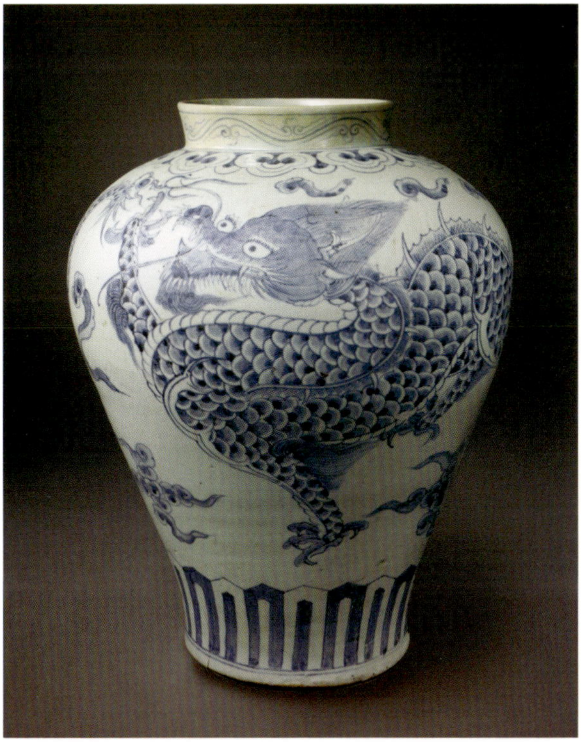

Oil on canvas, 31 15/16 x 25 9/16 in. (81.2 x 64.9 cm). Fogg Museum, Bequest of Charles E. Dunlap, 1966.47.

François Boucher French, 1703–1770 Jeanne-Antoinette Poisson, Marquise de Pompadour, 1750 later additions by c. 1760 and 1781

Boucher painted numerous portraits of the Marquise de Pompadour (1721–1764), the bourgeois consort of King Louis XV from 1745 to 1750. Although she was no longer the king's mistress at the time of this painting, she remained one of his closest associates. The cameo bracelet on her arm, which bears his profile, is oriented toward the viewer as if to emphasize her privileged relationship with the monarch. Boucher disguised her age and bathed her in her signature color, known as "Pompadour pink." He reshaped the canvas at several points during the process of completing the work; the painting is constructed from seven separate pieces of canvas, which were carefully sewn together. ER

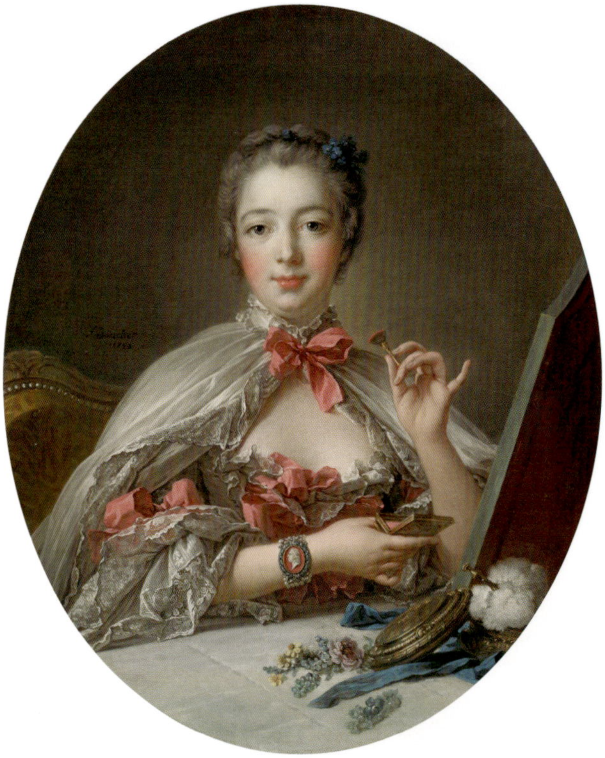

Oil on canvas, 36 x 29 1/2 in. (91 x 75 cm). Fogg Museum, Gift of Catherine Coolidge Lastavica, M.D., 2004.220.

Robert Feke
American, c. 1707–1752
Susannah Speakman Inman
1748

The native-born Robert Feke was the most significant portrait painter in the American colonies before John Singleton Copley. In this portrait, Feke depicts Inman (1727–1761) at age twenty-one, two years after her marriage to prosperous merchant Ralph Inman. The Inmans lived in a grand home on the current site of the Cambridge (Massachusetts) city hall. Feke's skill is apparent in his rendering of the drapery and texture of the sitter's satin dress and wrap, while her décolletage and charm suggest something of the liveliness and prosperity of Boston in that era. This painting remained in the family for over 250 years before it was generously donated to the museum in 2004. FW

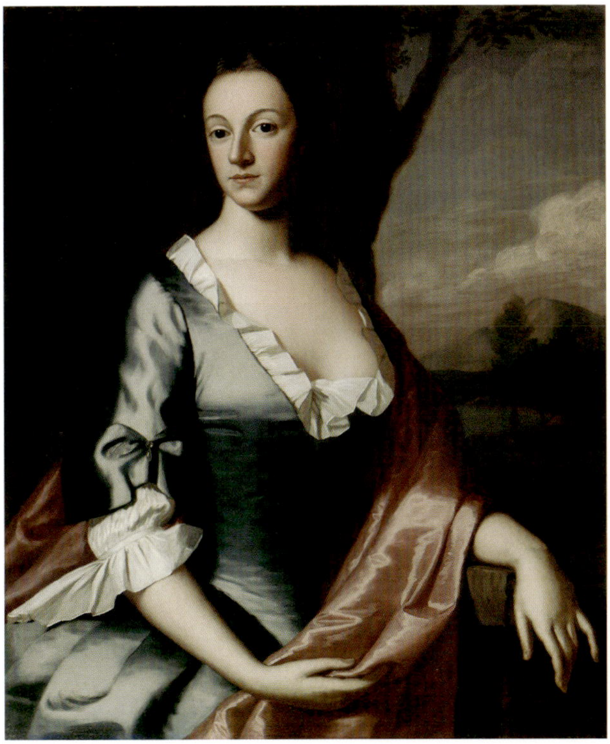

Carved and painted wood, 29 1/8 x 26 3/8 in. (74 x 67 cm). Arthur M. Sackler Museum, Fund for the Acquisition of Islamic Art, 1981.10.

Ceiling Panel
Islamic, Morocco
Saʿdid or ʿAlawid dynasty
16th–17th century

Decorative wooden ceilings are found in palaces, mosques, and homes throughout Morocco. Panels of cedar are carved and painted with complex, radiating geometric designs; the individual pieces are then fitted together to cover the wooden beam construction used extensively in Moroccan architecture. This particular design is centered on a twelve-pointed star with interlacing hexagons and five-pointed stars. The panel was likely constructed at the end of the reign of the Saʿdid dynasty (1509–1659) or early in the reign of the ʿAlawid dynasty, the current Moroccan royal family. AA

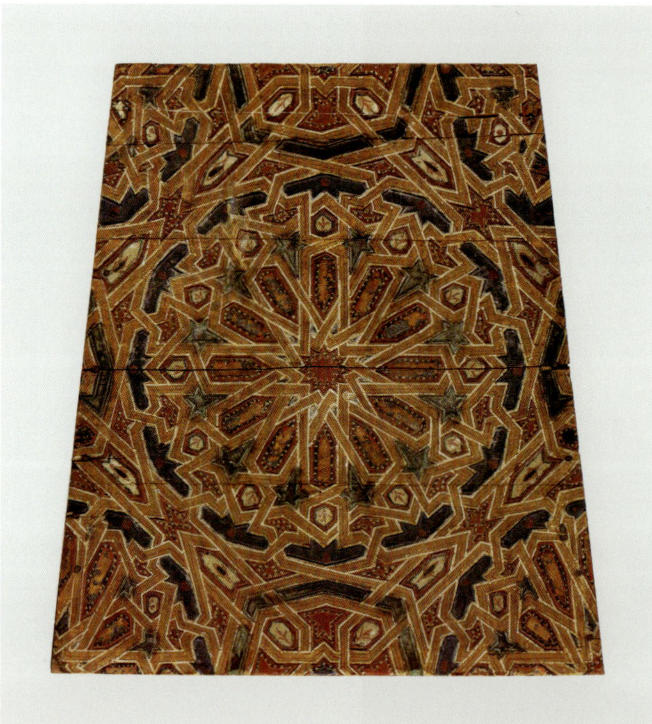

123 Mahogany and white pine with brass mounts, 101 3/4 x 48 x 24 5/8 in. (258.5 x 121.9 x 62.6 cm). Fogg Museum, Loan from Harvard University, 205.1972.

Attributed to Benjamin Frothingham Jr. American, 1734–1809 Bombé Secretary Desk c. 1760

This secretary shows American colonial furniture at its most sophisticated. Made by Charlestown, Massachusetts, cabinetmaker Benjamin Frothingham Jr. in the years before the American Revolution, it represents the height of the Massachusetts Chippendale style, with its three corkscrew finials, tight paw feet, curved molding, and Corinthian pilasters. The rare bombé (curving) base form was found only in works from Boston. Frothingham was known as a master of blocking, or creating tripartite vertical sections of alternating concave and convex decorative sections, which can be seen in the desk's interior. FW

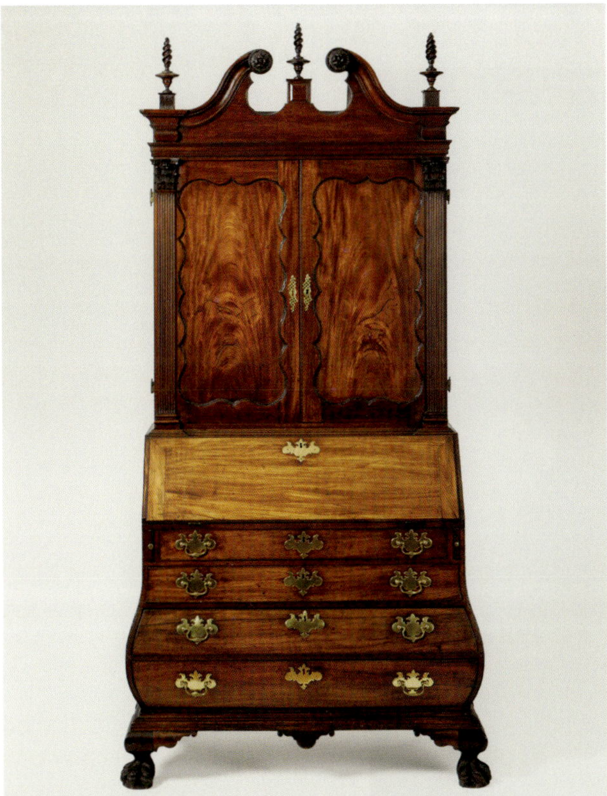

Oil on canvas, 50 1/8 x 39 13/16 in. (127.3 x 101.1 cm). Fogg Museum, Bequest of Ward Nicholas Boylston to Harvard College, 1828, H90.

John Singleton Copley
American, 1738–1815
Nicholas Boylston
1767

Portraits by Boston-born John Singleton Copley depicted the character and prosperity of New England's elite with a realism that was unrivaled in the colonial period. Nicholas Boylston (1716–1771), a prominent Boston merchant and one of Harvard's most important benefactors, commissioned this painting. His informal yet elegant dressing gown and turban, the ledger on the table, and the ship in the background speak of his wealth and profession. Harvard later commissioned a posthumous full-length portrait of Boylston, described by John Quincy Adams as "in a style of ease and amenity, which renders it singularly prepossessing. The expression of the countenance is admirable. [The physiognomist Johann Kaspar] Lavater would have said, I see there the genuine indications of intelligence, rectitude, and benevolence. That man must have been the delight of his friends." FW

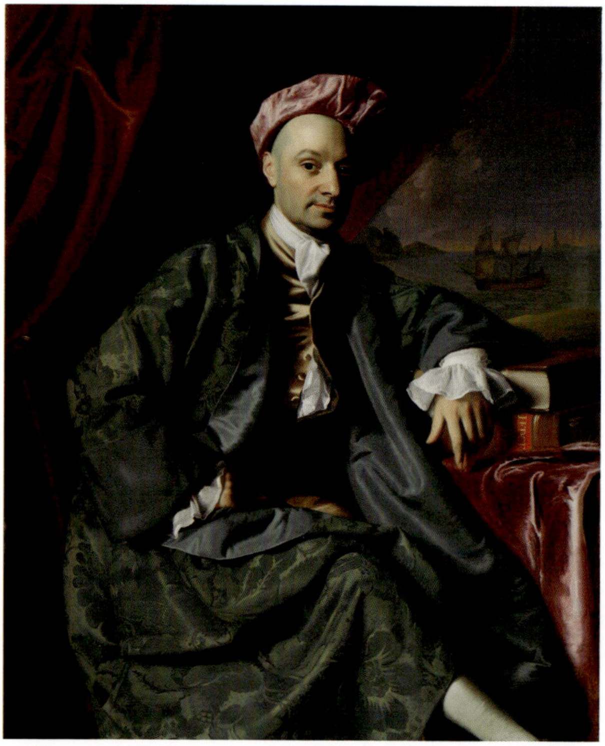

Oil on canvas, 95 x 57 3/8 in. (241.3 x 145.7 cm). Fogg Museum, Bequest of Grenville L. Winthrop, 1943.144.

Charles Willson Peale
American, 1741–1827
George Washington
1784

Charles Willson Peale, the first in a great family of American painters, commanded American forces as first lieutenant during the Revolutionary War. He knew General Washington (1732–1799) and painted his portrait from life on several occasions. This painting, once owned by Thomas Jefferson, was commissioned by Virginia governor Benjamin Harrison. A variation of Peale's "Annapolis" portrait (at the Maryland State House), this version also presents Washington standing before a tent with Yorktown Heights in the distance but without General Lafayette and Colonel Tench Tilghman, Washington's aide-de-camp at Yorktown. A document on the desk behind Washington reads "York Virginia October 17, 1781 / Articles of Capitulation." Officers in the background display French and American colors to mark their victory over the British. FW

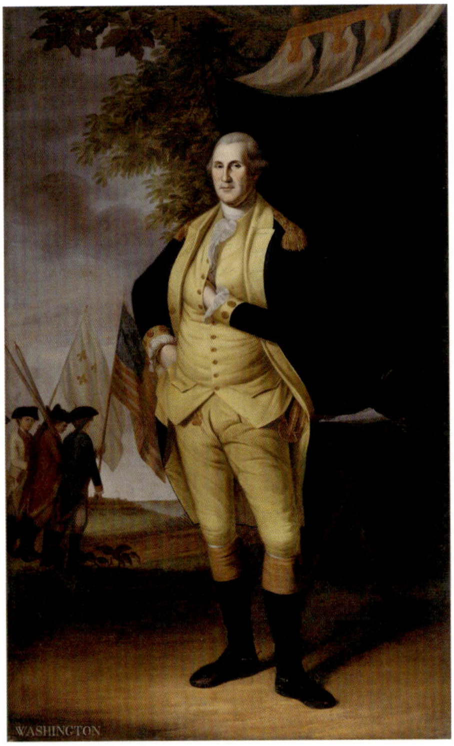

Etching and aquatint, 8 3/8 x 5 7/8 in. (21.3 x 15 cm). Fogg Museum, Gift of Philip Hofer, M4310.

Francisco de Goya
Spanish, 1746–1828
Love and Death
From the series *Los Caprichos*
1799

Goya was the Spanish court painter at Madrid under Carlos III and Carlos IV. In an attempt to avoid royal disapproval, he sold his set of eighty "caprices," *Los Caprichos*, which were slyly critical of the church and aristocracy, in secret. Goya tapped into the expressive capabilities of etching and aquatint with these darkly whimsical satires on contemporary social mores. / In this example, Goya produces a striking contrast between the stark white of the mortally wounded man and the shadowy garb of his lamenting companion. The abandoned sword implies that this lover has lost a duel. The couple slump against architectural ruins, a foreboding backdrop that reinforces the pathos of this desperate scene. SKS

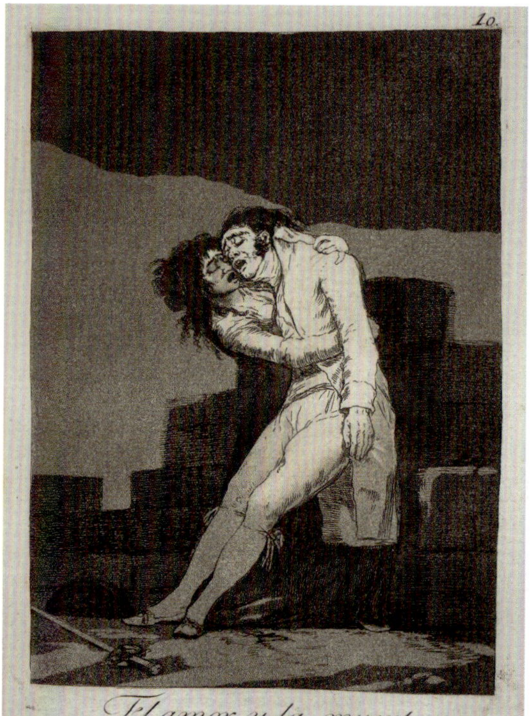

127 Opaque watercolor and gold on paper, 9 9/16 x 6 1/4 in. (24.3 x 15.8 cm). Arthur M. Sackler Museum, Gift of John Kenneth Galbraith, 1972.352.

A Nayika Yearning for Her Lover

Indian, Rajasthan, Kota

c. 1770

Collapsed upon crimson cushions, a lonely *nayika* (romantic heroine) gazes up at her handmaiden and confidante. The nayika's separation from her lover is referenced in a tiny vignette above: a crane in full flight departing from its mate against a starkly white sky. This spare painting is striking in its juxtaposition of luxury, eroticism, and visual austerity. A pierced railing in the foreground is the only signifier of a palatial setting. The nayika's courtly status is indicated by her jewelry and brocade garments as well as by the elegant wares assembled before her: gold and silver vases, trays, a spittoon, and an ornate hookah (water pipe). Fine brushstrokes are used to create the gently modeled faces and individual strands of wavy hair of the two heavy-eyed subjects. This emotive scene was painted in Kota and probably belonged to a nayika series featuring courtly lovers. KM

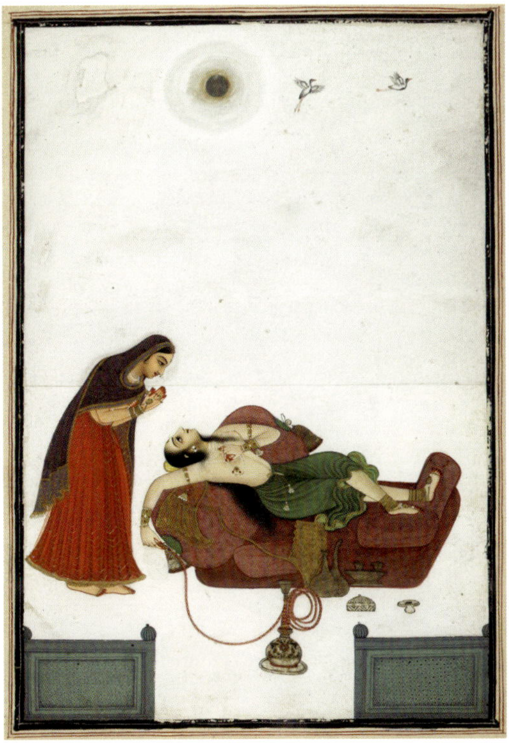

 Silver; 10 x 7 in. (25.4 x 17.8 cm), 47 oz., 15 pwt. Fogg Museum, Loan from Harvard University; Gift to Harvard College from the Honorable William Stoughton, 1701, 877.1927.A–B.

John Coney
American, 1655–1722
The Stoughton Cup
1701

John Coney was the most prolific and accomplished silversmith in America during the early eighteenth century, and the *Stoughton Cup* is an outstanding piece of early American silver. Massachusetts judge and acting governor William Stoughton (1631–1701; Harvard AB, 1650) funded construction of Harvard's original Stoughton Hall (1698–1781) and commissioned this cup for Harvard's commencement in 1701, shortly before his death. / According to tradition, the grace or loving cup was passed around the table after grace had been said as a symbol of hospitality. With its elegant curves and gadrooning (reverse fluting), the cup reflects wealthy New Englanders' taste for the baroque motifs of the English William and Mary style. Cast silver caryatids grace the handles, and on one side Coney engraved Stoughton's coat of arms surrounded by acanthus leaves. The cup is part of the collection of ceremonial silver that is displayed when a new Harvard president is installed. FW

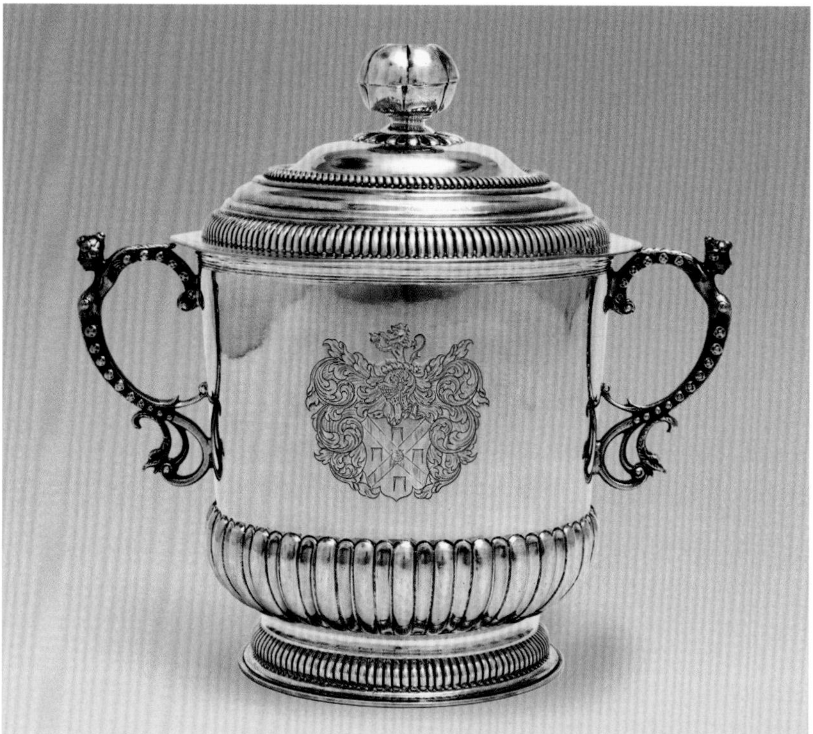

129 Blue-black and white jasperware; h. $10\,3/16$ in. (25.8 cm), diam. $7\,5/16$ in. (18.5 cm). Fogg Museum, Bequest of Grenville L. Winthrop, 1943.1181.

Josiah Wedgwood
British, 1730–1795
Portland Vase, First Edition
1790–95

Reproducing the *Portland Vase*, a Greco-Roman amphora from the first century AD, was the greatest challenge of Wedgwood's career. The vase, lent to Wedgwood by the Duke of Portland in 1786, was the most significant piece of cameo glass surviving from antiquity. Henry Webber and William Hackwood worked for four years to design a model for the copies that met Wedgwood's exacting standards. The first Wedgwood copy was exhibited in 1790, at a ticketed show. This example was from the first edition, which included approximately thirty copies. The number *9* and the name *J. Trevor*, which are written in pencil inside the lip of the vase, indicate its number in the first series and its original subscriber. ER

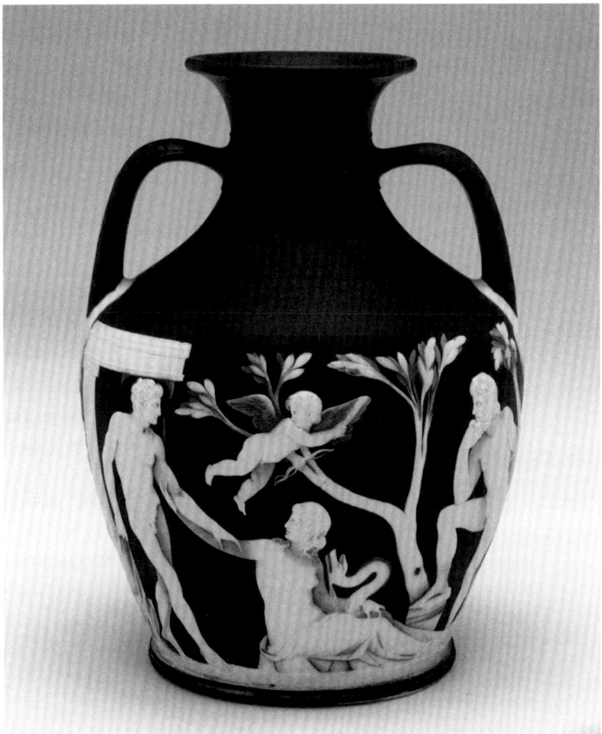

Graphite and black crayon on off-white antique laid paper; each page: 8 1/4 x 6 7/16 in. (21 x 16.4 cm). Fogg Museum, Bequest of Grenville L. Winthrop, 1943.1815.13.2 (verso), .3 (recto).

Jacques-Louis David French, 1748–1825 Two Studies of Napoleon, Nude, Crowning Himself From *Sketchbook No. 20* 1805–7

Jacques-Louis David was present at the coronation of Napoleon in 1804, and at the emperor's bidding, he produced the renowned painting of the elaborate ceremony, *The Coronation of the Emperor Napoleon I and the Crowning of the Empress Josephine at Notre-Dame on December 2, 1804* (1806–7, now in the Louvre). The Fogg owns two rare and important sketchbooks of studies for the enormous painting, which includes a cast of nearly two hundred participants. The figures are generally in the poses they assumed in the final work, indicating that the composition had already been established. Most of the drawings are squared for transfer to the canvas, and some of the figures are nude since the artist worked from models to fix the poses. David originally intended to represent Napoleon crowning himself, as seen in the sketches on these pages, but ultimately showed him placing the imperial diadem on the head of his kneeling wife, Josephine. MS

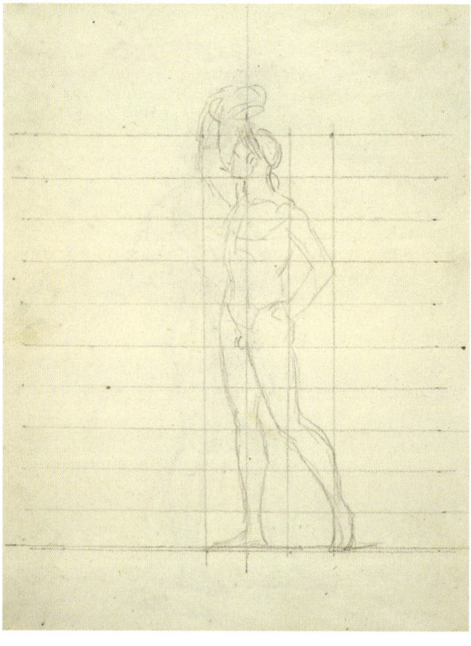

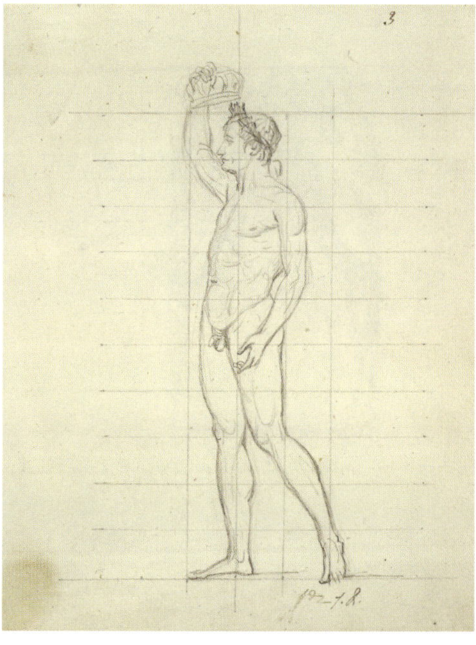

131 Oil on canvas, 38 1/2 x 29 1/8 in. (97.8 x 74 cm). Fogg Museum, Bequest of Grenville L. Winthrop, 1943.229.

Jacques-Louis David
French, 1748–1825
Emmanuel Joseph Sieyès
1817

David painted this arresting portrait of his friend when they were both in exile in Brussels, following their banishment from France in 1815. Sieyès (1748–1836) had written the influential pamphlet *What Is the Third Estate?* in 1789, and David had been a key figure in the formation of the French nation-state following the storming of the Bastille. In a manner typical of many of his portraits, David painted a Latin inscription at the top of the canvas identifying the sitter and his age. Though he has indicated that Sieyès is shown at the age of sixty-eight (in his sixty-ninth year), David depicted the politician as a much younger man with idealized features and a stylish wig. ER

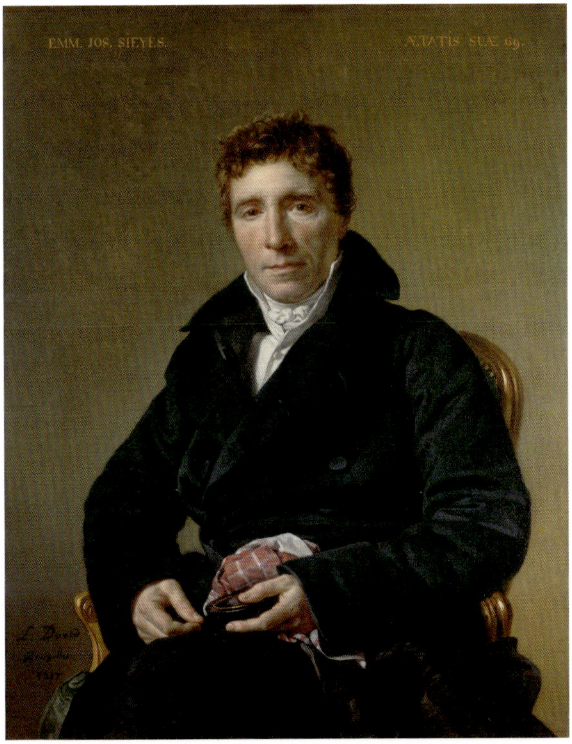

Oil on canvas, 57 x 28 in. (144.8 x 71.1 cm). Fogg Museum, Gift of the Estate of Harriet Anna Niel, 1945.27.

Ammi Phillips
American, 1788–1865
Harriet Leavens
c. 1815

Ammi Phillips was a highly prolific, untrained portrait painter who advertised his paintings as in "a correct style, perfect shadows" and with subjects wearing "elegant dresses in the prevailing fashion of the day." Harriet Leavens (1802–1830) is shown wearing a fashionable gown in the Empire style, adopted from France, and holding a parasol, another emblem of feminine status. / Phillips painted five portraits of members of the Leavens family; each was valued at $10 in the father's will. Characteristic of Phillips's "border" period (when he worked in the border area where New York, Connecticut, and Massachusetts abut), the painting has a plain background, pastel palette, and light shading. It has been admired over the years as a masterpiece of American "folk" painting, and was included in an informal exhibition of Phillips's portraits in the 1920s that coincided with a mounting nationalistic interest in American folk art and culture. FW

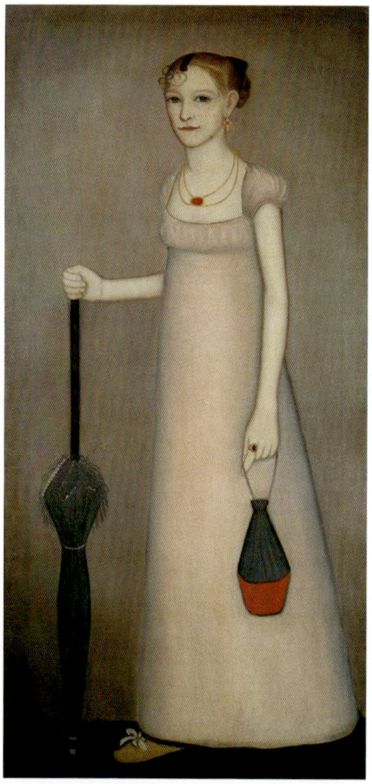

Graphite on white wove paper, 16 15/16 x 12 11/16 in. (43 x 32.3 cm) and 17 7/16 x 12 13/16 in. (44.3 x 32.6 cm). Fogg Museum, Bequest of Grenville L. Winthrop, 1943.840, .841.

Jean-Auguste-Dominique Ingres
French, 1780–1867

Portrait of Augustin Jordan and His Daughter, Adrienne, 1817

Portrait of Mme Augustin Jordan and Her Son, Gabriel, 1817

These pendant drawings are among the most imposing and affecting of the twenty-five portraits by Ingres in the Fogg collection. Augustin Jordan (1773–1849), secretary at the French embassy in Rome; his wife, Augustine-Louise-Euphrasie de Mauduit Du Plessis (1789–1847); and their children, Adrienne (six) and Gabriel (three), steadfastly engage the viewer. Augustin is represented in a voluminous greatcoat, his hat tossed hastily on a chair: he has just arrived home and is greeted by his daughter. His wife, draped in a cashmere shawl and leaning against a mantelpiece, occupies the domestic sphere. While each portrait can stand alone, the two drawings share a tender rapport. The intricate rhythm of the hands, father to daughter and mother to son, carries through between them and establishes an affectionate familial relationship. MS

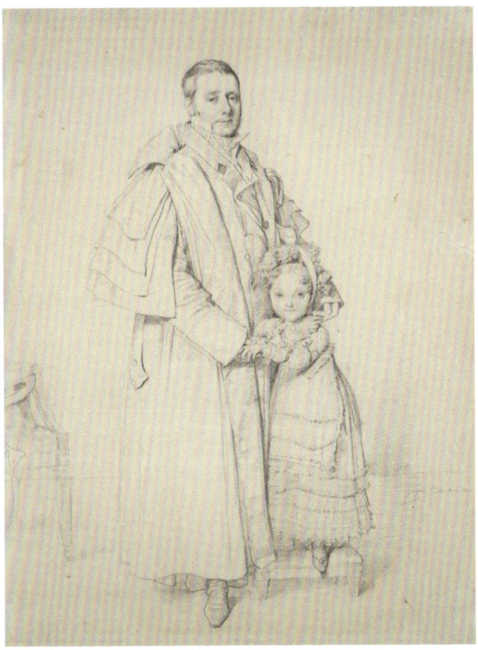

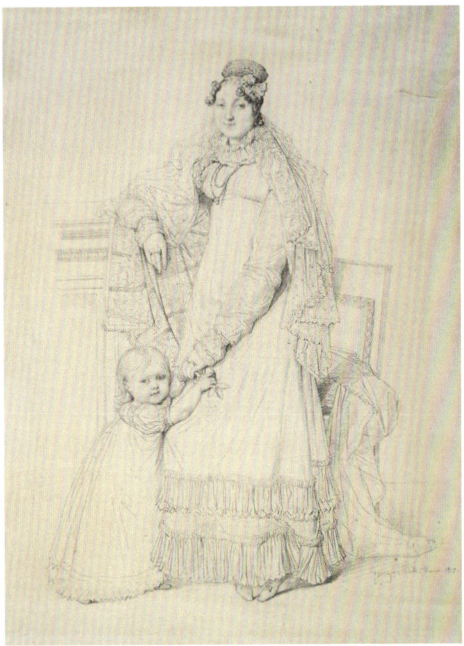

Black chalk, black crayon, white chalk, brown and blue-green watercolor, and white gouache on brown modern laid paper; 15 15/16 x 20 1/16 in. (40.5 x 51 cm). Fogg Museum, Bequest of Grenville L. Winthrop, 1943.824.

Théodore Géricault French, 1791–1824 The Mutiny on the Raft of the *Medusa* 1818

In 1816, the French frigate *Medusa* was shipwrecked off the African coast. Indignation with the government grew when it became known that the disaster was the result of the appointment of an incompetent captain, a royalist favorite, who saved himself and left most of his passengers to die gruesome deaths. / Informed by newspaper articles and the accounts of survivors, Théodore Géricault voiced the horror of the French people, making a critical political statement about a contemporary event: a new kind of history painting. In this drawing and several others, Géricault explored a mutinous episode related by the survivors; he ultimately chose to represent another part of the story in his final painting, *The Raft of the "Medusa"* (1819, Louvre). The mass of bodies in an array of poses shows his Renaissance and baroque roots, but the composition is not traditional: The eye is not led to the center of action but instead is forced to follow the strangely intertwined limbs. WL

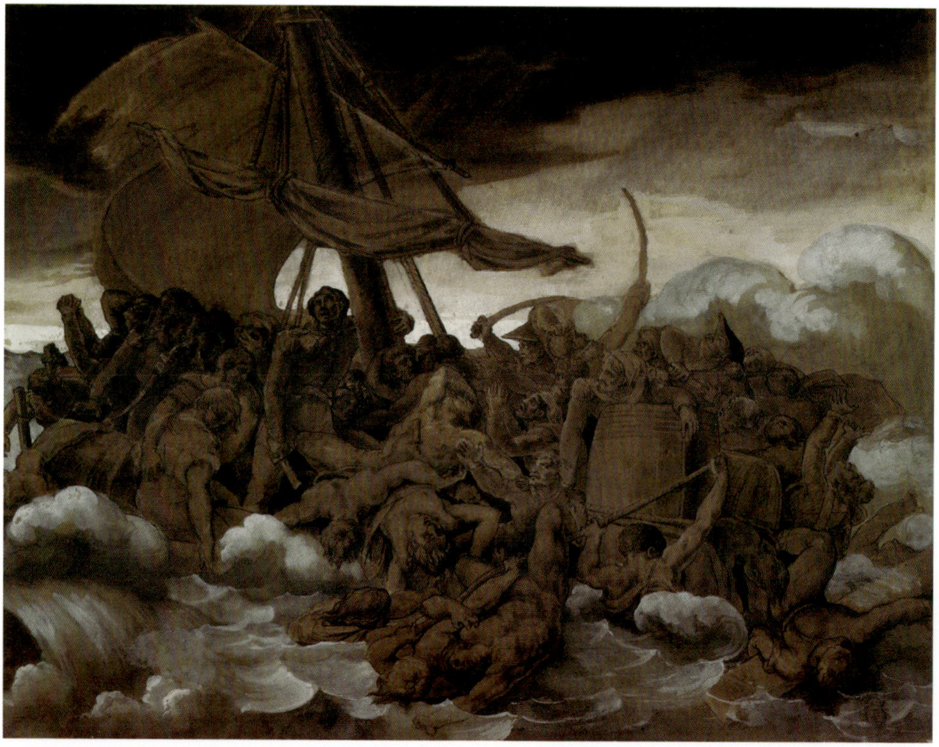

135 Double-page spread from the first of a pair of thread-bound ukiyo-e woodblock-printed books in *hanshi-bon* format: ink on paper; signed Gakyōrōjin Manji hitsu; 8 7/8 x 10 5/8 in. (22.5 x 27.1 cm). Arthur M. Sackler Museum, Bequest of the Hofer Collection of the Arts of Asia, 1985.783.1.

Katsushika Hokusai
Japanese, 1760–1849
The Appearance of Hōeizan

From *One Hundred Views of Mount Fuji*, vol. 1

Edo period, 1834

After the success of his color-print series on a related topic, seventy-five-year-old Hokusai embarked on the book project *One Hundred Views of Mount Fuji* (*Fugaku hyakkei*). This tour de force was executed in monochrome ink with highly detailed block carving and nuanced printing. Each double-page spread features one or two compositions showing the peerless mountain from various, often ingenious perspectives. This image gives a sense of the chaos and confusion of the volcano's last major eruption, in 1707, which resulted in the formation of a crater dubbed Hōeizan. The event predated Hokusai's lifetime, but that did not prevent him from expressing the destruction wrought by rocks, ash, broken bits of thatched and tiled buildings, and objects of daily use tumbling down on a terrified populace. This effective use of two-tone printing employs the darkest ink to describe the choking ash that threatens to engulf all, powerfully imagining the victims' experience. ARK

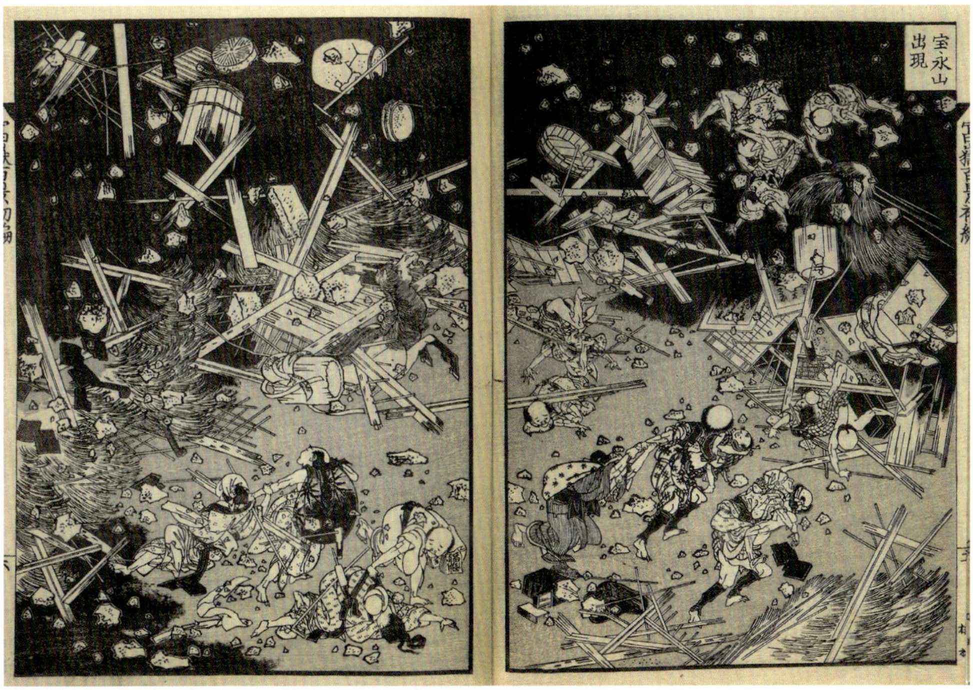

Oil on panel, 18 1/4 x 26 3/8 in. (46.4 x 67 cm). Fogg Museum, Daniel A. Pollack, Class of 1960, American Art Acquisition Fund, 2006.4.

Sarah Miriam Peale
American, 1800–1885
Still Life with Watermelon
1822

One of the first successful women painters in America, Sarah Miriam Peale was known for her miniatures and oil portraits of prominent figures and for her still lifes. She trained with her cousin Raphaelle Peale, son of Charles Willson Peale and founder of the still-life tradition in the United States. In 1817, she exhibited two flower paintings at the Pennsylvania Academy of the Fine Arts; seven years later, she and her sister, Anna Claypoole Peale, became the first women elected to the Academy. During her sixty-year career, Peale actively painted in Philadelphia, Baltimore, Washington, DC, and eventually St. Louis, where she was in high demand for her portraits and won prizes for her still lifes.

With its brilliantly executed fruit and leaves, asymmetrical composition, tumbling seeds, and play of shadows, *Still Life with Watermelon* is an exuberant work and an astonishing accomplishment for the twenty-two-year-old artist. FW

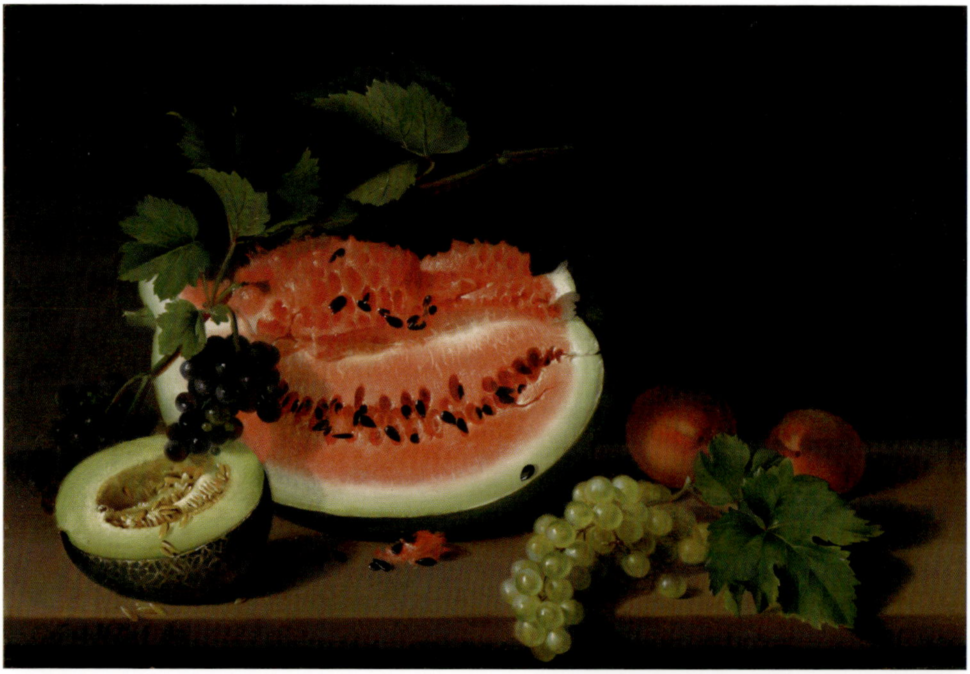

 Oil on canvas, 32 x 42 3/4 in. (81.3 x 108.6 cm). Fogg Museum, Gift of Grenville L. Winthrop, Class of 1886, 1942.220.

William Michael Harnett
American, 1848–1892
Still Life with Bric-a-Brac
1878

In his *Still Life with Bric-a-Brac*, a major early work, William Michael Harnett's careful execution anticipates his later trompe l'oeil style. Dry-goods importer William Hazelton Folwell commissioned this painting and owned many of the objects represented in it, including a Wedgwood reduced-scale copy of the famous Roman *Portland Vase* (a full-scale copy is included in this handbook on page 129), a bust of Minerva, "antiqued" sword, Persian torch stand, lacquer tray, European porcelain, and Greek vases. The Middle Eastern, European, ancient Greek, and Asian objects reflected the increasing cosmopolitanism of the Victorian era in the United States and the growing taste for collectible objects from a wide range of cultures. FW

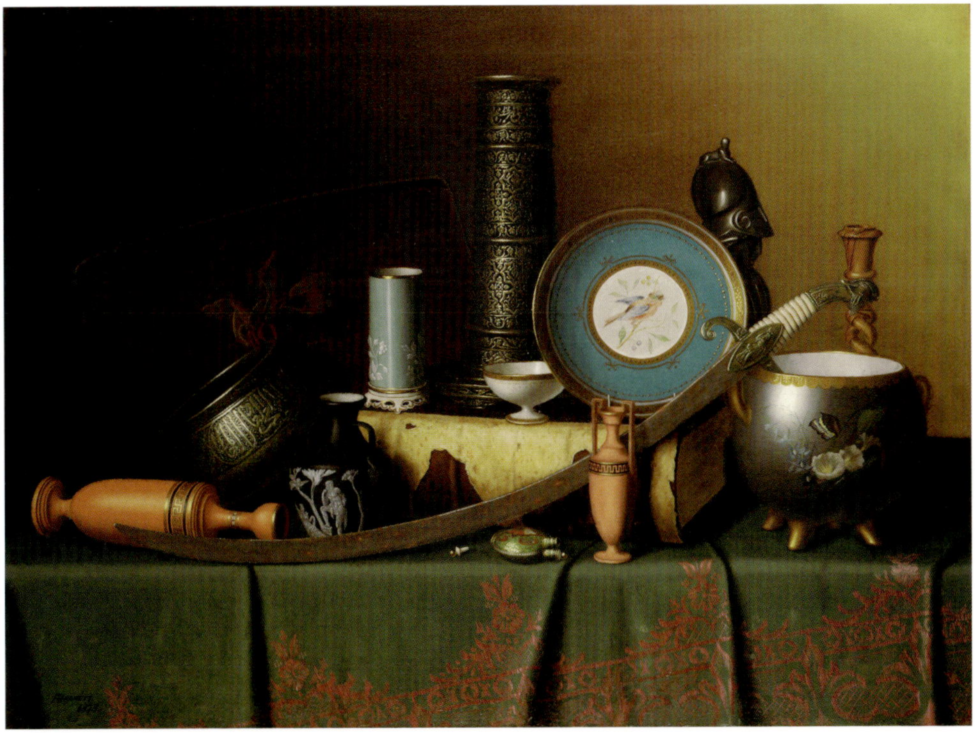

Oil on canvas, 64 1/2 x 95 in. (163.8 x 241.3 cm). Fogg Museum, Gift of Mrs. Edward W. Moore, 1956.62.

Washington Allston American, 1779–1843 Diana on a Chase 1805

This landmark painting demonstrates Washington Allston's ability to compete with his European contemporaries, who were working in Rome in the neoclassical style. The figures of Diana and her nymphs, hunting Aktaion, are small in scale compared with the grandiose landscape, which was inspired by the compositions of Claude Lorrain and Nicolas Poussin. Allston based the foliage, trees, and view of Mount Pilatus on plein-air sketches that are also in the Fogg's collection. / A graduate of Harvard University (class of 1800), Allston painted *Diana on a Chase* while in Rome with Samuel Taylor Coleridge and Washington Irving. Coleridge praised the painting for its "picturesque" and "coloristic" qualities. FW

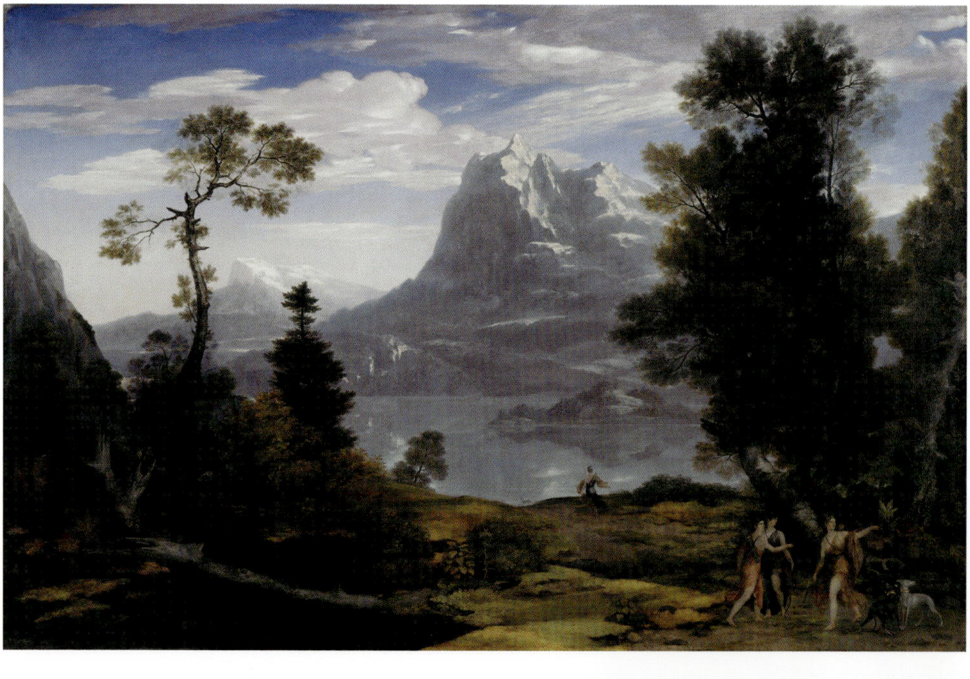

139 Watercolor and gouache, with extensive scratchwork, on cream wove paper; 3 1/4 x 5 5/16 in. (8.3 x 13.5 cm). Fogg Museum, Bequest of Grenville L. Winthrop, 1943.509.

Joseph Mallord William Turner
British, 1775–1851
Bally-burgh Ness
c. 1834–35

J. M. W. Turner's *Bally-burgh Ness* is an illustration for Sir Walter Scott's *The Antiquary*, the third of his many Waverley novels. Originally intended for an edition of the novels that was never published, this drawing was reproduced as one of six engravings after Turner in *Landscape-Historical Illustrations of Scotland and the Waverley Novels: From Drawings by J. M. W. Turner and Others*, a compendium of excerpts from the books. Turner's minute brushstrokes and brilliant use of color, enlivened by judicious scraping, effectively capture Scott's description of the scene: "The disk of the sun became almost totally obscured ere he had altogether sunk below the horizon, and an early and lurid shade of darkness blotted the serene twilight of a summer evening." One can barely make out the tiny figures of Sir Arthur Wardour, his daughter Isabella, and the beggar Edie Ochiltree marooned between the cliffs and the rapidly rising tide, which surges against the headland of Bally-burgh Ness. MS

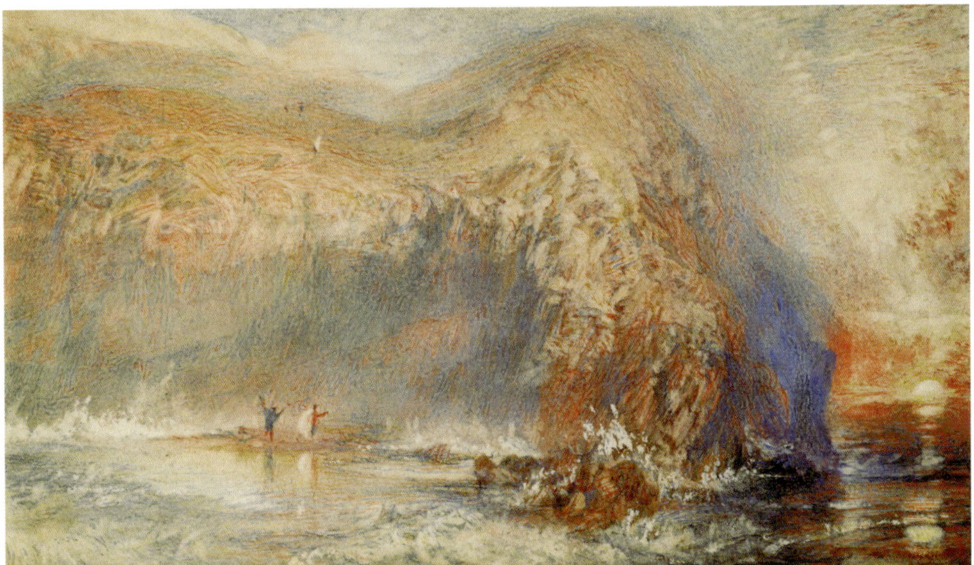

Ukiyo-e woodblock-printed *surimono* in *shikishi* format: ink, colors, and metallic pigments on paper; signed Go Hokkei; 8 5/16 x 7 3/16 in. (21.1 x 18.2 cm). Arthur M. Sackler Museum, Gift of the Friends of Arthur B. Duel, 1933.4.1856.

Totoya Hokkei
Japanese, 1780–1850
The Hero Zhang Shun Representing Water

From the series *Five Elements of the Water Margin*, with poems by Seiyōkan Umeyo (Baise) and Garyūen

Edo period, probably 1832

Surimono are lavish, privately commissioned prints made for exchange during the latter half of Japan's Edo period (1615–1868). Combining symbolic imagery with poetic texts, they were popular in urban literary circles such as the Hanazono Group, which commissioned this striking print. Zhang Shun was one of 108 heroes from the Chinese adventure *Tales of the Water Margin*. A giant whose preternatural strength and swimming ability enabled him to survive as a fisherman and bandit before joining the rebels' righteous cause, he personified water in this series that matched *Water Margin* warriors with the Five Elements. Totoya Hokkei depicted the half-nude, muscle-bound hero clambering over rocks entwined with the line of an anchor. It is unclear if this represents a particular exploit of Zhang Shun, who bravely faced a watery death only to emerge from the depths and possess his brother's body in order to smite a cowardly enemy. ARK

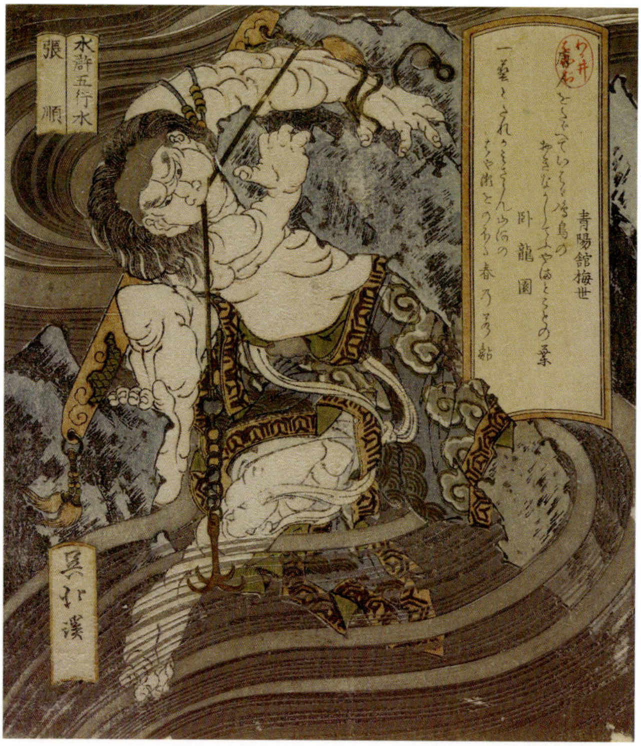

141 / Vegetable-dyed banana fiber, plain weave; 56 x 55 3/16 in. (142.2 x 140.2 cm). Arthur M. Sackler Museum, Gift of Margot Warner, 1984.255.

Long Olive-Green Robe
Ryūkyū (Okinawa)
late 18th–early 19th century

The Ryūkyū archipelago comprises thirty-six small islands linking the southern tip of Japan to the northeastern shore of Taiwan. Officially regarded as Japan's Okinawa prefecture, these islands have a complex cultural history, with Japanese, continental Asian, and Pacific Island influences that contributed to yet did not supersede a strong local character. / This garment represents the height of Ryūkyū textile craft. Less florid than the Chinese-style costumes worn by royalty during formal ceremonies or the vibrant stencil-dyed robes of entertainers, such fine banana-fiber robes were worn only by high-ranking members of the Ryūkyū court. Because it incorporates very long fibers, this robe was probably made using plants cultivated on the imperial plantation, since only royalty could afford to grow their crops so tall. To achieve the rich green color, the fabric was first dyed yellow and then indigo blue. Sadly, very little Okinawan cultural property has survived, making this robe even more rare. ARK

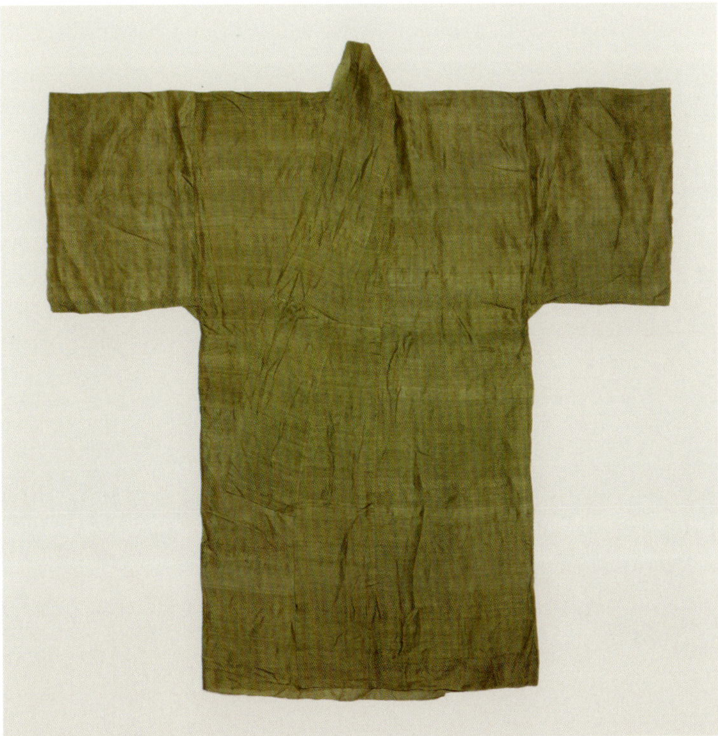

Watercolor, black ink, graphite, and black chalk on off-white antique laid paper; 14 5/8 x 20 9/16 in. (37.2 x 52.3 cm). Fogg Museum, Bequest of Grenville L. Winthrop, 1943.446.

William Blake British, 1757–1827 The Demons Tormenting Ciampolo the Barrator 1824–27

A contemporary account held that Blake made his 102 illustrations to Dante Alighieri's *Divine Comedy* "during a fortnight's illness in bed" in 1824. This might explain the sketchy quality of some of the watercolors. This drawing illustrates one section of the eighth circle of Dante's Hell, where sinners are plunged into boiling pitch and guarded by ten demons called the Malebranche (Evil Claws). Blake portrayed the moment when the demon Libicocco "with his grapnel seized him by the arm / So that, by rending, he tore off a tendon." Blake planned to produce engravings of all the illustrations, but at his death in 1827 he had finished only seven plates, including one after *The Demons Tormenting Ciampolo*. The Fogg owns twenty-three watercolors from the *Divine Comedy* series as well as impressions of the seven engravings. WL

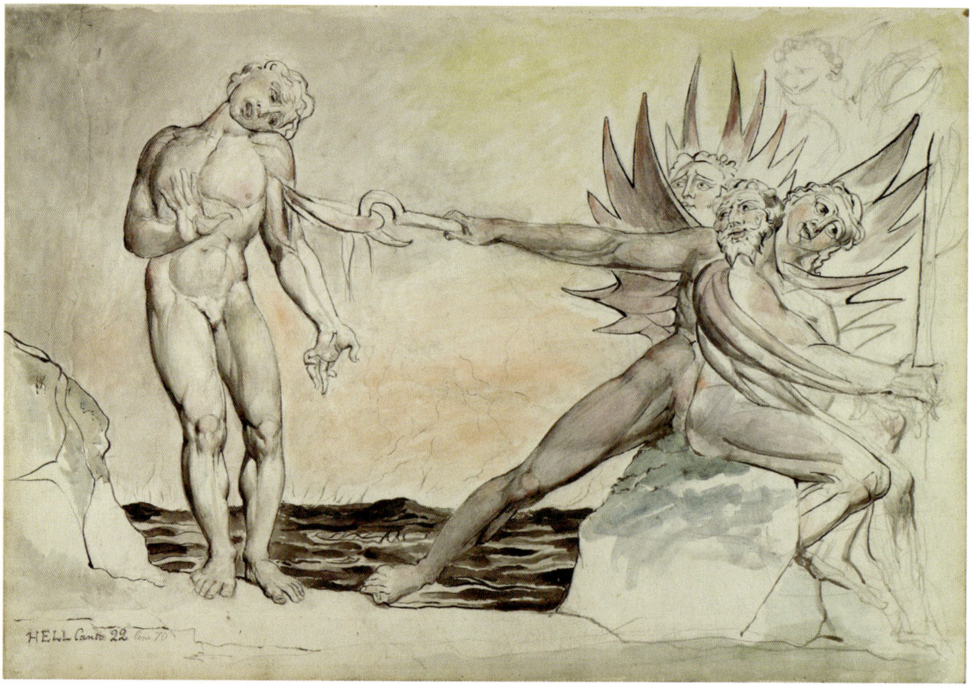

143 Lithograph, 6 3/4 x 9 3/8 in. (17.1 x 23.8 cm). Fogg Museum, Gray Collection of Engravings Fund, G8232.

Eugène Delacroix
French, 1798–1863
Lion Devouring a Horse
1844

Eugène Delacroix's vibrant coloristic paintings and painterly lithographs embodied the essence of romanticism, marking the artist's sworn opposition to the linear classicism of Jean-Auguste-Dominique Ingres and Jacques-Louis David. A journey to Morocco and Algeria in 1832 fueled Delacroix's interest in orientalism, perhaps by offering a glimpse of Barbary lions in their diminishing natural habitat. He probably drew this ravening beast at the Jardin des Plantes zoo in Paris. Others, including his illustrious predecessor Rubens, had sketched animals in captivity. Yet only Delacroix could have reenvisioned this lion's frenzied eyes and the trail of his claws through equine flesh on the lithographic stone with such gut-wrenching tactility. SKS

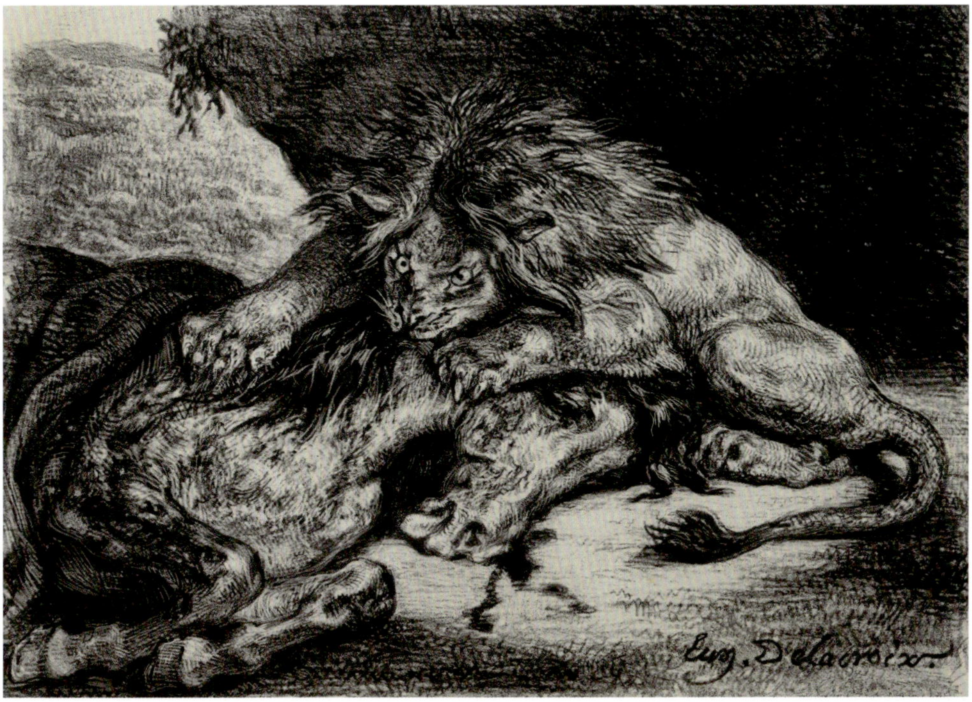

Lithograph, hand colored; 9 7/16 x 9 1/8 in. (23.9 x 23.2 cm). Fogg Museum, Anonymous Fund for the Acquisition of Prints Older than 150 Years, M26366.

Honoré Daumier French, 1808–1879 "Mister, that won't do! ... You have to make it right for me, mister!!!" 1837

Painter, printmaker, and caricaturist par excellence, Honoré Daumier cast his knavish everyman Robert Macaire in more than one hundred different roles and vocations in the French newspaper *Le Charivari* from 1836 to 1838. Daumier used his protagonist to demonstrate his disdain for the July Monarchy and its oligarchy, so Macaire and his rakish schemes generally failed. Here, deeply indignant at being forced to admit he cannot repay a debt, Macaire demands satisfaction for that humiliation—by challenging his bewildered, sleepy creditor to a duel. This unique sheet, signed by the colorist Edouard Bouvenne, served as the coloring template for hand-painting the deluxe second edition of the print. SKS

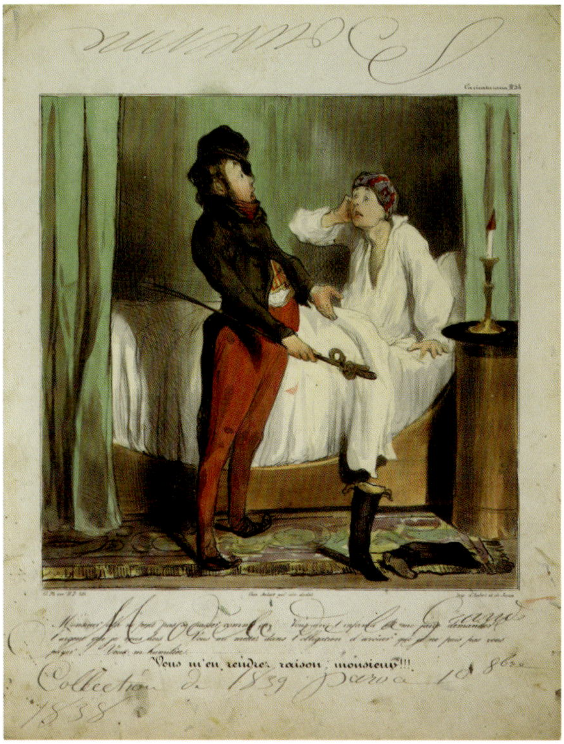

145 Oil on canvas mounted on wood panel, 28 3/8 x 39 1/2 in. (72.1 x 100.3 cm). Fogg Museum, Bequest of Grenville L. Winthrop, 1943.251.

Jean-Auguste-Dominique Ingres
French, 1780–1867
Odalisque with a Slave
1839–40

Ingres completed this painting to fulfill a commission of 1821 and to repay a portion of the debt he owed to his patron Charles Marcotte d'Argenteuil. Ingres painted several odalisques, participating in the French fascination with northern Africa and the Middle East as sites of colonization. This composition exaggerates the erotic aspects of his subject by showing the interior of a harem occupied by a concubine, a musician, and a eunuch, each of whom have different skin tones to emphasize the hierarchy of their social status. When the painting was exhibited publicly five years after its execution, it brought Ingres great acclaim as a painter of the female nude. ER

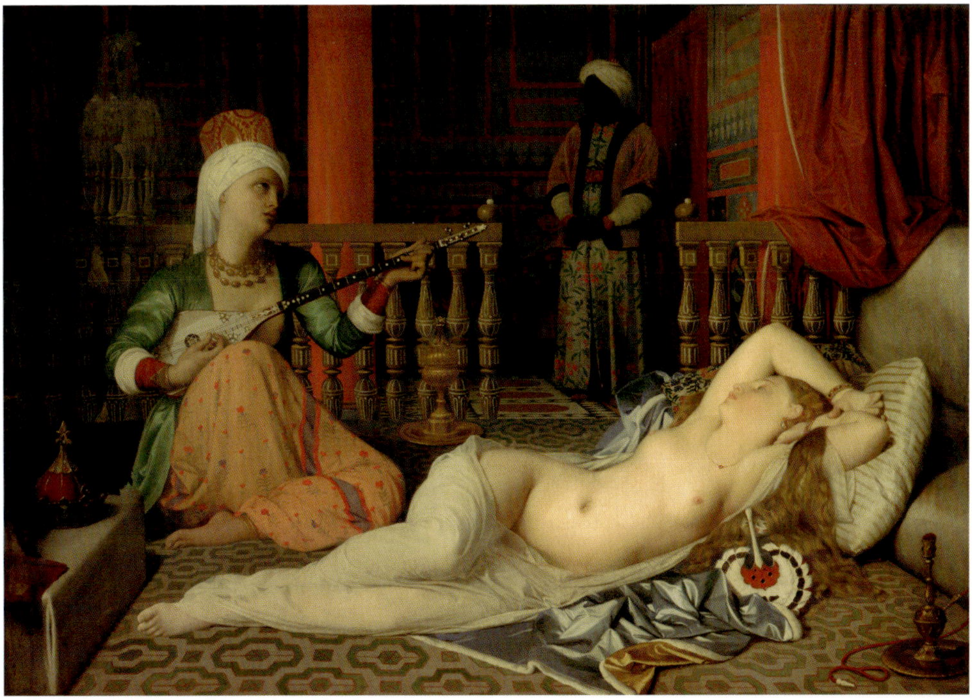

Salted paper print from a calotype negative, 7 11/16 x 6 1/8 in. (19.5 x 15.5 cm). Fogg Museum, Gift of Stuart Cary Welch, Jr., P1973.55.

Harriet Ann Tucker
British, b. 1809
Untitled
1845

The English amateur photographer William Henry Fox Talbot developed one of the two initial photographic technologies and the first negative-based process that produced multiple positive prints. The process, which he named "calotype" (from the Greek *kalos*, "beautiful"), was largely the province of amateurs. Among them were some of the earliest women photographers, including Talbot's wife, Constance, and several friends and relatives; Harriet Ann Tucker has been connected to this circle through her association with the writer and photographer Pauline Trevelyan. / This image exemplifies the soft, speckled, low-contrast appearance of early calotypes, which can resemble drawings more than modern photographs. Isolating her sitter in a closely framed vignette and concentrating on the broad divisions of light and shadow formed around her folded arms, Tucker emphasizes the dreamy state of her model, who gazes upward, away from the book before her. BF

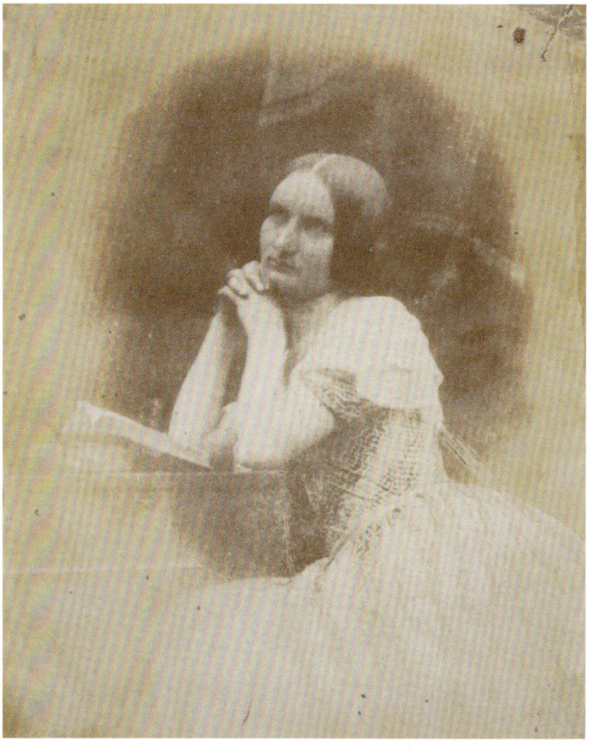

147 / Full-plate daguerreotype, 8 1/16 x 6 1/8 in. (20.5 x 15.5 cm). Fogg Museum, Loan from the Massachusetts General Hospital Archives and Special Collections, 9.1979.

Southworth & Hawes
American, active 1843–61
John Collins Warren
c. 1855

Announced in France in 1839, the daguerreotype (named for its inventor, Louis-Jacques-Mandé Daguerre) was the earliest publicly revealed photographic process. In contrast with Fox Talbot's calotype, daguerreotypes were unique objects—sharply detailed images on a metal support—and were largely created in professional studios. / Albert Sands Southworth and Josiah Johnson Hawes's firm was known for the unusual artistry of its portraits of Boston's elites and intellectuals. Depicted here is John Collins Warren (1778–1856), a founding member of Massachusetts General Hospital and the doctor responsible for the first demonstration of ether as a surgical anesthetic. Eschewing the allover clarity of typical daguerreotype portraiture, and modeling the lighting after Rembrandt, Southworth & Hawes posed Warren before a background of deep shadows and murky grays, using a strong overhead light to spotlight his face, cast shadows below his brow, and accentuate the folds of his skin. BF

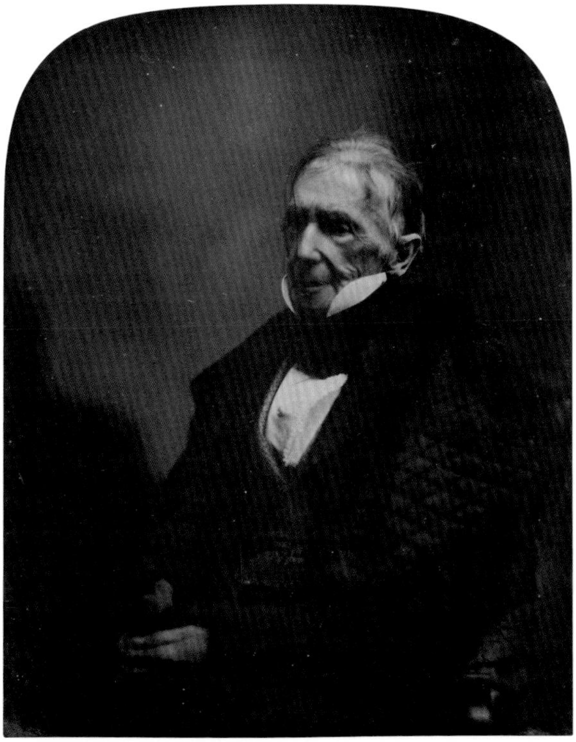

Marble, 28 x 19 1/2 x 14 in. (71.1 x 49.5 x 35.6 cm). Fogg Museum, Transfer from Harvard College, gift of Mrs. T. O. Richardson, 1958.180.

Hiram Powers
American, 1805–1873
America
c. 1854–65

The best-known U.S. sculptor of his day, Hiram Powers first specialized in portrait busts of leading political figures. In 1837, he moved to Florence, where he began making idealized sculptures of classical and biblical subjects. Just as the United States had fashioned its government after Greek and Roman models, Powers drew on classical sources for this allegorical representation of America. Wearing a crown of thirteen stars representing the original colonies, America appears as a Greek goddess in white marble, a departure from earlier representations of her as a Native American. Upon seeing this work, Nathaniel Hawthorne declared, "It has great merit, and embodies the ideal of youth, freedom, progress and whatever we consider as distinctive of our country's character and destiny." FW

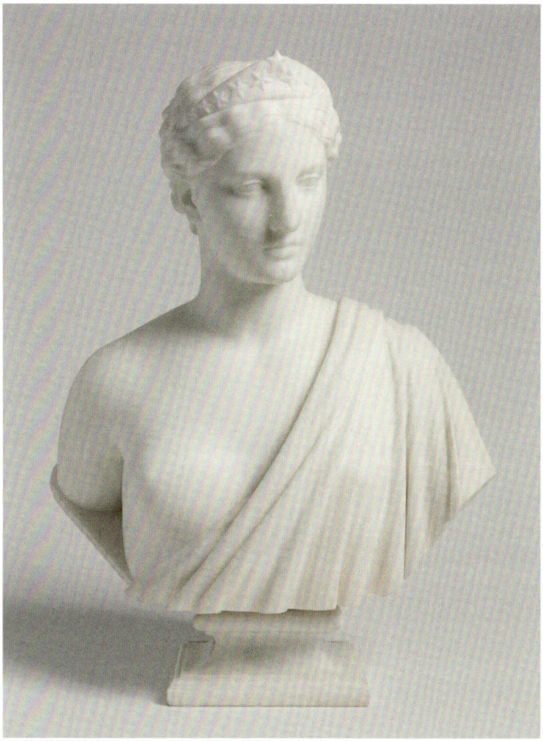

149 / Oil on canvas, 35 1/8 x 29 1/2 in. (89.2 x 74.9 cm). Fogg Museum, Gift of Grenville L. Winthrop, Class of 1886, 1942.193.

Charles Bird King
American, 1785–1862
The Vanity of the Artist's Dream
1830

Notable for both its skillful rendering and sardonic humor, *The Vanity of the Artist's Dream* ranks as one of the most significant American still lifes from the period before the Civil War. Charles Bird King depicts a cupboard piled high with the essential supplies of a painter—palette, brushes, and drafting tools—along with letters and books, including a tattered volume entitled *The Pleasures of Hope*. In the center, King includes a cast of the head of the famous classical sculpture *Apollo Belvedere*, which American artists frequently studied and copied. A note tacked to the cupboard frame declares these goods to be "the property of an Artist" offered in a "Sheriff's Sale." This pioneering work in the trompe-l'oeil manner functions as an allegorical portrait of the artist and also suggests his disillusionment over the low esteem in which art was held in America at that time. FW

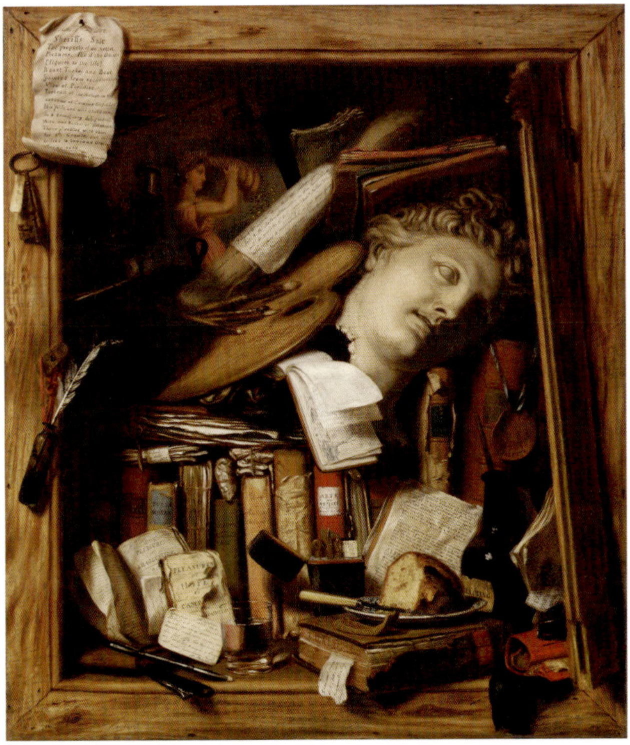

Album page with two albumen silver prints and hand coloring; sheet as shown: 11 3/8 x 9 1/8 in. (28.9 x 23.2 cm). Fogg Museum, Purchased through the generosity of Melvin R. Seiden, P1982.359.67.

Mary Georgiana Caroline Cecil Filmer, British, 1838–1903
Untitled
c. 1865

Lady Mary Filmer of Kent produced an album titled *My Book* that chronicles her connections to the court of Queen Victoria and other society figures. Her album is an imaginative combination of hand decoration, family photographs, and *cartes de visite* (small-format photographs that were in widespread circulation in the 1860s) of royalty and other notable figures. / This page marks the marriage of Albert Edward, Prince of Wales (1841–1910; later King Edward VII), to Princess Alexandra of Denmark (1844–1925; later Queen Alexandra), adorned with the equipment of the sporting life and the flag of Denmark. In other pages, Filmer's more radical cutting and reassembly of her source photographs evidences the nineteenth-century use of collage techniques usually associated with modern photomontage. Filmer's album, like other Victorian photographic albums, intertwines private and public photographs, linking photography to social identity. BF

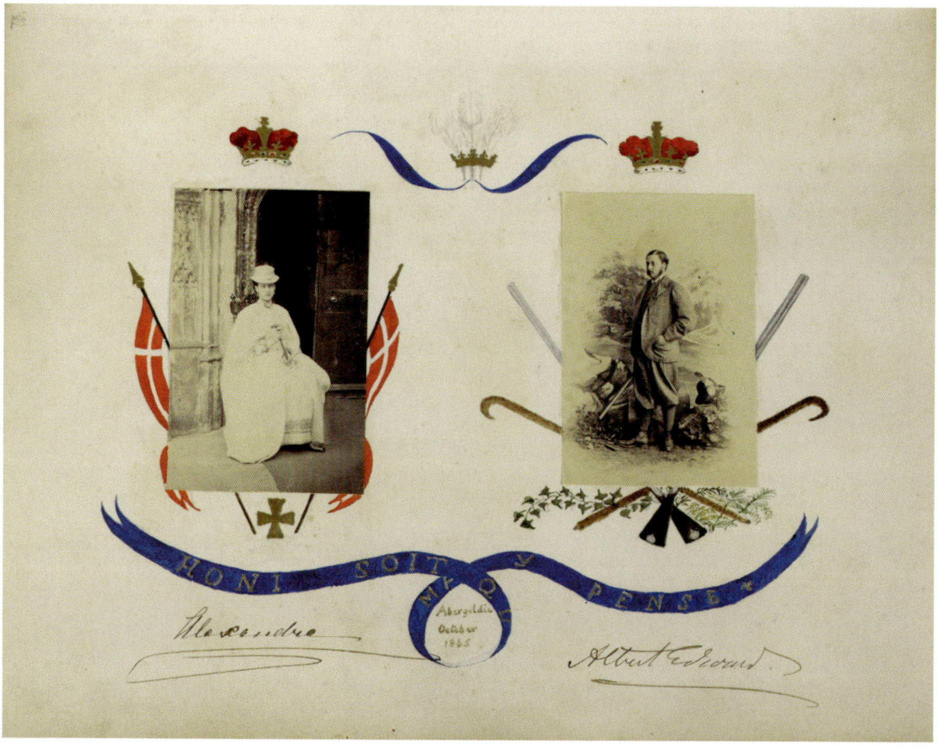

151 Opaque watercolor and gold on paper; inscribed (top left) in Devanagari script bicteriya maharani (Victoria Maharani); 10 1/4 x 8 1/16 in. (26.1 x 20.5 cm). Arthur M. Sackler Museum, Gift in gratitude to John Coolidge; Gift of Leslie Cheek Jr.; Anonymous Fund in memory of Henry Berg; Louise Haskell Daly, Alpheus Hyatt, Richard Norton Memorial Funds; and through the generosity of Albert H. Gordon and Emily Rauh Pulitzer; formerly in the collection of Stuart Cary Welch, Jr., 1995.139.

Victoria Maharani with the Princess Royal
Indian, Rajasthan, Colonial period c. 1845

In a surprising Rajput portrait, Queen Victoria coddles her daughter, Princess Victoria Adelaide Mary Louise, under her ermine cloak and against her bosom. Its subject certainly recalls imagery of the Christian Madonna and Child, which was familiar to some Indian court ateliers even before the period of British colonial rule in India. This painting also references a popular contemporary print from Britain depicting Victoria and her daughter. Long-standing examples of mother-and-child representation also existed in India for artists to draw upon, from sculpted icons of *matrkas* (mothers), often holding children, to images of Yashodhara nursing the divine infant Krishna. Queen and princess are rendered in an Indian visual language with stylized features and bold, flat colors. Depicted as regal and maternal, Victoria embodies the ideal maharani, or great queen, in an Indian worldview. KM

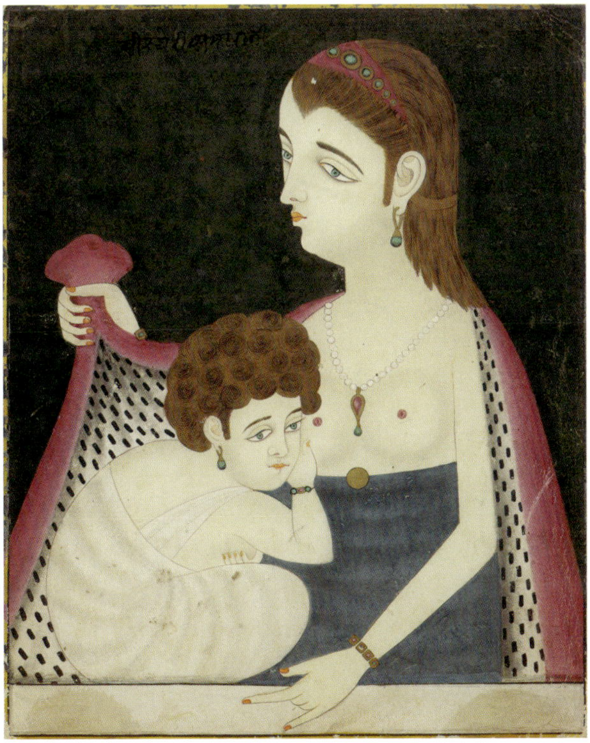

Left: Salted paper print, 17 15/16 x 15 7/16 in. (45.5 x 39.2 cm); right: albumen silver print; image: 3 3/8 x 2 1/16 in. (8.5 x 5.3 cm). Fogg Museum, On loan from the Historical Photographs and Special Visual Collections Department, Fine Arts Library, Harvard College Library, Bequest of Evert Jansen Wendell, 119.1976.240, 120.1976.1770.

Mathew B. Brady & Studio
American, c. 1823–1896
Colonel Elmer Ephraim Ellsworth, 1861

Silsbee, Case, & Co., after Mathew B. Brady & Studio
Colonel Elmer Ephraim Ellsworth, c. 1861

Mathew Brady was a major chronicler of eminent Americans and of the Civil War, two subjects that converged in his portrait of Elmer Ellsworth (1837–1861). He photographed Ellsworth on his entry to the Union army, posing the soldier for a large-format portrait in an unusually spare studio setting. Brady marketed such portraits as "Imperial Photographs" because of their size. More elaborate versions than Ellsworth's, featuring extensive hand coloring, could cost as much as five hundred dollars. / Ellsworth turned out to be one of the first casualties of the war and became a posthumous celebrity whose memory was invoked in enlistment campaigns. In the process, Brady's original image became the basis for much cheaper, easily obtained *cartes de visite* produced both within and outside of his studio. The small card shown here substantially alters Brady's original, reworking parts of the portrait and adding a drawn landscape to locate Ellsworth in an imagined military setting. BF

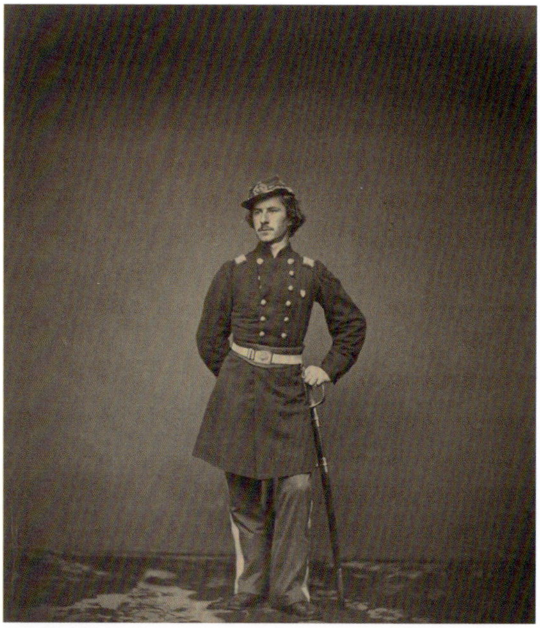

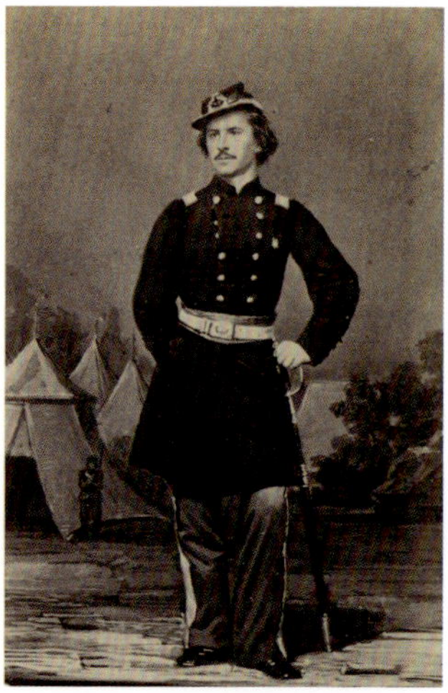

Oil on canvas, 26 3/4 x 53 3/4 in. (68 x 136.5 cm). Fogg Museum, Gift of Mr. and Mrs. Frederic Haines Curtiss, 1940.298.

Winslow Homer
American, 1836–1910
Pitching Quoits
1865

Winslow Homer initially established his reputation as an illustrator of Civil War scenes, and his earliest paintings depict the camp life of the Union army in Virginia. Here Homer shows soldiers playing quoits, a forerunner of horseshoes in which heavy objects are tossed onto a stake. The red and blue uniforms and tasseled caps indicate that the players are members of the Fifth New York Volunteers, also known as Duryée's Zouaves or the Red Devils. This corps was one of several whose uniforms were modeled on the original Zouaves, Algerian mercenaries recognized for their bravery in battle. This work was exhibited at the National Academy of Design in New York in 1865 and contributed to Homer's being elected to full membership that year. FW

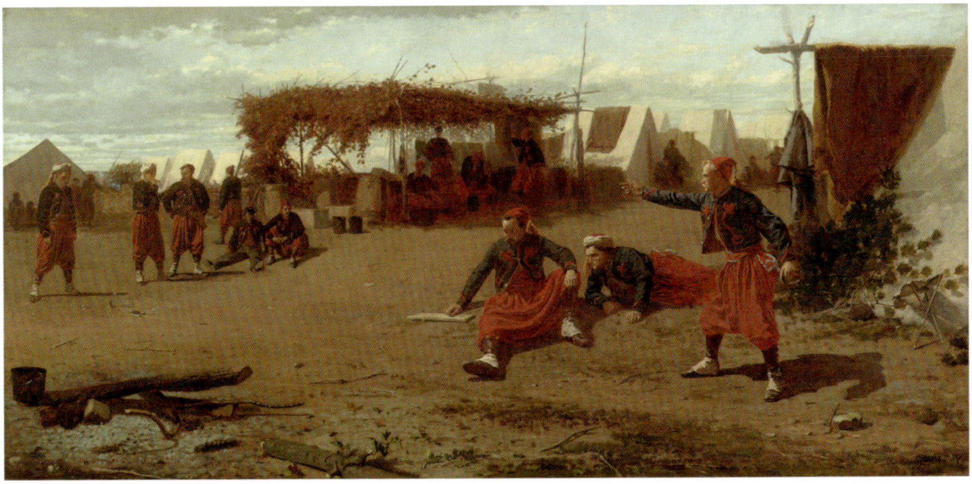

Lithograph, 19 1/8 x 24 1/2 in. (48.6 x 62.3 cm). Fogg Museum, Program for Harvard College Fund, M13710.

Édouard Manet
French, 1832–1883
The Balloon
1862

Édouard Manet produced this lithograph (the second one he made) for a portfolio that was never completed; only five proof impressions were ever printed. The image is a compilation of different views of the August 15, 1862, Fête de l'Empereur, which took place on the Esplanade of the Seine. Manet is historically accurate in showing the balloon as a highlight of the festival, a propagandistic display intended to celebrate the ascendancy of the Second Empire. His decision to undermine that triumph by placing a crippled boy in the foreground between two crosslike poles—as if he were a surrogate for Christ—is, however, pure artistic license. The bold strokes of Manet's lithographic crayon conflate the real and the imaginary, giving the scene the feeling of actuality. SKS

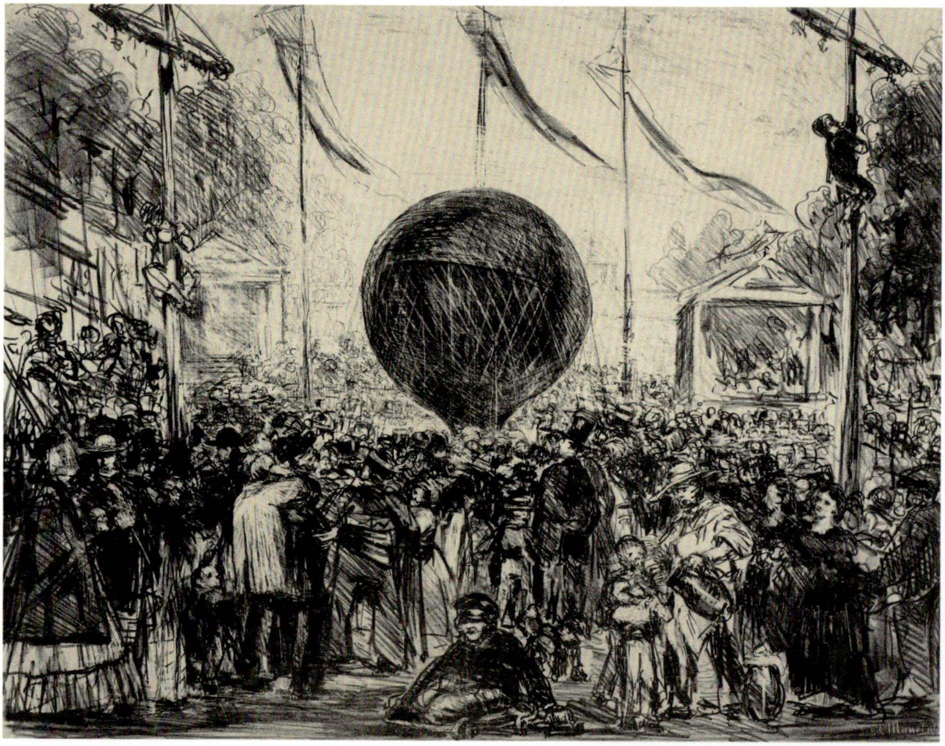

155 Watercolor and gouache over graphite on white wove paper on two sheets, joined; 8 11/16 x 22 3/16 in. (22.1 x 56.4 cm). Fogg Museum, Bequest of Grenville L. Winthrop, 1943.387.

Édouard Manet
French, 1832–1883
Race Course at Longchamp
1864

The opening in 1857 of the Longchamp racetrack in the Bois de Boulogne in Paris and the running of the first Grand Prix de Paris in 1863 sparked a racing mania. Paintings and sculptures of the racehorses, the tracks, and the elegant spectators became popular. Édouard Manet's 1864 watercolor of the Longchamp track, painted on two joined sheets of paper, is one of several versions of the subject. Manet's ingenuity lay in the unusual viewpoint; he was possibly the first Western artist to depict a race from the middle of the track, with the horses coming toward him. The flurry of the race and the wealthy crowd showing off *la grande bataille des robes* (the great battle of dress) equally caught Manet's fascination. WL

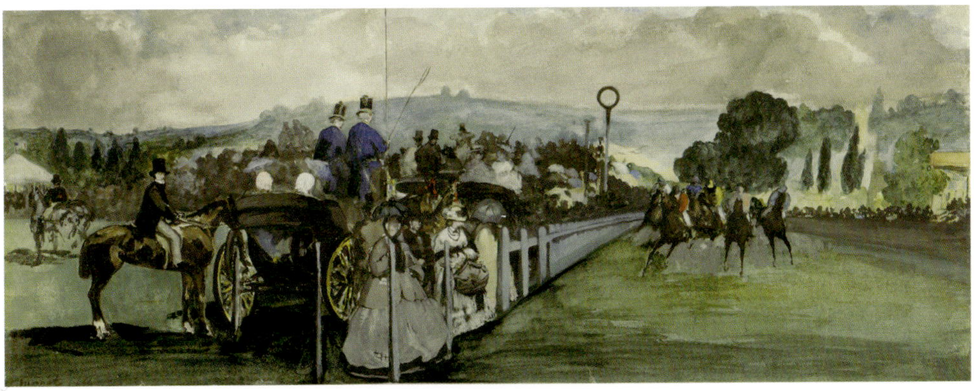

Oil on linen, $43\,5/8 \times 35\,1/2$ in. (110.8 x 90.2 cm). Fogg Museum, Bequest of Mrs. William Hayes Fogg, 1895.698.

Albert Bierstadt
American, 1830–1902
Rocky Mountains, "Lander's Peak"
1863

Bierstadt's western landscapes won him enormous popularity during the 1860s. *Rocky Mountains, "Lander's Peak"* was one in a series of paintings modeled on sketches and photographs he had made while with Frederick W. Lander's 1859 expedition to the Rockies to survey alternate routes for the Overland Trail in California. Bierstadt went in search of new subject matter that would distinguish him from the other artists painting the Hudson River Valley; he intended to sketch the wild scenery and to "study the manner and customs of the Indians" in preparation for larger studio paintings—reinventions or rearrangements of reality. / The *New York Times* praised Bierstadt's exhibition of 1864, which most likely included this painting: "In the large saloon, Mr. Bierstadt exhibited a remarkably fine landscape, with great tumultuous mountains, and wild flashes of aerial light, and distant visions of feathery waterfalls and streaming masses of clouds hurtling through it." FW

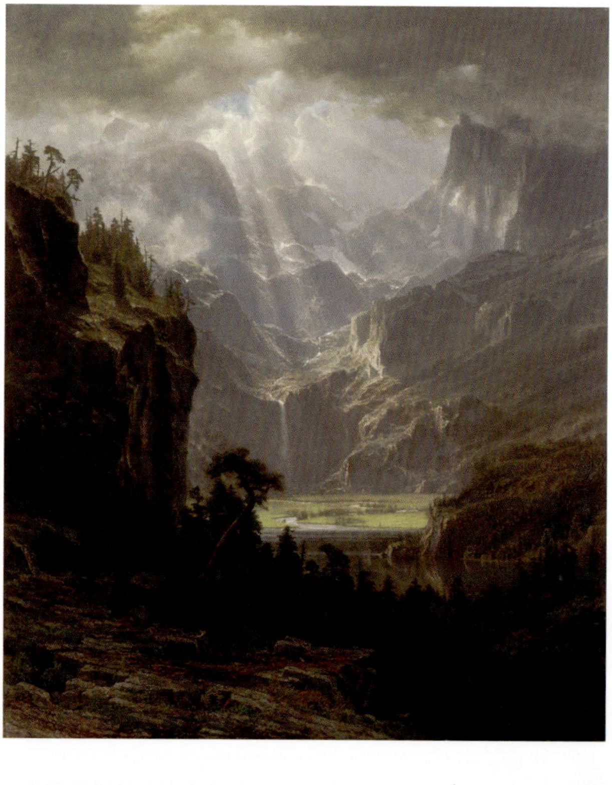

 Oil on canvas, 31 1/8 x 38 3/4 in. (79.1 x 98.4 cm). Fogg Museum, Gift of Mr. and Mrs. Joseph Pulitzer Jr., 1957.163.

Claude Monet
French, 1840–1926
La Porte d'Amont, Étretat
c. 1868–69

Monet painted the cliffs bordering the fishing village of Étretat several times, but he depicted the landscape from this particular vantage point only once. The blustery winds of the Normandy coastline often complicated his process of working outdoors, *en plein air*, but Monet continued to use this method of painting in order to capture the natural effects of the cliffs in a more immediate way. Many artists visited Étretat to paint the landscape, but Monet was unique in his use of large, flat brushstrokes to capture the chromatic variation of the landscape and to make his painting appear spontaneous. ER

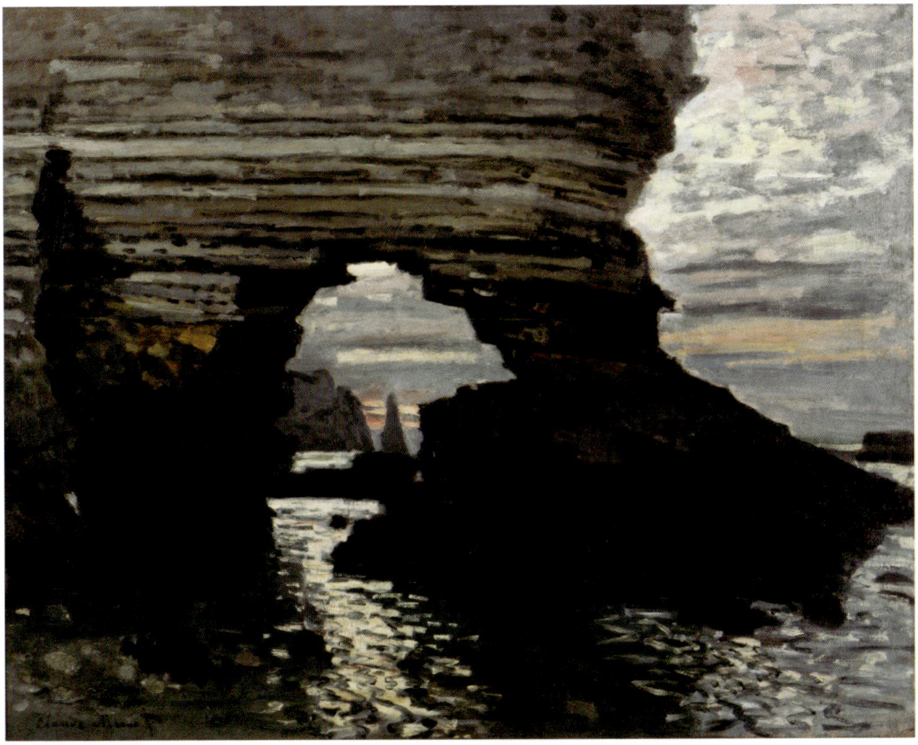

 Oil on canvas, 63 x 63 1/4 in. (160 x 160.7 cm). Fogg Museum, Gift of Mr. and Mrs. F. Meynier de Salinelles, 1937.78.

Frédéric Bazille
French, 1841–1870
Summer Scene
1869

Bazille originally conceived of this work as a major statement about the history of art. Many of the figures are repeated from old master paintings, and they were all painted nude, which was a pioneering reversal of the long tradition of depicting the eroticized nude as a female body. Fearing the critics' disapproval, Bazille covered his figures in swimsuits before submitting the painting for public exhibition. Nevertheless, when it appeared at the Salon of 1870, it had a tremendous impact on many artists. These included Thomas Eakins, who saw the painting and later painted his own bathing scene composed entirely of male nudes. ER

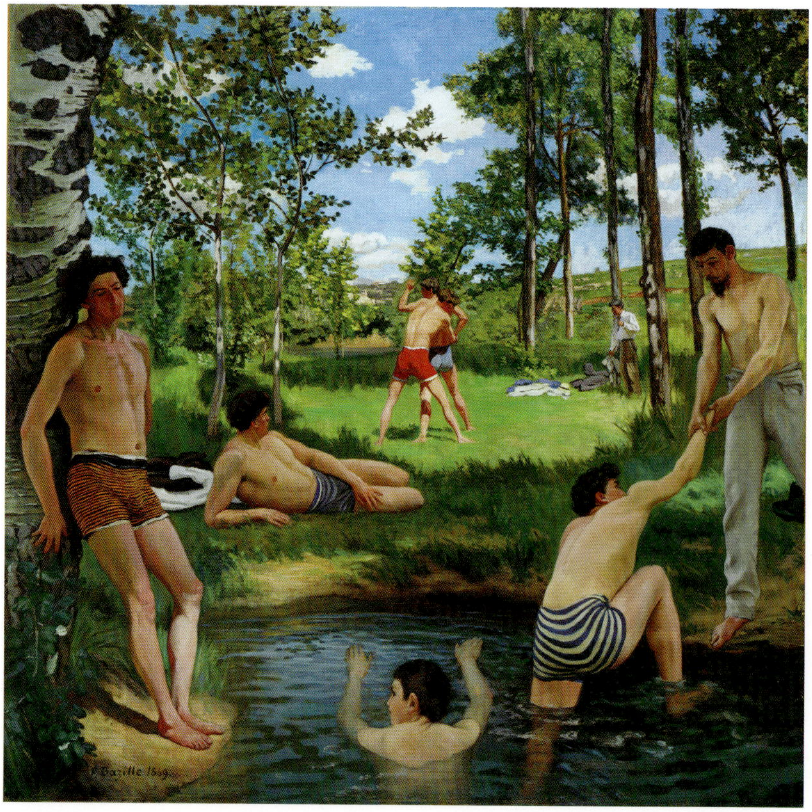

 Watercolor over graphite on white wove paper, $13^{7}/_{8}$ x $19^{15}/_{16}$ in. (35.2 x 50.7 cm). Fogg Museum, Anonymous gift, 1939.230.

Winslow Homer
American, 1836–1910
Hunter in the Adirondacks
1892

Over the course of four decades Winslow Homer continually returned to New York's Adirondack Mountains, producing about seventy watercolors that are among the highlights of his oeuvre. He managed to give a traditional American subject, the woodsman, a new vitality. The artist's enchantment with nature is captured in rapturous colors, laid down on the paper in unusually free, broad strokes. His intention was not only to paint the motif but also to portray the quality of light in the shade of the woods. Homer manipulated the watercolor layers to reveal the poetic effect of the light filtered through the branches and leaves. The numerous verticals of the thin trunks, the big sunlit fallen tree on which the hunter rests his left foot, and the slightly diagonal tree against which he is silhouetted create a dynamic composition. WL

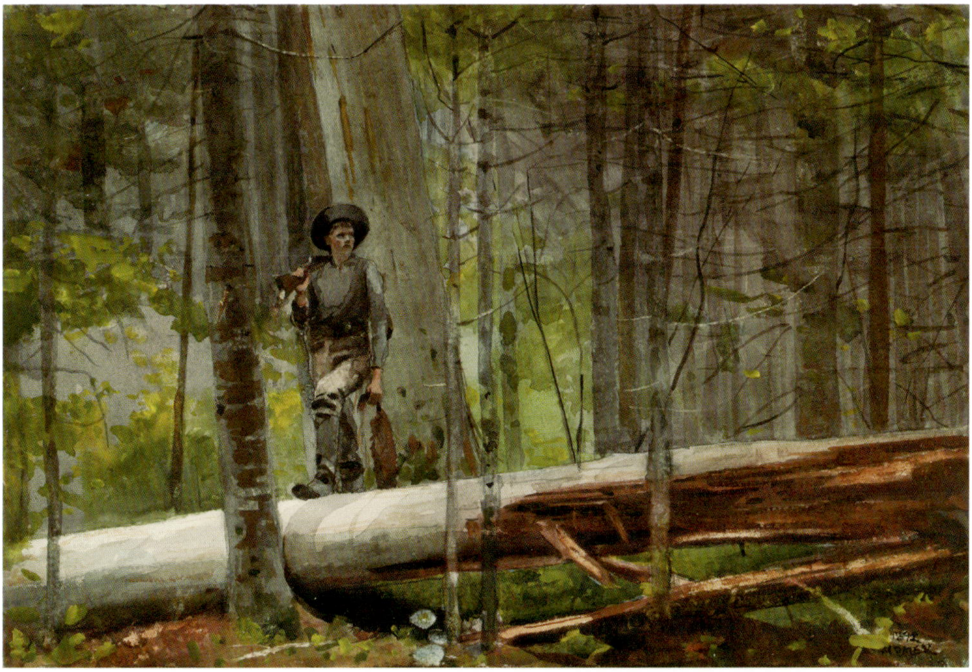

Watercolor, gouache, and metallic paint on white paper mounted on very fine canvas; $47\frac{15}{16}$ x $17\frac{15}{16}$ in. (121.7 x 45.5 cm) and $48\frac{1}{8}$ x 18 in. (122.2 x 45.7 cm). Fogg Museum, Bequest of Grenville L. Winthrop, 1943.460, .461.

Edward Burne-Jones
British, 1833–1898
Day and *Night*
1870

Edward Burne-Jones painted the large watercolors *Day* and *Night*, along with four panels depicting the seasons, for the shipping magnate and collector Frederick R. Leyland's house in London. The youthful figure of Day, wreathed in morning mist and holding a torch, is poised at the threshold of a new-made day above an imaginary seaport. Night, in front of a star-spangled sky and dusky sea, extinguishes her torch and summons sleep. William Morris composed quatrains for each of the six panels, including *Day* and *Night*: "I am Day I bring again/Life and Glory Love and Pain/Awake arise from death to death/Through me the worlds tale quickeneth" and "I am Night & bring again/Hope of pleasure rest from pain/Thoughts unsaid twixt life and death/My fruitful silence quickeneth." MS

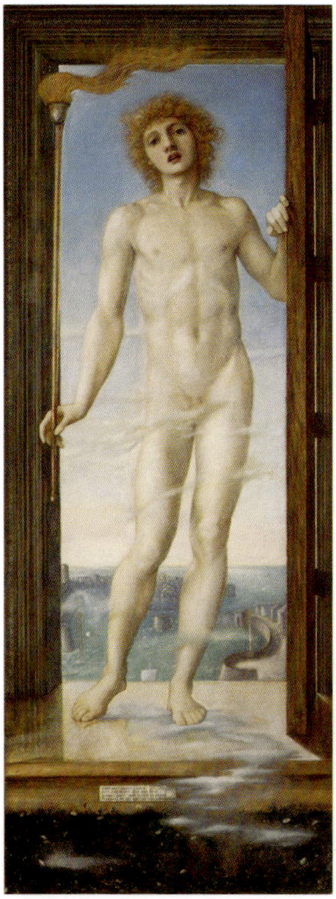

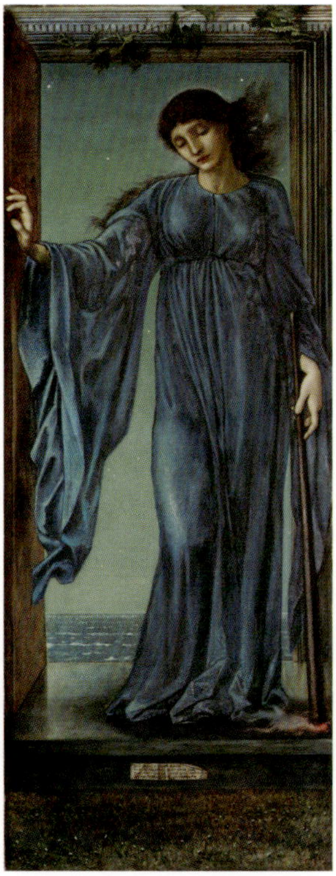

161 Oil on canvas, $53\frac{7}{8}$ x 38 in. (136.8 x 96.5 cm); predella: $13\frac{7}{8}$ x $37\frac{7}{8}$ in. (35.2 x 96.2 cm). Fogg Museum, Bequest of Grenville L. Winthrop, 1943.202.

Dante Gabriel Rossetti
British, 1828–1882
The Blessed Damozel
1871–78

This is Rossetti's most famous painting, an erotic variation on the Italian Renaissance type of the enthroned Virgin Mary. The work was commissioned in 1871 by William Graham, a merchant and Pre-Raphaelite patron, as an illustration to Rossetti's poem "The Blessed Damozel." Rossetti produced many "double works of art"—paintings paired with poems—but this is a unique instance in which the poem preceded the painting. Rossetti also designed the gold frame around this canvas, as he had done for many of his paintings. He later produced a smaller, somewhat different version of this painting (Lady Lever Art Gallery, Port Sunlight, National Museums Liverpool). ER

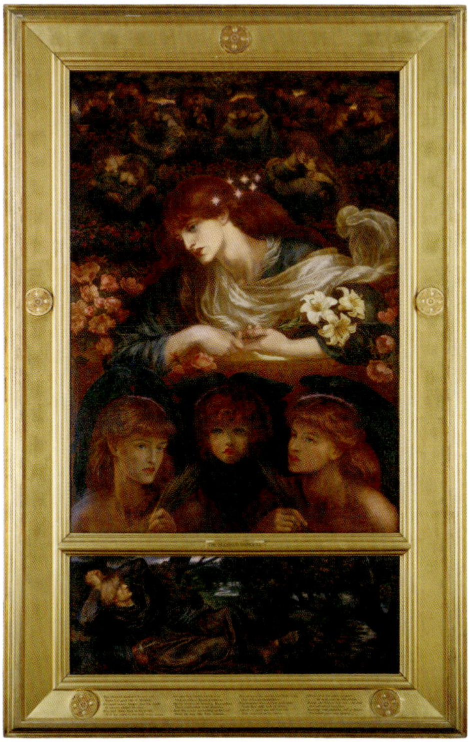

Oil on panel, 17 3/8 x 24 in. (44.1 x 61 cm). Fogg Museum, Bequest of Grenville L. Winthrop, 1943.176.

James Abbott McNeill Whistler
American, 1834–1903
Nocturne in Blue and Silver
c. 1871–72

A forerunner of modernism, Whistler reacted against the highly detailed paintings of the Victorians and embarked on a series of paintings he called "nocturnes"—nighttime seascapes and cityscapes emphasizing tone and mood. In *Nocturne in Blue and Silver*, he represented the Battersea shore in London as hazy, abstracted forms in shades of blue and gray. The painting was among those exhibited at London's Grosvenor Gallery in 1877, and in a scathing review, critic John Ruskin berated Whistler for "flinging a pot of paint into the public's face." Whistler sued Ruskin for libel, and in the ensuing trial, the defense counsel presented this painting as evidence to support its case. Ultimately, Whistler won the case but was awarded only one farthing in damages. FW

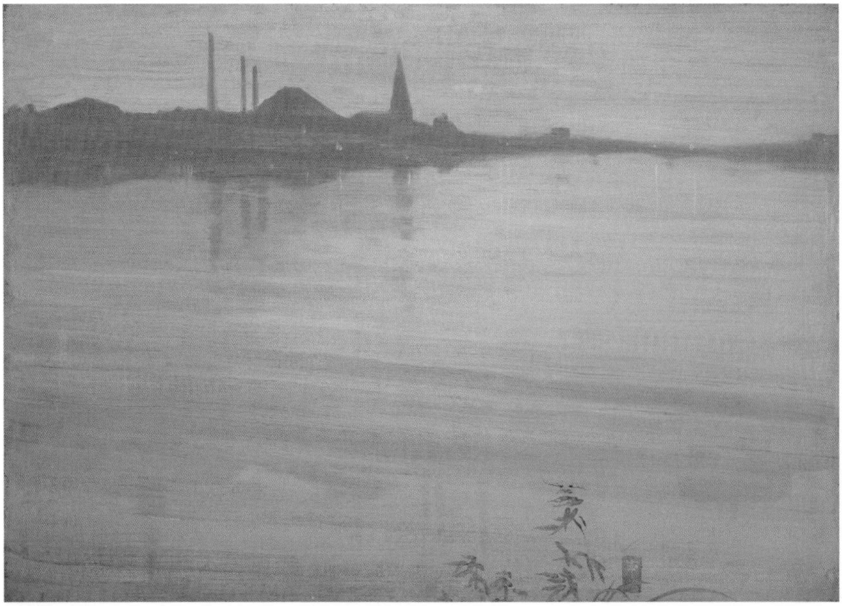

Oil on canvas, 19 1/16 x 39 1/8 in. (48.4 x 99.4 cm). Fogg Museum, Bequest of Mrs. William Hayes Fogg, 1895.716.

Sanford Robinson Gifford
American, 1823–1880
Leander's Tower on the Bosporus
1876

Sanford Robinson Gifford made his reputation by painting light-filled views of New York's Catskill Mountains. In response to growing interest in European and "Oriental" subjects in art, he turned increasingly to international subjects after traveling throughout Europe and the Near East in 1868–69. In this painting, he applied his luminist style to the legendary Leander's Tower, which stands in the Bosporus within view of Constantinople (Istanbul). According to Greek myth, Hero and Leander were lovers separated by the Hellespont (Dardanelles). Hero dwelt in a tower, where she lit a lamp each night to guide Leander as he swam to her. One night a storm blew out the lamp, and Leander drowned. Grief-stricken, Hero threw herself from the tower and died. FW

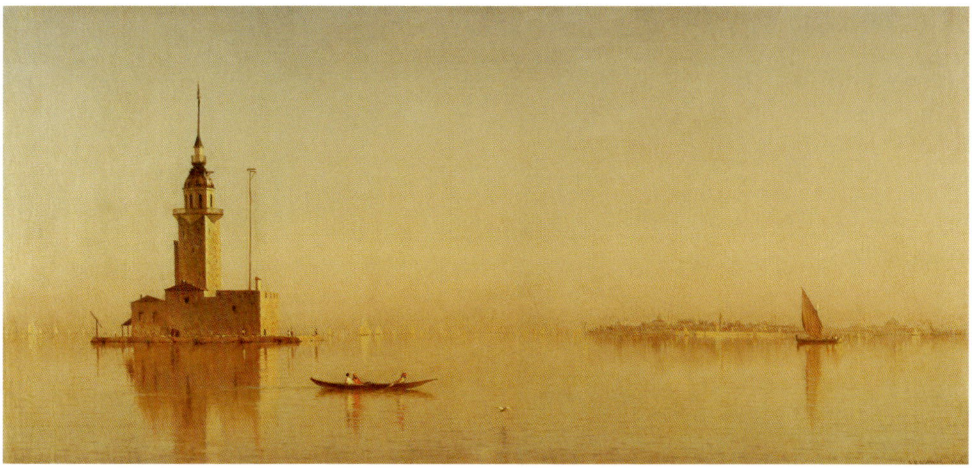

Hand-colored quarter-plate tintype, $3\frac{15}{16} \times 2\frac{7}{16}$ in. (10 x 6.2 cm). Fogg Museum, Gift of Dr. Andrew S. Dibner, P2003.131.12.

Untitled
American
c. 1870–95

Tintypes, like daguerrotypes before them, were unique photographs produced on metal supports. They required significantly less expensive materials than daguerrotypes, however, and were one of the cheapest forms of photographic portraiture in the second half of the nineteenth century. They were frequently produced by itinerant portraitists rather than commercial studios, thus making individual and family portraits accessible to those unable to afford more costly processes. While inexpensive and portable, some tintypes also evidence great care: This well-preserved example reveals sensitivity in rendering the subject's comportment before the camera and skill in the subtle retouching of her cheeks. This picture is one of a large collection of tintypes from before the Civil War to after the turn of the twentieth century assembled by Dr. Andrew Dibner and donated to the Fogg in 2003. BF

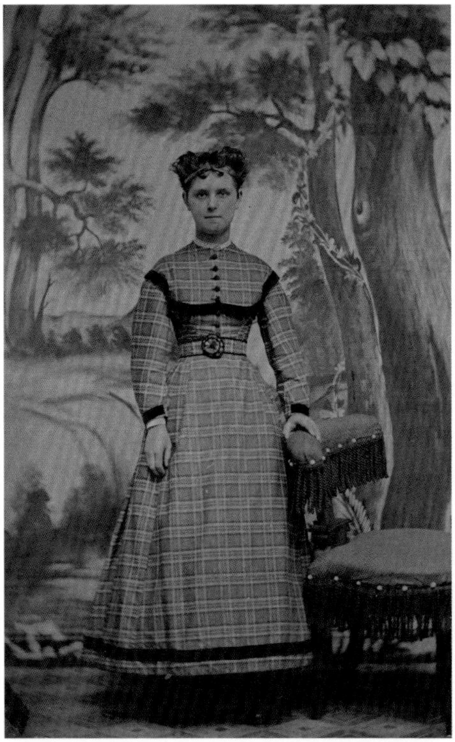

165 Albumen silver print; image: 7 7/8 x 10 13/16 in. (20 x 27.4 cm). Fogg Museum, On deposit from the Carpenter Center for the Visual Arts, Transfer from the Museum of Comparative Zoology Library, Gift of the U.S. War Department, 1877, 2.2002.1085.

Timothy O'Sullivan
American, 1840–1882
Historic Spanish Record of the Conquest. South Side of Inscription Rock, N.M. No. 3, 1873

Timothy O'Sullivan produced photographs of the American West as a member of the Army Corps of Engineers surveys led by Clarence King and Lt. George M. Wheeler between 1867 and 1874. Working alongside teams of scientists and cartographers in this post-Civil War effort to map national territory and resources, O'Sullivan documented the surveys' activities but also aimed to make photography an instrument of measurement comparable with other instruments used in the survey. This photograph, taken in New Mexico during the 1873 Wheeler survey, records the content and scale of an inscription by early Spanish explorers; it also asserts photography's ability to convey the factual and quantitative information found in the inscription and yardstick. As twentieth-century photographers discovered O'Sullivan's work, they began to evaluate it by modernist aesthetic standards, and his scientific images entered artistic and museum discourses. BF

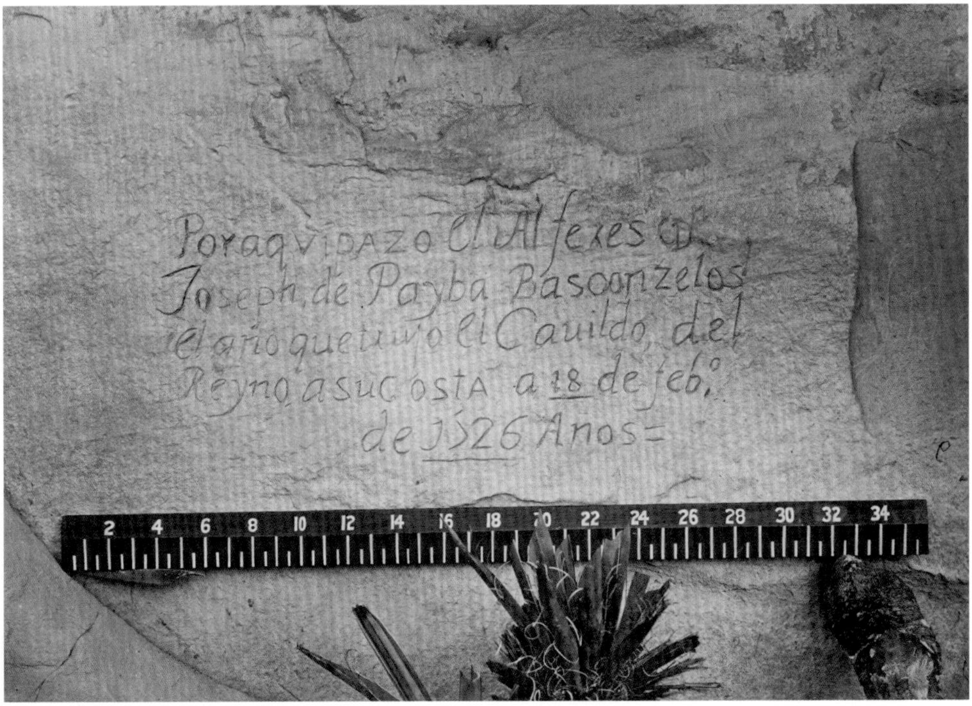

Oil on canvas, 18 x 23 5/8 in. (45.7 x 60 cm). Fogg Museum, Bequest from the Collection of Maurice Wertheim, Class of 1906, 1951.47.

Edgar Degas French, 1834–1917 The Rehearsal c. 1873–78

One of Degas's earliest paintings of ballet dancers, this work was initially exhibited at the Fogg Museum in 1911, during the artist's first solo exhibition at a museum. Degas reworked this composition several times, and evidence of his changes can be seen beneath the first layer of paint—in the repositioning of the violinist's right leg, for example. Degas was allowed to circulate freely to observe the ballet classes and backstage activities. He would then paint the rituals of the performances from memory back in his studio. / This is the only painting from the 1911 exhibition in the museum's collection. ER

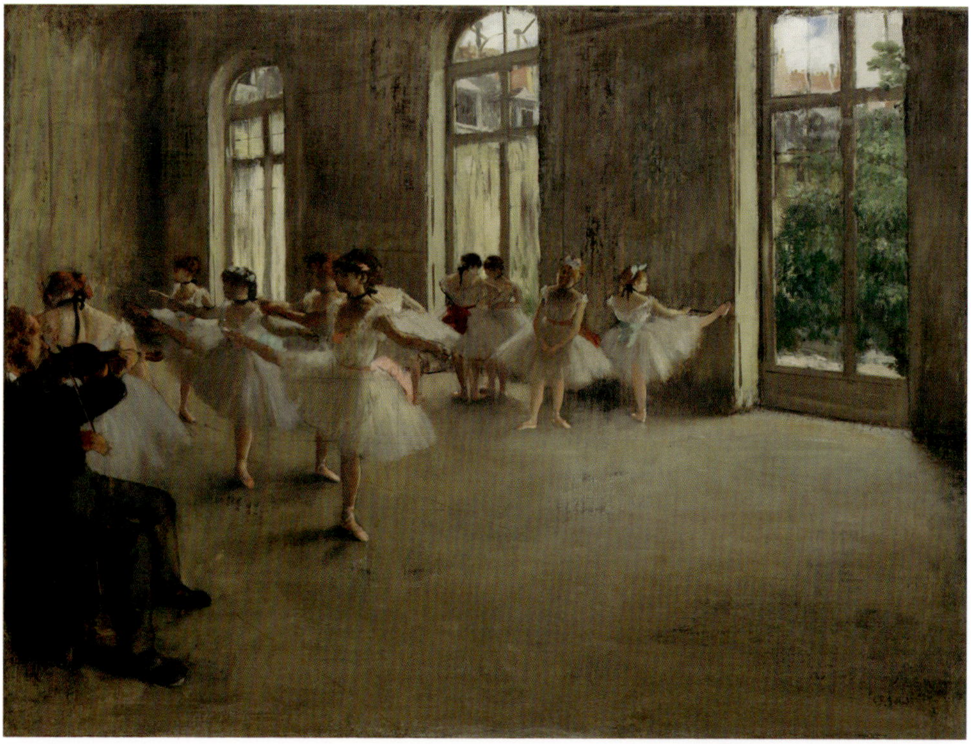

167 Charcoal and red-brown pastel on cream wove paper, 30 3/4 x 22 7/8 in. (78.1 x 58.1 cm). Fogg Museum, Partial and promised gift of Emily Rauh Pulitzer in honor of James Cuno, 2002.303.

Edgar Degas
French, 1834–1917
Dancers, Nude Study
1899

This drawing, conceived as part of a group of drawings and pastels showing nude or clothed dancers arranged in different ways, provides insight into the complex and innovative working practice that characterizes the late oeuvre of Edgar Degas. When he worked in series, he repeated compositions with subtle changes, which allowed him to research his subjects and "correct" himself. The art dealer Ambroise Vollard, who once owned this drawing, explained that Degas's perfectionism lay at the base of his persistent repetition of motifs. This drawing recalls the observation of art historian Eugenia Parry Janis: "The arrangement of five ballet girls adjusting their clothing or scratching has become a set of angles and a pattern of linear and tonal oppositions." WL

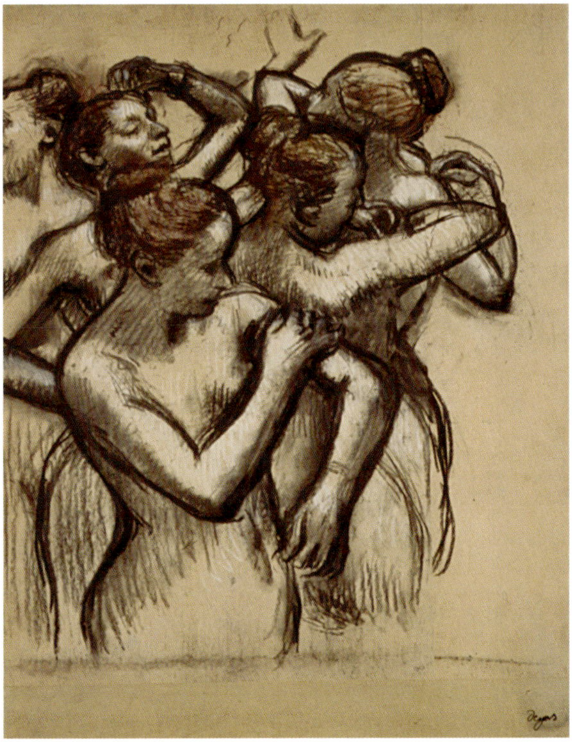

Oil on canvas, 21 1/4 x 17 3/4 in. (54 x 45.1 cm). Fogg Museum, Bequest of Grenville L. Winthrop, 1943.150.

John Singer Sargent
American, 1856–1925
The Breakfast Table
1883–84

John Singer Sargent's extraordinary, intimate painting *The Breakfast Table* depicts the artist's sister Violet reading at a dining table in Nice, where his family was living in a rented house. With quick brushwork, he renders elegant household objects and decorations, including a Japanese print in the background, paintings, silver service, table linens, and a vase of roses, all featured within a rich, shadowed interior. Here, Sargent captures both the look of a room and the quiet thoughtfulness of his younger sister. / Sargent was one of Grenville L. Winthrop's favorite American painters, and the Winthrop gifts between 1939 and 1942 and bequest of 1943 brought to the Fogg ten oil paintings, eleven watercolors, and forty-four drawings by this outstanding expatriate artist. FW

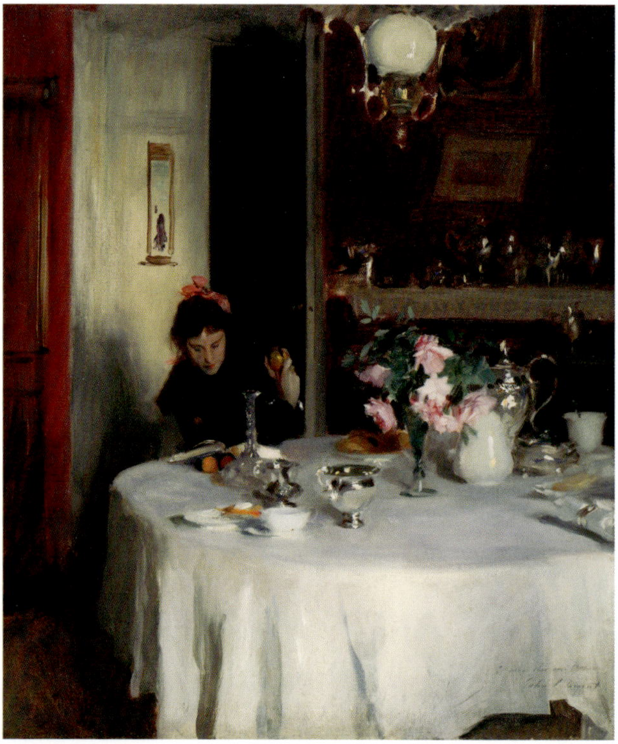

Oil on canvas, $23^{1}/_{2}$ x $19^{1}/_{2}$ in. (59.7 x 49.5 cm). Fogg Museum, Gift in part of Mrs. John Whiteman (Alice Kurtz); purchase in part with funds contributed by friends of John Coolidge, Director, 1948–1968, 1969.1.

Thomas Eakins
American, 1844–1916
Miss Alice Kurtz
1903

In 1903, William B. Kurtz, a Philadelphia banker, commissioned Thomas Eakins to paint this portrait of his daughter, Alice. Kurtz had been a penmanship student of Benjamin Eakins, the artist's father. Thomas Eakins believed in unflinching honesty and truthfulness in all of his work, whether anatomical or perspective studies, views of rowers on the Schuylkill River, or portraits. Unlike many of his contemporaries who idealized their female subjects, he depicted women realistically and often referred to their intellectual, musical, or athletic prowess and to their vulnerability. The Kurtz family objected to this portrayal of Alice—specifically, to her muscular shoulder line, sharply delineated bones and tendons, and sunburnt face, all of which reference Alice's athleticism and her love of outdoor tennis. FW

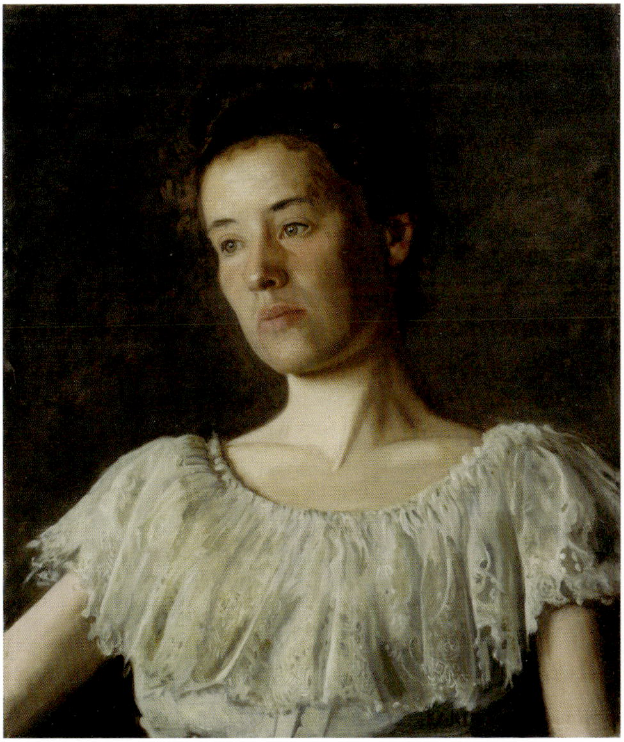

Oil on canvas, 24 x 19 11/16 in. (61 x 50 cm). Fogg Museum, Bequest from the Collection of Maurice Wertheim, Class of 1906, 1951.65.

Vincent van Gogh
Dutch, 1853–1890
Self-Portrait Dedicated to Paul Gauguin
1888

One of five self-portraits that van Gogh completed during his residence in Arles (1888–89), this painting was part of a portrait exchange between van Gogh, Paul Gauguin, and Émile Bernard. The inscription along the top of the canvas reads, "A mon ami Paul Gauguin." In this self-portrait, van Gogh deliberately transformed and exaggerated his own features; he wrote to Gauguin that he wanted to convey the impression of a simple Buddhist monk. Because van Gogh sent the work to Gauguin before the paint had dried, the portrait was slightly damaged during transport and Gauguin had to make some small restorations to repair it. In the collection of the Neue Staatsgalerie in Munich since 1919, this painting, denounced by the Nazis as "degenerate" and purged from the museum's holdings, was sold at auction in Switzerland in 1939. ER

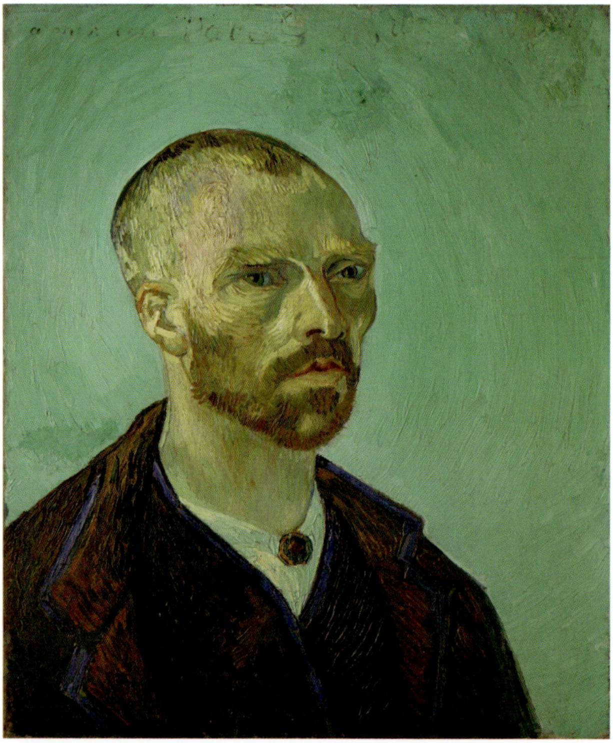

171 Brown ink over graphite on white wove paper, 19 7/16 x 14 15/16 in. (49.4 x 38 cm). Fogg Museum, Bequest of Grenville L. Winthrop, 1943.515.

Vincent van Gogh
Dutch, 1853–1890
Peasant of the Camargue
1888

"You are shortly to make the acquaintance of Master Patience Escalier, a sort of 'man with a hoe,' formerly cowherd of the Camargue," Vincent van Gogh wrote to his brother Theo on August 11, 1888. That summer in Arles, the artist focused on drawing figures with a reed pen; the most ambitious drawings were executed on heavy paper and sent to Theo. The variety of the vigorous marks van Gogh coaxed from the reed pen makes his technique profoundly original. Indeed, this portrait is one of the most poignant examples of van Gogh's virtuosity as a draftsman. WL

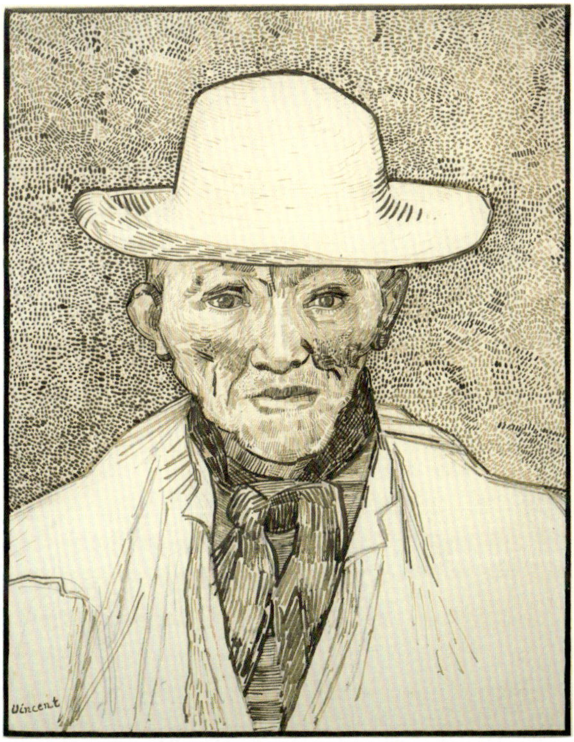

Black and gray ink and red and green watercolor on cream wove paper, 11 1/4 x 7 1/16 in. (28.6 x 18 cm). Fogg Museum, Bequest of Grenville L. Winthrop, 1943.656.

Aubrey Beardsley
British, 1872–1898
Isolde
1895

Aubrey Beardsley, who said he would go anywhere to hear Richard Wagner's music "decently rendered," was enchanted with the composer's work. He owned copies of books about and by Wagner, including the libretto for *Tristan and Isolde*. Beardsley's drawings like *Isolde*, exemplifying the Art Nouveau movement, greatly influenced the art of illustration and page design. On an almost flat background consisting of a red curtain and the white of the paper, the figure of Isolde stands out like an ornamental gem. With two hands she brings a chalice to her mouth, convinced it contains poison, although it actually holds a love potion. WL

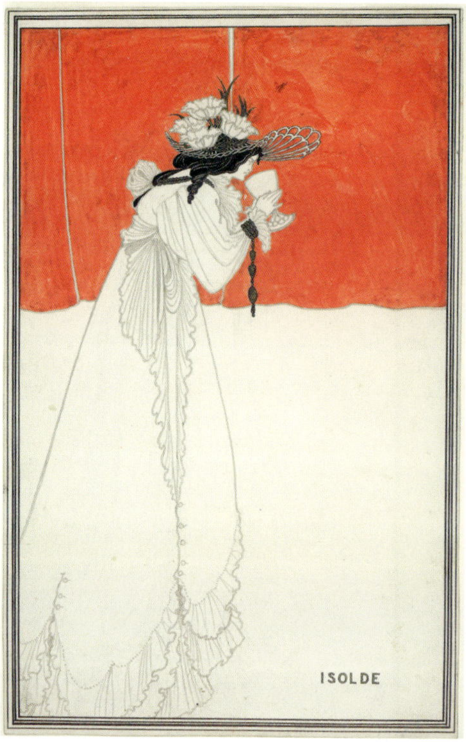

 Color lithograph, 20 3/8 x 15 3/4 in. (51.7 x 40 cm). Fogg Museum, Program for Harvard College Fund, M13499.

Henri de Toulouse-Lautrec
French, 1864–1901
The Seated Clowness

From the portfolio *Elles*

1896

The first plate of Toulouse-Lautrec's famous portfolio of the daily life of prostitutes, *Elles*, reveals the redoubtable clowness Cha-u-Kao in a moment of distracted repose. Toulouse-Lautrec often depicted this distinctive model, dancer, and circus acrobat, although he never showed her performing as a clown. She is always costumed in her black leggings; off-kilter, beribboned white topknot; and enormous feathery yellow collar. Hardly humorous, these trappings become a kind of battle armor. Even in an inactive moment, Cha-u-Kao's posture remains guardedly provocative—particularly the placement of her hands between her wide-open legs. The coy anonymity of the departing masked figures in the background reinforces the bluntness of the clowness's gaze as it targets her next potential client—the viewer. SKS

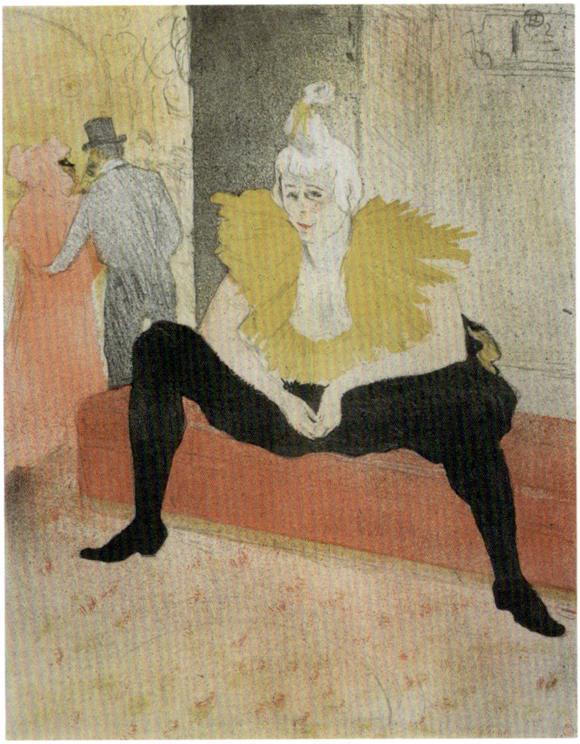

Oil and mixed media on canvas, 72 13/16 x 53 5/8 in. (185 x 136.2 cm). Fogg Museum, Bequest of Grenville L. Winthrop, 1943.262.

Gustave Moreau
French, 1826–1898
The Infant Moses
c. 1876–78

In this spectacular depiction of a biblical story, Moreau has filled the canvas with symbolic and allegorical features. The fantastical landscape and dramatic light rays emanating from the child's temples announce the painter's inventive interpretation of the early days of Moses's life. Moreau considered several old master paintings as sources for this composition, but he chose Pierre-Paul Prud'hon's portrait of Napoleon's son, *The King of Rome Sleeping* (1811), as his inspiration for the baby Moses. He even made a wax study of the child before completing the painting, which was a rare practice for this artist. ER

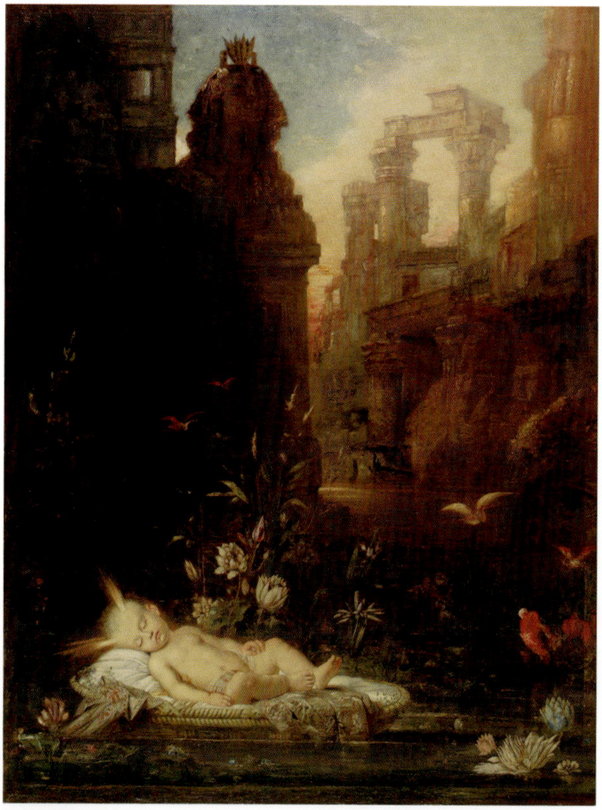

 Oil on canvas, 30 x $32^7/_8$ in. (76.2 x 83.5 cm). Busch-Reisinger Museum, Gift of Hans H. A. Meyn, BR53.60.

Lovis Corinth
German, 1858–1925
Salomé
1899

Depictions of the biblical seductress Salomé, whose erotic dance enticed King Herod to accede to her demand for the head of John the Baptist, captured the imaginations of late-nineteenth-century artists and intellectuals in Europe, and the theme was used repeatedly around the turn of the twentieth century, particularly after the 1893 publication of Oscar Wilde's play *Salomé*. Lovis Corinth's rendering of Salomé at the moment of the presentation of John the Baptist's head is unusually vivid. While many artists present an isolated dancing figure, thus casting Salomé as an embodiment of the femme fatale, Corinth composed a more comprehensive scene. Its emphasis on the result of the fatal dance and Salomé's grotesque gesture of opening her victim's eye led critics of the day to charge that Corinth's depiction was more perverse than those of his contemporaries. SK2 & EMR

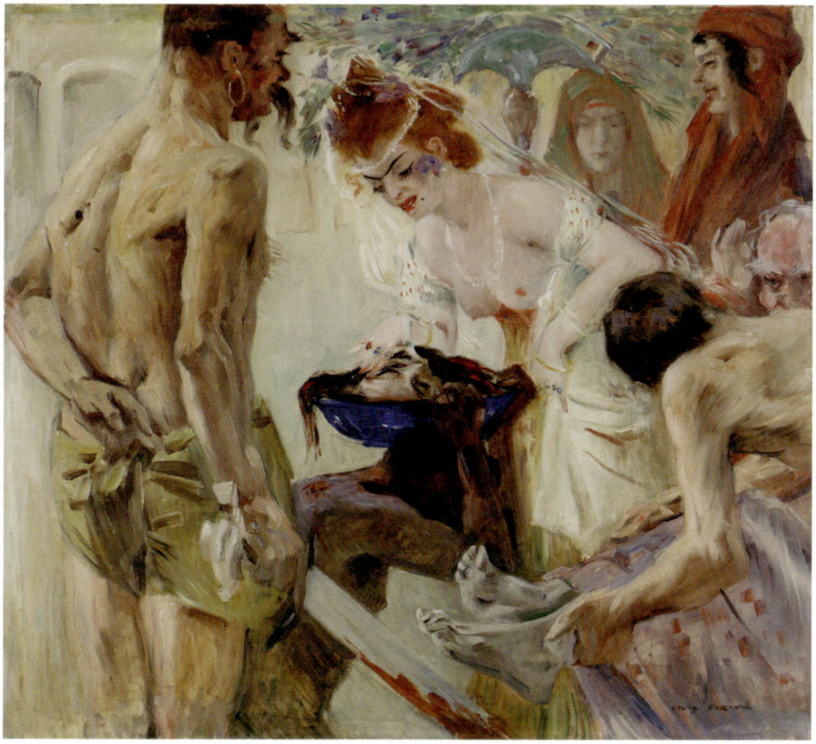

Drypoint, 5 x 5 in. (12.7 x 12.7 cm). Fogg Museum, Gift of Marjorie B. and Martin Cohn in honor of Emily Rauh Pulitzer, M26274.

Edgar Degas
French, 1834–1917
Leaving the Bath
1879–80

Degas's intimate images of bathers revived an artistic subject that had historically been legitimated through the depiction of biblical and mythological figures. By the late nineteenth century, such narrative legitimation was no longer necessary. The technical experimentation Degas lavished on this particular intaglio image is astounding in its masterful range of textures and contrasts. An obsessive twenty-two states survive bearing subtly varying drypoint lines, augmented with aquatint shading in later states. This print is the unique remaining impression of the fifth state. It was once owned by Alexis Roualt, a close friend of Degas, at whose home the artist began work on the plate for the print. SKS

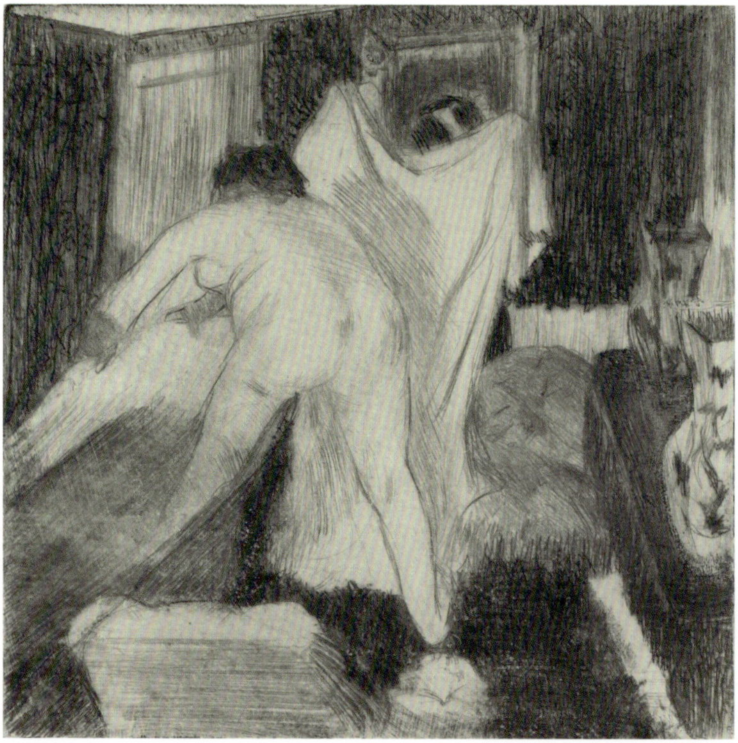

177 Bronze with black patina, $32\frac{11}{16} \times 33\frac{7}{16} \times 15\frac{11}{16}$ in. (83 x 85 x 39.8 cm). Fogg Museum, The Lois Orswell Collection, 1998.307.

Auguste Rodin
French, 1840–1917
Iris, Messenger of the Gods
c. 1890–91

Originally conceived as part of a monument to novelist Victor Hugo, *Iris* was intended to be the personification of Glory that hovered above the French writer. Rodin later returned to studies for this monument and elaborated larger, independent sculptures, as with *Iris*. Here Rodin does not depend on traditional goddess iconography (wings, veils, weapons) but instead depicts a state of forceful, kinetic energy. He omits the figure's head and left arm in order to focus on the tension of the stretched limbs, creating a state of equilibrium in the strong, angular silhouette. The frank modeling of the figure's genitals is emphasized by the revealing pose; during the 1890s this piece was one of the most controversial works to be found in Rodin's studio. EL

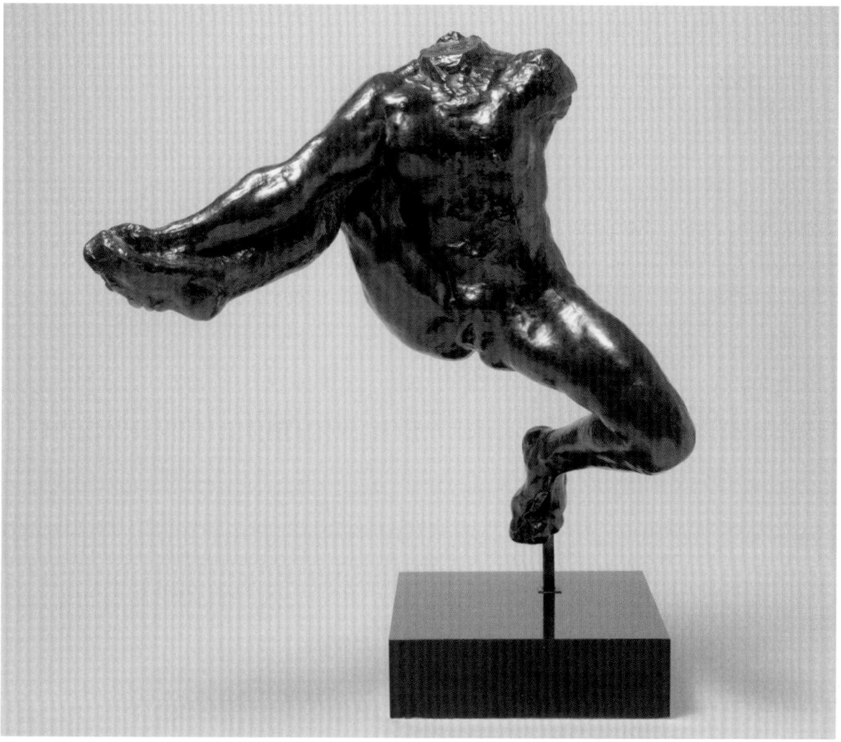

Drypoint, softground etching, and aquatint; 5 states (4, 9, 12, 14, 17) of 17, 12 9/16 to 12 11/16 x 9 5/8 to 9 13/16 in. (31.9 to 32.2 x 24.4 to 25 cm). Fogg Museum, Gift of Dr. Ernest G. Stillman, Class of 1907, by exchange, 2006.24.1, .2, .4, .7, .8.

Mary Cassatt
American, 1844–1926
The Bath
1890–91

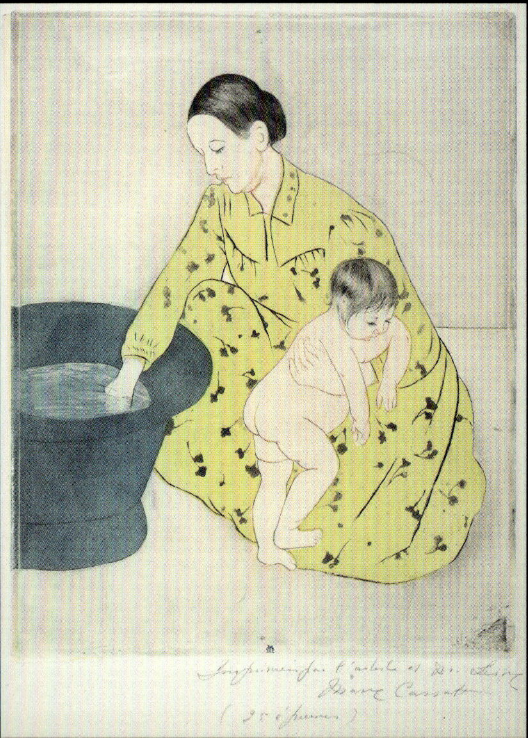

The Pennsylvania-born Cassatt lived most of her life in Paris, where she became the only American to exhibit with the impressionists. Her favorite subjects were mothers with children and women engaged in intellectual, social, and cultural activities. In 1890, Cassatt viewed an exhibition of Japanese woodblock prints at the École des Beaux-Arts, which inspired her to explore color printmaking. With strong graphic lines, flat shapes, bold colors, and decorative patterns intentionally echoing the woodcuts, *The Bath* reflects the influence of Japanese design on her work. / In renderings of this print, Cassatt experimented extensively with drypoint, color etching, and aquatint, all complicated technical processes that require separate plates for the lines and the tonal areas. She also investigated the effects of varying the paper, ink, and density of plate tone. Four proofs from Cassatt's seventeen different states appear here with the final composition. These impressions come from the collection she maintained in her studio until her death. SKS & FW

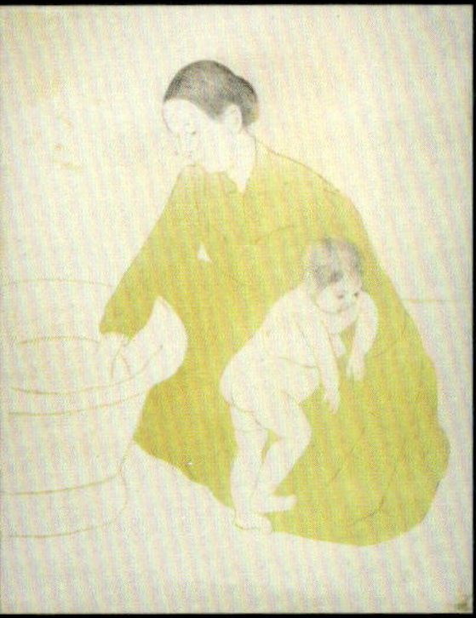
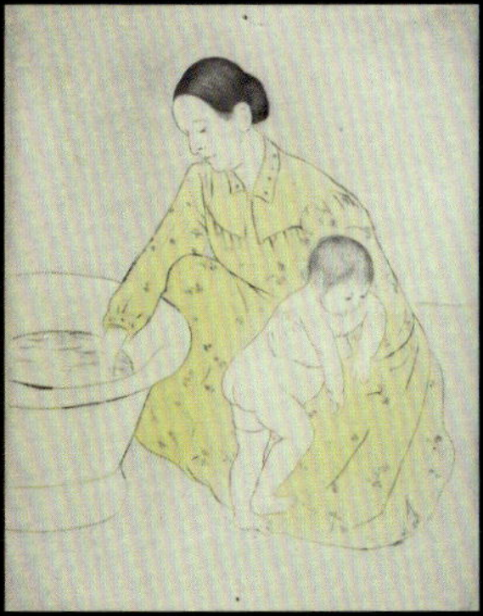
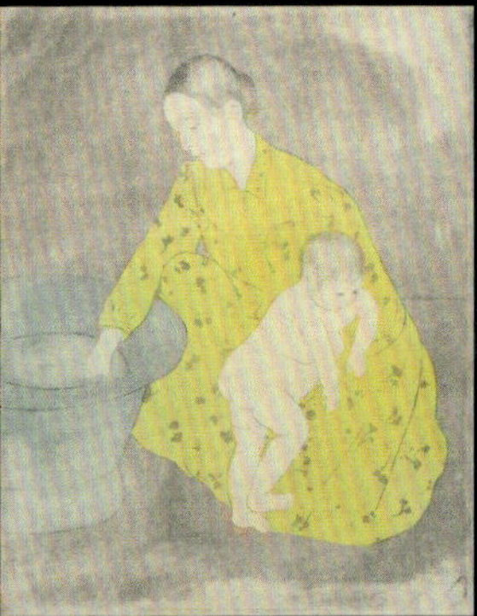
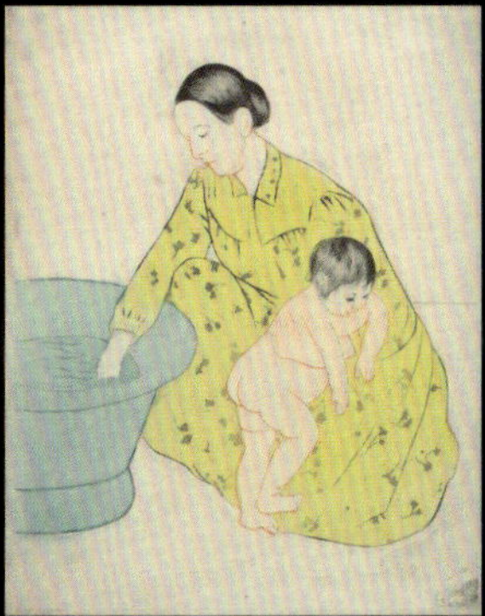

Hand-colored lithograph, 18 7/16 x 13 9/16 in. (46.8 x 34.4 cm). Fogg Museum, Purchase through the generosity of Lynn and Philip A. Straus, Class of 1937, M20224.

Edvard Munch
Norwegian, 1863–1944
Attraction I

From the portfolio *The Mirror*

1896

An unsettling blue laced with melancholy desire and northern half-light permeates this black-and-white lithograph, which the Norwegian symbolist Edvard Munch additionally enhanced with hand coloring. His beloved Oslo fjord and its dark cluster of linden trees radiate imminent, Edenic danger. The chalk-white tendrils of the woman's hair ensnare her lover in greedy lines scratched deep into the lithographic stone. Munch trimmed this impression, accentuating the arch above the starry sky, pasted it onto a cardboard backing, and signed his name underneath. The work appeared in an 1897 exhibition of *The Mirror*, an unfinished print portfolio that also included a lithographic version of *The Scream*. SKS

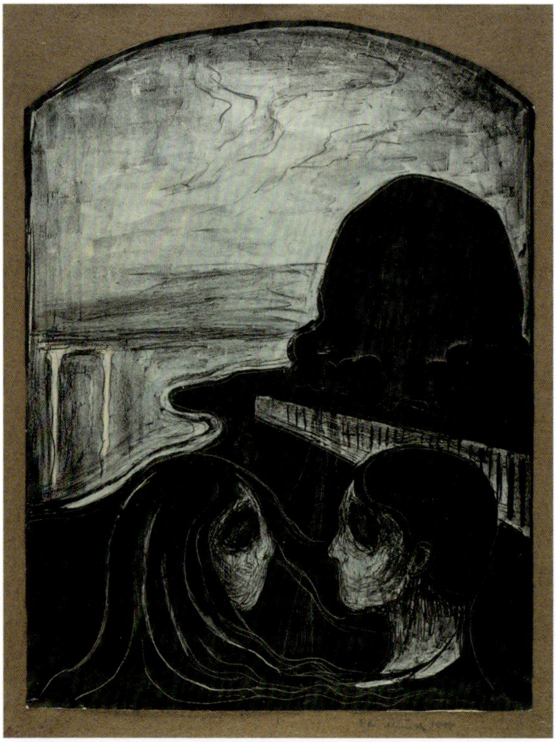

181 Oil on canvas, 44 1/4 x 38 3/8 in. (112.4 x 97.5 cm). Fogg Museum, Bequest from the Collection of Maurice Wertheim, Class of 1906, 1951.57.

Pablo Picasso
Spanish, 1881–1973
Mother and Child
c. 1901

One of the earliest and largest paintings from Picasso's Blue Period, *Mother and Child* comments on the social injustice of poverty. Artistically, Picasso was influenced by the elongated figures of El Greco and Catalan Gothic sculpture. Yet it was the people he saw on the streets of Barcelona and the prostitutes with venereal diseases in the Saint-Lazare hospital-prison in Paris who perhaps had a more profound effect on him. / Interestingly, this image was painted on a canvas that originally featured a portrait of the artist's friend Max Jacob. The impastoed contours of Jacob's head are still visible to the left of the mother's head. DC & MB

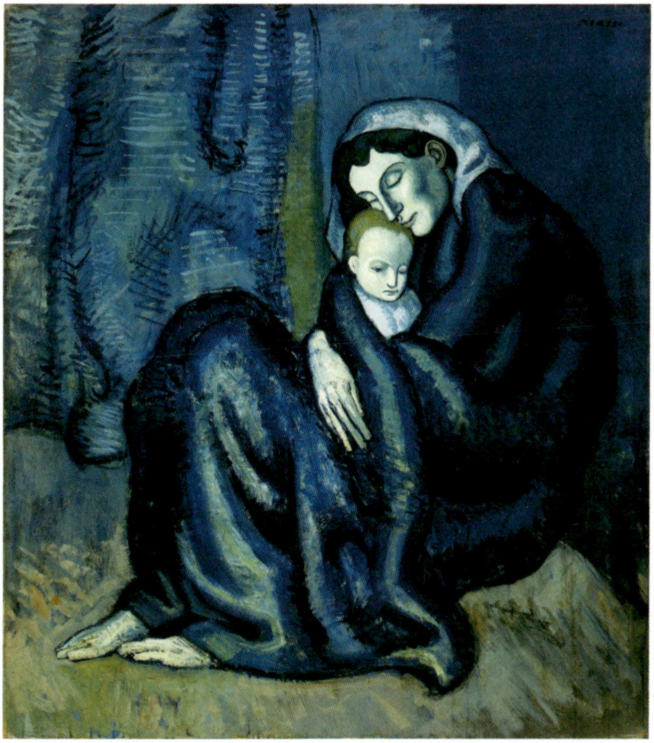

Bronze, h. 23 3/8 in. (59.4 cm). Fogg Museum, Bequest of Frances Leventritt in honor and in memory of M. Victor Leventritt, Harvard Class of 1935, 2005.174.

Henri Matisse
French, 1869–1954
Madeleine I
1901

Throughout his career, Henri Matisse turned to sculpture to refresh and reinvigorate his painting, and he has been increasingly recognized as a great sculptor in his own right. This famous bronze, one of his earliest, is a landmark in his artistic development: Its radical *contrapposto* led him to a lifelong exploration of the expressive possibilities of the female nude. Unlike its weighty male counterpart, *Le Serf* (1953.42, also in the Fogg collection), *Madeleine I* is all life and movement. Its twisting limbs keep the viewer circling the work, unable to find a frontal view or any stable vantage point. HC

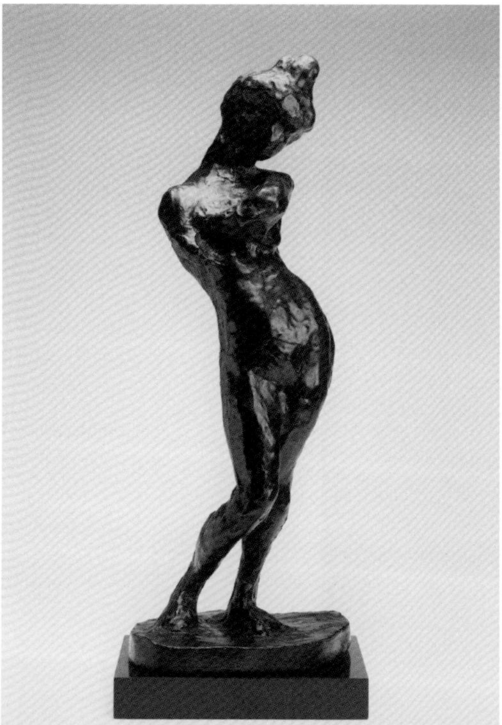

183 / Woodcut, 18 9/16 x 15 1/16 in. (47.1 x 38.3 cm). Fogg Museum, Francis H. Burr Memorial and Alpheus Hyatt Funds, M13022.

Henri Matisse
French, 1869–1954
The Large Woodcut Nude
1906

Henri Matisse may be best remembered for the brashly unprecedented color relationships of his fauve paintings and the bright cut-out shapes of the *Jazz pochoir* stencils, but he also completed four important black-and-white woodcuts around 1906–7. This monumental nude was the largest. Although he quickly abandoned the medium, Matisse intimately grasped its expressive capabilities, flattening his model into contorted planes that echo the blaze of background lines. A similar aesthetic in monochrome printmaking spanned his career, and he produced over eight hundred designs in monotype, drypoint, etching, lithography, and linocut. SKS

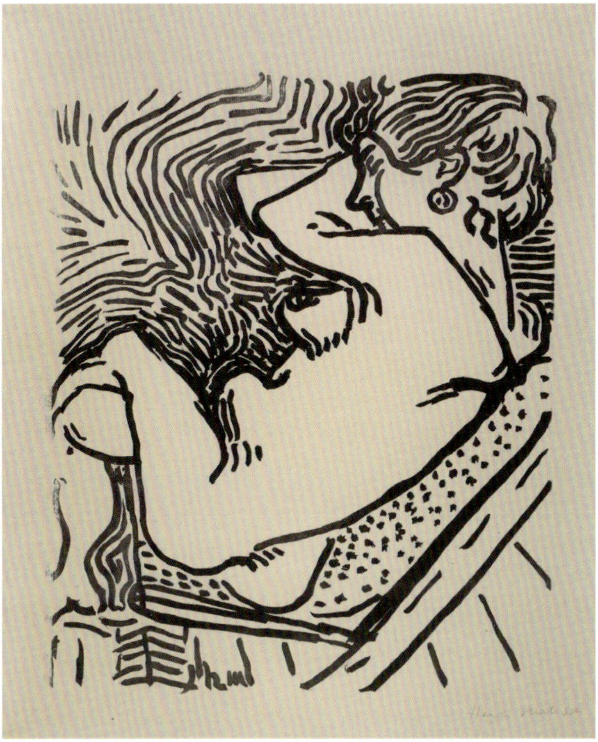

Charcoal on blue-green wove paper, 24 7/8 x 19 in. (63.2 x 48.3 cm). Fogg Museum, Gift of Mrs. Francis Ormond, 1937.9.23.

John Singer Sargent
American, 1856–1925
Standing Male Nude
c. 1890–1915

This drawing is from an album of thirty charcoal studies of male figures by John Singer Sargent. The works were probably made for the artist's pleasure in drawing unabashed, dramatically posed male models, although he may have used them for reference in other works. Here Sargent magnificently conjures a strong sense of space; the twist of the right shoulder toward us, the right arm overlapping the pole, and the diagonal hatchings of the background contrasted with the opposing diagonal line of the shoulders convey depth within the image. The figure's control of space is as powerful as in some of Sargent's famous pictures of costumed females. But the most virtuoso element is Sargent's mastery of the charcoal. His manipulation of the medium displays a wide range of its effects, varying from rich velvety blacks to a subtle range of grays. WL

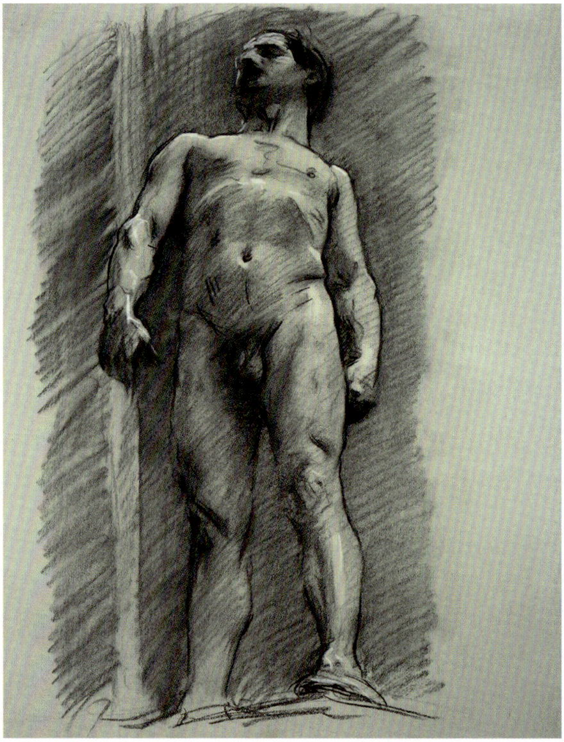

185 Black ink and red gouache on off-white laid paper, $25\frac{1}{8} \times 17\frac{13}{16}$ in. (63.8 x 45.2 cm). Fogg Museum, The Lois Orswell Collection, 1998.234.

Pablo Picasso
Spanish, 1881–1973
Standing Nude Woman
1907

In 1906–7, when Picasso was developing *Les Demoiselles d'Avignon*, he was also exploring the possibilities of rendering figures in space in unconventional ways. Leaving academic practice behind, he experimented with volume and flatness, classical and primitive, masculine and feminine. At that time Picasso was very impressed by sculpture, both by contemporary artists such as Paul Gauguin and by works from other cultures, and during the winter of 1906–7 he made several wooden sculptures that must be seen in relationship to this drawing. The masklike face and the ambiguous anatomy give the figure an inhuman character. A fascinating tension is created by the hatching lines that give the body a tangible three-dimensionality and the red gouache contour that flattens it. WL

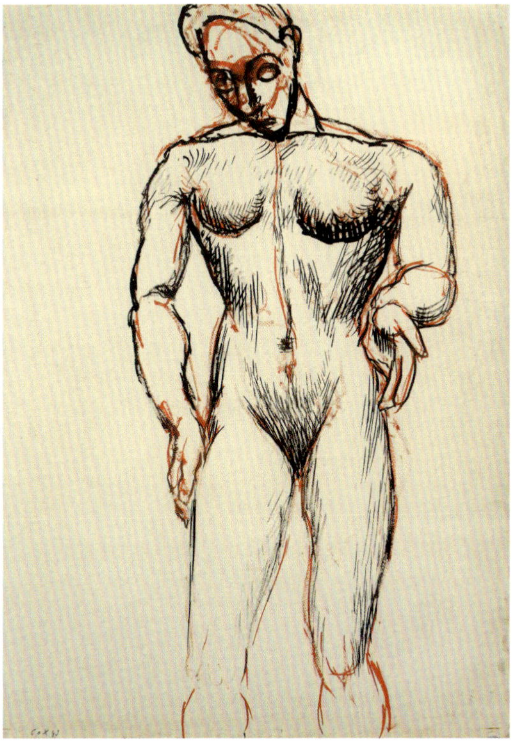

Platinum print; image: 6 1/2 x 4 5/16 in. (16.5 x 11 cm). Fogg Museum, On deposit from the Carpenter Center for the Visual Arts, The Social Museum Collection, 3.2002.357.1.

Frances Benjamin Johnston
American, 1864–1952
Untitled
c. 1900

Harvard professor Francis Greenwood Peabody founded the Social Museum of Harvard University in 1903 as the cornerstone of the new Department of Social Ethics. With an aim to "collect the social experience of the world as material for university teaching," he sought materials documenting solutions to social problems and organized them for comparative study. In his emphasis on rigorous classification and rational comparison, he envisioned the Social Museum serving the social sciences as other museums served fields like anthropology, art history, and natural history. He conceived of these materials as a basis from which to guide changes in industrial and social life. / Photographs formed a substantial portion of the Social Museum collection, reflecting the central role of the medium in the progressive movement. Like many social activists, Peabody understood photographs as incorruptible specimens, as factual records with a special power to persuade. Yet the

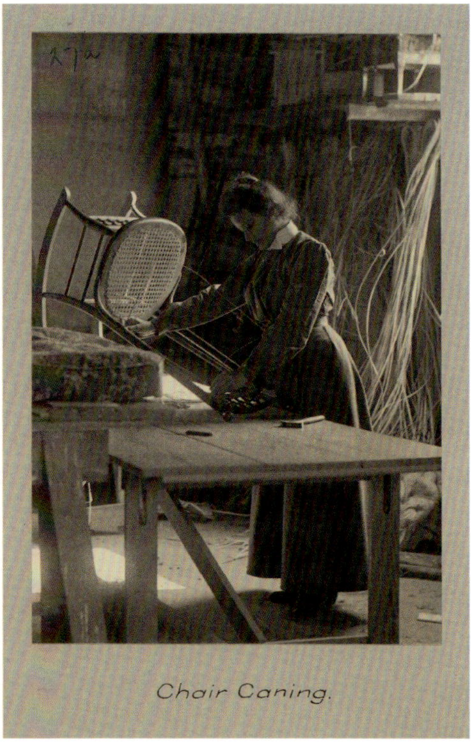
Chair Caning.

Gelatin silver print; image: 14 7/16 x 17 3/16 in. (36.6 x 43.6 cm). Fogg Museum, On deposit from the Carpenter Center for the Visual Arts, The Social Museum Collection, 3.2002.515.

Lewis Wickes Hine
American, 1874–1940
Untitled
From the Pittsburgh Survey
1907

images he collected encompass a variety of formats and approaches and reveal the diverse photographic practices that preceded the codification of a social documentary style. They demonstrate the need for action in some cases and the efficacy of reform efforts in many others. / These prints by photographers Frances Benjamin Johnston and Lewis Wickes Hine illustrate the range of the Social Museum photographs. Johnston's exquisite platinum print was commissioned to document the beneficial effects of training at the Hampton Normal and Agricultural Institute in Virginia. Hine's enlarged gelatin silver print is mounted on an original exhibition board from the 1907 Pittsburgh Survey, a pioneering investigation of workers' living and working conditions. / Nearly 4,500 photographs survive from the original Social Museum Collection, which was rescued by Harvard's Carpenter Center for the Visual Arts in the late 1960s and placed on deposit at the Fogg in 2002. BF

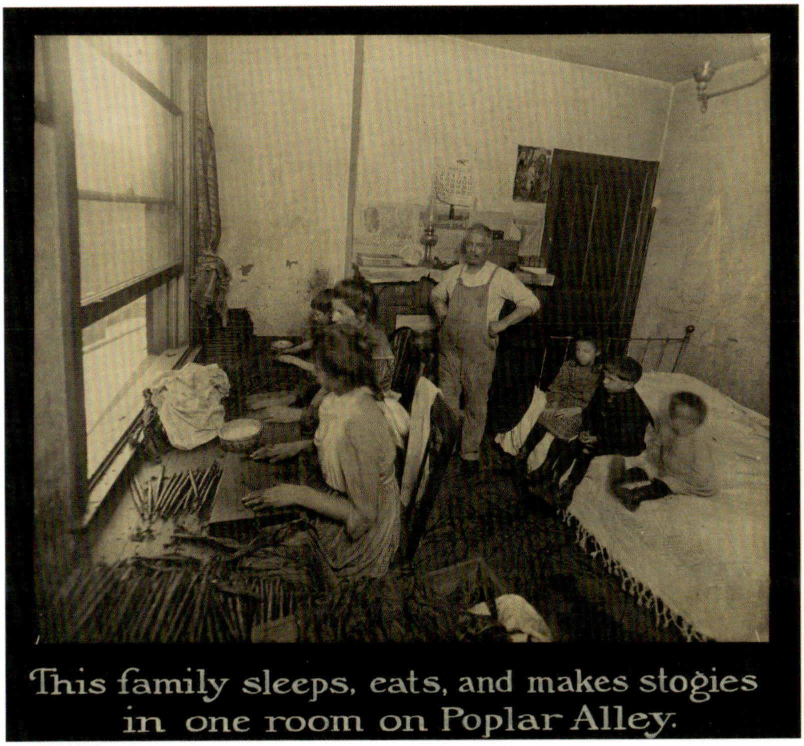

 Oil and casein on canvas, 39 3/4 x 39 3/4 in. (101 x 101 cm). Busch-Reisinger Museum, Gift of Otto Kallir, BR66.4.

Gustav Klimt
Austrian, 1862–1918
Pear Tree
1903, later reworked

Gustav Klimt developed a lush, decorative style that has become synonymous with fin-de-siècle Vienna. Close up, the flickering surface of *Pear Tree* disintegrates into thousands of luminous flecks of paint, evocative of both Byzantine mosaics, which Klimt had seen in Ravenna, Italy, shortly before working on this canvas, and postimpressionist paintings. Emilie Flöge, Klimt's muse and mistress, owned this painting, which allowed him to repaint sections of the canvas later. / Klimt's square canvas borrows the dominant geometric motif of the Vienna Secession, of which he was a founding member. The Secession sought to give modern Vienna a style of its own, freed from the constraints of history and nature. HH

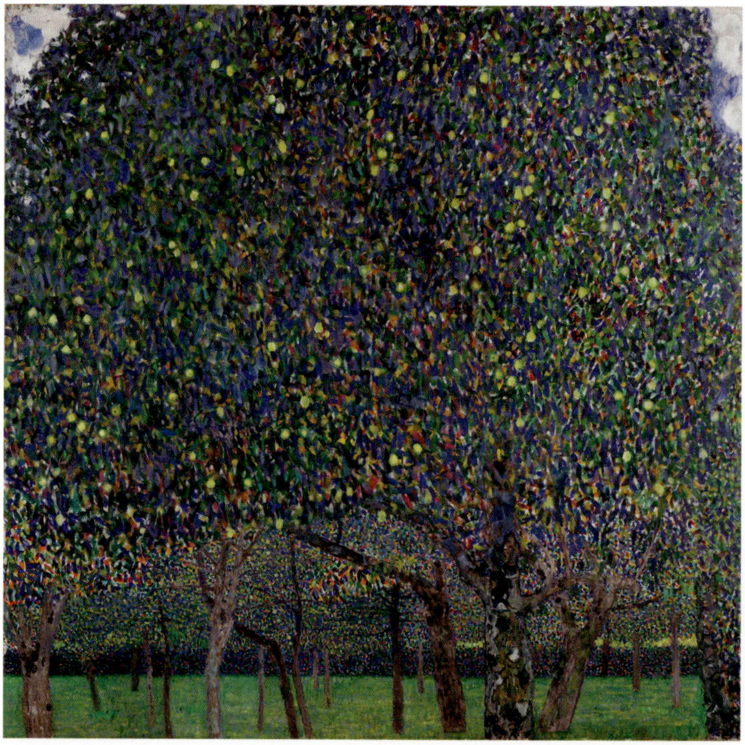

Oil on canvas, 13 x 16 1/8 in. (33 x 41 cm). Fogg Museum, Purchase through the generosity of Emily Rauh Pulitzer, Myron Laskin, George David, Ellen Abbott Gilman Trust, Jessie Lie Farber, Frances H. Burr Memorial Fund and the Director's Discretionary Fund; and through the generosity of Philip and Lynn Straus, Marshall Field, Irvin and Rebekah Taube, John and Jill Walsh, and Richard E. Oldenburg in honor of James Cuno, 2001.117.

Georges Braque
French, 1882–1963
The Bay of Estaque
1908

Following Paul Cézanne's death in 1906 and major shows of his work in Paris, Georges Braque traveled south, following in Cézanne's footsteps. This oil sketch recalls Cézanne's paintings of the same site from the 1880s, but something new is stirring, something that led Matisse to call it (or another work much like it) the first cubist painting. "Braque had come back from the Midi with a landscape of a village by the seashore, seen from above," Matisse recalled in 1951. "There was a large background of sea and sky into which he had continued the village roofs." In other words, Braque used a single sign—a tan triangle—to represent rooftops in the foreground, hills in the background, and ambiguous reflections of both on the sea surface. This act of abbreviation was a key step in cubism's campaign to make painting less like pictures to be looked at and more like a language to be read. HC

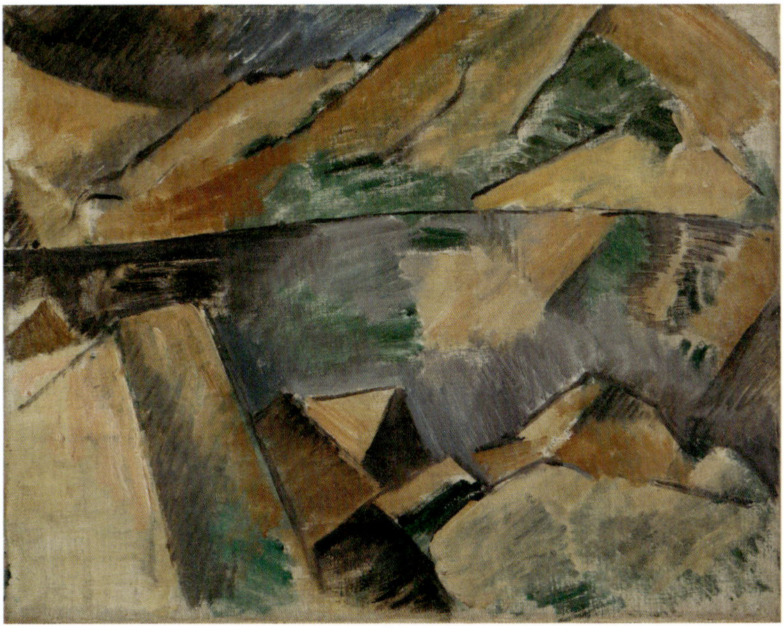

Watercolor over graphite on white wove paper, 9 15/16 x 14 in. (25.3 x 35.6 cm). Fogg Museum, Bequest of Grenville L. Winthrop, 1943.313.

John Singer Sargent
American, 1856–1925
The Grand Canal, Venice
c. 1902

After an initial visit to Venice in 1880, John Singer Sargent returned almost annually from 1902 to 1914, during which time he depicted the city's popular sights with great inventiveness and verve in numerous watercolors, including *The Grand Canal, Venice*. Watercolor proved to be an ideal medium for Sargent in these later views of Venetian canals and buildings: With quick yet fluent brushwork, he illuminated the shifting effects of water and light while also capturing the form of the city's many monuments. This particular watercolor is unusual in its fresh, unfaded condition and its depiction of a broad, recognizable view of the Grand Canal rather than Sargent's more typical fragmentary views of buildings and boats. FW

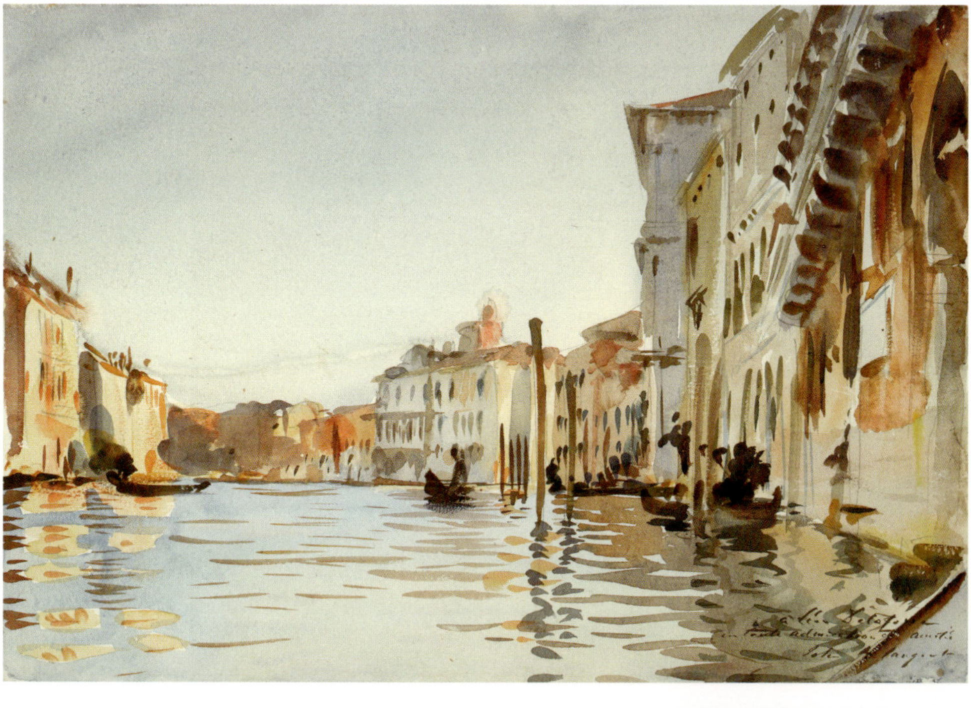

Oil on canvas, $8^{7}/_{16}$ x $13^{5}/_{8}$ in. (21.5 x 34.6 cm). Fogg Museum, Anonymous gift in memory of Eric Schroeder, 1972.12.

Pablo Picasso
Spanish, 1881–1973
The Pomegranate
1911–12

Analytic cubism reached its maximum difficulty in 1911. In these works, careful touches of browns and grays and ambiguously intersecting planes combine with flickering lights and a play of transparency and opacity to produce still lifes, figures, landscapes, or combinations thereof. Here Picasso signifies (more than depicts) such habitués of the café table as a pipe, dice, a glass, a cigarette, bottles, and the title's pomegranate, which seems split between the cluster of seeds at right and the round, crowned fruit at left. At the upper right, *Cafe 3* looms in front of the objects, suggesting a view through a windowpane and helping to compress the space behind it. This may have been the first time that Picasso, following Braque's lead, included letters and numbers in a painting. HC

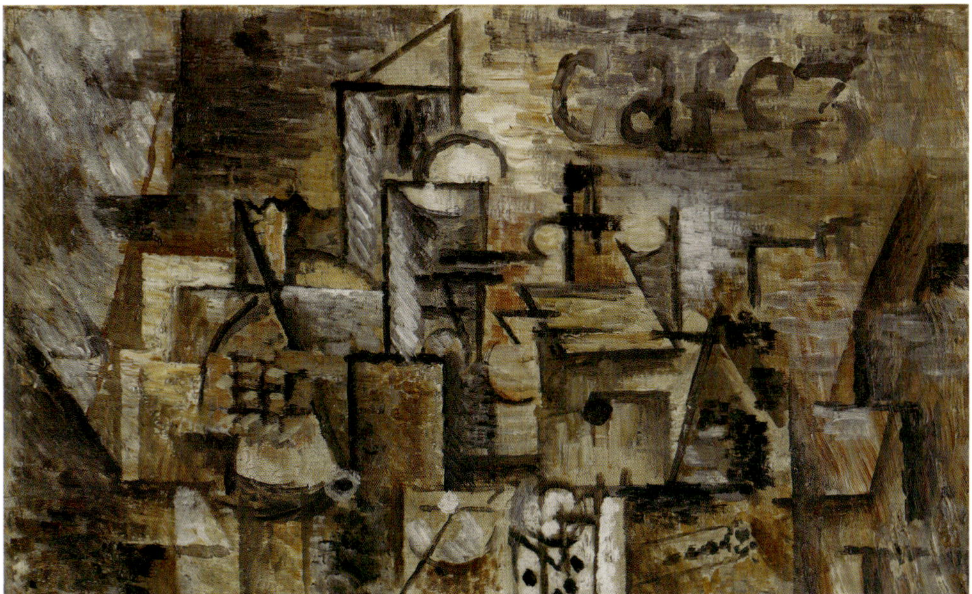

 Autochrome, 4 1/2 x 6 1/2 in. (11.5 x 16.5 cm). Fogg Museum, Richard and Ronay Menschel Fund for the Acquisition of Photographs, P2005.16.

George Henry Seeley
American, 1880–1955
Untitled
c. 1908

Pictorialist photographer George Seeley was a student of Frederick Holland Day and a member of Alfred Stieglitz's Photo-Secession group from 1904 to 1910. Like other photographers of his day, he explored a range of photographic techniques, including the newly introduced autochrome color process. The first commercially viable color process, autochrome used dyed starch grains suspended between layers of glass, and the picture took the form of a transparency best seen when lit from behind. / Pictorialism aligned photography with aesthetic ideas from other media. Here Seeley's subject and formal treatment combine to evoke a symbolist painting. He tightly frames these decorative objects and relates them through color and shadow. The flowers in the vase cast shadows into the bowl and across the tapestry, while the tapestry pattern echoes their form. The palette of reds, greens, and yellows common to the objects and the granularity of the autochrome process unify the image. BF

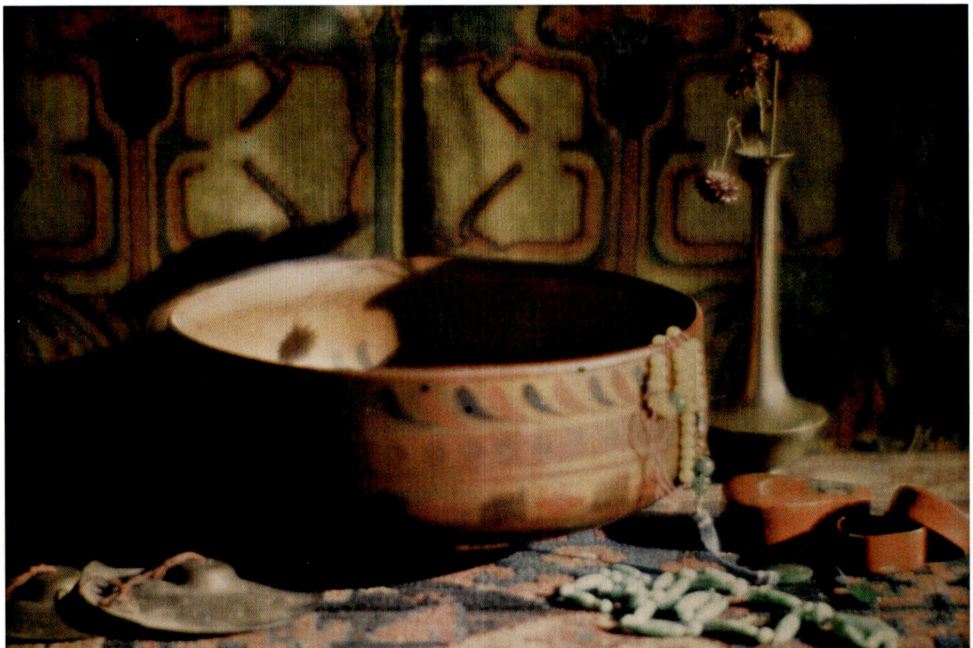

193 Oil on panel, 12 3/4 x 16 in. (32.4 x 40.6 cm). Fogg Museum, Bequest from the Collection of Maurice Wertheim, Class of 1906, 1951.51.

Henri Matisse
French, 1869–1954
Still Life with Apples
1916

In 1916 Matisse finished such major works as *The Moroccans* and *Bathers by a River*. This canvas, although tiny by comparison, has all the drama and tension of its great contemporaries—in the play of sober black and gray against vivid color and the contrast of repeated curves against right angles. The choice of apples and the radical tipping-up of the tabletop recall Cézanne's still lifes, but color is arguably more important here than motif or structure. The cracked surface testifies to Matisse's struggle to find just the right shades of gray, black, and blue, while the acid hues of the apples appear to have been applied as a decisive final touch. HC

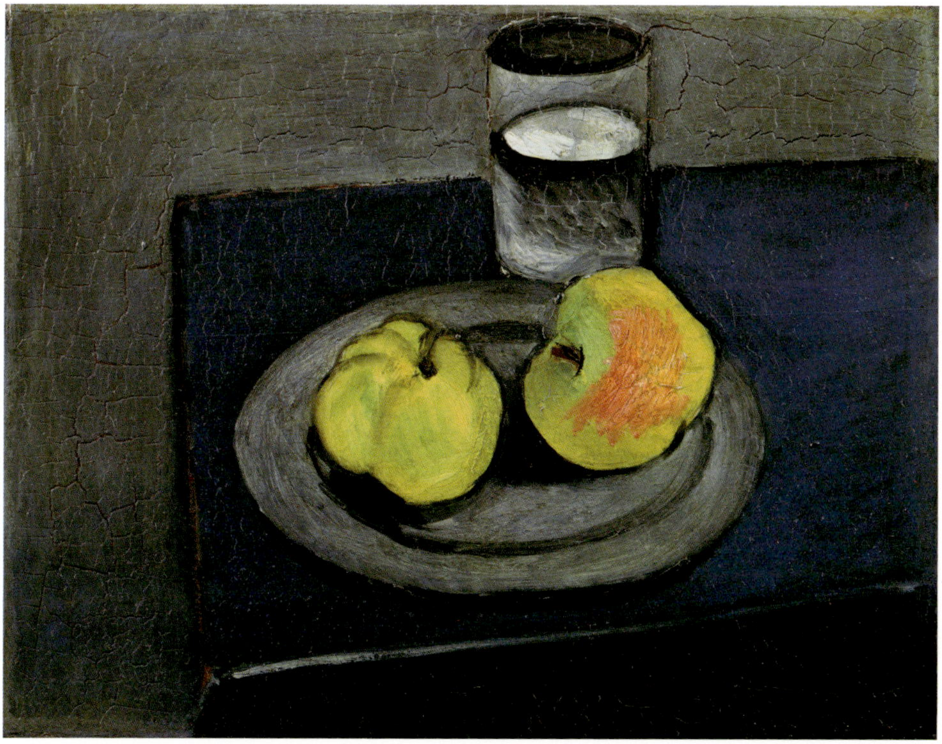

Wood, 65 1/8 x 16 3/4 x 18 1/8 in. (165.4 x 42.6 x 46 cm). Fogg Museum, Gift in part of William A. Coolidge, Joseph H. Hazen Foundation Inc., Mrs. Max Wasserman; purchase in part, Francis H. Burr Memorial and Alpheus Hyatt Funds, 1968.2.A–C.

Constantin Brancusi
Romanian, 1876–1957
Caryatid II
1914, reworked 1926

Reacting against Auguste Rodin's aptitude as a modeler, Constantin Brancusi revived carving as a modern sculptural possibility. He named this work after the classical architectural element of a figure-shaped column, but his decision to use wood reflects his interest in Romanian folk art. References to African tribal art also abound, for example, in the anthropomorphic legs and belly and the frontal presentation of the whole. (The figurative aspect was even more obvious before Brancusi cut down the legs in 1926.) He once used the piece as the base for another sculpture: Unraveling the distinction between a work and its base was one of Brancusi's great legacies to contemporary sculpture and installation. HC

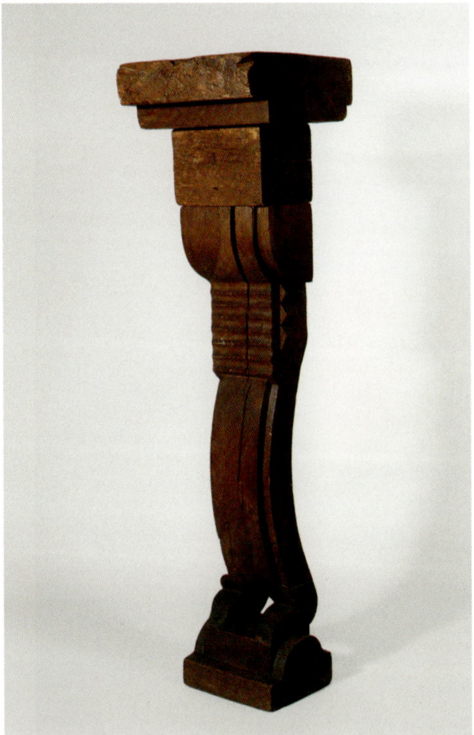

Mahogany, 35 3/4 x 22 x 11 3/8 in. (90.8 x 55.9 x 28.9 cm). Fogg Museum, Gift of Dr. and Mrs. John P. Spiegel, 1956.200.

Elie Nadelman American, 1882–1946 The Pianiste c. 1920–22

Elie Nadelman was already a distinguished artist in Europe before coming to the United States in 1914. An avid collector of folk arts and crafts, he founded the Museum of Folk and Peasant Arts in Riverdale, New York, in 1926 and incorporated elements of folk art into his sculpture. *The Pianiste* balances the severity and simplification of forms with graceful and whimsical details, including the rounded delicate hands of the musician, the bows on the figure's dress and in her hair, and the slight smile on her face. Today Nadelman is considered one of the major American sculptors of the early twentieth century. FW

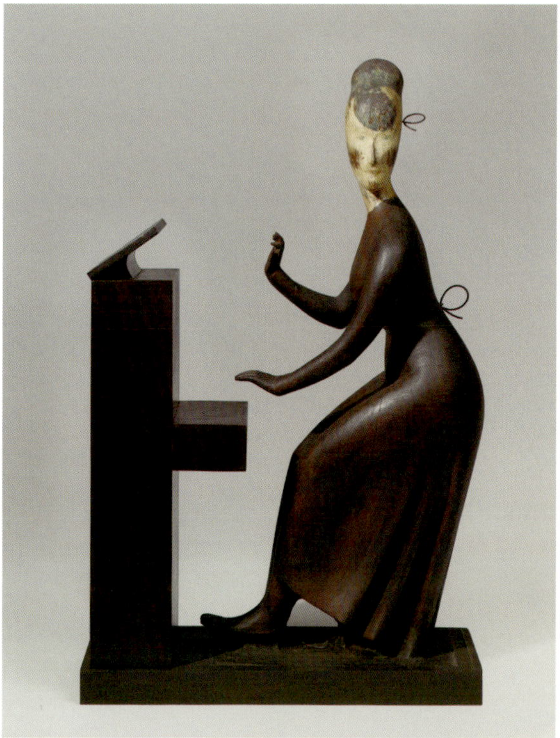

Oil on canvas, 47 5/8 x 72 1/16 in. (121 x 183 cm). Busch-Reisinger Museum, Promised gift from an anonymous donor, 21.1991.

Franz Marc
German, 1880–1916
Grazing Horses IV (The Red Horses)
1911

Throughout his brief career, Franz Marc sought to invent a style of spiritual art for the modern age that would express the unity of the world. He experienced his major breakthrough in 1911 when, with stark simplicity and using complementary colors and animals as symbols, he came to depict creatures that still lived in innocent harmony with nature during an increasingly turbulent time. His masterpiece from that year, the monumental painting *Grazing Horses IV*, can be read as an attempt to unify and balance opposing principles, which he believed could be expressed through the use of color. This is one of the few paintings in which Marc presents complete, unfragmented depictions of his favorite subject, the horse, which he took as his personal symbol and regarded as an expression of power, purity, intelligence, and sensitivity. SK2

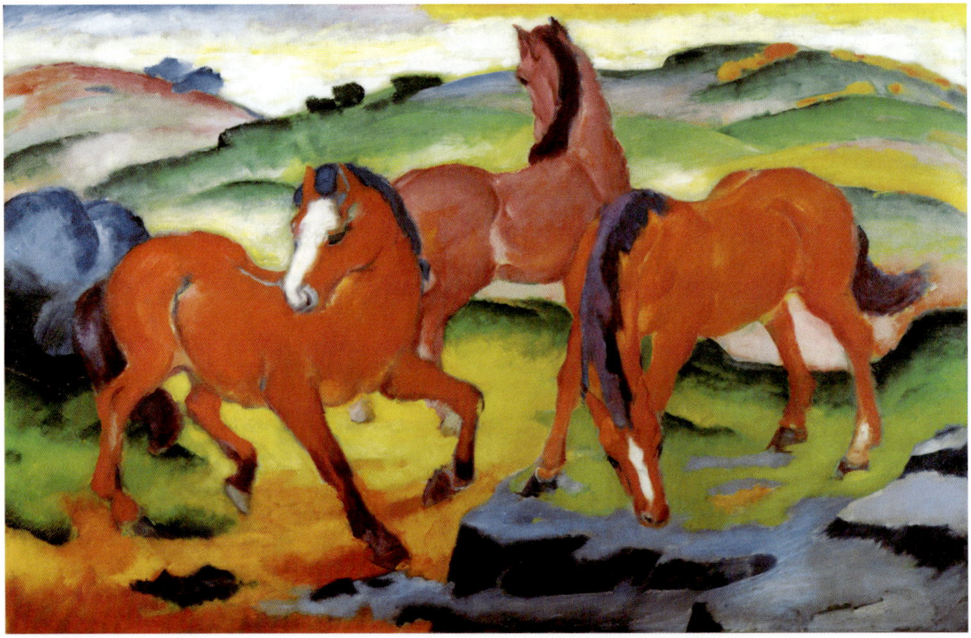

 Distemper on burlap, 47 5/16 x 35 1/8 in. (120.2 x 89.2 cm). Busch-Reisinger Museum, Association Fund, BR53.102.

Otto Mueller
German, 1874–1930
Nude in a Landscape
c. 1925

By the 1920s, many German artists had abandoned depictions of landscapes and nature, preferring to focus on urban scenes that conveyed their critique of what was increasingly seen as a corrupt society. In contrast, Otto Mueller, who was affiliated with the German expressionist group Brücke, continued his search for an expression of humankind's harmony with nature, an interest he had begun to explore in the previous decade. Mueller frequently painted his romantic partners, and his paintings of women in landscapes are regarded today as some of the most striking nude compositions of the early twentieth century. *Nude in a Landscape*, an important work in his oeuvre, is one of only a few of Mueller's paintings owned by an American museum. It is painted directly on burlap, without a ground layer, using distemper, a glue-based paint whose matte surface gives the work a natural, rough-hewn look. SK2

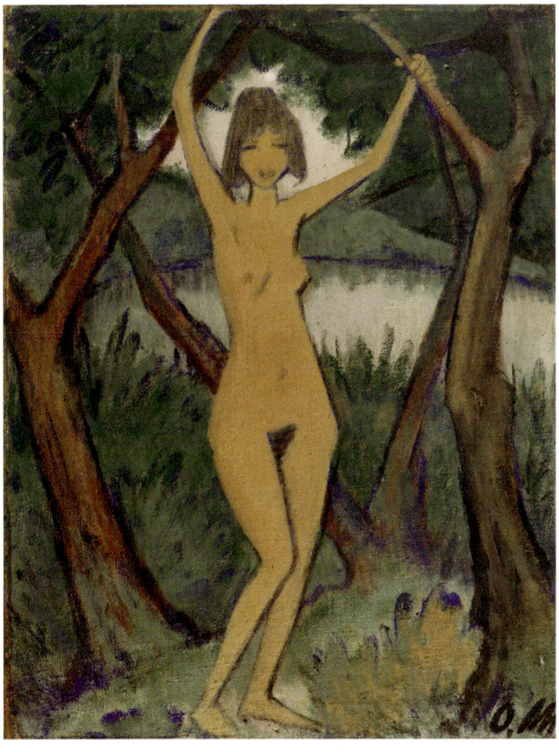

Collage with printed papers, 12 3/16 x 9 in. (31 x 22.8 cm). Busch-Reisinger Museum, Gift of Rose Fried Gallery, BR56.46.

Hannah Höch
German, 1889–1978
On a Tulle Net Ground
1921

The seemingly abstract patterns of Hannah Höch's collage are sewing patterns for tulle nets and embroidery taken from German women's magazines of the early 1920s. At that time, Höch worked as a graphic designer in the handicrafts department of a Berlin publishing house, and she transformed many of the images from society magazines into critical commentary on Weimar society. Höch fuses the traditional world of domestic craft with the avant-garde sensibility of Dadaist collage. HH

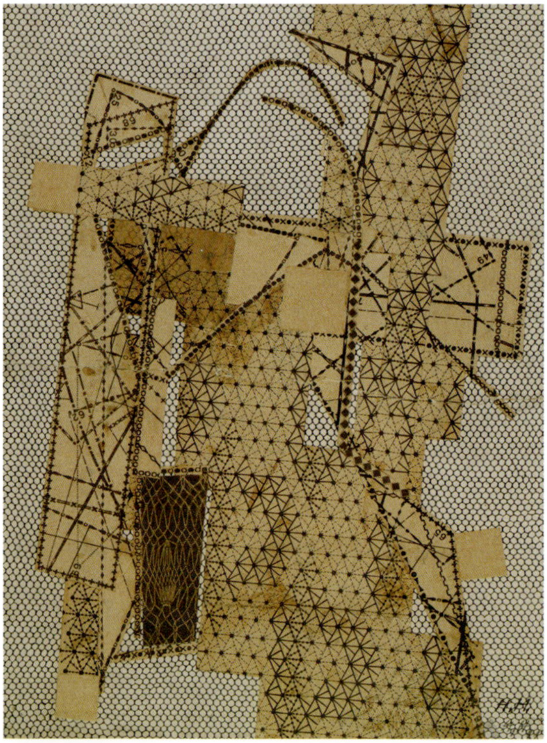

 / Oil on canvas, 22 1/2 x 16 3/4 in. (57.2 x 42.5 cm). Busch-Reisinger Museum, Association Fund, BR49.303.

El Lissitzky
Russian, 1890–1941
Proun 12E
1923

While other Soviet artists renounced easel painting in favor of strictly utilitarian types of art making, El Lissitzky remained committed to the utopian potential of painting, a position articulated in his neologism *proun*, meaning "project for the affirmation of the new." Through his prouns, Lissitzky rescued painting from its traditional, historical use for adorning churches, state buildings, or bourgeois homes. His ideas became extremely influential among avant-garde artists working in Germany. / *Proun 12E* is typical of Lissitzky's intriguing constructions of space, in which objects seem to defy gravity and project forward from the picture plane. The proun leaves behind the Renaissance convention of a picture as a window onto an alternate reality. A flat band runs across the width of the canvas, providing an anchor to the other objects that are built up like a relief. HH

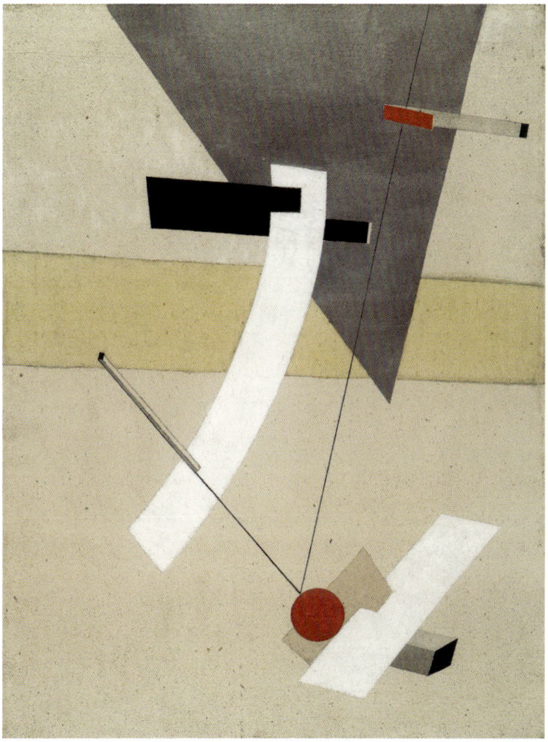

Oil on canvas, 15 3/8 x 13 11/16 in. (39 x 34.7 cm). Busch-Reisinger Museum, Anonymous gift in honor of Martin and Paul F. Sanders; purchase through the generosity of Emily Rauh Pulitzer and the Friends of the Busch-Reisinger Museum; Alpheus Hyatt Purchasing Fund; and Esperia Foundation Fund, in memory of Donald Outerbridge, 2000.1.

Piet Mondrian
Dutch, 1872–1944
Composition with Blue, Black, Yellow, and Red
1922

Piet Mondrian was a pioneering figure in the development of abstraction, perhaps the single most important innovation in twentieth-century art. In 1917, he cofounded with Theo van Doesburg (1883–1931) the Dutch artists' group De Stijl, which aimed to purify the arts of extraneous elements and integrate the arts into modern life. By 1920, Mondrian had developed neoplasticism, a new mode of abstraction, through which he sought to express universal principles by reducing painting to its essentials of pure color and line. / *Composition with Blue, Black, Yellow, and Red* is an exceptional example of Mondrian's most important innovation and is unusual, moreover, in that it is one of only a few of his paintings that was never damaged, cleaned, restored, or reframed. Its pristine state offers a rare opportunity to study the artist's technique, marked by the animating contrast between the shiny black lines and the matte and textured surfaces of the color fields. SK2

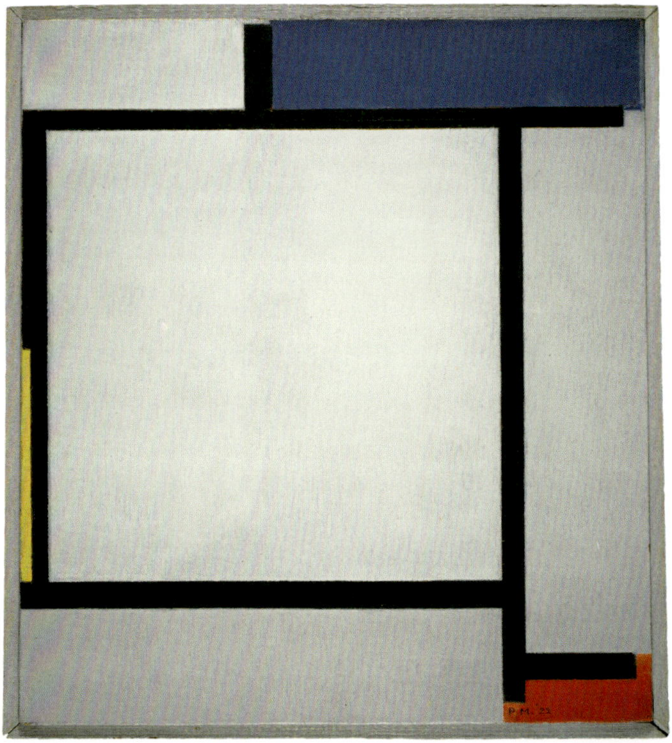

Oil on canvas, 16 x 12 1/2 in. (40.6 x 31.8 cm). Fogg Museum, Gift of Dr. Ernest G. Stillman, Class of 1907, by exchange, 2006.49.

Georgia O'Keeffe
American, 1887–1986
Red and Pink
1925

Red and Pink is the first work by Georgia O'Keeffe to enter the Fogg collection. O'Keeffe is chiefly known for still lifes painted in the late 1920s of plants, shells, and bones, but abstraction was never far from her work. Created as a commission for the Cheney Brothers Silk Company, this work shows her evolving notions of abstraction while maintaining an essential connection to organic forms. The undulating cascade of tendrils, suggestive of the interior spaces of the body, has a surrealist intensity, and the cropping of the composition recalls the close-up techniques of modernist photography. EL

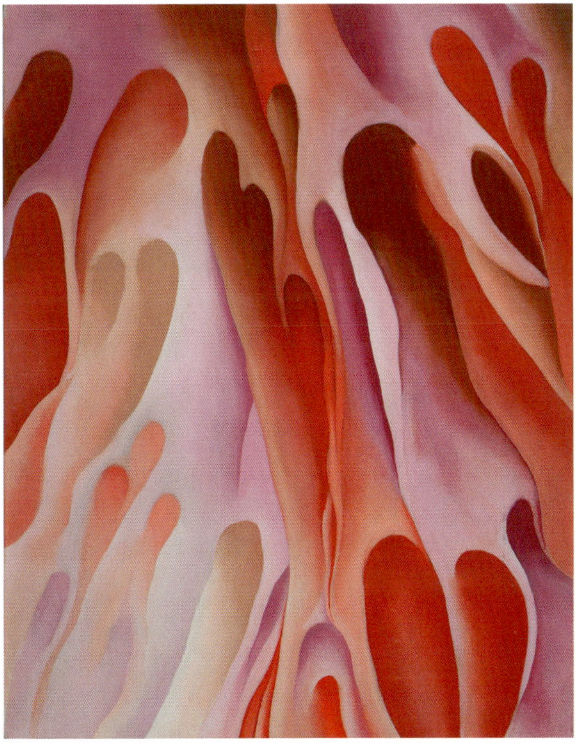

Oil on canvas, 38 7/8 x 96 3/8 in. (98.7 x 244.8 cm). Busch-Reisinger Museum, Edmée Busch Greenough Fund, BR50.415.

Erich Heckel
German, 1883–1970
To the Convalescent Woman (Triptych)
1912–13

As a founding member of the German expressionist group Brücke (Bridge), Erich Heckel strove to depict the individual psychological condition. This triptych, showing his fiancée, Siddi Riha, convalescing after a long illness, mirrors the exhausted state of German society in the years immediately before World War I.

Dressed comfortably in loose clothing rather than the carefully structured garments prescribed by good society, and lounging on pillows reminiscent of an orientalist scene, Riha inhabits a world removed from civilized, urban life. She is flanked by flowers, primitivist sculpture, and an African textile, symbols of health and rejuvenation that imply recovery is not to be found in Berlin's department stores but requires a return to the wellsprings of civilization. In 1937, the Nazis condemned Heckel and other modern artists as "degenerate," and this painting was removed from the Museum Folkwang in Essen. The Busch-Reisinger Museum acquired it in 1950. HH

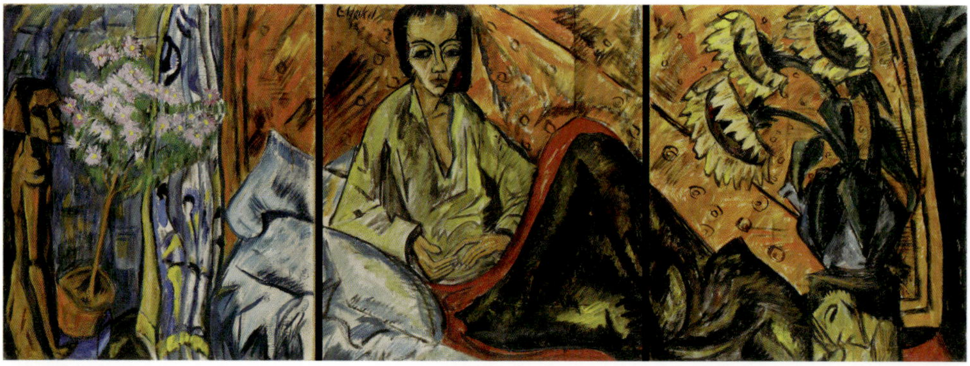

 Silk, 70 3/8 x 46 3/8 in. (178.8 x 117.8 cm). Busch-Reisinger Museum, Association Fund, BR48.132.

Anni Albers
German, 1899–1994
Wall Hanging
1926

Like other women in the early 1920s, when Anni Albers matriculated at the Bauhaus, she was channeled by the school to the traditionally feminine field of textile arts. In 1926, she began working with double and jacquard looms, and this wall hanging shows her technical skill at creating complex weaves. She carefully plotted the design of her textiles in advance, deriving the pattern from the repetition of numbers in nature. With only three warp and two weft yarns, Albers created a rich variety of color and pattern in this textile. The Busch-Reisinger Museum also owns the preparatory sketch for this work, which clearly shows her detailed numbering system. / The museum acquired the sketch and textile directly from the artist in 1948. Albers's parents had previously used the hanging as a cover for their grand piano, which infuriated their daughter. As she explained, the "tapestries are, to my mind, a kind of picture." HH

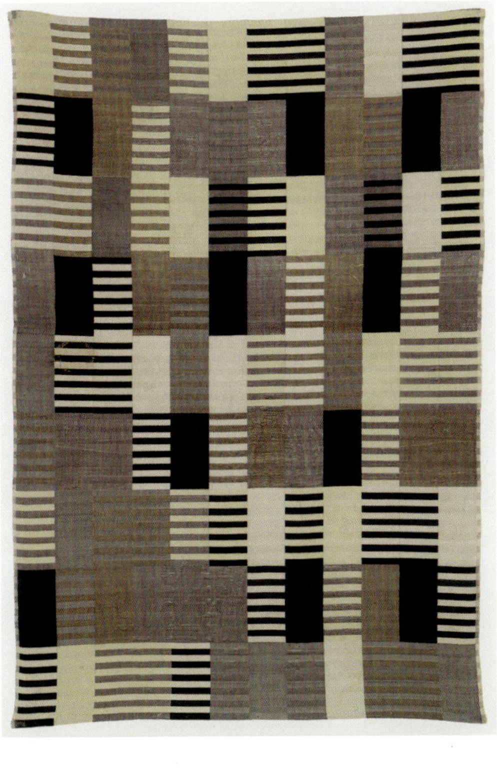

Oil on canvas, 17 1/4 x 28 in. (43.8 x 71.1 cm). Busch-Reisinger Museum, Purchase in memory of Eda K. Loeb, BR56.414.

Lyonel Feininger
American, 1871–1956
Bird Cloud
1926

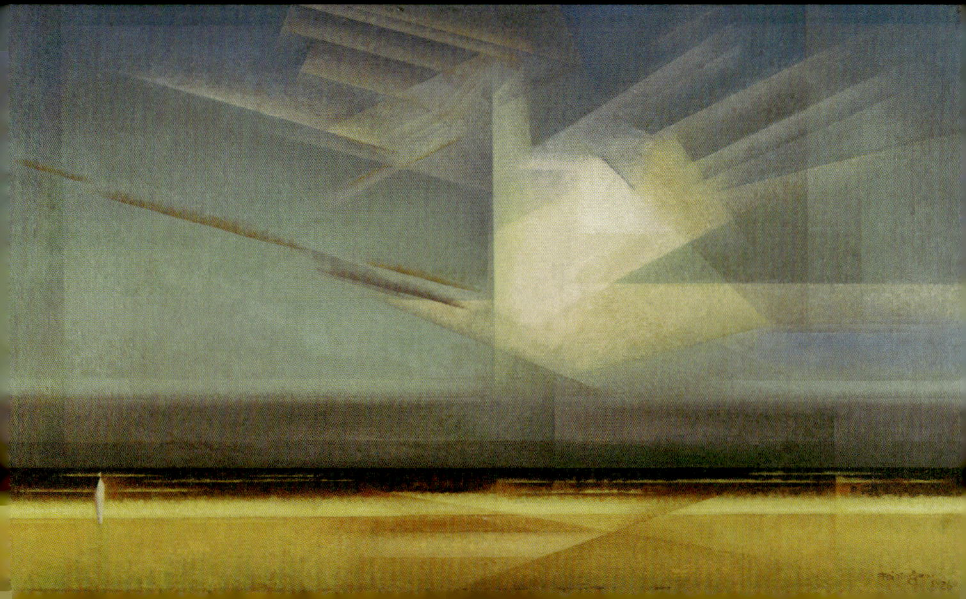

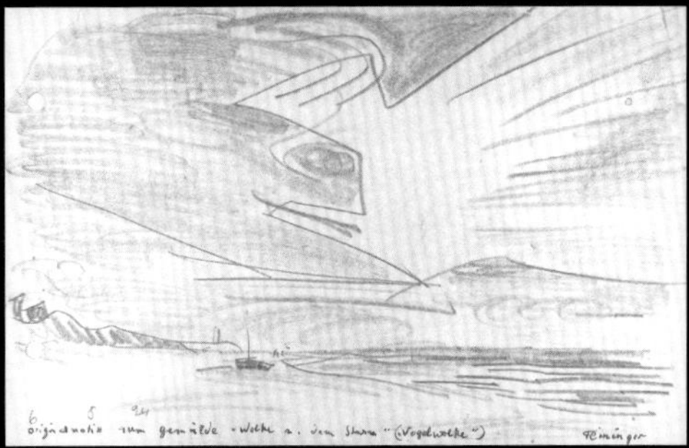

Original "nature note" for the painting *Bird Cloud*, dated 8/6/1924. Graphite on cream wove paper, 5 9/16 x 8 1/2 in. (14.1 x 21.6 cm). Busch-Reisinger Museum, Gift of T. Lux Feininger, 1986.312.

Born in the United States to German parents, Lyonel Feininger was an important artist and teacher at the Bauhaus, active in painting, printmaking, and photography. With more than 23,000 paintings, sketches, comic strips, photographic negatives, and documentary materials spanning his entire career, the Busch-Reisinger has one of the most comprehensive Feininger collections in the world. / *Bird Cloud* is a carefully composed picture of luminous geometric planes and diagonals. A large crystalline cloud in the shape of a bird dominates the sky and hovers near a solitary figure at the edge of the sea. Feininger based his paintings on his "nature notes," quick sketches he made in the open air, many of which are also in the Busch-Reisinger collection. In 1924, he began visiting Deep, a small village on the Baltic Sea remarkable for its isolation and nearly primordial atmosphere. There he sketched the emptiness of the landscape and captured many bizarre effects of nature. Later, often only after many years, Feininger distilled the sketches into paintings, when a "yearning for form" compelled him to extract the ultimate significance from his initial observations. The subject of a figure awed by the vastness of nature unites Feininger's cubist experimentations with the early nineteenth-century German Romantic tradition. HH

Oil on canvas, 28 3/4 x 21 3/4 in. (73 x 55.3 cm). Fogg Museum, Louise E. Bettens Fund, 1933.97.

Charles Sheeler
American, 1883–1965
Upper Deck
1929

Charles Sheeler was one of the founders of precisionism, a distinctly American style of painting that largely depicted industrial and mechanical subjects with exacting realism. This canvas, one of the most famous of the movement, unites motif and manner by rendering the mechanical shapes of modern industry with photographic clarity. Due in part to strategic simplifications such as omitting extraneous mechanical elements, the resulting image is almost as abstract as it is realistic, which made the acquisition a bold one for its time. Fogg Museum director Edward Forbes wrote in 1933, "I like the picture very much indeed and am glad to have it in our museum. As it is so unlike our other pictures, it will be a little hard to exhibit." EL

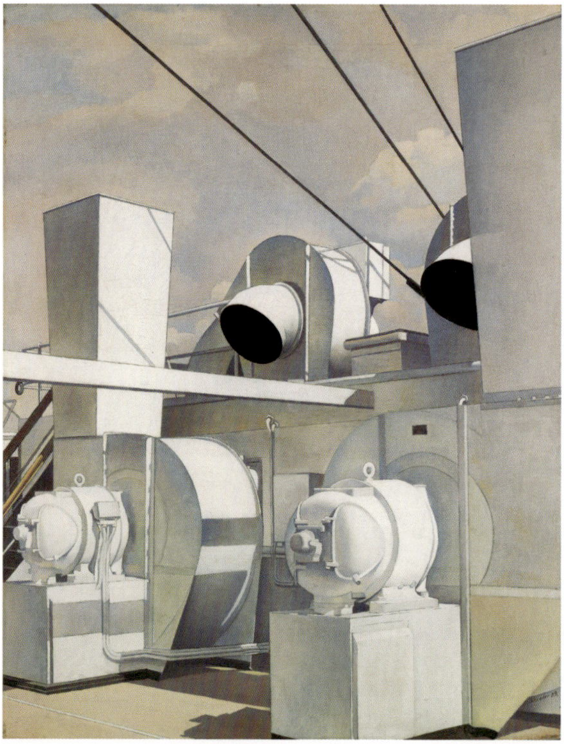

207 Aluminum, steel, nickel-plated brass, other metals, plastic, wood, and electric motor; 59 1/2 x 27 1/2 x 27 1/2 in. (151.1 x 69.9 x 69.9 cm). Busch-Reisinger Museum, Gift of Sibyl Moholy-Nagy, BR56.5.

László Moholy-Nagy
Hungarian, 1895–1946
Light Prop for an Electric Stage (Light-Space Modulator)
1930

Early in his tenure at the Bauhaus, the renowned school of art and architecture in Weimar, Germany, László Moholy-Nagy developed an interest in stage design and the creative use of electric light and metal. In 1923, he described an idea for an apparatus for the demonstration of special lighting and motion effects, an idea realized in 1930 when he unveiled *Light Prop for an Electric Stage* at an exhibition in Paris. Today this work, also known after the artist's death as the *Light-Space Modulator*, represents a milestone in the history of sculpture: It is one of the first kinetic sculptures, and its integration into the surrounding environment and use of industrial materials and movement manifest a complete break with traditional sculpture, presaging many important developments of later decades. SK2

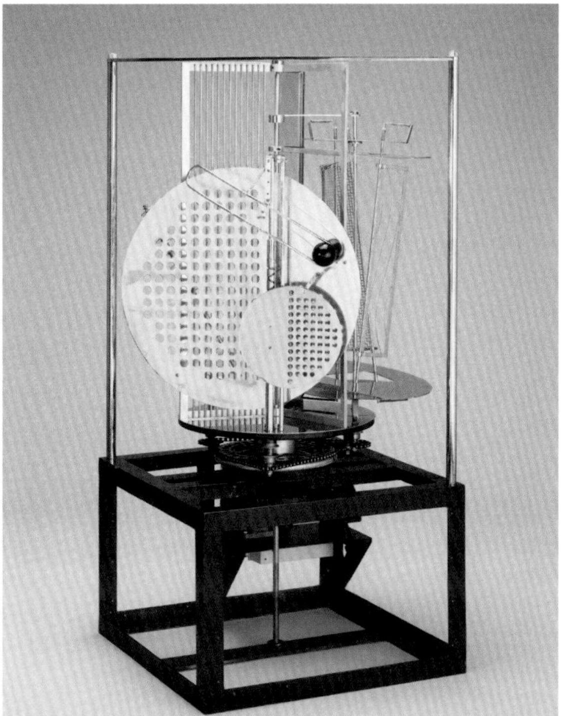

Oil on canvas, 54 15/16 x 37 5/8 in. (139.5 x 95.5 cm). Busch-Reisinger Museum, Association Fund, BR41.37.

Max Beckmann
German, 1884–1950
Self-Portrait in Tuxedo
1927

Max Beckmann painted *Self-Portrait in Tuxedo* at the height of his fame, and it has long been regarded as one of his masterpieces. After its completion, it was exhibited in a special Beckmann room in the Berlin National Gallery and became one of the most celebrated self-portraits of its time. In 1937 the Nazis declared Beckmann's works "degenerate," confiscated the painting, and sold the work abroad. The Busch-Reisinger Museum purchased it in 1941, the first modern painting to enter the collection. The year it was painted, Beckmann wrote an article in which he stressed the role of the artist in the development of a new culture and state, an idea perhaps reflected in this monumental self-portrait. For all the ambiguity in the masklike face, *Self-Portrait in Tuxedo* captures Beckmann at his most confident, the artist depicting himself in a position of power and control. SK2

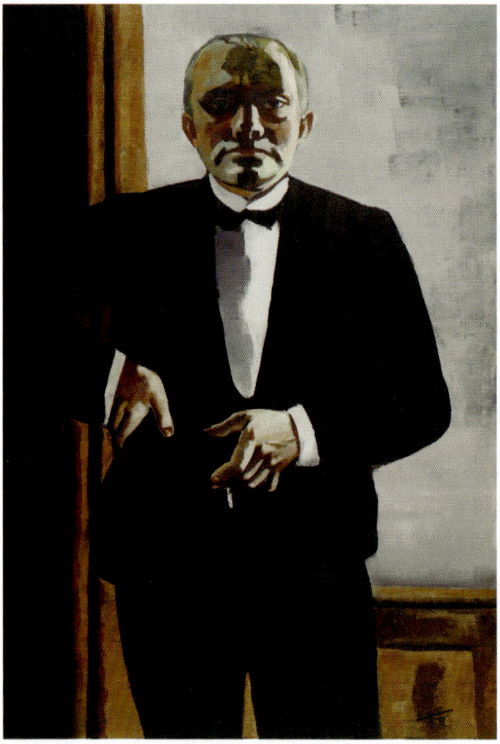

 Solarized gelatin silver print, 11 5/8 x 8 11/16 in. (29.5 x 22 cm). Fogg Museum, Robert M. Sedgwick II Fund, P1977.20.

Man Ray
American, 1890–1976
Femme (Mary Gill)
1930

Man Ray's career bridges New York Dadaism and Paris surrealism, but the latter phase, beginning with his move to Paris in 1921, gave rise to his most innovative photographic work. Taking up a range of experimental photographic techniques from the new vision photography of the 1920s that emphasized the physical and chemical properties of the medium, Man Ray instead used these techniques for subjective and psychological expression. Exposing this print to additional light during development—a technique known as solarization, in which unpredictable changes emerge in the gray tones of the print—he joined his photographic process to a surrealist interest in chance operations and inner states. The resulting effects render Mary Gill as an emblem of inwardness and strange juxtaposition, locating her in a dream state and focusing our attention on the interplay between her facial expression and her seemingly free-floating hand. BF

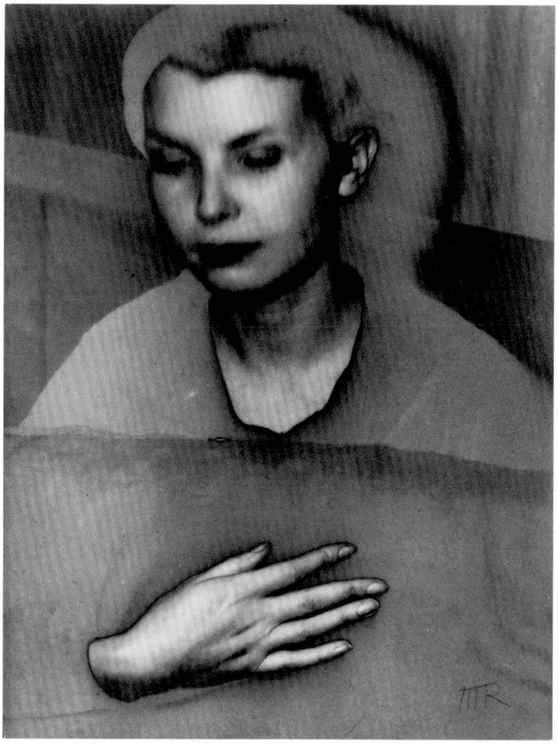

Watercolor over graphite on rough white wove paper, 16 5/8 x 25 11/16 in. (42.3 x 65.3 cm). Fogg Museum, Louise E. Bettens Fund, 1930.462.

Edward Hopper
American, 1882–1967
Highland Light
1930

Edward Hopper is best known for his moving depictions of desolate urban and rural spaces. Working at various times in graphite, oil, and watercolor, he derived a uniquely American subject matter from empty streets, motels, gas stations, homes, and lighthouses. For this watercolor, he used a light palette and simple geometric forms to represent a lighthouse and surrounding buildings in North Truro on Cape Cod, Massachusetts, where he and his wife, Josephine Nivison Hopper, spent summers. In Hopper's notebook, his wife described the watercolor: "Explosive sky–white in back of buildings, ragged cutoff white, blue beyond. Sultry colored ground & road." FW

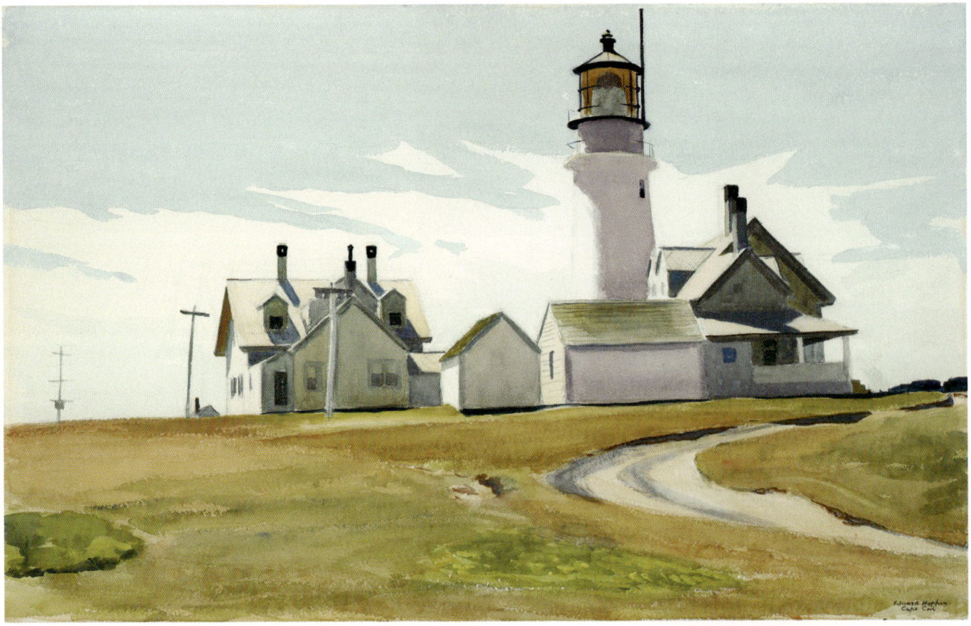

211 / Lithograph, 10 3/8 x 14 15/16 in. (26.3 x 37.9 cm). Fogg Museum, Louise E. Bettens Fund, M11047.

Thomas Hart Benton
American, 1889–1975
Wreck of the Old 97
1944

Thomas Hart Benton was an American regionalist painter known for his sculptural, stylized images. This widely available lithograph vividly reimagines a popular folk song about a railroad catastrophe of September 27, 1903. The Old 97 was a fast mail train famous for its punctuality. Following orders to complete a trip on time, the operator increased speed but lost control of the engine, plunging into a ravine in Danville, Virginia. At least nine people died. Woody Guthrie's 1944 recording of a traditional ballad about the wreck may have been inspired by Benton's print. As Benton wrote, "The song doesn't say who saw the affair, but somebody must have, and it could just as well have been people like those in the wagon. I put 'em in anyhow." By showing the reactions of bystanders, Benton invents a suspenseful prelude to this deadly clash between human and machine. SKS

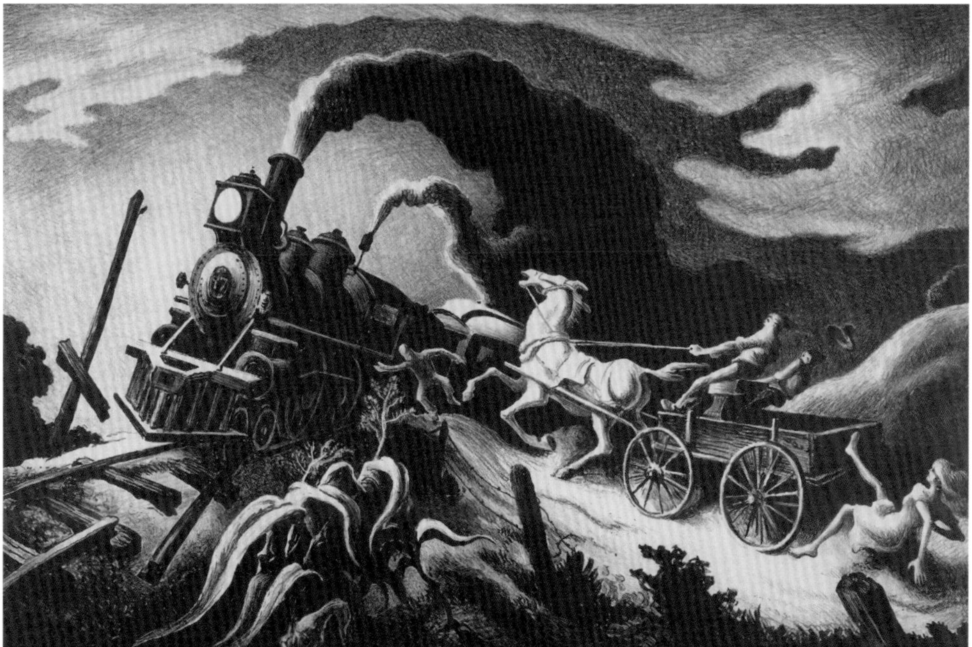

Lithograph; image: 20 3/4 x 15 3/4 in. (52.7 x 40 cm). Fogg Museum, Louise E. Bettens Fund, M10183.

David Alfaro Siqueiros Mexican, 1898–1974 Emiliano Zapata 1931

The social activist artist David Alfaro Siqueiros depicted several Mexican national heroes in monumental fashion—from Cuauhtémoc, the valiant Aztec defender against the Spanish conqueror Hernán Cortés, to the more recently deceased revolutionary Emiliano Zapata. Government troops assassinated Zapata in 1919 after he had helped topple previous regimes. Zapata's rallying cry of "Tierra y Libertad" (Land and Liberty) struck a chord with Siqueiros and other Communist sympathizers interested in agrarian reform. Zapata's gaucho attire and his placement in the outdoors emphasize his link with the land. Siqueiros created the drawing for this lithograph shortly after being released from prison, where he had served six months for participating in a May Day Communist rally. SKS

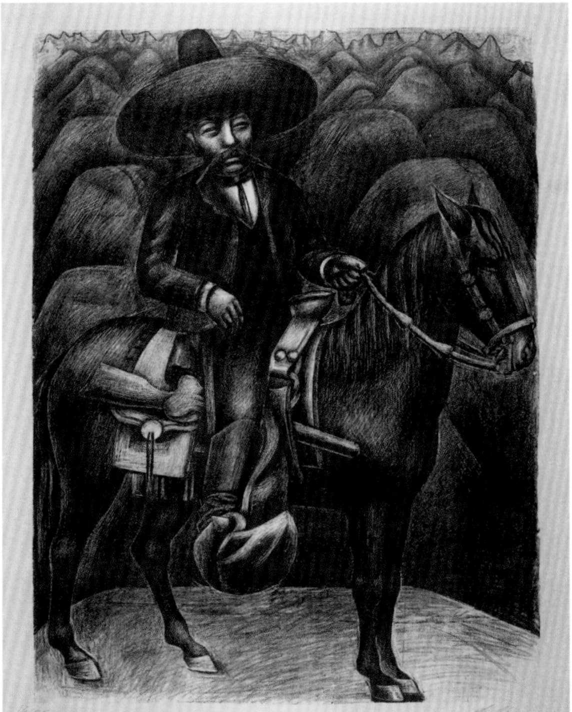

213 / Gelatin silver print, 6 3/4 x 9 1/16 in. (17.2 x 23 cm). Fogg Museum, Gift of Bernarda Bryson Shahn, P1970.2464.

Ben Shahn
American, 1898–1969
Untitled
1933–34

A painter and photographer committed to progressive politics and politically engaged artistic production, Ben Shahn took New York's Lower East Side as a primary subject in the early 1930s. This photograph offers an image of isolation within the crowded diversity of an impoverished section of the city, using an architectural detail to suggest the social separation belied by the physical proximity of the Greek American businessman and the African American laborer. / This print is one of over five thousand images included in Bernarda Bryson Shahn's gift to the Fogg of her late husband's photographic archives. The collection contains prints, negatives, and contact strips, including a large selection of his work made under the New Deal for the Resettlement Administration/Farm Security Administration. Together with the Steven Lee Taller Ben Shahn Archive, also at Harvard, it forms a prominent resource for research into Shahn's photography, life, and contemporaries. BF

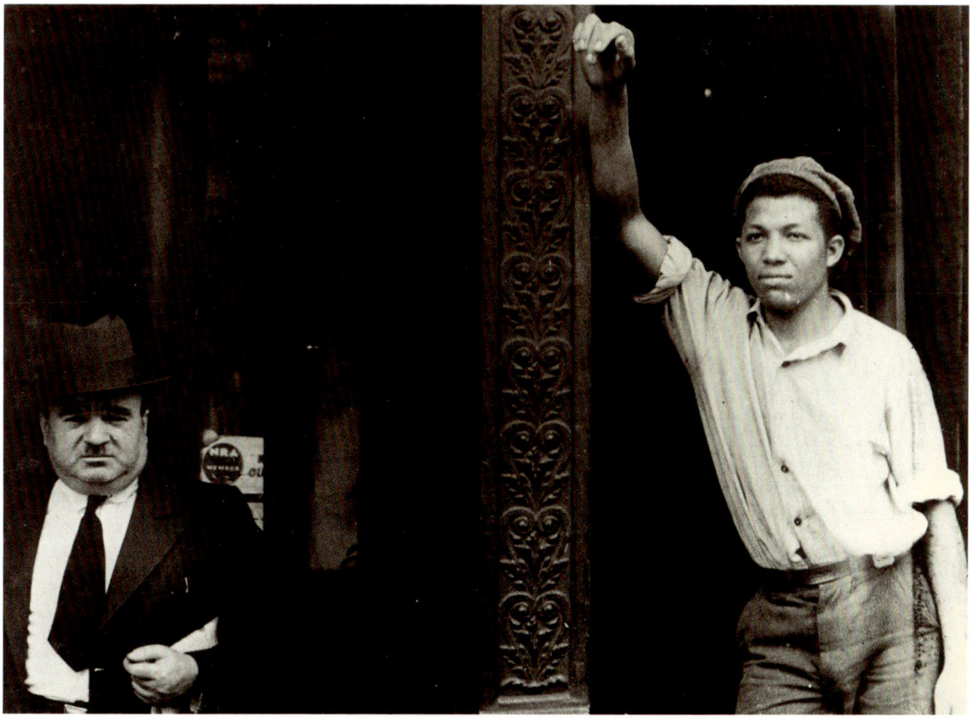

Oil on canvas, 28 7/8 x 36 1/4 in. (73.3 x 92.1 cm). Fogg Museum, Gift of Mr. and Mrs. Joseph Pulitzer Jr., 1966.138.

Pablo Picasso
Spanish, 1881–1973
Plaster Head with Bowl of Fruit
1933

This painting, an example of Picasso's growing interest in surrealism, is a witty meditation on art and representation. On the left is a sculpture on a pedestal—a portrait of his lover Marie-Thérèse Walter—and on the right is a bowl of fruit. By depicting the work of art realistically and the ordinary objects abstractly, Picasso alerts us to the power of the artist to transform reality and reorder the hierarchies of representation. EL

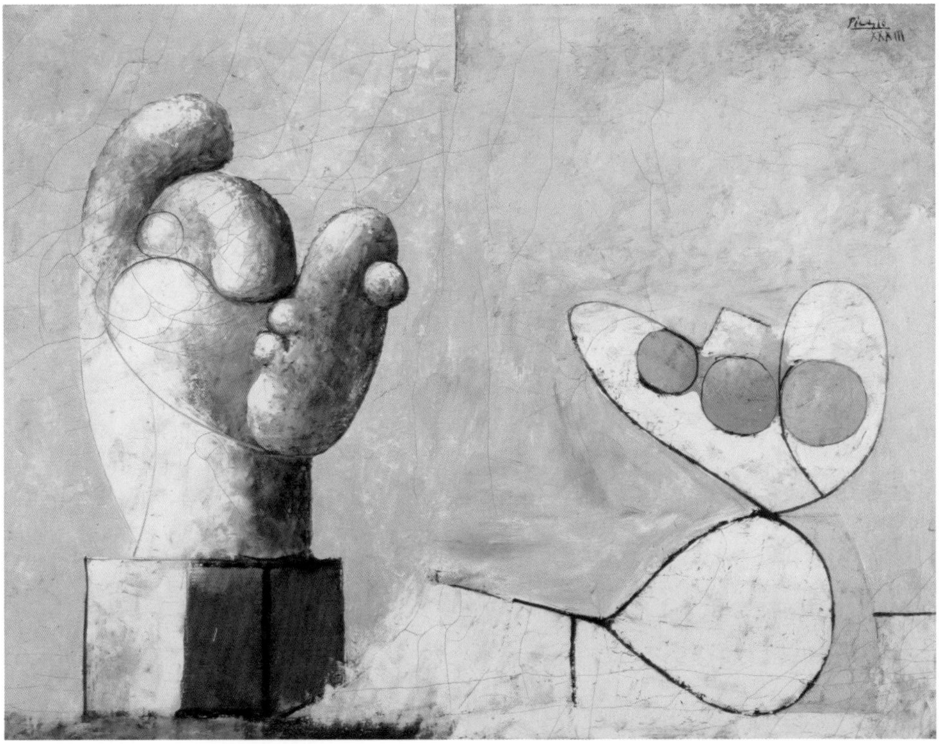

Gouache and graphite on off-white wove paper, 13 1/4 x 11 in. (33.6 x 28 cm). Fogg Museum, Gift of Mr. and Mrs. Josep Lluis Sert, 1964.58.

Joán Miró
Spanish, 1893–1983
Figures by the Sea
1934

Figures by the Sea is one of six works by Joán Miró from architect Josep Lluis Sert's collection that are now in the Fogg. Presumably, the drawing was the model for a *pochoir* (stencil print) in a special issue of the Catalan journal *D'Aci i D'Alla* in 1934, supervised by Sert, a friend of Miró. The bodies of the male and female figures on the shore are constructed of swollen lobular forms—perfectly suited for the stenciled shapes required by pochoir. The physical agitation of the figures is at odds with the placid beach scene, conveying a sense of anxiety that perhaps reflected Spain's political turmoil in the 1930s. MS

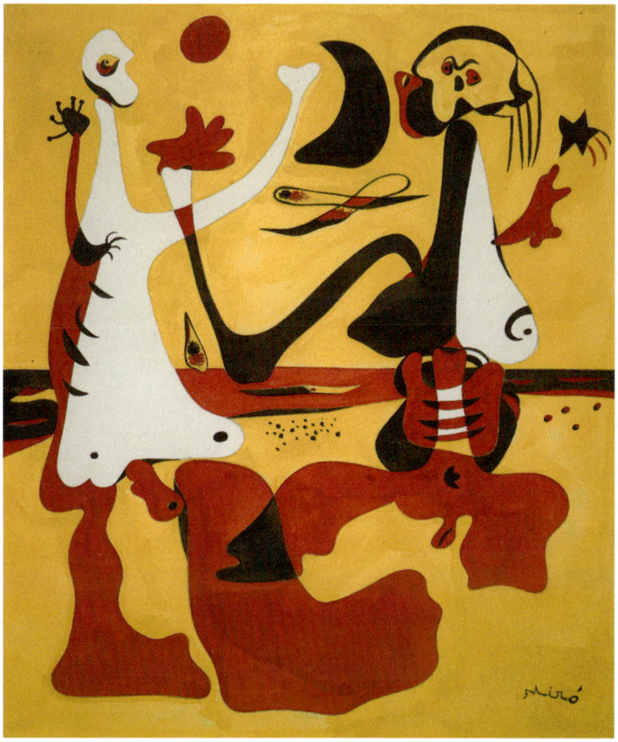

Oil on canvas, 27 1/2 x 13 3/4 in. (69.8 x 34.9 cm). Fogg Museum, Gift of Mr. and Mrs. Arnold S. Askin, 1980.72.

Pierre Bonnard
French, 1867–1947
Still Life: Basket of Fruit
c. 1936

Pierre Bonnard returned to three subjects throughout his career: his wife, Marthe; the gardens and trees around his home; and still life. This painting has the dazzling colored touches of Bonnard's mature style, a synthesis and extension of a French painterly tradition reaching back to Monet, Seurat, and Delacroix. The sophisticated play of abstraction and figuration, with its suggestions of disguise and disclosure (a figure seems to hide on the far side of the table amid a profusion of dissolving objects), is characteristic of Bonnard's greatest works, which combine lyricism with anxiety. HC

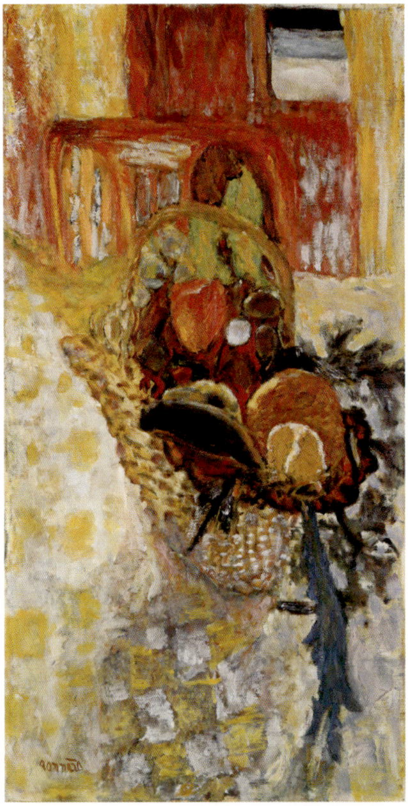

217 Oil and watercolor on paper with a chalk ground, mounted to card; 9 7/16 x 9 3/16 in. (23.9 x 23.3 cm). Busch-Reisinger Museum, Gift of Richard M. Bennett, 2005.113.

Paul Klee
Swiss, 1879–1940
Falling Asleep
1935

Falling Asleep represents a transitional moment in the life and career of Paul Klee, who taught at the Bauhaus in the 1920s. One of the leading art theoreticians of the twentieth century, Klee is known particularly for his innovative work with color. This drawing was completed shortly after he was forced to return to his native Switzerland as the National Socialists rose to power. It features rich jewel tones that refer back to the artist's experimentation with light begun at the Bauhaus, while the pared-down composition of the central figure anticipates the starkly reduced linear forms that typify the final works of his career. The drawing is notable in that it was created from a larger work: After drawing an artist's easel in a landscape, Klee cut the drawing, rotated it, and reworked this section by adding a circle, thereby creating a new work. SK2 & EMR

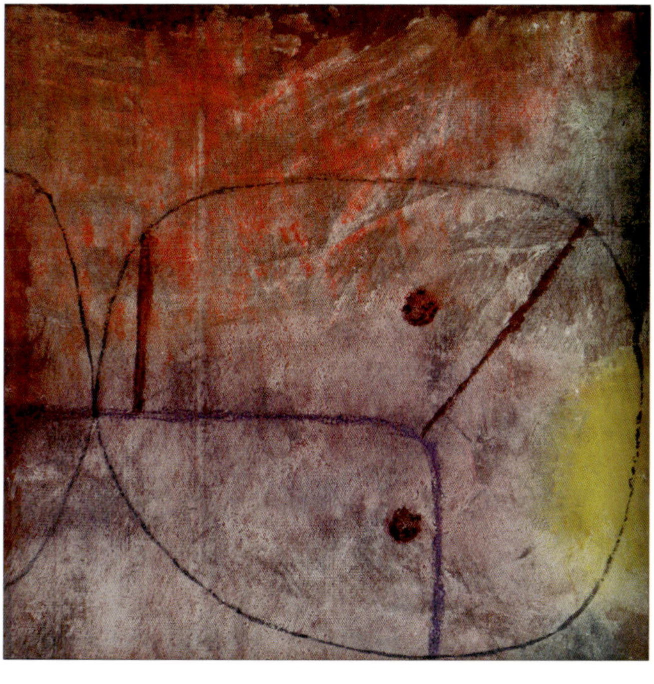

Graphite and colored wax crayon with stumping on off-white wove paper edged with lavender paper at left and right, 19 15/16 x 26 1/16 in. (50.7 x 66.2 cm). Fogg Museum, Gift of Lois Orswell, 1977.176.

Arshile Gorky
American, 1904–1948
Untitled
1944

Arshile Gorky's work has often been seen as the bridge between surrealism and abstract expressionism. His drawings from the 1940s were informed by his response to the natural world: In many of them, relics of vegetal, floral, and even bovine forms emerge, heightened and transformed into a personal vocabulary. These drawings typically featured a dynamic interplay between colored crayon smudges and fluent graphite lines. In *Untitled* (1944), the surface is animated by a more aggressive, vigorous attack. The colored patches, judiciously spread across the sheet, are drawn together into a net of harshly scribbled graphite. MS

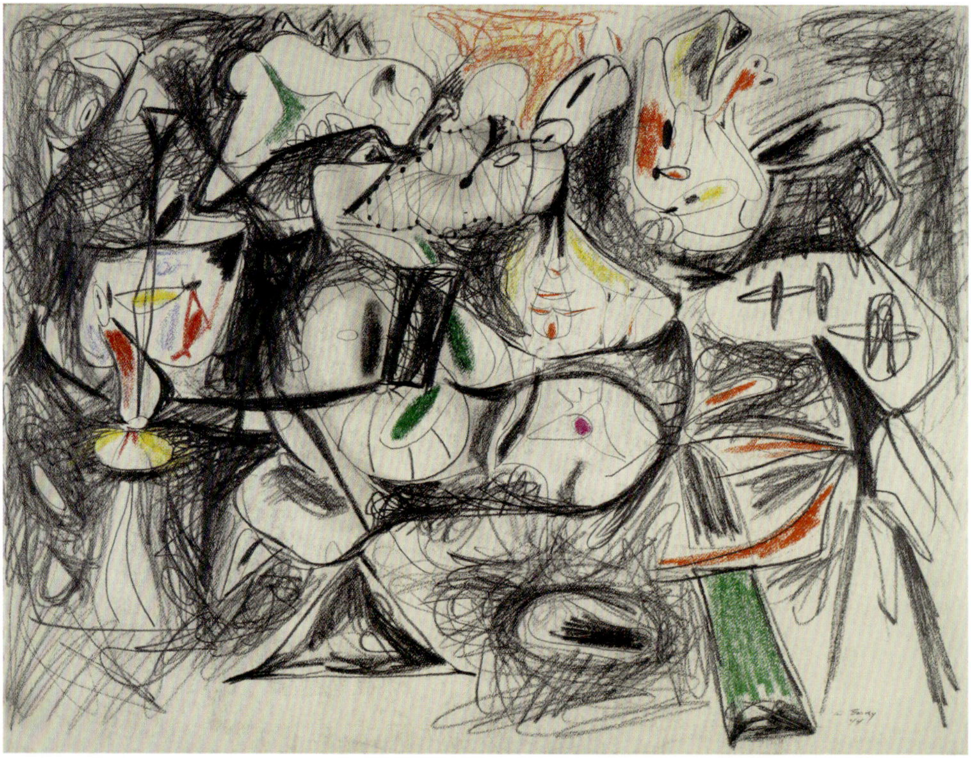

219 Mixed media on canvas, 110 x 36 1/8 in. (279.4 x 91.8 cm). Fogg Museum, Mr. and Mrs. Reginald R. Isaacs and Family and purchase through the Contemporary Art Fund, 1965.554.

Jackson Pollock
American, 1912–1956
No. 2
1950

With the rise of abstract expressionist painting in the United States during and after World War II, the center of the art world moved from Paris to New York. The painter who soon came to epitomize this shift was Jackson Pollock. Working on the floor of a barn in Springs, Long Island, Pollock danced around and into his paintings. Using the brush as a stick, he directed the flow of paint from a can through the air onto the canvas. This allowed him to "be in the painting," as he said, which meant he could give his abstractions an unprecedented physicality while also allowing a free flow of decision and revision, which he associated with the expression of his unconscious. *No. 2* has the distinction of being the tallest painting in Pollock's oeuvre. HC

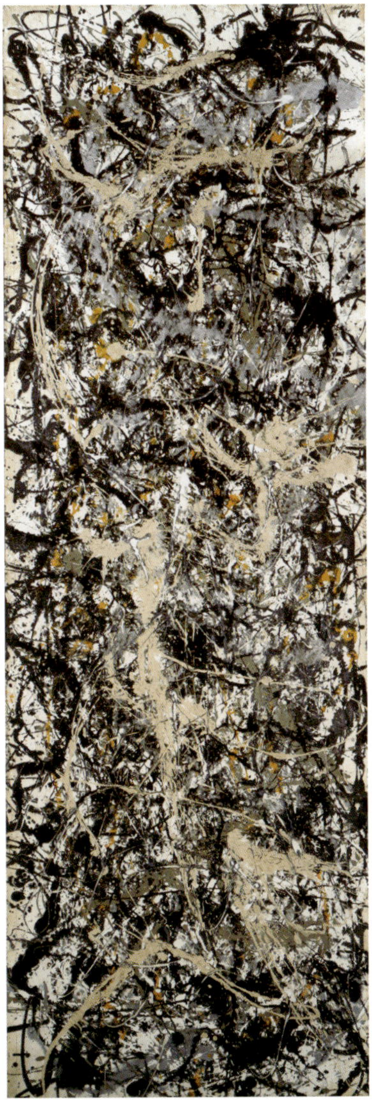

Gelatin silver print, 13 3/8 x 10 3/16 in. (34 x 25.8 cm). Fogg Museum, Gift of Carl Chiarenza and Heidi Katz, P1999.52.

Aaron Siskind
American, 1903–1991
The End of the Civic Repertory Theatre 1
1938

Aaron Siskind was a defining figure in photographic aesthetics and education. He began photographing within the New York Photo League, an organization of progressive documentary photographers, and was central in the development of the League's collective working methods. From the 1930s into the 1950s, Siskind's photography evolved from its documentary roots toward a style emphasizing formal relationships found within flat surfaces, with affinities to the work of New York school artists like his close friend Franz Kline. / Siskind's images of New York's Civic Theater were made midway in this evolution. This photograph was part of an extended series documenting the partially demolished theater. Here, amid the Great Depression and the collapse of his first marriage, Siskind centered a fallen head in a field of diverging angles and truncated forms to create a more general symbol of dissolution and decay. BF

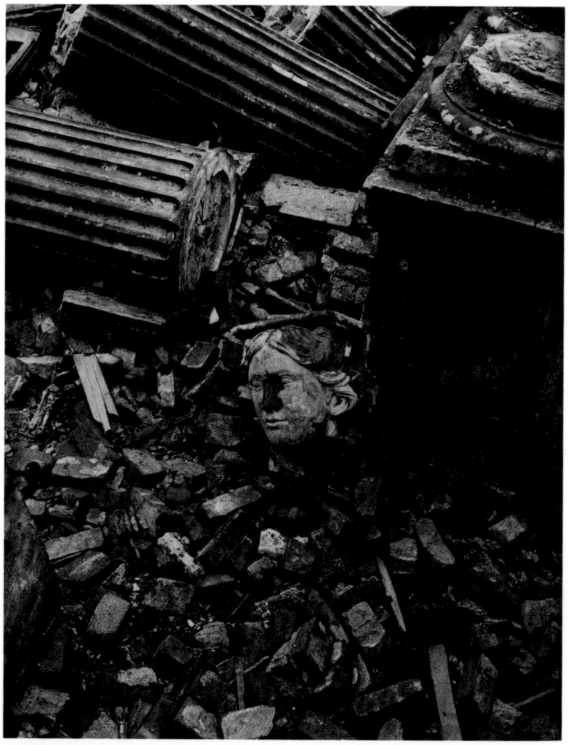

Oil on canvas, 58 1/8 x 77 1/2 in. (147.6 x 196.9 cm). Fogg Museum, Gift of Lois Orswell, 1971.121.

Franz Kline
American, 1910–1962
High Street
1950

Every major abstract expressionist painter had a breakthrough experience. Franz Kline's came in 1950 when he unveiled a set of black-and-white abstractions at his first solo exhibition. Although these works are often read as landscapes or pictographs, Kline worked hard to undermine the viewer's impulse to see them as black figures floating on white grounds. He accomplished this by bracing his compositional structures against the canvas edge and by working the white paint as aggressively as the black. / Despite the spontaneous look of the results, Kline's action, in this and other paintings, was carefully deliberated in preliminary sketches. Jackson Pollock and Willem de Kooning better deserve the label "action painter," coined by a critic in 1952. HC

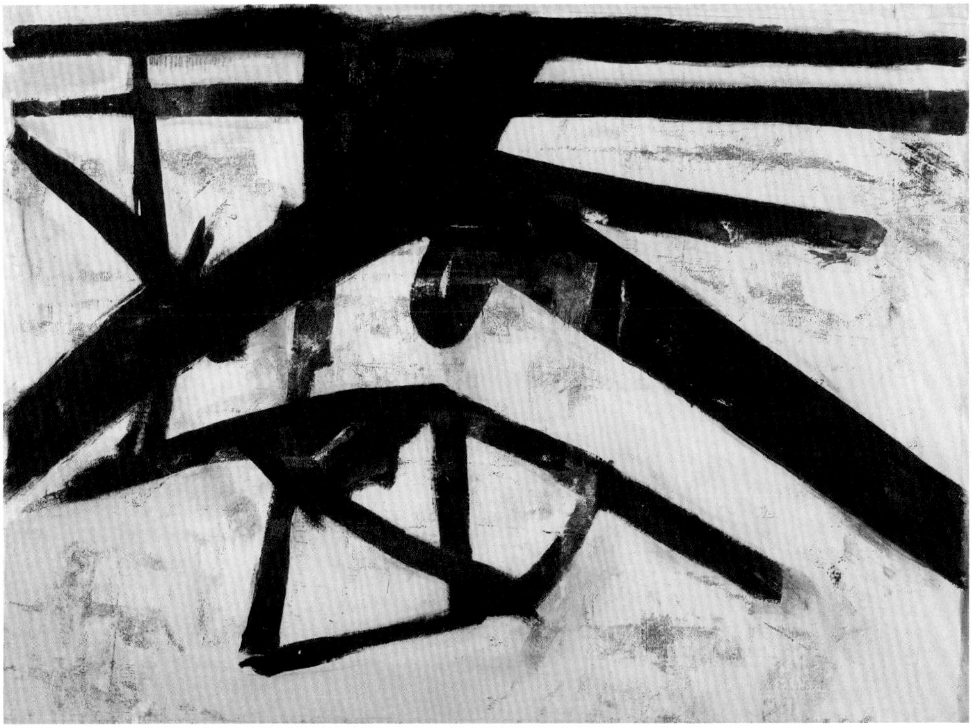

Black ink, blue-gray watercolor, brown wash, white gouache, collage, graphite, and touches of red chalk on cream wove paper; 10 x 7 5/16 in. (25.4 x 18.5 cm). Fogg Museum, Gift of David Smith, 1966.36.

David Smith
American, 1906–1965
Studies for *Home of the Welder*: Wife as Locomotive Parts
1945

David Smith enjoyed a particularly inventive period just after World War II, writing in 1945 that "right now I have drawings and thinkings for a year's labor." This drawing from a dismantled sketchbook is a study for his steel sculpture *Home of the Welder* (1945, Tate, London). The sculpture, which takes the form of a sort of unfolded room, manifests some of Smith's (the "welder") personal preoccupations: totems, the family, fertility. His inscriptions refer to sculptural components—a mirror reflecting the figure of a woman, a millstone, a blooming "tit flower"—and details of fabrication. The drawing of "the woman" composed of locomotive parts at the top left is on a separate sheet of paper adhered to the sketchbook sheet. MS

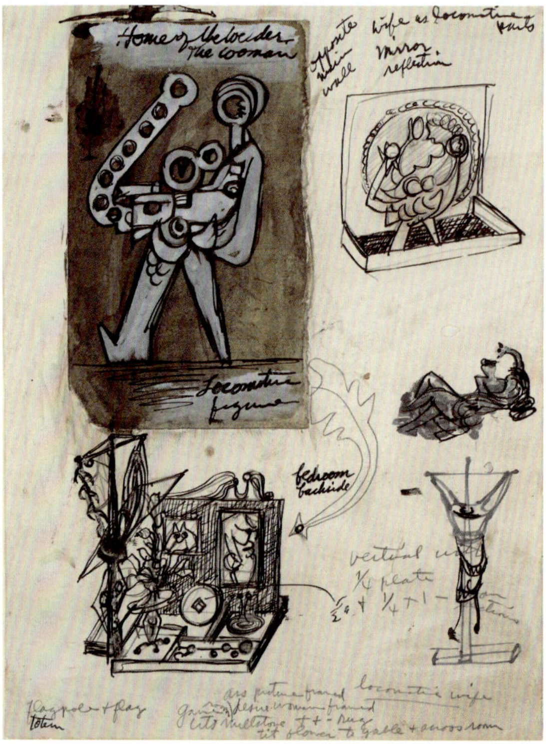

223 Welded steel, painted cadmium red; $69\frac{1}{2} \times 70\frac{1}{2} \times 18\frac{1}{2}$ in. (176.5 x 179.1 x 47 cm). Fogg Museum, Gift of Lois Orswell, 1994.20.

David Smith
American, 1906–1965
Fish
1950–51

Among American sculptors, only David Smith created a body of work that could compete with the triumphant abstract expressionist canvases of the 1950s. His art, while renowned for the muscular balancing of heavy elements, also had its painterly side: Witness his scandalous introduction of color into his work, interest in "drawing in space," preference for frontal orientation, and general refusal to have his works duplicated by casting, thus giving them the uniqueness of paintings. All this is evident in *Fish*, one of his first truly mature works, in which he has taken hints from Picasso (the use of found objects, welded together) and Calder (the sense of humor and movement) and made them his own. HC

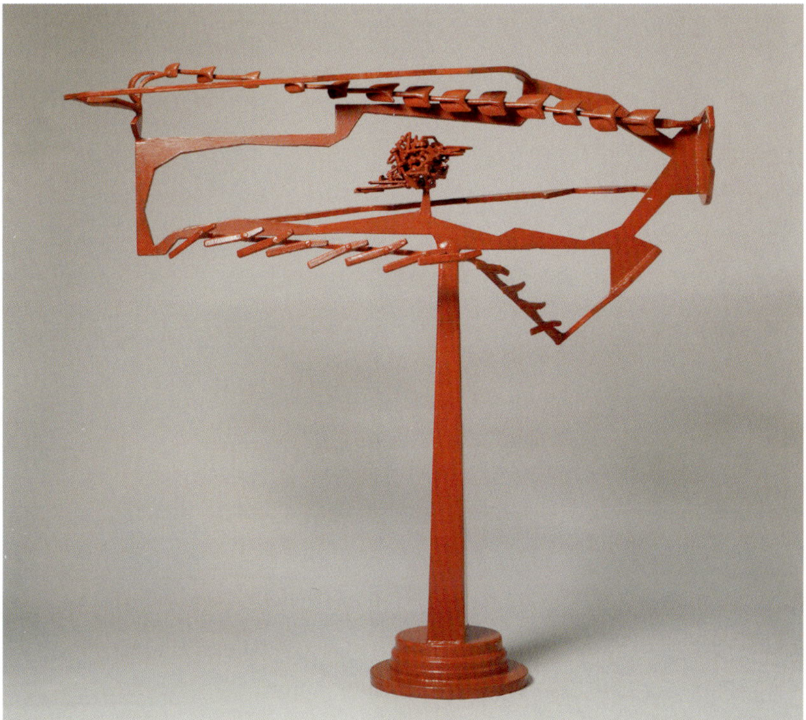

Hand-painted gelatin silver print, 19 7/8 x 15 7/8 in. (50.5 x 40.4 cm). Fogg Museum, On deposit from the Carpenter Center for the Visual Arts, American Professional Photographers Collection, 4.2002.757.1.

Harry Annas
American, 1897–1980
Untitled
1949

Harry Annas, a studio portraitist from Lockhart, Texas, is one of about twenty-five professional photographers whose studio materials form the American Professional Photographers Collection, comprising approximately 1,500 prints and over 15,000 negatives. The collection was assembled in the 1970s by Barbara Norfleet, photography curator at Harvard's Carpenter Center for the Visual Arts from 1972 to 2001, who recognized the materials as evocative documents of idealized social life in middle-class America. / Annas's portrait is a hand-painted image built up over an enlarged gelatin silver print. The collection also holds a contact print with the original notes instructing the colorist on the varied tones of the boy's shirt. That image shows that the foreground, middleground, and sky of the imaginary setting correspond to the floor, molding, and wall of the studio setting, with the painted tree at right masking the edge of a doorway. BF

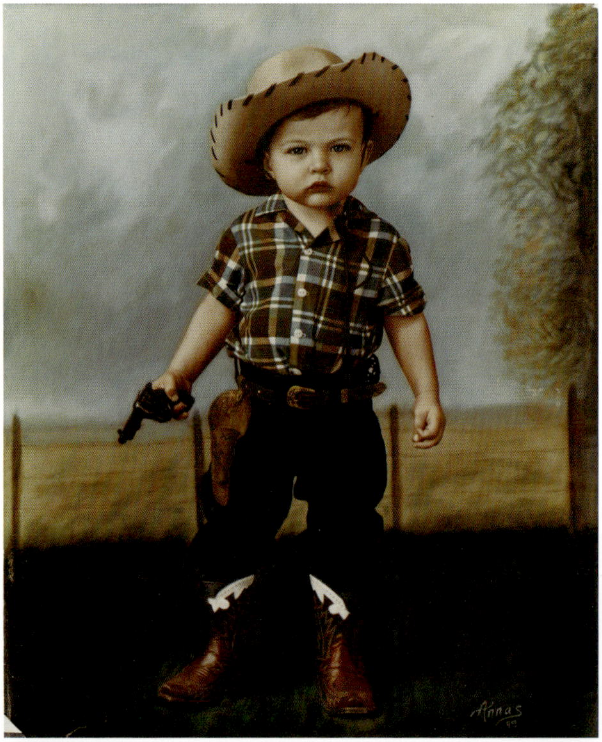

 Gelatin silver print; image: 13 9/16 x 9 3/16 in. (34.4 x 23.4 cm). Fogg Museum, On deposit from the Carpenter Center for the Visual Arts, 2.2002.339.

Robert Frank
American, b. 1924
U.S. 90, en route to Del Rio, Texas From *The Americans*
1955

A Swiss photographer who arrived in the United States in 1947, Robert Frank was the first foreign recipient, in 1955–56, of the prestigious Guggenheim Fellowship in photography. He toured the United States during his fellowship year and, from the negatives produced on that trip, selected the images for his landmark 1959 publication, *The Americans*. This controversial volume was criticized for its images of 1950s America as a place marked by racial and economic tensions but was also widely influential within photography circles because of Frank's combination of formal rigor and social insight. Here, in the book's final image, he depicts his road-weary family parked by a Texas roadside. He offers a glimpse of the private moments and long distances that lie between the other pictures in the volume, while drawing together three icons of the 1950s: the nuclear family, the car, and the open road. BF

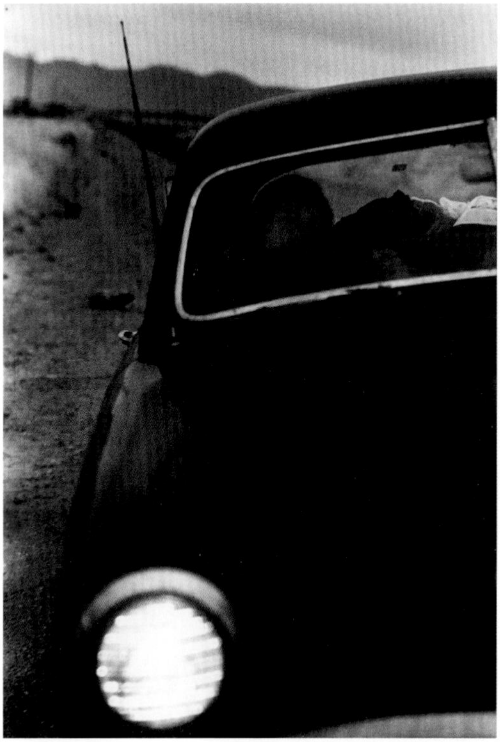

126 Mixed media, closed box: 7 7/8 x 7 7/8 x 3 5/16 in. (20 x 20 x 8.3 cm). Fogg Museum, Barbara and Peter Moore Fluxus Collection, Margaret Fisher Fund, and gift of Barbara Moore/Bound & Unbound, M26448.

Various American Artists
Flux Year Box 2
late 1960s

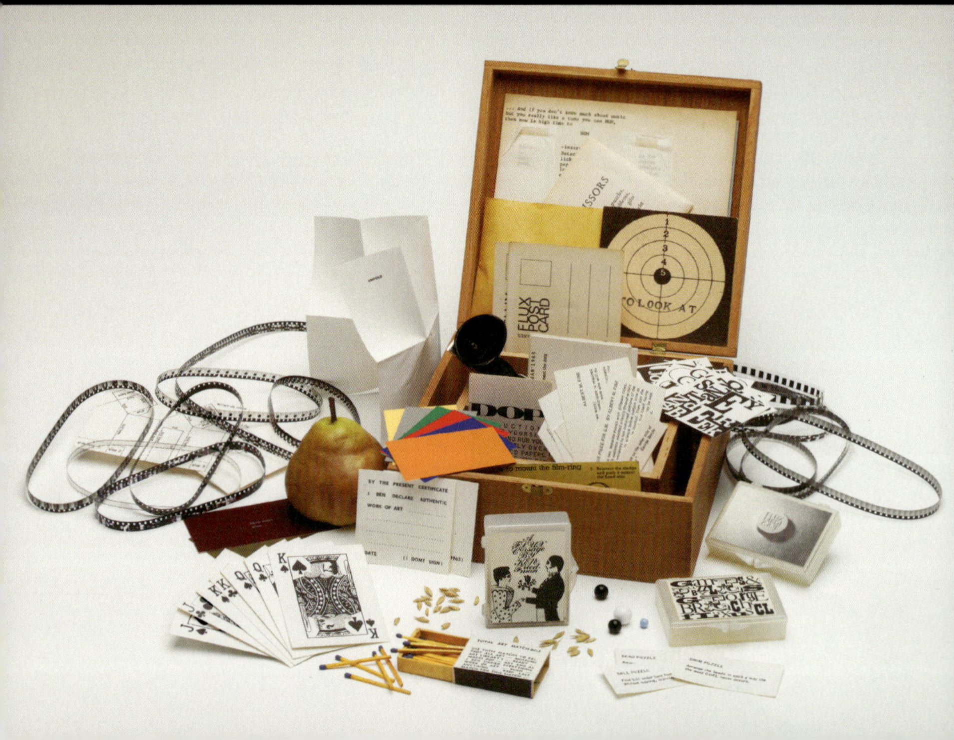

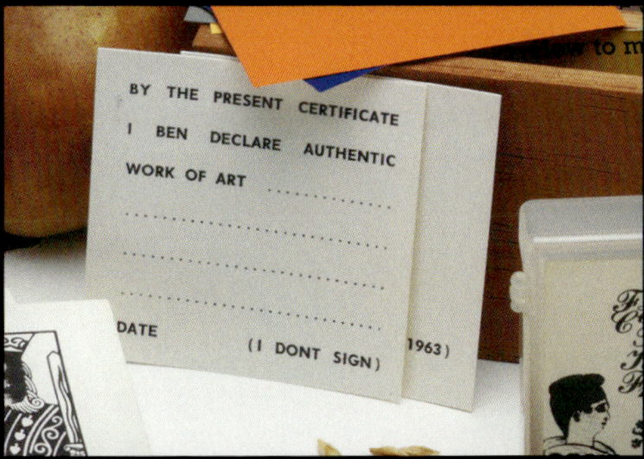

Ben Vautier (American, b. 1935), *Flux Declarations*, offset lithograph cards, from *Flux Year Box 2*.

A product of the 1960s avant-garde movement known as Fluxus, this screen-printed wooden box contains forty works by various Fluxus artists. *Flux Year Box 2* embodies editor, designer, and publisher George Maciunas's desire to expand the potential of the boxed anthology portfolio to include printed material, small readymade objects, miniature Fluxus boxes, and 8 mm film loops with a small, hand-operated viewer. George Brecht, Ken Friedman, Shigeko Kubota, Claes Oldenburg, Yoko Ono, Ben Vautier, and Robert Watts are among the artists represented in this edition. / *Flux Year Box 2* is one of more than one hundred objects in the Barbara and Peter Moore Fluxus Collection, an intact, first-owner collection now in the Harvard Art Museum that features a remarkable range of Fluxus editions, prototypes or models for editions, and early and rare examples of many key multiples. The collection places the Art Museum's Fluxus holdings among the most significant in North America. JP

Acrylic resin paint on canvas, 91 3/4 x 156 in. (233.1 x 396.2 cm). Fogg Museum, Gift of Lois Orswell and Gifts for Special Uses Fund, 1965.28.

Morris Louis
American, 1912–1962
Blue Veil
1958–59

Morris Louis was the chief proponent of the post-abstract expressionist style known as color field painting. Although familiar with Jackson Pollock's pouring and dripping technique, he also learned from Helen Frankenthaler, who in 1952 started staining her canvases with washes of thinned pigment. In the Veil series, Louis fused paint and canvas, figure and ground, to create vast polychrome fields whose decorative power recalls Matisse's largest paintings. To create such a huge work in his small studio, Louis worked with gravity: He stapled the loose canvas to a wooden bar and then manipulated the angle of the cloth to control the sequential flows of paint. HC

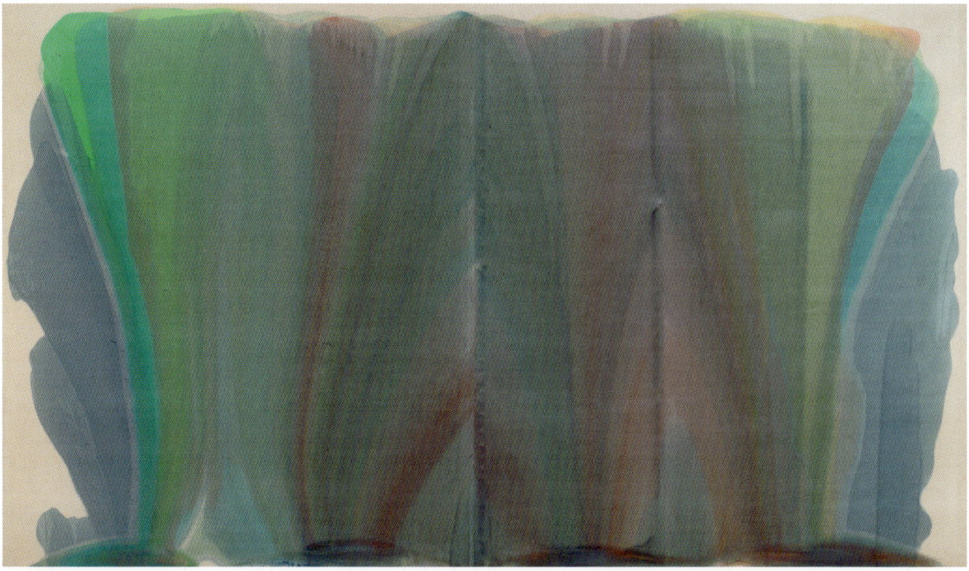

229 Chromogenic print, 18 5/16 x 23 1/16 in. (46.5 x 58.5 cm). Fogg Museum, On deposit from the Carpenter Center for the Visual Arts, 2.2002.3137.

Richard Misrach
American, b. 1949
Submerged Gas Pumps, Salton Sea
1983

Richard Misrach takes the desert Southwest of the United States as his major subject and in 1979 began an extended body of work known by the title *Desert Cantos*. Misrach's ongoing series frequently complicates our ideas of nature by turning the aesthetics of landscape photography toward instances of human interaction with the land, as in this image of the Salton Sea in California. The once-submerged basin known as the Salton Sink was inadvertently reflooded around 1905 as a result of canal and irrigation projects; over the next half-century, tourism and resort construction came to the area but had to contend with the lake's frequently shifting water levels. Depicting in 1983 the outdated artifacts of such construction reflected in the waters of later flooding, Misrach compresses several layers of the lake's history. BF

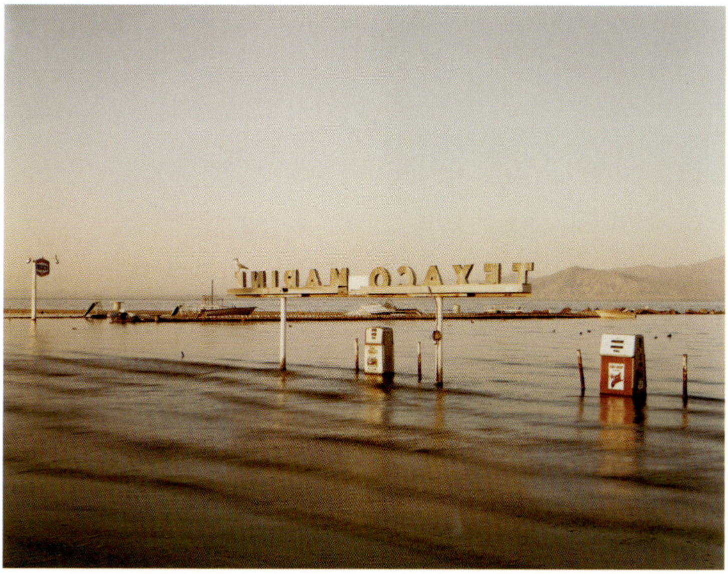

Lithograph, 25 9/16 x 20 7/8 in. (65 x 53 cm). Fogg Museum, Deknatel Purchase Fund, M20193.

Jasper Johns
American, b. 1930
Coat Hanger I
1960

Jasper Johns consistently pushed the boundaries of abstract representation by using everyday objects such as flags, cans, and targets in multidimensional artworks. His Coat Hanger series, from early in his career, comprised a drawing, a painting, and two different lithographs. The use of this commonplace item imparted an aura of realism to the abstract backdrops. The drawing in the series created a trompe l'oeil effect, and Johns reified the illusion by attaching an actual coat hanger to the subsequent painting. He refers obliquely to this deft integration of pictorial device and actual object in this lithograph, the third work in the series. The image remains subtly deceiving as it hints at the coat hanger's material presence by depicting it as a three-dimensional object. Johns reworked the second lithograph, *Coat Hanger II*, from the same stone, but the starker contrast with the background diminishes its illusionism. SKS

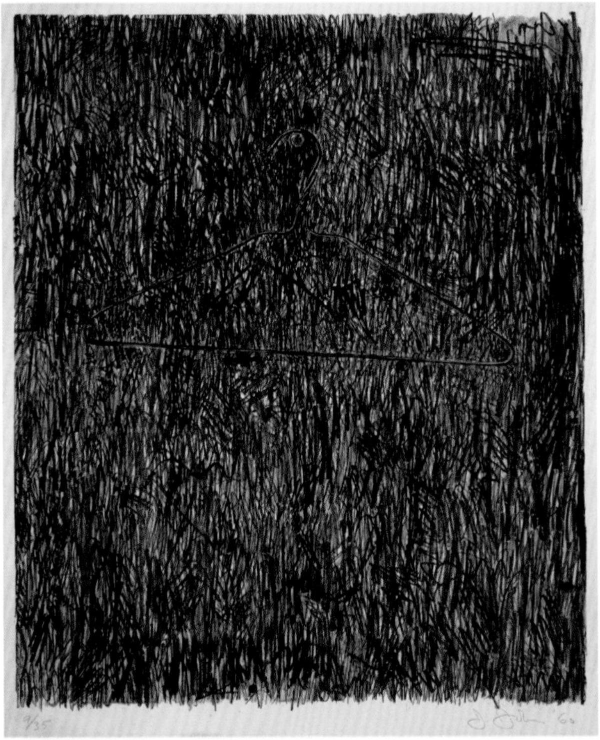

231 Charcoal, graphite wash, and graphite with polyester resin-molded hand, string, paintbrush, and wooden ruler on off-white wove paper; 50 x 34 1/2 x 4 in. (127 x 87.6 x 10.2 cm). Fogg Museum, Gift of Sarah-Ann and Werner H. Kramarsky, 2002.94.

Jasper Johns
American, b. 1930
Wilderness I
1963–70

Wilderness I, first drawn in 1963 and revisited and completed in 1970, refers to Johns's meditations on the subject of artistic practice. The back of a stretched canvas, complete with stretcher keys wedged under the corners, appears in the lower half. The artist is embodied by a resin cast of his hand and, at the bottom of the frame, a ruler—a "foot." Doubled images engage in a dialogue between physical objects, representation, and language: the traced outline of the suspended brush, hastily inscribed letters below the stenciled words describing the primary colors, a silhouette and washy shadow behind the hand. MS

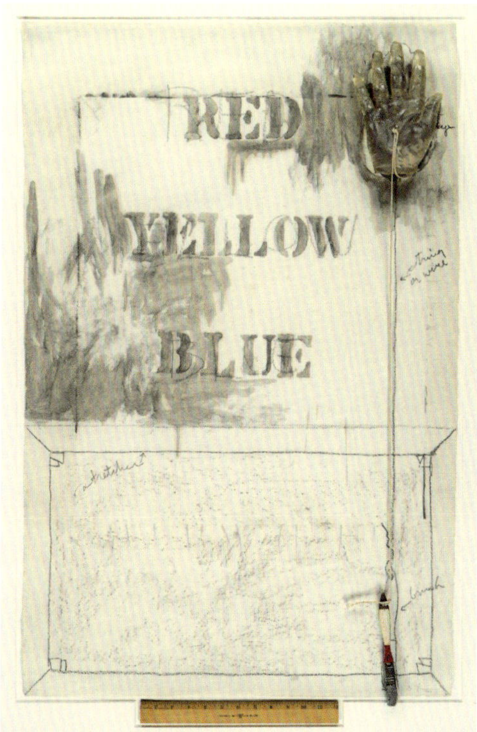

Screen print, 35 1/16 x 23 1/16 in. (89 x 58.5 cm). Fogg Museum, Gift of John and Kimiko Powers, M15531.

Andy Warhol
American, 1928–1987
Chicken Noodle Soup
1968

From the portfolio *Campbell's Soup I*

Chicken Noodle Soup epitomizes Warhol's stance that art lovers are also consumers. His choice of the familiar Campbell's soup can as a leitmotif in paintings and prints underscores the role of artworks as mechanically produced, interchangeable commodities. The ten flavors from Warhol's screen print portfolio also included *Tomato*, *Pepper Pot*, and *Consommé (Beef)*. Proclaiming that he would like to be a machine, Warhol oversaw the production of art by other hands at his Factory, turning this authorlessness into his signature style. The magnified scale of the screen print suggests that, like the American Dream, the can is both boundless and empty. SKS

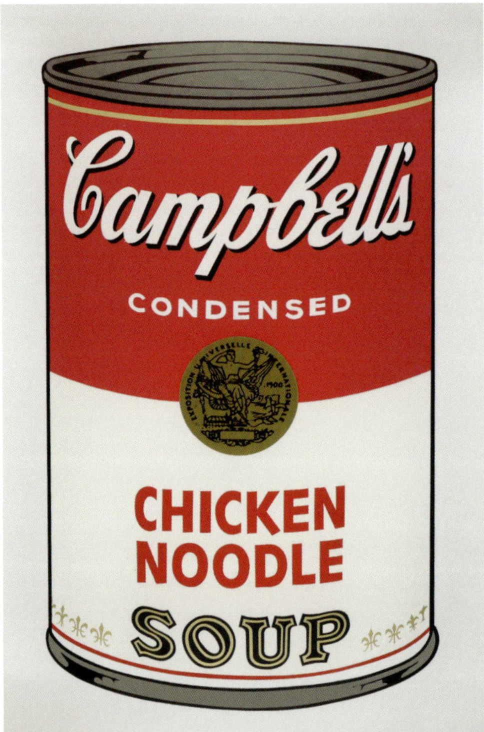

233 Two bottles of soda water, felt, and printed labels in a wooden box, its cover printed in black ink; box: 10 7/8 x 6 1/2 x 3 9/16 in. (27.7 x 16.5 x 9 cm). Busch-Reisinger Museum, The Willy and Charlotte Reber Collection, Edmée Busch Greenough Fund, 1995.214.A–D.

Joseph Beuys
German, 1921–1986
Everess II 1
1968

Controversial postwar artist Joseph Beuys sought to democratize art and involve the viewer in what he termed "social sculpture." He is remembered today for his multiples—works of art that, like prints, are created in editions. Multiples mark an important break with traditional conceptions of the unique work of art, and they were of particular importance to Beuys, who is reported to have stated, "If you have all of my multiples, you have all of me." / In 1995, the Busch-Reisinger Museum acquired a near-complete set of Beuys multiples, making Harvard's collection among the most comprehensive in the world. *Everess II 1* is an intriguing example of the artist's call for active participation. The instructions printed on the box direct the collector to empty the contents of one of the bottles and throw the cap "as far as possible," a condition that most were unlikely to fulfill. SK2

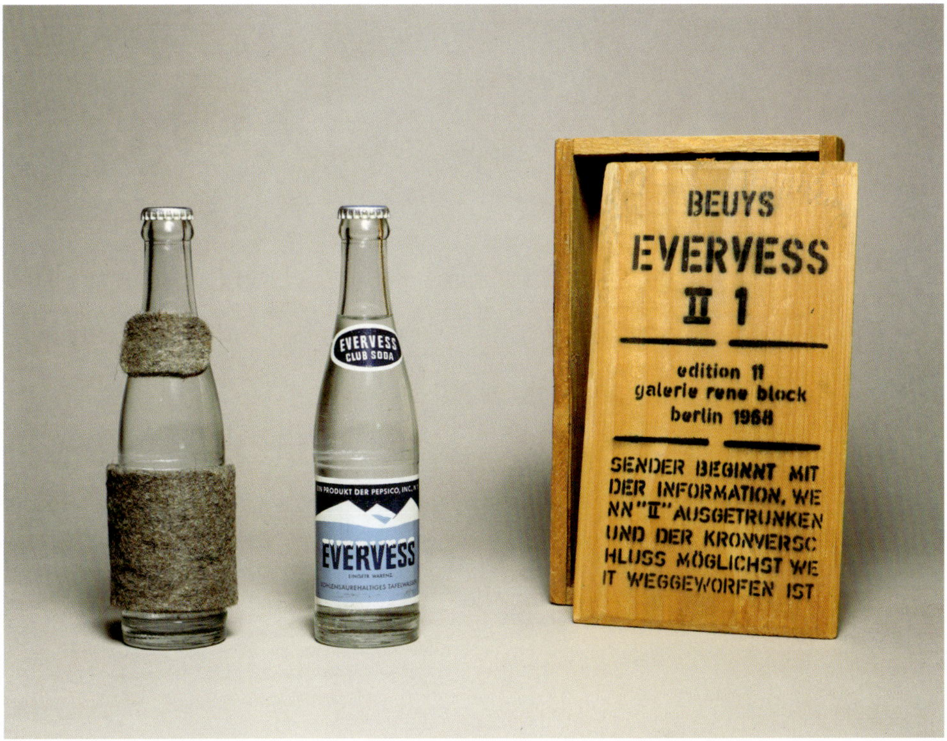

Oil on canvas, 63 x 51 in. (160 x 129.5 cm). Busch-Reisinger Museum, Edmée Busch Greenough Fund and purchase through the generosity of Gabriele Geier, Edythe and Eli Broad, the Broad Art Foundation, Emily Rauh Pulitzer; and Melva Bucksbaum and Raymond Learsy in honor of James Cuno, 2001.51.

Georg Baselitz
German, b. 1938
Curly Head
1967

Georg Baselitz's skepticism toward the coercive powers of representation derived in part from his upbringing in East Germany. Moving to the West, he rejected the dominant mode of abstract painting and developed a personal style of expressionist figuration. His fracture paintings of the late 1960s deliberately disturb painterly conventions of perspective, pictorial unity, and propriety. *Curly Head* defies viewer expectations of a quiet, pastoral scene and instead disorients, with three horizontal bands discontinuous in scale and color. With the fracture paintings Baselitz began testing the limits of figurative painting, which led him, starting in 1969, to paint images upside down in order to emphasize painterly effects over subject matter. HH

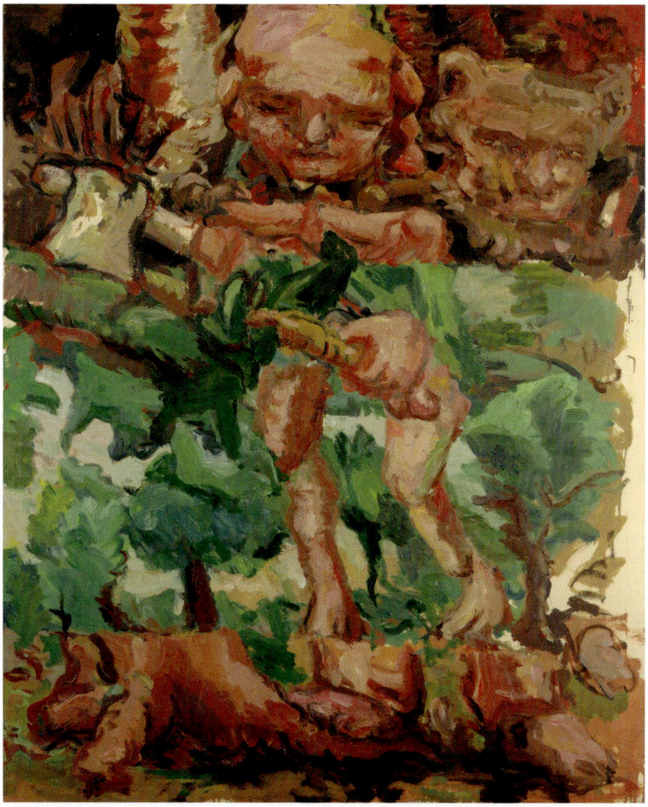

 Oil on Masonite, 12 1/8 x 14 in. (30.8 x 35.6 cm). Fogg Museum, Louise E. Bettens Fund, 1976.9.

Philip Guston
American, 1913–1980
The Three
1970

In 1970, the eminent abstract expressionist Philip Guston began exhibiting nonabstract, figural canvases whose readability scandalized fellow New York school painters. Guston had previously worked as a muralist for the WPA in the 1930s and 1940s, and *The Three* reflects his concern for social justice and his early training as a cartoonist. In the painting, three hooded figures reminiscent of Ku Klux Klansmen huddle together conspiratorially, creating a sense of menace and claustrophobia that is emphasized by the schematically rendered buildings and oppressive skyline. EL

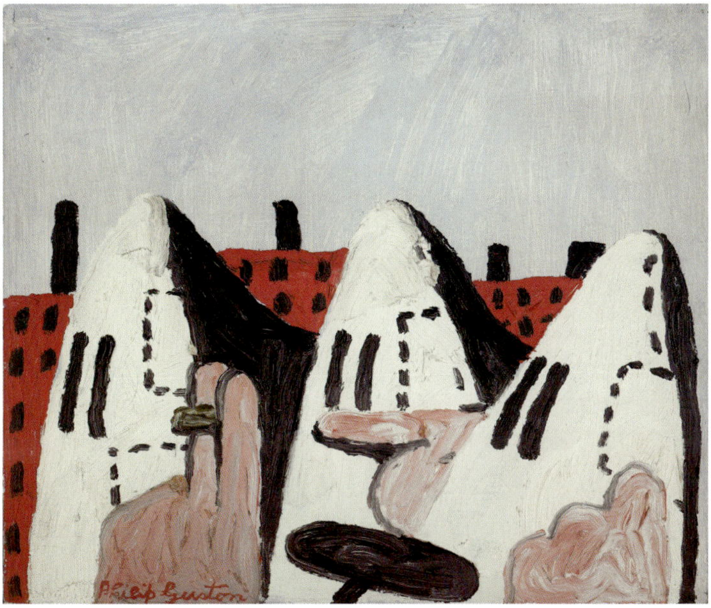

Gelatin silver print, 14 15/16 x 14 15/16 in. (38 x 38 cm). Fogg Museum, National Endowment for the Arts Grant, P1972.6.

Diane Arbus, American, 1923–1971
This is Eddie Carmel, a Jewish giant, with his parents in the living room of their home in the Bronx, New York, 1970

Diane Arbus explored the psychological dimension of charged political times through photography. The effectiveness of her work often hinged upon the disjunction between the strangeness of her subjects and the formal order of her photographic vision. Centering this image on the physical space between Eddie and his parents, and echoing the curve of his shoulder in the darkened corners of the print, the photograph suggests both claustrophobia and emotional distance. / This print comes from Arbus's *A Box of Ten Photographs* (issued in 1971, the year of her death); the Fogg's portfolio is one of only a few copies known to be printed by the artist herself. Its acquisition by former curator of photography Davis Pratt in 1972 reflects not only his prescient support of her work but also the Fogg's early and ongoing interest in the personal documentary tradition stretching from Robert Frank to Nan Goldin. BF

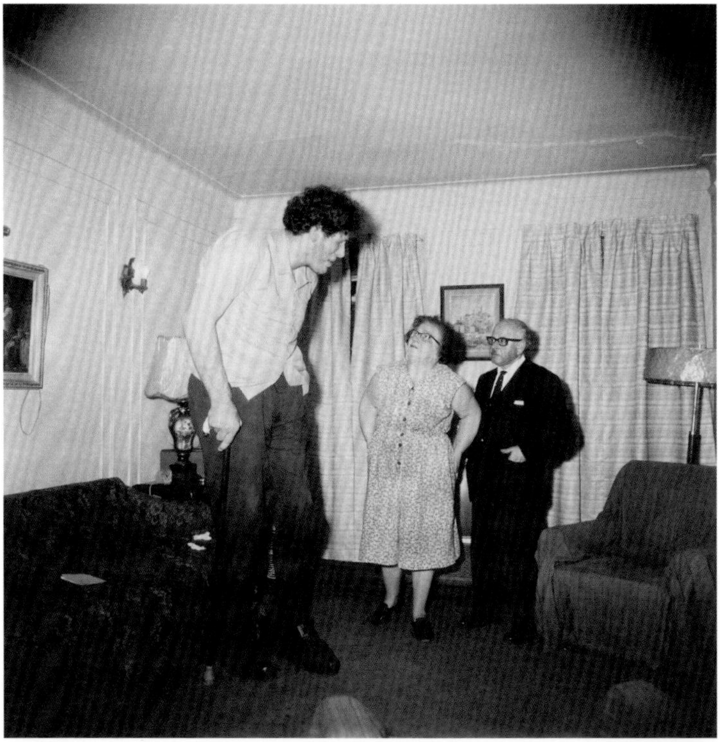

237 Gelatin silver print, 8 3/4 x 13 in. (22.3 x 33 cm). Fogg Museum, On deposit from the Carpenter Center for the Visual Arts, 2.2002.1638.

Lee Friedlander
American, b. 1934
Mount Rushmore, South Dakota
1969

Lee Friedlander's ironic photograph of tourists viewing Mount Rushmore bridges two major projects that underscore his interest in the artist's book as a means to present his work. Made during the evolution of an innovative and irreverent series of self-portraits that led to his first publication, *Self-Portrait*, in 1970, this picture includes the artist's reflection suspended in a complex layering of bodies seen outside, through, and reflected in the panes of glass. However, this image was published instead in his 1976 book *The American Monument*, which largely depicts less famous monuments obscured and ignored within their environments. BF

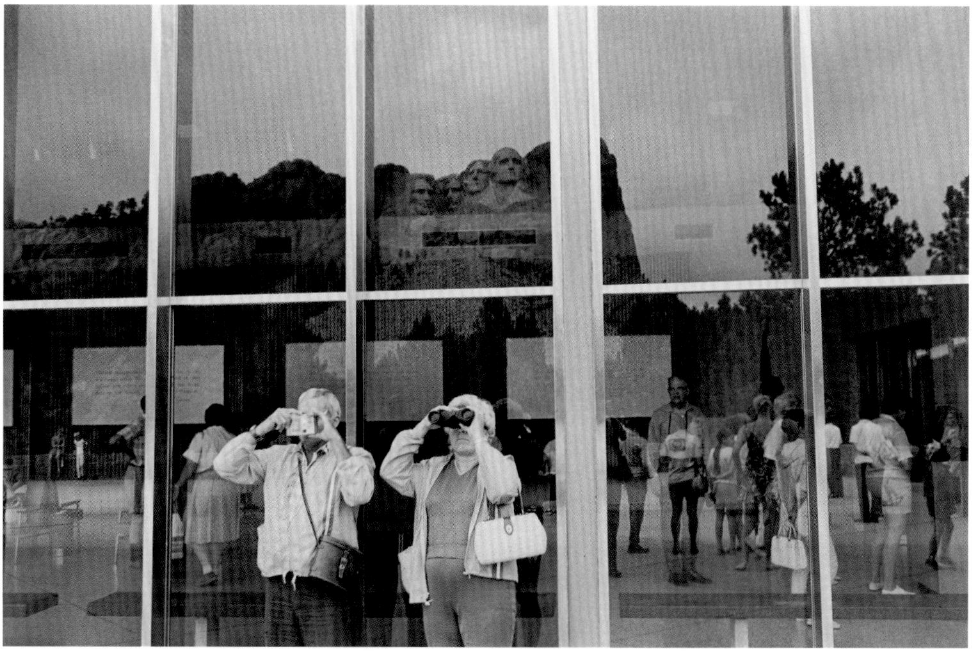

Graphite, gouache, crayon, black ink, and collage on thin cream wove paper; 8 7/16 x 10 15/16 in. (21.5 x 27.8 cm). Fogg Museum, Margaret Fisher Fund, 2003.73.

Eva Hesse
American, 1936–1970
Untitled
1962

Although Eva Hesse is best known as a sculptor, in the early 1960s she identified herself as a painter. During that time, she produced a series of painterly drawings that have a presence and monumentality belying their small scale. *Untitled* (1962) is a tangle of scrubbed gouache and furiously scribbled lines. Centered on a pair of bull's-eyes (the one at the right was cut from another drawing and attached as a collage element), the composition is characteristically askew—an example of what Hesse referred to as "wild space." The armature is unstable, allowing the eye no comforting purchase, and the whole seems in danger of collapsing. MS

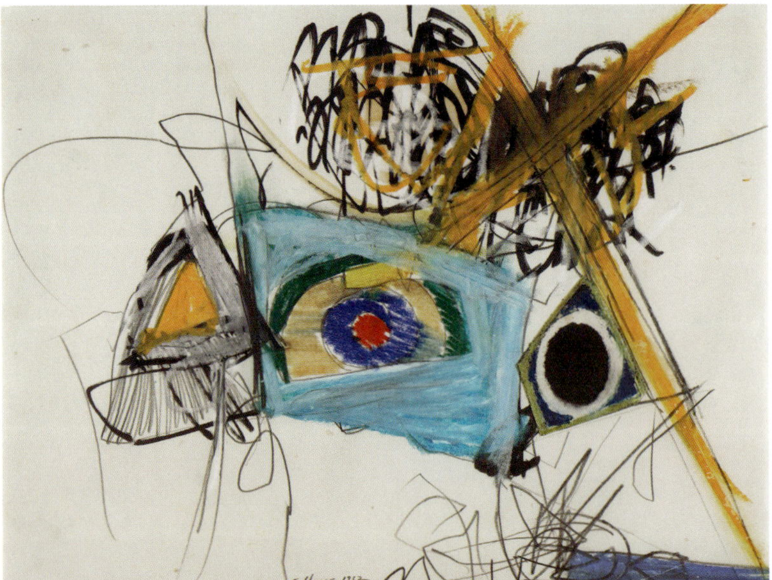

Oil on canvas, 102 3/8 x 78 3/4 in. (260 x 200 cm). Busch-Reisinger Museum, Gift of Lufthansa German Airlines, 1984.194.

Gerhard Richter
German, b. 1932
Said
1983

Gerhard Richter's abstract pictures investigate basic principles of painting and experiment with color in relation to physical mass, texture, and surface. Richter created *Said* with conventional materials and tools—acrylic primer, standard oil paints from tubes, linseed oil as a diluent, canvas, and brushes. However, in addition to brushes of various sizes, he used a piece of Plexiglas glued to a handle to create the yellow smears and speckles that spread across the center of the painting. In works like *Said*, color reveals the various manipulations of the artist's array of instruments, media, and techniques. / The painting's title refers both to the surname of the German-Egyptian psychoanalyst Mohamed Said El-Safti (1924–2001), a friend of the artist, and to the past tense of the English verb "to say"—an apt conjunction, given psychoanalysis's reliance on the spoken word. CS

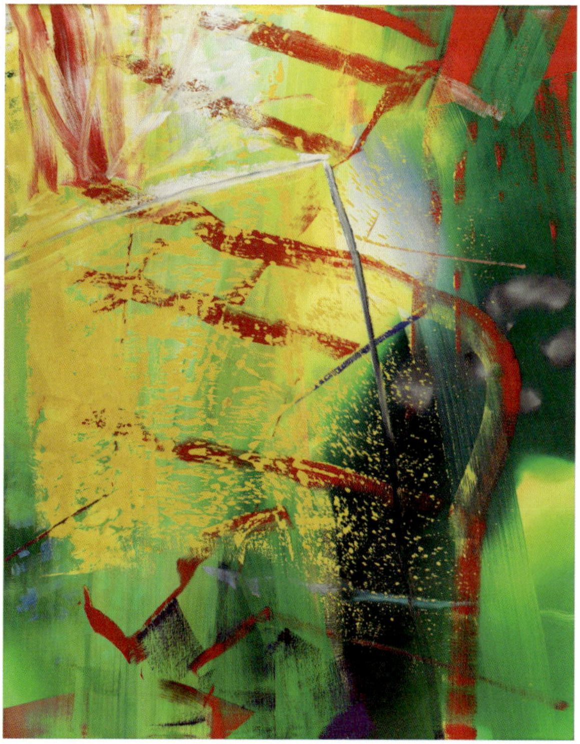

Ashes and acrylic on gelatin silver prints, mounted to board; 39 11/16 x 27 15/16 x 3 1/8 in. (100.8 x 71 x 8 cm). Busch-Reisinger Museum, Purchase in honor of Arend Oetker through the generosity of a group of Friends of the Busch-Reisinger Museum, 1993.205.

Anselm Kiefer
German, b. 1945
The Heavenly Palaces: Merkabah
1990

According to the Kabbalah, the mystical approach to study of the Torah, one must travel through seven celestial regions to reach the throne of God, known as Merkabah, the place where God becomes visible. Anselm Kiefer, one of Germany's leading postwar artists, made this journey the theme of *The Heavenly Palaces: Merkabah*, the organization of which is structured after a mystic's journey. / Books have always been a central component of Kiefer's oeuvre as both subject and medium, and since the 1970s he has incorporated original photography into his work. In *The Heavenly Palaces: Merkabah*, Kiefer combines photographs taken in his studio, a repurposed brickworks, with materials such as ashes and acrylic. Visual and structural interest arises from the contrast between the flat surfaces of the photographs and the three-dimensionality of the reworked sections, while the resulting tension between figuration and abstraction approaches the possibility of representing God. SK2

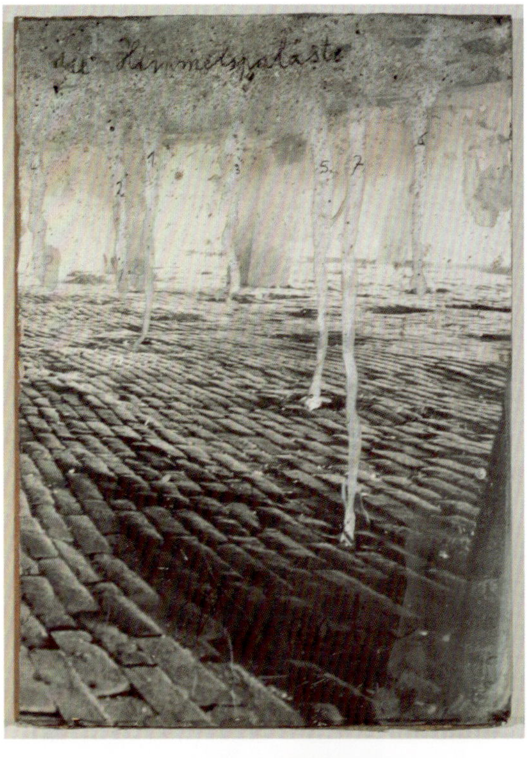

16 mm color anamorphic film, 63 min. Fogg Museum, The Jorie Marshall Waterman '96 and Gwendolyn Dunaway Waterman '93 Fund in honor of James Cuno, 2003.9.3.

Tacita Dean
British, b. 1965
Banewl
1999

Tacita Dean's rhythmic and meditative film tracks a total eclipse of the sun at a dairy farm on the western coast of England. As the sky darkens and lightens again, images of a herd of Holstein cows at pasture are interspersed with shots of the overcast sky, providing a veiled glimpse of the changing position of the sun. The lulling, ambient noise of the farm—mooing cows and crashing waves—comprises the soundtrack. Dean filmed the eclipse for two hours and forty minutes in August 1999 and then compressed the time frame. The distorted events, along with the lushly saturated colors, give the work the peculiar quality of a landscape painting come to life. EL

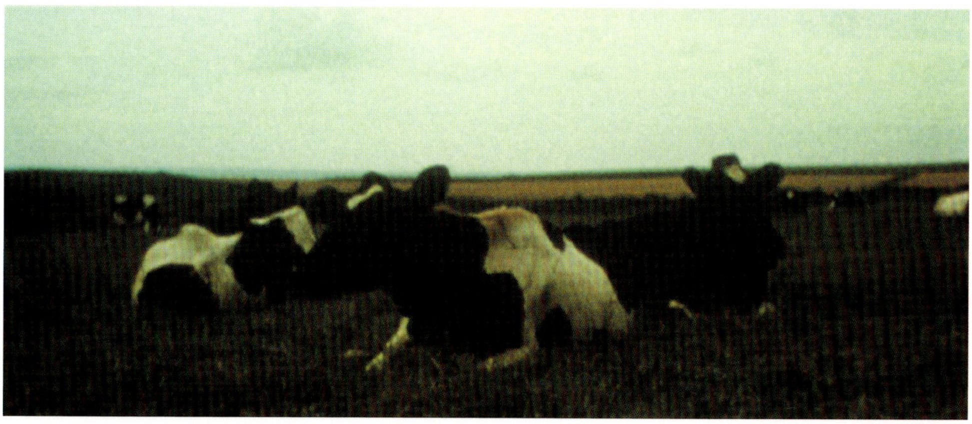

Cibachrome, 29 x 40 in. (73.6 x 101.6 cm). Fogg Museum, Gift of Nan Goldin in memory of Jeffrey Weinberger, P1994.1.

Nan Goldin
American, b. 1953
Self-Portrait in Blue Bathroom, London
1980

Nan Goldin's self-portrait comes from an extensive and largely autobiographical series, *The Ballad of Sexual Dependency*, which depicts the environments and intimate activities of the drag queens, drug users, and other individuals who have composed her subculture "family." The original series was a slideshow of seven hundred images set to music, which migrated from clubs to galleries before appearing at the Whitney Biennial in 1985. From this evolving presentation, Goldin selected images for publication as a book by the Aperture Foundation in 1986. / In this introspective picture, atypical of the emotionally raw imagery of the slideshow and the book, we witness Goldin distancing and isolating herself through the framing device of the mirror while allowing the broad expanse of blue to carry the scene's melancholy tone. Harvard has enjoyed a special connection with the artist: She performed the *Ballad* here in 1988, and her parents donated a group of early works to the Fogg in 2003. BF

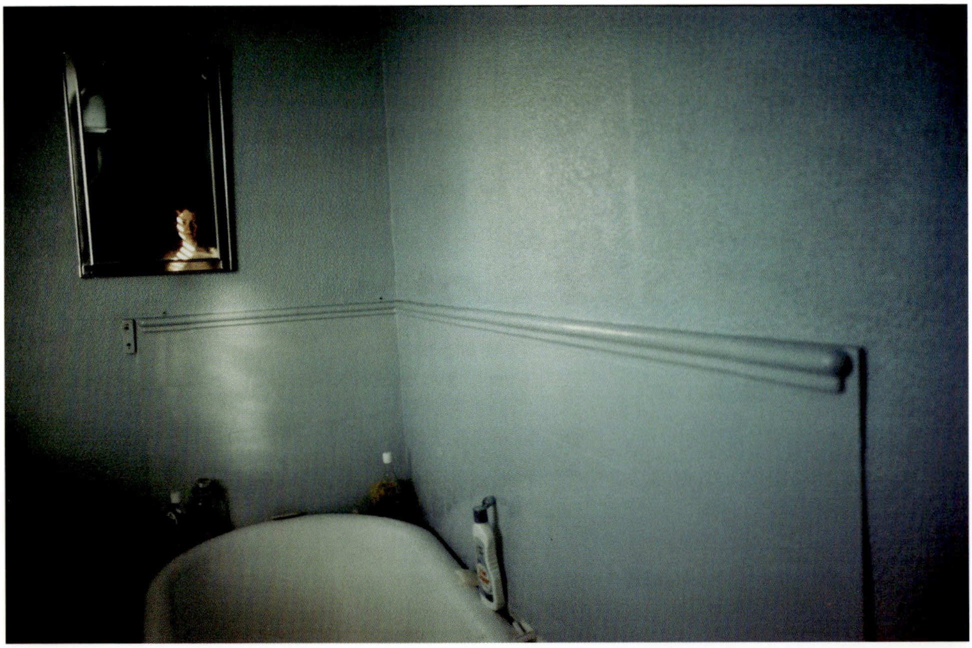

243 Chromogenic print, 60 x 48 in. (152.4 x 121.9 cm). Fogg Museum, Richard and Ronay Menschel Fund for the Acquisition of Photographs, P2005.11.

Gary Schneider
American, b. 1954
Helen
2000

Gary Schneider's photographs frequently engage with issues of duration and interaction, interests shaped by his experience in film and performance art. This work derives from the expansion of his black-and-white durational portraits—images of sitters before a large-format camera, their faces selectively illuminated with a penlight for an hour or more—into color photography. Although Schneider shortened his exposure times in the color medium, these new works are still artifacts of the interaction of photographer and sitter: The differing highlights in Helen's eyes point to the piecemeal illumination of her face, and the asymmetry of her upper face reveals a change of position during exposure. The standardized format of the series, isolating each face in a black ground, emphasizes the differences between Schneider's subjects, and the large scale of the works allows the faces to open into abstract passages of color and texture. BF

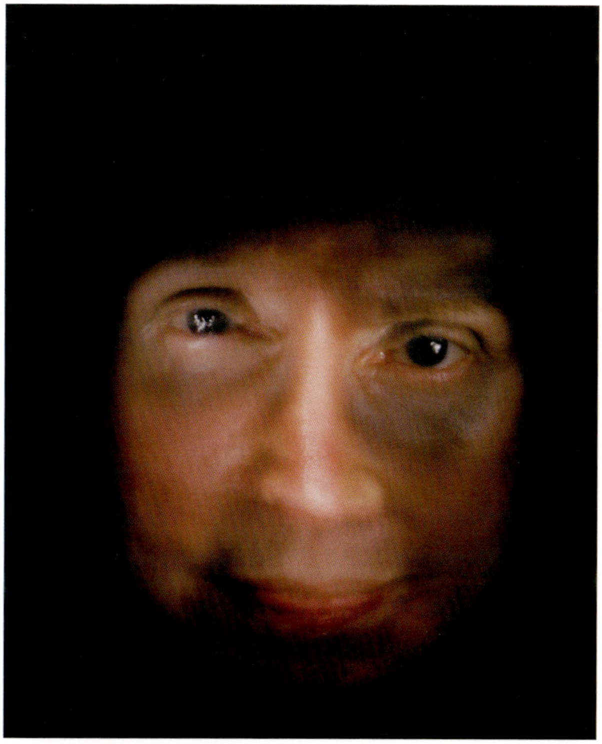

 Pink marble, 35 x 27 x 21 in. (88.9 x 68.6 x 53.3 cm). Fogg Museum, Gift of José M. Soriano Sr., 2005.3.

Louise Bourgeois
American, b. 1911
Nature Study
1986

Influenced by minimalism and abstraction, Louise Bourgeois's work is strongly rooted in the surrealist practice of mining the unconscious. Bourgeois, one of the few surviving artists of the modernist period, developed a vocabulary of ambiguously symbolic, suggestive, biomorphic shapes that address themes of fear, anger, and betrayal. Here, a polished pink tube coils around a pair of tenderly folded hands atop a massive, rough-cut block of marble. The contrasting surfaces and bulky materiality of the marble show that Bourgeois is as interested in exploring the sensual properties of the material as in the images she elicits from it. EL

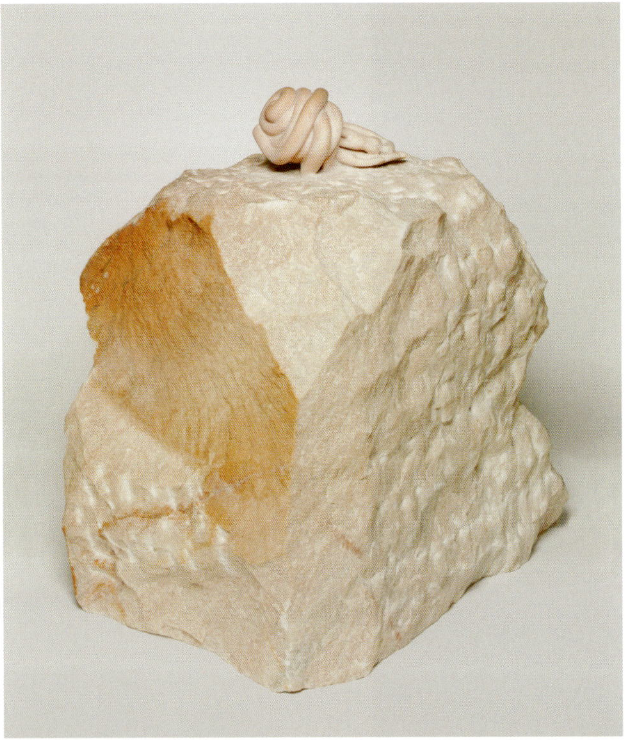

245 Wax and glass beads; 27 x 28 x 28 in. (68.6 x 71.1 x 71.1 cm), including 23 strands of beads, each 1–15 ft. long. Fogg Museum, Promised gift in part of Barbara Lee and Emily Rauh Pulitzer and purchase in part from the Joseph A. Baird Jr., Francis H. Burr Memorial, and Director's Acquisition Funds, 1997.82.

Kiki Smith
American, b. 1954
Pee Body
1992

Pee Body is one of the many works by American artist Kiki Smith that explore the female body and its private performance of basic bodily functions. Shifting the focus from exterior appearance to the interior processes of waste and regeneration, Smith subverts the sculptural tradition of the eroticized female form. Here, the life-size body of a woman, molded in sweet-smelling beeswax, crouches on the gallery floor, with sparkling yellow beads streaming out behind her. The visceral subject matter is tempered by the delicate materials—wax and glass—and by the bowed head and folded arms that suggest a private, introspective state and a fragile, vulnerable human body. EL

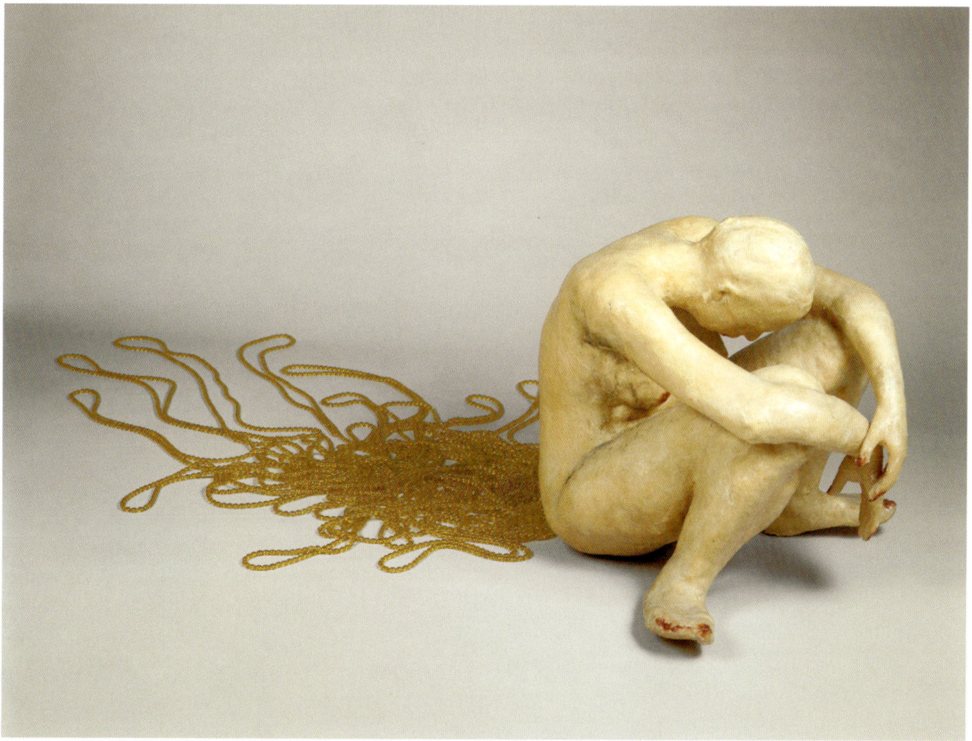

Offset lithography on wallpaper, 94 7/8 x 29 5/8 in. (241 x 75 cm). Fogg Museum, Purchase through the generosity of John Silberman, 2006.291.

Robert Gober
American, b. 1954
Hanging Man/Sleeping Man
1989

Robert Gober's provocative installations comprise painstakingly handmade sculptures, drawings, and printed objects that evoke disconcerting spaces and situations. Gober sometimes designs printed wallpaper as backdrops for his installations. This example of wallpaper—a small section on rollers—shows images of a lynched black man juxtaposed with images of a white man in bed. The sources for the designs were a racist 1920s Texas cartoon and a contemporaneous Bloomingdale's advertisement for bed linen. By subverting the decorative medium of wallpaper, Gober positions issues of race, violence, and culpability within an ambivalent sphere of dreams, with multiple, sometimes uneasy, interpretations. SKS & EL

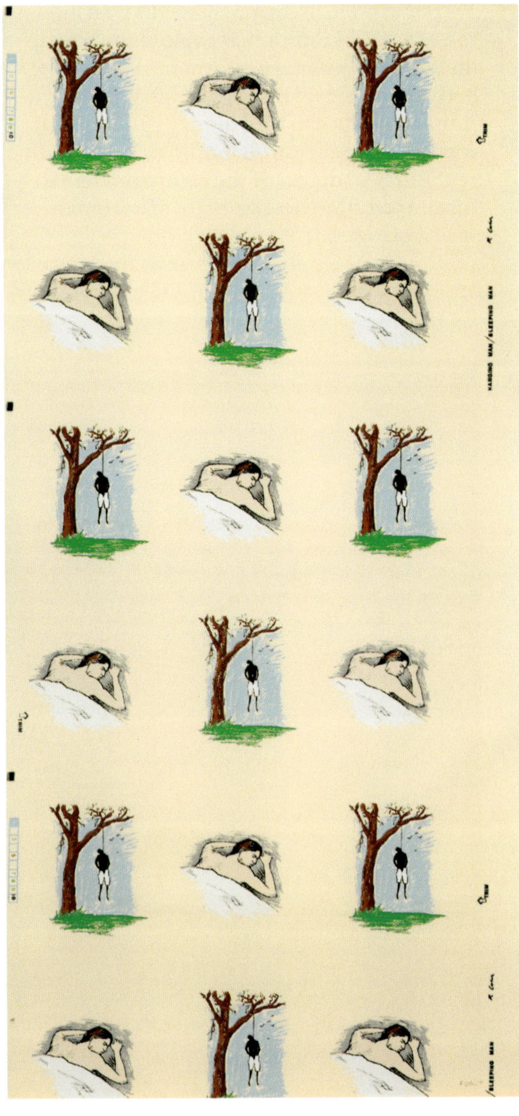

247 Four monochrome chromogenic print panels with sandblasted text on glass; each sheet: $23\frac{7}{16} \times 19\frac{1}{2}$ in. (59.5 x 49.5 cm). Fogg Museum, Richard and Ronay Menschel Fund for the Acquisition of Photographs, P2001.28.1–.4.

Carrie Mae Weems
American, b. 1953
You Became a Scientific Profile / A Negroid Type / An Anthropological Debate / & A Photographic Subject
1995–96

From the series *From Here I Saw What Happened and I Cried*

Invited to respond to an exhibition on the portrayal of African Americans in early photography, Carrie Mae Weems produced a thirty-two-panel installation based on appropriated photographs spanning issues of slavery, emancipation, and civil rights. Weems enlarged her source photographs, produced them in red, and presented them in circular mats with overlaid texts. / These four panels, which are also a stand-alone work, depict two African-born slaves and their American-born daughters. They derive from daguerreotypes commissioned by Harvard scientist Louis Agassiz in 1850 to support his argument for the separate origins of different races; the works were discovered at the Peabody Museum in 1975. Weems's captions emphasize Agassiz's original presentation of the slaves as scientific specimens, yet she addresses these historical subjects in the second person, returning our attention to the individuality stripped away by slavery and science alike. BF

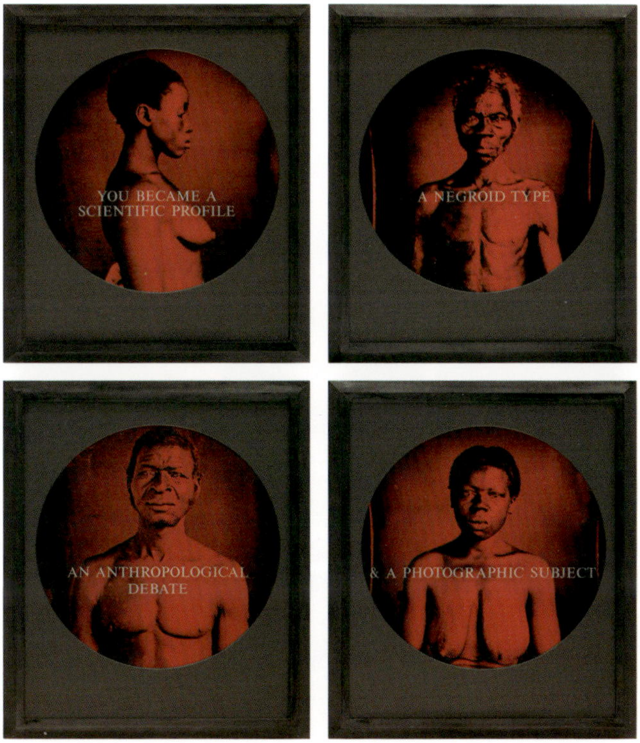

Gelatin silver print, 6 5/8 x 9 5/8 in. (16.8 x 24.5 cm). Fogg Museum, Richard and Ronay Menschel Fund for the Acquisition of Photographs, P2004.32.

Shōmei Tomatsu
Japanese, b. 1930
Untitled (Yokosuka)
1959, printed 1974

From the series
Chewing Gum and Chocolate

After narrowly surviving World War II as an adolescent in Japan, Shōmei Tomastu came to examine what he described as the postwar "Americanization" of his country. The photograph here captures what he perceived as the two dominant aspects of this transformation: the ongoing presence of American soldiers in Japanese cities and the concomitant spread of U.S. products and consumer culture. It is one of the first images in an extended series titled *Chewing Gum and Chocolate* that draws together these two concerns. In this case, it does so quite directly by juxtaposing the girl in the foreground viewed through the bubble she blows, as if through the lens of U.S. commerce, and the soldier in the background. BF

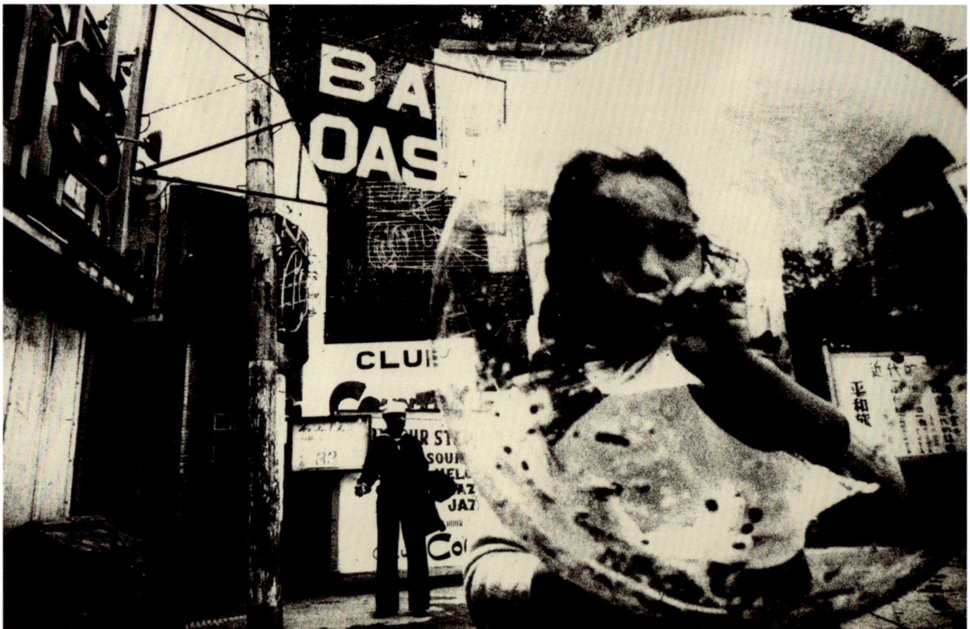

 Chromogenic print, 19 1/2 x 29 1/4 in. (49.5 x 74.3 cm). Arthur M. Sackler Museum, Gift of José M. Soriano, 2005.11.

Raghubir Singh
Indian, 1942–1999
Mango Season, Crawford Market, Mumbai, Maharastra
1993

At the main wholesale produce market in Mumbai (Bombay), vendors quench their thirst during the hot mango season while others scurry to reload their baskets. Shot in vivid color, this lively scene, with its wide focal frame preserving busy and blurry rather than cleanly cropped edges, is typical of Singh's oeuvre. Influenced by Henri Cartier-Bresson's concept of the "decisive moment," Singh believed that photography required a special mix of skill and intuition to best capture action on the streets. Though based in New York, he had a sustained photographic relationship with India, the country of his birth. Singh viewed his photographs of Mumbai as a turning point in his work because they fully engage contemporary urban life in India. SG

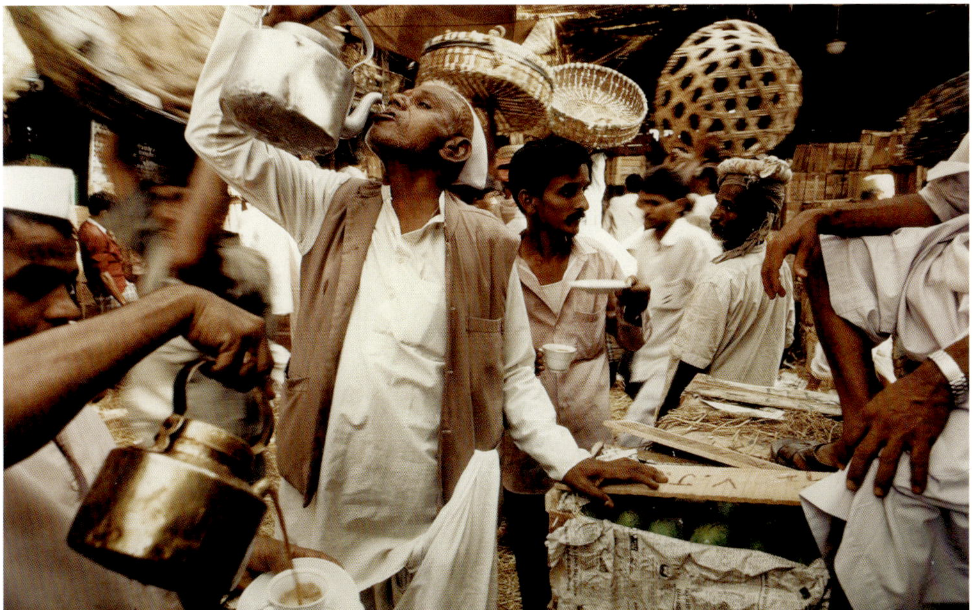

Woodcut, 47 5/8 x 32 1/16 in. (120.9 x 81.5 cm). Fogg Museum, Margaret Fisher Fund, M25274.

Fang Lijun
Chinese, b. 1963
1998.11.2
1998

Fang Lijun trained in Beijing, adopting the stylized ambivalence of China's cynical realism movement in the 1990s after the violent suppression of protest at Tiananmen Square in June 1989. His compositions depict a recurring bald-headed protagonist who exhibits a variety of emotions, ranging from laughter to the despair of this work. The reflection of the setting sun on the water illuminates a rocklike figure with his head in his hands. The size and vertical orientation of the sheet evoke those of a scroll, and Fang exhibited similar woodcuts on silk scrolls at the 1999 Venice Biennale. While the work is traditionally Chinese in format, its expressive simplicity and the bold cutting style enhance the woodcut's connection to Western printmaking traditions. SKS

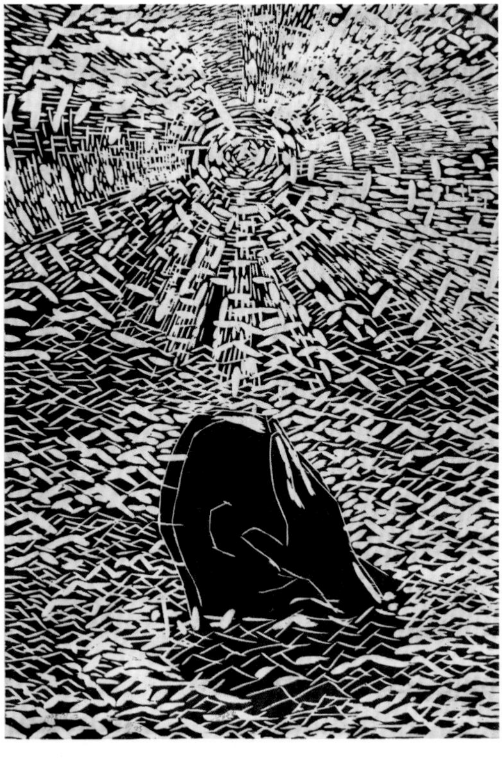

251 Gunpowder on paper, 118$\frac{9}{16}$ x 158$\frac{11}{16}$ in. (301.2 x 403 cm). Fogg Museum, The Jorie Marshall Waterman '96 and Gwendolyn Dunaway Waterman '92 Fund, 2000.60.1.

Cai Guo-Qiang
Chinese, b. 1957
The Century with Mushroom Clouds: Project for the 20th Century, 1996

Cai Guo-Qiang was born in Quanzhou, Fujian Province, China. He has worked in Japan and now lives and works in New York, but his art draws heavily from ancient Chinese history and tradition, here dramatically reconfigured through experimental media. For this painting, the artist exploded gunpowder across the surface of the paper, creating a field of shapes resembling mushroom clouds. The smoky delicateness of the clouds is weighed against the destructive potential of the atomic bomb, the symbol of annihilation in the twentieth century. The work was originally part of a site-specific installation that included army footage of nuclear bomb tests, a selection of the artist's books, tables and chairs, postcards depicting nuclear explosions, hot pots for making medicinal mushroom tea, and live crabs that inhabited the space for the duration of the exhibition. EL

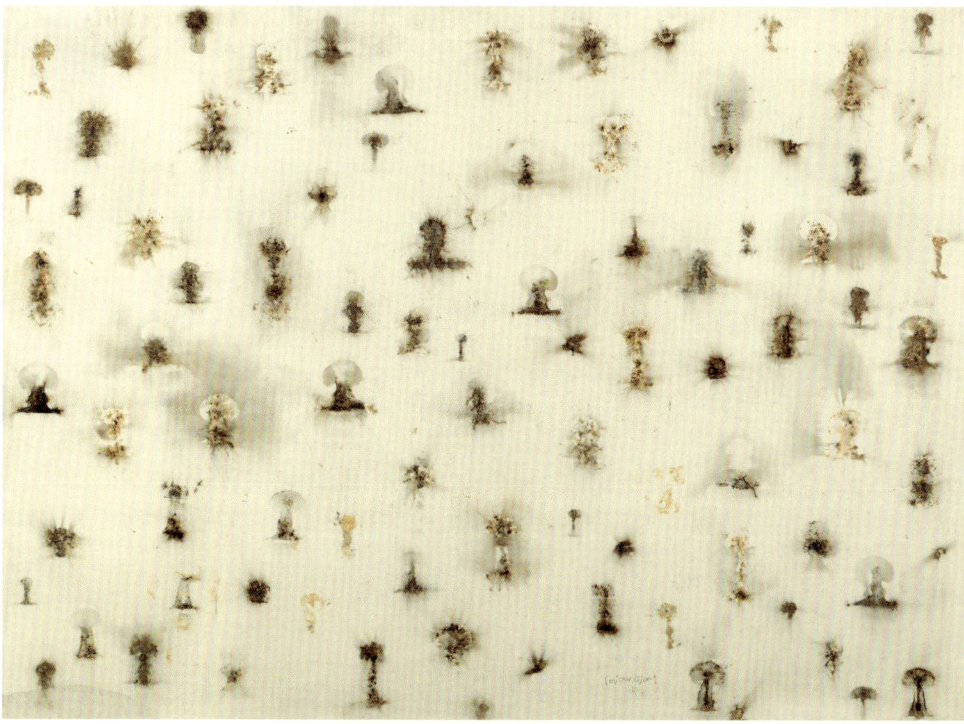

Acrylic on canvas, 60 x 61 in. (152.4 x 154.9 cm). Fogg Museum, Purchase through the generosity of William Danoff, Fifth Floor Foundation, the Charles Engelhard Foundation, Catherine and Paul Buttenwieser Foundation, Laura-Lee W. Woods, an anonymous donor, Bruce A. Beal, and the Broad Art Foundation, 2000.240.

Ed Ruscha
American, b. 1937
Highland Franklin Yucca
1999

Ed Ruscha's lushly rendered work is part of a series of mountain paintings depicting postcard views of mountains Ruscha imagines might be seen from a particular intersection in Los Angeles. The smoky, smeared quadrant of beige paint in the lower right adds unexpected and enigmatic dimension to the painting, and the similarity of the pristine Himalayan mountain to the Paramount Pictures logo alludes to the faux Hollywood glamour of Los Angeles. The intersecting lines of text are arbitrary street names and represent both a visual and conceptual mapping: They meld the pragmatic grid of American city planning with the conceptual grid of European modernist painting. This visually dramatic composition is only one example of the Fogg's considerable collection of Ruscha's work. EL

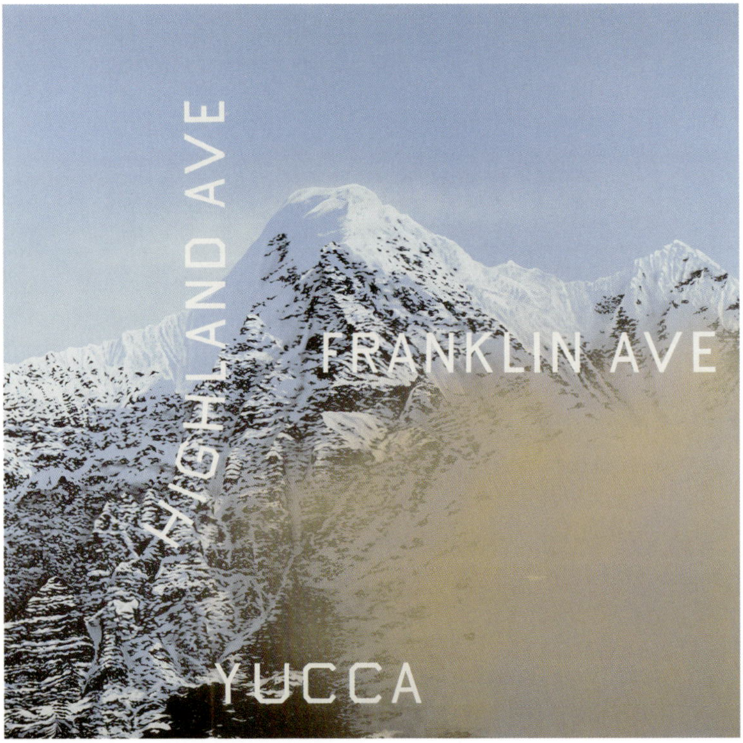

253 Chromogenic print on paper, face mounted to Plexiglas; 80 11/16 x 141 3/4 in. (205 x 360 cm). Busch-Reisinger Museum, Purchase through the generosity of Edythe and Eli Broad, the Broad Art Foundation, and the Friends of the Busch-Reisinger Museum, 2000.6.

Andreas Gursky
German, b. 1955
Los Angeles
1999

This expansive night view of Los Angeles exemplifies the work of Andreas Gursky, who has become known for his iconic images of the contemporary world. His large-format photographs typically focus on anonymous crowds and the environments in which people live and work, capturing global landmarks and sites of leisure, consumption, and commerce that are at once generic and highly specific. The panoramic view in *Los Angeles* seems familiar as an archetype, presenting an almost cinematic impression of one of the world's most media-driven cities while managing to capture remarkably precise detail. Gursky recalls the exquisite composition and scale of monumental landscape painting, invoking the laws of classical perspective by bringing the city's avenues to a point of careful convergence. He plays with our perception of photography as an objective medium, subtly bending the horizon through a wide-angle lens and cropping out extraneous or distracting details. SK2 & EMR

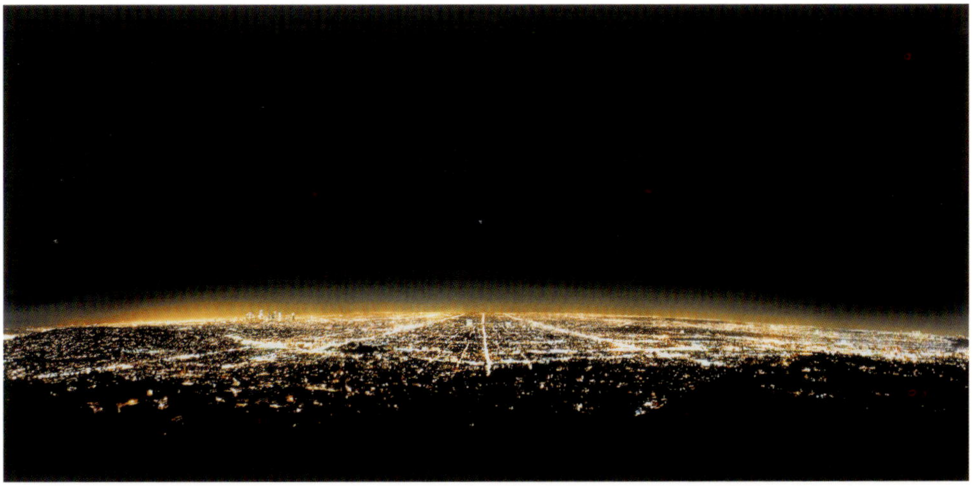

254 / Lithograph and screen print, 71 7/8 x 35 7/16 in. (182.6 x 90 cm). Fogg Museum, Margaret Fisher Fund, M22001.

Robert Rauschenberg
American, 1925–2008
Booster
1967

In 1967, Robert Rauschenberg's *Booster* was the largest lithograph ever made, and in both size and technical complexity, it offered a challenge to the medium of painting. The publisher, Gemini G.E.L., worked with the artist to allow for variations in the printing process, accommodations that call into question the work's status as a multiple. Referencing his radical use of three-dimensional objects in his paintings, Rauschenberg reproduces his body in a life-size X-ray and includes a chart of the sun's movements for 1967. This juxtaposition relates Rauschenberg's skeleton to the grandeur of the cosmos; his title also links the work to the technology of space travel. SKS

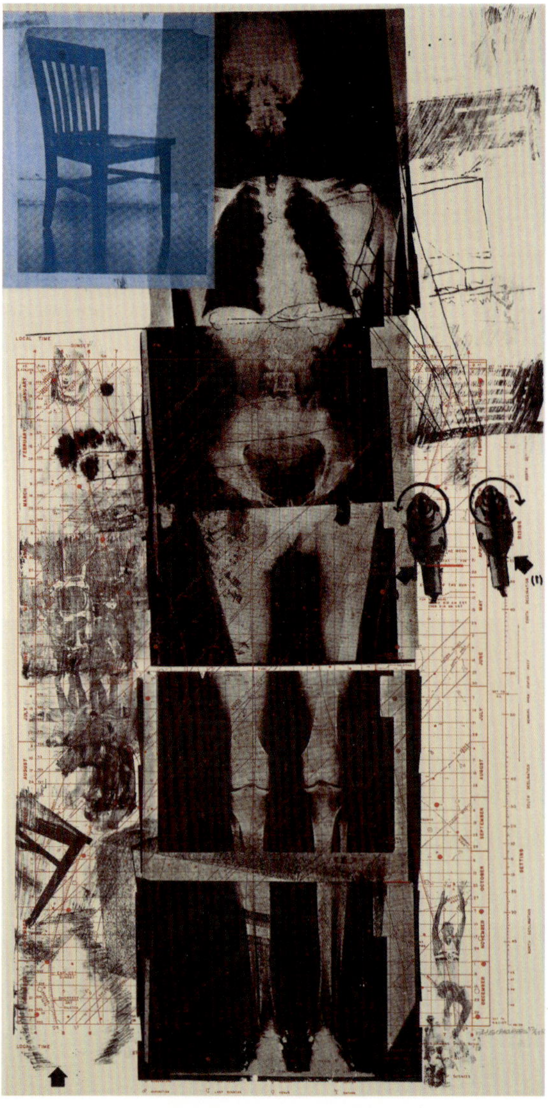

Portfolio of 45 Lightjet C-prints in a box; each print: 15 3/4 x 11 13/16 in. (40 x 30 cm). Fogg Museum, The Jorie Marshall Waterman '96 and Gwendolyn Dunaway Waterman '92 Fund, 2004.46.9, .39, .4, .40.

Paul McCarthy American, b. 1945 (in collaboration with Damon McCarthy) Piccadilly Circus, 2003

Since the late 1960s, West Coast artist Paul McCarthy has dedicated himself to spectacularly grotesque explorations of the hidden dysfunctions of American life, creating disturbing scenarios of sex, violence, and contamination. The scenes of defilement and degradation in the *Piccadilly Circus* performance are typical of McCarthy's disgusting and darkly humorous projects that question authority and subvert American pop-culture symbols. The forty-five photographs in this series show actors wearing giant prosthetic heads representing George W. Bush, the Queen Mother, and Osama bin Laden. The figures engage in improvised, carnivalesque rituals in a hauntingly deserted bank, using viscous goo, pieces of furniture, power tools, and prosthetic tubes. Relying heavily on sticky condiments and recognizable cultural icons, McCarthy's work is at once horrifying and funny, revolting and absurd. EL

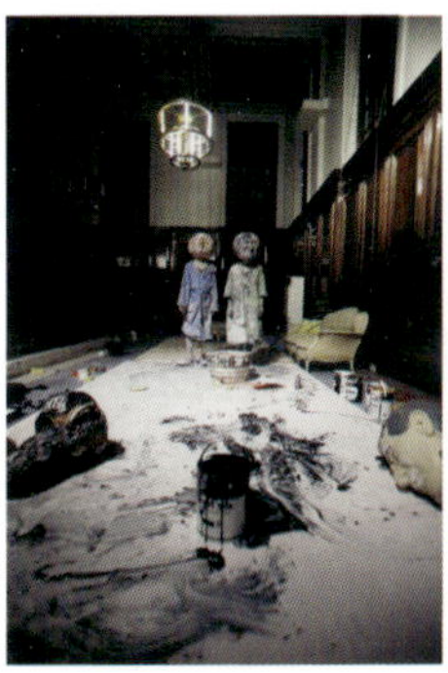
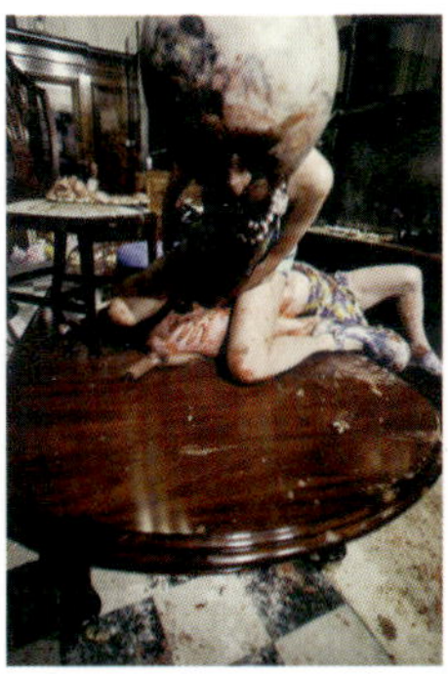
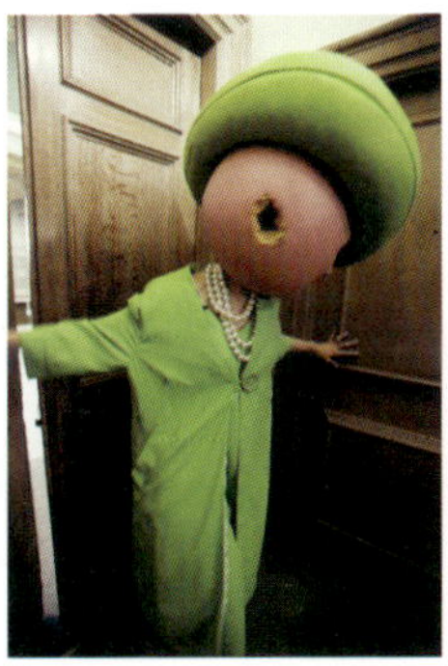
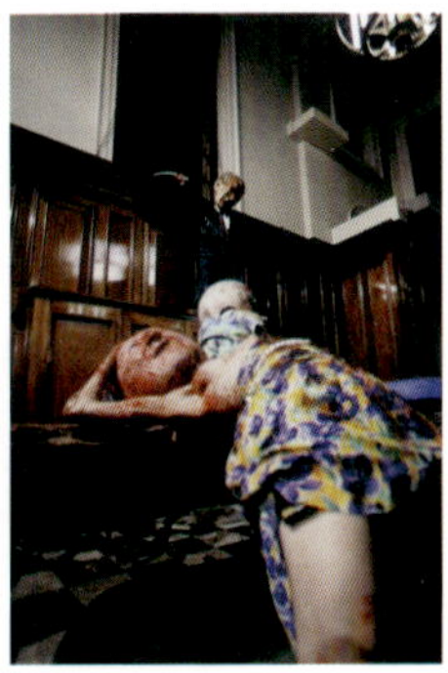

 Photogravure and mixed media, 24 1/2 x 35 1/2 in. (62.2 x 90.2 cm). Fogg Museum, Margaret Fisher Fund, 2006.82.

Ellen Gallagher
American, b. 1965
Abu Simbel
2005–6

Ellen Gallagher replaced the photogravure of the monumental Egyptian temple at Abu Simbel in Sigmund Freud's office with this print during a 2005 installation at the Freud Museum in London. She incorporated a wide variety of mixed media and pop culture references to raise complicated issues of race, history, and identity. The most colorful augmentation on the nineteenth-century original is a fur-trimmed spaceship resembling the one in jazz musician Sun Ra's blaxsploitation film *Space Is the Place*, which carries the earth's black population to a utopian planet of their own. During the rescue, the ship attacks Egypt's colossal sculptures of Pharoah Ramses II with fireballs; the decapitated heads below indicate that in this instance, the Egyptian ruler has become a symbol of black oppression by other blacks. SKS

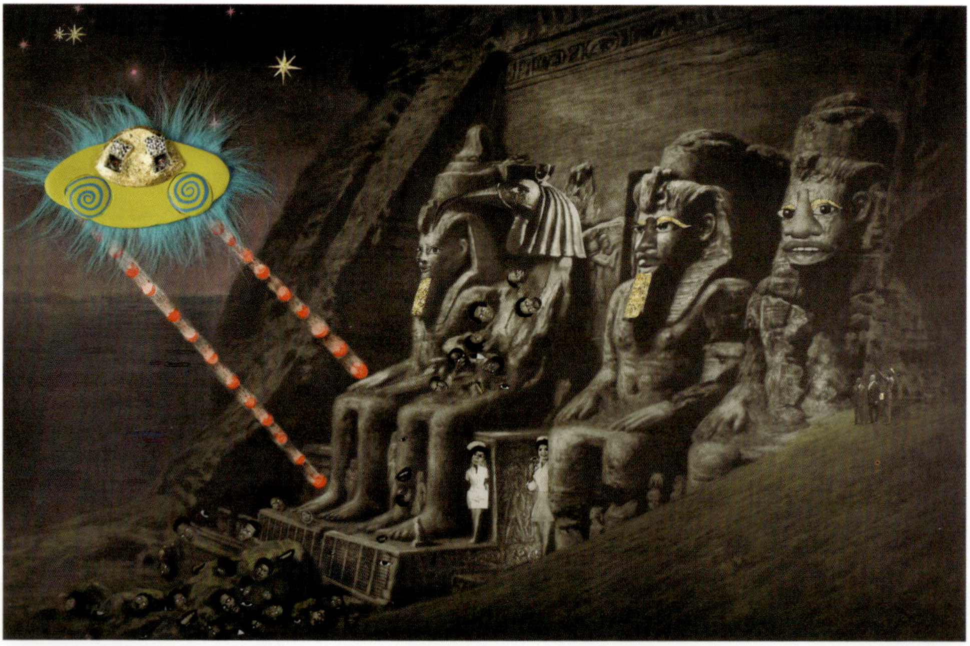

For more information and additional resources at the Harvard Art Museum including online collections, exhibitions, databases, technical studies, provenance research, and curatorial and conservation fellowships, please visit our website: www.harvardartmuseum.org.

Resources

Fogg Museum: Harvard's oldest art museum, the Fogg has collections spanning the history of Western art from the Middle Ages to the present, with particular strengths in Italian early Renaissance, British Pre-Raphaelite, and nineteenth-century French art. The Wertheim Collection is one of America's finest collections of impressionist and postimpressionist art. The Fogg also includes the Agnes Mongan Center for the Study of Prints, Drawings, and Photographs.

Busch-Reisinger Museum: The Busch-Reisinger is the only museum in America devoted to promoting the informed enjoyment and critical understanding of the arts of Central and Northern Europe, with a special emphasis on the German-speaking countries. The museum has especially important holdings of German expressionist, Austrian Secession, and 1920s abstract art, and material related to the Bauhaus, including archives of Lyonel Feininger and Walter Gropius. In addition to notable collections of late medieval, Renaissance, and baroque sculpture, sixteenth-century painting, and eighteenth-century porcelain, the Busch-Reisinger has recently focused on deepening its holdings of postwar and contemporary art from German-speaking Europe. The collection of unique and editioned works by the postwar artist Joseph Beuys is among the world's most comprehensive.

Arthur M. Sackler Museum: The Sackler Museum includes superb collections of ancient, Asian, and Islamic and later Indian art. Among its highlights are the world's finest collections of archaic Chinese jades and Japanese surimono, as well as outstanding Chinese bronzes, ancient ceremonial weapons, and Buddhist cave-temple sculpture; Chinese and Korean ceramics; and Japanese woodblock prints, calligraphy, narrative paintings, and lacquer boxes. The Sackler is also home to paintings, drawings, and calligraphy from Iran, India, and Turkey, as well as to one of the nation's most important teaching collections of Greek, Roman, Egyptian, and Near Eastern art, with significant holdings of Greek and Roman sculpture, Greek vases, and ancient coins.

Straus Center for Conservation and Technical Studies: The Straus Center is the oldest research center in the United States for the scientific study of works of art. It contains archives and special collections of materials for research including X-radiographs, pigment samples, and painting materials.

Archives in the Mongan Center: The Mongan Center contains several artists' archives, including the Christopher Wilmarth Archive, the Stuart Davis papers, and the Ben Shahn Archive.

Archaeological Exploration of Sardis: This program of excavation and research is focused on the site of ancient Sardis, Turkey. The Sardis records from 1958 to the present are housed at the Harvard Art Museum.

Center for the Technical Study of Modern Art: This research center holds primary sources that document the materials and techniques of modern and living artists.

Harvard Art Museum Archives: The Archives contain the records of the institution from 1895 to the present, including correspondence, records of exhibitions, and materials documenting the study and teaching of art history and curatorship, and materials about the museum's works of art and their history.

Abu Simbel (Ellen Gallagher), 256
Actor Arashi Wakano I as Aburaya Osome (Torii Kiyomasu II, attrib.), 107
Albers, Anni, 203
Algardi, Alessandro, 96
Allston, Washington, 138
America (Hiram Powers), 148
Angelico, Fra, 57
Annas, Harry, 224
Appearance of Hōeizan (Katsushika Hokusai), 135
Aqa Mirak, attrib., 69
Aqa Riza (Riza ʿAbbasi), 83
Arbus, Diane, 236
Arch of Titus (Giovanni Battista Piranesi), 114
Aryballos in the Shape of a Hare (Greek), 10
Attraction I (Edvard Munch), 180

Balloon (Édouard Manet), 154
Bally-burgh Ness (Joseph Mallord William Turner), 139
Bamboo through the Four Seasons (Yu Tŏk-chang [Su-un and Ka-san-ŭng]), 109
Banewl (Tacita Dean), 241
Baselitz, Georg, 234
Bath (Mary Cassatt), 178–79
Bay of Estaque (Georges Braque), 189
Bazille, Frédéric, 158
Beardsley, Aubrey, 172
Beckmann, Max, 208
Bedoli, Girolamo Mazzola, 76
Benton, Thomas Hart, 211
Bernini, Gian Lorenzo, 97
Beuys, Joseph, 233
Bierstadt, Albert, 156
Bird Cloud (Lyonel Feininger), 204–5
Bizarre Silk Panel (French), 108
Black-Figure Skyphos: Preparation of Clay or Agricultural Scene (Theseus Painter, attrib.), 11
Blake, William, 142
Blessed Damozel (Dante Gabriel Rossetti), 161
Blue Veil (Morris Louis), 228
Bodendeich, Jacob, 105
Bombé Secretary Desk (Benjamin Frothingham Jr., attrib.), 123
Bonnard, Pierre, 216
Booster (Robert Rauschenberg), 254
Botticelli, Sandro, studio of, 63
Boucher, François, 120
Bourgeois, Louise, 244
Bouts, Albrecht, 62
Bowl with Flower and Scallops (Islamic), 37
Bowl with Hadith Inscriptions (Islamic), 39
Brady, Mathew B., & Studio, 152
Brancusi, Constantin, 194
Braque, Georges, 189
Breakfast Table (John Singer Sargent), 168
Broad-Shouldered Jar with Dragon Decor (Korean), 119
Bruegel the Elder, Pieter, 88–89
Buonarroti, Michelangelo, 74
Burne-Jones, Edward, 160
Bust of an Attendant Bodhisattva (Chinese), 34

Cai Guo-Qiang, 251
Calabash-Shaped Bottle with Blue Splashes (Chinese), 36
Canaletto, 115
Capital with Four Scenes from the Story of Samson (French), 40
Caryatid II (Constantin Brancusi), 194
Cassatt, Mary, 178–79
Ceiling Panel (Islamic), 122
Century with Mushroom Clouds: Project for the 20th Century (Cai Guo-Qiang), 251
Ceremonial Stand and Round-Bottomed Jar (Korean), 33
Charger with Blossoming-Peony Decor (Chinese), 54
Charger with Courtly Couple Encircled by Bands of Poetry (Islamic), 45
Chicken Noodle Soup (Andy Warhol), 232
Christ on the Cross between the Virgin and Cardinal Torquemada and Saint John the Evangelist (Fra Angelico), 57
Coat Hanger I (Jasper Johns), 230
Colonel Elmer Ephraim Ellsworth (Mathew B. Brady & Studio), 152
Colonel Elmer Ephraim Ellsworth (Silsbee, Case, & Co.), 152
Commemorative Head of a King (Nigerian), 82
Composition with Blue, Black, Yellow, and Red (Piet Mondrian), 200
Coney, John, 128
Copley, John Singleton, 124
Corinth, Lovis, 175
Curly Head (Georg Baselitz), 234
Cylinder Seal: Presentation Scene (Mesopotamian), 6

Dancers, Nude Study (Edgar Degas), 167
Daumier, Honoré, 144
David, Jacques-Louis, 130, 131
Day (Edward Burne-Jones), 160
Day of Judgment (Aqa Mirak, attrib.), 69
Dean, Tacita, 241
Death with Left Hand Raised (German), 92
Death with Outstretched Right Hand (German), 92
Degas, Edgar, 166, 167, 176
Dekadrachm of Syracuse (Greek), 16
Delacroix, Eugène, 143
della Bella, Stefano, 113
Demons Tormenting Ciampolo the Barrator (William Blake), 142
Demosthenes (Roman copy of a Greek original), 21
Denarius of Marcus Iunius Brutus and Lucius Plaetorius Caestianus (Roman), 18
Descent into Limbo (Master of the Osservanza), 56
Diana on a Chase (Washington Allston), 138
Drachm of Lucius Verus, with the Nile and the Nilometer (Roman), 19
Dürer, Albrecht, 66, 67

Eakins, Thomas, 169
Earplugs with Relief Decorations (Chimu), 60
Emiliano Zapata (David Alfaro Siqueiros), 212
Emmanuel Joseph Sieyès (Jacques-Louis David), 131
End of the Civic Repertory Theatre 1 (Aaron Siskind), 220
Enthroned Lion-Headed Deities (Egyptian), 1
Evervess II 1 (Joseph Beuys), 233

Falling Asleep (Paul Klee), 217
Fang Lijun, 250
Farm on the Amsteldijk (Rembrandt van Rijn), 99
Feininger, Lyonel, 204–5
Feke, Robert, 121

Femme (Mary Gill) (Man Ray), 209
Figures by the Sea (Joán Miró), 215
Figures from the Annunciation (Sadiqi Beg), 80
Filmer, Mary Georgiana Caroline Cecil, 150
Fish (David Smith), 223
Five Views of an Elephant Combat (Shaykh Taju, attrib.), 111
Flux Year Box 2 (various American artists), 226–27
Foliate Flowerpot and Basin (Chinese), 55
Folio from a Qur'an, Sura 4: 161–62 (Islamic), 44
Folio from a Qur'an, Sura 49: 16 (Islamic), 38
Fragonard, Jean-Honoré, 117
Frank, Robert, 225
Friar Angelo Feretti as Saint Peter Martyr (Lorenzo Lotto), 79
Friedlander, Lee, 237
Frothingham Jr., Benjamin, attrib., 123
Funerary Relief of a Woman (Roman), 27

Gaddi, Taddeo, 48
Gallagher, Ellen, 256
Garden Carpet (Islamic), 87
Gentileschi, Orazio, 93
George Washington (Charles Willson Peale), 125
Géricault, Théodore, 134
Gifford, Sanford Robinson, 163
Gober, Robert, 246
Goldin, Nan, 242
Goldsmith's Designs and Other Studies (Michelangelo Buonarroti), 74
Goltzius, Hendrick, 90
Gorky, Arshile, 218
Goya, Francisco de, 126
Grand Canal, Venice (John Singer Sargent), 190
Grave Stele of a Young Girl, "Melisto" (Greek), 17
Grazing Horses IV (The Red Horses) (Franz Marc), 196
Gursky, Andreas, 253
Guston, Philip, 235

Hanging Man/Sleeping Man (Robert Gober), 246
Harnett, William Michael, 137
Harriet Leavens (Ammi Phillips), 132
Head of a Winged Genie (Neo-Assyrian), 7
Head of Julia Domna (Roman), 25
Heavenly Palaces: Merkabah (Anselm Kiefer), 240
Heckel, Erich, 202
Helen (Gary Schneider), 243
Hero Zhang Shun Representing Water (Totoya Hokkei), 140
Hesse, Eva, 238
High Street (Franz Kline), 221
Highland Franklin Yucca (Ed Ruscha), 252
Highland Light (Edward Hopper), 210
Hine, Lewis Wickes, 186–87
Historic Spanish Record of the Conquest. South Side of Inscription Rock, N.M. No. 3 (Timothy O'Sullivan), 165
Höch, Hannah, 198
Hog (Rembrandt van Rijn), 98
Hokkei, Totoya, 140
Hokusai, Katsushika, 135
Holy Family Enthroned with Saints Sebastian, Catherine of Alexandria, and Francis (Giovanni Battista Tiepolo), 116
Homer, Winslow, 153, 159
Hopper, Edward, 210
Hunter in the Adirondacks (Winslow Homer), 159

Idyll: A Woman with a Child and a Halberdier in a Landscape (Titian, attrib.), 72
Incense Burner in the Form of a Lion (Indian), 53
Infant Bacchus Entrusted to the Nymphs of Nysa; The Deaths of Echo and Narcissus (Nicolas Poussin), 100, 101
Infant Moses (Gustave Moreau), 174
Ingres, Jean-Auguste-Dominique, 133, 145
Iris, Messenger of the Gods (Auguste Rodin), 177
Iskandar's Iron Cavalry Battles King Fur of Hind (Islamic), 50
Ismael, Persian Ambassador at Constantinople in 1557 (Melchior Lorch), 81
Isolde (Aubrey Beardsley), 172
It's the Day for the Garden! (Mahesh, attrib.), 86

Jade Configuration of Dragon, Bird, and Snake (Chinese), 14–15
Jeanne-Antoinette Poisson, Marquise de Pompadour (François Boucher), 120
John Collins Warren (Southworth & Hawes), 147
Johns, Jasper, 230, 231
Johnston, Frances Benjamin, 186–87

Kiefer, Anselm, 240
King, Charles Bird, 149
Kiyomasu II, Torii, attrib., 107
Klee, Paul, 217
Kleophrades Painter, attrib., 12
Klimt, Gustav, 188
Kline, Franz, 221
Kōdaiji Scroll Box with Lozenge and Crest Design (Japanese), 102

La Porte d'Amont, Étretat (Claude Monet), 157
Lamentation of Christ (Albrecht Dürer), 67
Landscape with Farmhouse (Hendrick Goltzius), 90
Large Dish with Flying Cranes (Islamic), 85
Large Jade Disk (Chinese), 14–15
Large Woodcut Nude (Henri Matisse), 183
Last Judgment (Jan Provoost), 68
Leander's Tower on the Bosporus (Sanford Robinson Gifford), 163
Leaving the Bath (Edgar Degas), 176
Light Prop for an Electric Stage (Light-Space Modulator) (László Moholy-Nagy), 207
Lion Devouring a Horse (Eugène Delacroix), 143
Lippi, Filippo, 59
Lissitzky, El, 199
Long Olive-Green Robe (Ryūkyū), 141
Lorch, Melchior, 81
Los Angeles (Andreas Gursky), 253
Lotto, Lorenzo, 79
Louis, Morris, 228
Love and Death (Francisco de Goya), 126

Madeleine I (Henri Matisse), 182
Mahesh, attrib., 86
Man of Sorrows (Albrecht Bouts), 62
Manet, Édouard, 154, 155
Mango Season, Crawford Market, Mumbai, Maharastra (Raghubir Singh), 249

Marc, Franz, 196
Mariette, Jean and Pierre-Jean, 112–13
Master of the Osservanza, 56
Mater Dolorosa (Albrecht Bouts), 62
Matisse, Henri, 182, 183, 193
McCarthy, Paul, 255
McDaniel Painter, attrib., 13
Medal of Girolamo Savonarola (Italian), 70
Meissen Porcelain Manufactory, 118
Meleager (Roman copy of a Greek original), 20
Miró, Joán, 215
Misfortunes of Silenus (Piero di Cosimo), 64
Misrach, Richard, 229
Miss Alice Kurtz (Thomas Eakins), 169
"Mister, that won't do! ... You have to make it right for me, mister!!!" (Honoré Daumier), 144
Mitsunobu, Tosa, 65
Moholy-Nagy, László, 207
Mondrian, Piet, 200
Monet, Claude, 157
Moon and Melon (Zhu Da [Bada Shanren]), 106
Moreau, Gustave, 174
Mother and Child (Pablo Picasso), 181
Mount Rushmore, South Dakota (Lee Friedlander), 237
Mueller, Otto, 197
Munch, Edvard, 180
Mutiny on the Raft of the "Medusa" (Théodore Géricault), 134

Nadelman, Elie, 195
Nature Study (Louise Bourgeois), 244
Nayika and Her Lover (Indian), 104
Nayika Yearning for Her Lover (Indian), 127
Nemesis, or *The Large Fortune* (Albrecht Dürer), 66
Nicholas Boylston (John Singleton Copley), 124
Night (Edward Burne-Jones), 160
1998.11.2 (Fang Lijun), 250
No. 2 (Jackson Pollock), 219
Nocturne in Blue and Silver (James Abbott McNeill Whistler), 162
Nude in a Landscape (Otto Mueller), 197
Nude Youth (Taddeo Zuccaro), 77

Odalisque with a Slave (Jean-Auguste-Dominique Ingres), 145
O'Keeffe, Georgia, 201
On a Tulle Net Ground (Hannah Höch), 198
Openwork Pin Head (Iranian), 8
O'Sullivan, Timothy, 165

Peale, Charles Willson, 125
Peale, Sarah Miriam, 136
Pear Tree (Gustav Klimt), 188
Peasant of the Camargue (Vincent van Gogh), 171
Pee Body (Kiki Smith), 245
Phillips, Ammi, 132
Pianiste (Elie Nadelman), 195
Piazza San Marco, Venice (Canaletto), 115
Picasso, Pablo, 181, 185, 191, 214
Piccadilly Circus (Paul McCarthy), 255
Picture Contest (Tosa Mitsunobu and Reizei Tamehiro), 65
Piero di Cosimo, 64
Piranesi, Giovanni Battista, 114
Pitching Quoits (Winslow Homer), 153
Plaster Head with Bowl of Fruit (Pablo Picasso), 214
Pollock, Jackson, 219
Pomegranate (Pablo Picasso), 191
Portland Vase, First Edition (Josiah Wedgwood), 129
Portrait of a Lady with Earrings (Roman), 24
Portrait of Augustin Jordan and His Daughter, Adrienne (Jean-Auguste-Dominique Ingres), 133
Portrait of Mme Augustin Jordan and Her Son, Gabriel (Jean-Auguste-Dominique Ingres), 133
Poussin, Nicolas, 100, 101
Powers, Hiram, 148
Prince Shōtoku at Age Two (Japanese), 46–47
Proun 12E (El Lissitzky), 199
Provoost, Jan, 68
Putto as Hercules (Meissen Porcelain Manufactory), 118

Queen Arsinoë II as Hathor (Egyptian), 5

Race Course at Longchamp (Édouard Manet), 155
Rauschenberg, Robert, 254
Ray, Man, 209
Red and Pink (Georgia O'Keeffe), 201
Red-Figure Bell Krater: Phlyax Scene (McDaniel Painter, attrib.), 13
Red-Figure Kalyx Krater: Return of Hephaistos to Olympos (Kleophrades Painter, attrib.), 12
Rehearsal (Edgar Degas), 166
Rembrandt van Rijn, 98, 99
Richter, Gerhard, 239
Riemenschneider, Tilman, and workshop, 71
Ritual Wine-Pouring Vessel with Tiger and Owl Decor (Chinese), 3
Rocky Mountains, "Lander's Peak" (Albert Bierstadt), 156
Rodin, Auguste, 177
Rossetti, Dante Gabriel, 161
Rubens, Peter Paul, 94, 95
Ruscha, Ed, 252

Sadiqi Beg, 80
Said (Gerhard Richter), 239
Saint Anthony Abbot (Tilman Riemenschneider and workshop), 71
Saint Jerome in the Desert with Saints John the Baptist and Ansanus (Filippo Lippi), 59
Saint Longinus (Gian Lorenzo Bernini), 97
Saint Theodore (Byzantine), 29
Salomé (Lovis Corinth), 175
Salvator Mundi (Sandro Botticelli, studio of), 63
Sarcophagus: Amazonomachy (Roman), 26
Sargent, John Singer, 168, 184, 190
Schneider, Gary, 243
Seated Buddha (probably Shakyamuni) (Chinese), 35
Seated Buddha Shakyamuni Flanked by Standing Bodhisattvas (Korean), 58
Seated Buddha Shakyamuni with Flaming Shoulders (Chinese), 30
Seated Clowness (Henri de Toulouse-Lautrec), 173
Seeley, George Henry, 192
Segmented Maebyŏng Bottle (Korean), 41
Self-Portrait Dedicated to Paul Gauguin (Vincent van Gogh), 170
Self-Portrait in Blue Bathroom, London (Nan Goldin), 242
Self-Portrait in Tuxedo (Max Beckmann), 208